The Frankfurt Parliament
1848–1849

The Frankfurt Parliament 1848-1849

FRANK EYCK

MACMILLAN
London · Melbourne · Toronto
ST MARTIN'S PRESS
New York
1968

Published by
MACMILLAN AND CO LTD
Little Essex Street London w c 2
and also at Bombay Calcutta and Madras
Macmillan South Africa (Publishers) Pty Ltd Johannesburg
The Macmillan Company of Australia Pty Ltd Melbourne
The Macmillan Company of Canada Ltd Toronto
St Martin's Press Inc New York

Library of Congress catalog card no. 68–14232

Printed in Great Britain by
ROBERT MACLEHOSE AND CO LTD
The University Press, Glasgow

To the Memory of my Father

Contents

List of Tables

List of Illustrations

Preface

THIS study was undertaken because there is – surprisingly enough – no full-length history of the Frankfurt Parliament, not even in German. The lapse of time allows greater detachment, yet also adds to the difficulties. Periodically disturbed conditions in Europe, resulting early on in the dispersal and partial disappearance of the assembly records during the summer of 1849, have put many obstacles in the way of research. Frontier changes in Europe affecting the territories which sent members to the Frankfurt Parliament have led to the splitting up of archives. The National Socialist régime in Germany, the division of the country in 1945 and political barriers to the interchange of information have between them led to the loss of much valuable primary material and have often made the collection of data more difficult and sometimes impossible.

On the positive side, the author was fortunate enough to establish a fruitful collaboration with the German Federal Archives in Frankfurt am Main and he wishes to thank Oberarchivrat Dr W. Latzke and Archivrat Dr R. Moldenhauer of the Bundesarchiv, Aussenstelle Frankfurt, as well as Oberarchivrat Dr W. Klötzer of the Stadtarchiv in Frankfurt, for all the help they have given him over the years. Documents studied include the papers of two committees of the Frankfurt Parliament, the Economic Committee (*Volkswirtschaftlicher Ausschuss*) and the Naval Committee (*Marineausschuss*), the minutes of one of the parliamentary groups (*Westendhall*, Moderate Left), some of the press hand-outs issued by parliamentary groups in the assembly and, above all, biographical material on members of the Frankfurt Parliament. Help given by the Historical Institute of the Polish Academy (Polska Akademia Nauk, Instytut Historii) and by the archives of the German nobility (Deutsches Adelsarchiv) in Marburg an der Lahn is gratefully acknowledged.

Much of the information about the Frankfurt Parliament has never been systematically arranged. The records are often incomplete and sometimes faulty. Even a list of constituencies which sent deputies to the Frankfurt Parliament and shows changes in representation could only be compiled by the author with some difficulty. Punched cards were used in order to analyse the biographical data and to relate these to particular attitudes, for instance to the question of Prussian hegemony and to political ideology. It is hoped that these researches allow a clearer picture to be given than has hitherto been possible not only of the background to decisions made by the assembly, but also of the pattern of German public opinion generally. The author's thanks are due in connection with the compiling and analysis of the punched cards to the assistance given by colleagues in the Faculty of Social Studies at Exeter, including Mr P. J. Fletcher, Dr H. E. S. Fisher and Mr F. M. M. Lewes.

Those who read the book in typescript included Dr G. P. Gooch, O.M., and Professor W. N. Medlicott, who have both taken a great interest in the author's academic career, and the help given by their valuable comments is acknowledged with gratitude. The book could not have been written without the financial support of the German Academic Exchange Service (Deutscher Akademischer Austauschdienst), the British Academy and the University of Exeter, for research travel in Germany and other expenses. Thanks are given to these bodies, and to Professor F. Barlow and the author's colleagues in the Department of History at Exeter who enabled him to take a term's study leave. The distance from major academic libraries was overcome with the help of the London Library and of the Inter-Library loan service in the Exeter University Library under Mrs Mary Connolly, which supplied the author's book needs and put him much in their debt.

Last, not least, the author wishes to thank his wife for helping to compile a list of constituencies and their representatives, and for assisting in the filling in of 800 forms detailing biographical information for the punched cards, as well as for her sympathy and support while he was writing this book.

FRANK EYCK

Department of History, University of Exeter

Abbreviations in the Footnotes

ADB   *Allgemeine Deutsche Biographie.*
BSTH   Kosch, *Biographisches Staatshandbuch.*
GJNB   Wininger, *Grosse Jüdische Nationalbiographie.*
MdR   Schwarz, *Mitglied des Reichstags*
NDB   *Neue deutsche Biographie.*
NÖB   Bettelheim, *Neue Österreichische Biographie.*
ÖBL   *Österreichisches Biographisches Lexikon.*
Umrisse *Biographische Umrisse der deutschen konstituirenden Nationalversammlung.*

Volume and page numbers without a preceding title refer to Wigard, *Stenographischer Bericht.*

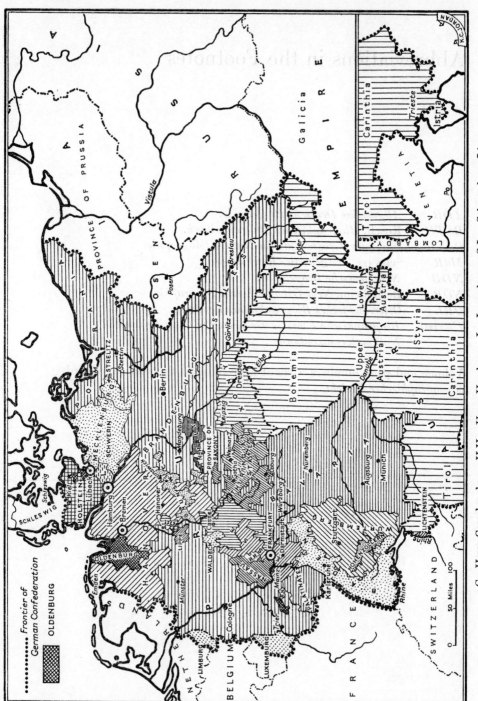

C=Hesse-Cassel exclave H.H.=Hesse-Homburg L=Lauenburg S.L.=Schaumburg-Lippe

The German Confederation, January 1848

1 The Background

i. Advantages and disadvantages of political interest in subject – The German Confederation – Germany and France

THE first German National Assembly which sat at Frankfurt between May 1848 and May 1849, most of the time in St Paul's Church (Paulskirche), known as the Frankfurt Parliament, has never ceased to attract considerable interest on the part of historians and politicians. This attention is well deserved. It is quite impossible for the historian to account for the Bismarckian creation or for the origin of German political parties without going back to the Frankfurt Parliament. Similarly, to the politician, this parliament is either an example to be emulated or a relic of the past to be eradicated. In view of the troubled course of German history, the first German National Assembly has kept its topicality and freshness. The achievements or misdeeds of 1848 in Germany have not – like the monster Chartist petition of April 1848 in England – been simply relegated to the pages of history. In 1918 and in 1945, a return to the forgotten lessons of the Frankfurt Parliament seemed essential. Even now hardly a year passes without some reference to the ideals of St Paul's Church.

The historian is flattered by current political interest in his problems. Yet his task is made none the easier by it. The pages of history are not only a record of the past, but a guide for future action. The politically active have always looked to history for support in their political struggles. The official German school of historians after 1870 was not only concerned to justify the Bismarckian solution, but also to prevent a return to what it regarded as the confusion and lack of purpose of the Frankfurt Parliament. Anti-Bismarckian historians, on the other hand, have tried to discover as many positive achievements as possible at Frankfurt which could be used to mould Germany more to their liking. Indeed after what appeared to them as the interlude of the Bismarckian Reich, the founders of both the Weimar Republic and the Federal Republic had, in certain ways, to go back to 1848. Thus, too often, German history has been interpreted as a series of right and wrong turnings. This is understandable and almost inevitable with a country which has had as turbulent a history as Germany. The question of what had gone wrong, between 1914 and 1918, between 1933 and 1945, was a powerful incentive to historical research. However stimulating, to pose the problem in this way is to invite difficulties. The texture of historical events is broken. The course of things is seen from one aspect only. Developments are selected which illustrate this particular side, others are omitted. The author is committed in advance to a certain position which deprives him of the freedom of movement every historian should have. He is defending one side, criticising the other, instead of being above both. In the concrete terms of the pre-Bismarckian period, these writers are bound to support all 'liberals' or 'progressives' against the 'reactionaries' who impeded progress. The liberals are the heroes. The reactionaries, with Metternich at their head, are the villains. Frederick William IV as a person, and the German Confederation as an institution, never leave the dock. These 'democratic' historians assume their guilt. Anything about the heroes which does not fit into the theory is quietly omitted.

To get away from this kind of approach is not as easy as it may appear. In Germany, historians have not unnaturally been sensitive to the effect their writings were likely to have on the political future of the country. At a time of rising National Socialist agitation before 1933, for instance, a historian who believed in the importance of preserving the Weimar Republic might well have felt that any exposure of liberal shortcomings in 1848 could do political harm. It is always more comfortable for the historian to be on the side of 'progress' than to expose himself to the accusation that he might have a blind spot for tyranny, and that he is insensitive to the sufferings of the persecuted and to the importance of human and political freedom. This risk will have to be taken. A sustained effort should be made to apply the same standards to all the parties involved, whether for or against freedom of speech. Those who opposed the immediate granting of all civil rights were not necessarily opposed to them in principle. Some of them might have judged that the time to grant them had not yet come. Many reforms have failed because they were forced through too quickly. This is a matter of historical fact and does not imply any lack of attachment to civil liberty on the part of the historian. While he may and perhaps ought to have his own views as to what form of government he may favour for a particular country *today*, he must not subject his historical vision to political and ideological blinkers. Whether immediately successful or not, every approach to the problems of 1848, from the extreme right to the extreme left, must be examined on its merits. Thus it will not do to regard as pure obstructionists those who insisted on maintaining the Austrian connection. This is done by many historians, supporting the exclusion of Austria from Germany, whether pro- or anti-Bismarck. If one side was entitled to its aims, so was the other. It is absurd to regard political agitation as honourable and high-minded if directed towards Prussian leadership and as an intrigue if opposed to it.

Historians have tended to accept without too close scrutiny the thesis of the German liberals and radicals of 1848 that the German Confederation had become obsolete. On this the Prussian and liberal schools of historians – which overlap to some extent – have been agreed. Both have ridiculed the slow machinery and inefficiency of the Confederation and the absurdity of the division of the country into so many states. Where the Confederation awoke from its slumbers and roused itself to action – or was roused to it by Metternich – it is condemned for the oppression it carried out. The Confederation cannot but do wrong.

The Confederation came into existence at Vienna in 1815 to provide a framework for the German states after the Napoleonic interlude which had followed the final collapse of the Holy Roman Empire nine years earlier. Various other schemes were considered, including the creation of a new imperial crown, but these were not found to be feasible. There is no evidence that the divisions in Germany had by then been so far overcome as to allow the formation of a unified German state. In spite of the wave of German national feeling which swept the country between 1812 and 1815, the bonds of loyalty which tied Germans to their state, whether it was Prussia, Bavaria or even Coburg, were still strong. Often unwittingly, writers trying to explain the rise of the German national movement have tended to antedate its beginnings and to exaggerate its strength. Then there have been others who for political purposes tried to create a history for their people, as was the habit with the new nations and not only with the Germans. The differences between the strength of national feeling in 1870 and 1815 have often been blurred by the emotion which nationalism generates. The outburst of German feeling during the final years of the Napoleonic period was due to several factors, not all of which fit easily into the nationalist pattern. The whole question is complicated by the ambivalent German relationship with France in the early decades of the century which was resolved in 1870. In 1814 France was the enemy. The French had invaded and subjected much of the country, and Germans from all parts helped as *Germans* and as Prussians, Bavarians or whatever they were, to drive them out. The German attitude was also part of a general European revulsion against Napoleonic tyranny. But France was not only an enemy, it was also a friend, in a sense in which it had ceased to be by 1870. In the first half of the nineteenth century, France was a spiritual home for many Germans, and Paris was sought out by a constant stream of German pilgrims of widely differing political views and social backgrounds. Some of them took up prolonged residence there, either from choice, like Wilhelm von Humboldt, or from necessity, like Heinrich Heine. Paris was a cultural centre without its equal in Germany. Germans were forever drawing on French political ideas, and the history of Germany between 1815 and 1850 would have been quite different without their impact. The French came to Germany during the revolutionary and Napoleonic era not only as conquerors but as political mentors. French theories of government, from the concept of nationality to the new position of the citizen, were no less welcome in Germany at that time because of their association with the conquering armies. The lines of nationality had not yet been so definitely drawn. The princes of the Confederation of the Rhine – and for a time even Frederick William III of Prussia – found little difficulty in co-operating with Napoleon because he was French. The Southern states which were given great accessions of territory by Napoleon also owed much to the bureaucratic system which they took over from him. The Code Napoléon became a prized possession of the territories left of the Rhine which retained it after 1815. Paradoxically, the French with their new emphasis on the responsibility of the citizen made possible the wave of popular national feeling which drove the often unwilling German princes into the fight against the French. Unfortunately for Germany, the political ideas which had come from France did not all point in one direction, not even the dominant ones, such as those which might be regarded as official French policy in Germany during the Napoleonic era. That was not only due to these ideas being a mixture of the revolutionary heritage and of their adaptation by Napoleon. Even the original ideas of the 1790s as applied to government by the French authorities both in France and elsewhere had curiously contradictory effects on the position of the individual. On the one hand, there was the affirmation of certain inalienable rights belonging to everybody, irrespective of social position, wealth, religion or any other factor. On the other hand, there was a deliberate strengthening of the power of the state. Whatever the differences within the ruling republican groups in France, this dual emphasis on the rights of the individual and on the importance of strengthening the state was *on the whole* common ground. In theory there need be no conflict between the two aims. For the intention was that the state would be run in the interests of the citizens forming it. But already during the 1790s in France it had become clear that even the existence of some democratic institutions did not necessarily resolve the conflict between individual liberty and the power of the state. A dilemma existed before the advent of Napoleon and arises quite apart from nationalism. This point is of importance in connection with the Frankfurt Parliament, because there were hardly any groups in the Centre or on the Left of the assembly which were uninfluenced by these basic pre-Napoleonic French concepts. The problem is present in a particularly acute form with the liberals in the Frankfurt Parliament, and it has sometimes been thought that this dilemma was due entirely to fundamental contradictions between liberalism and nationalism. Yet there was already a potential contradiction in the pre-Napoleonic French political principles which provided a starting point for German liberalism in the first half of the nineteenth century. Naturally the doctrine of nationalism cannot be entirely separated from the whole problem. For the French spread this theory across the European continent during the 1790s as one of the consequences which sprang from the changed position of the citizen in the state. Self-determination was the next step to self-government. If men were citizens of a republic rather than subjects of a prince, their say could not be confined to control over the affairs of the state in which they happened to find themselves. They could secede from a state with which they disagreed and form a new one or join another one. The right of the citizen to settle his own fate could not be inhibited by state frontiers. There were considerable elements of friction here between the rights of the individual and those of the community, but they were not necessarily without hope of reconciliation.

Napoleon did nothing to resolve the conflict between individual and community in the ideas which he took over from the revolutionary régime. He strengthened both the individual and the state, as is seen best in the Code Napoléon. Safeguards for the individual, such as the jury system, were found side by side here with the most cruel punishments. Second-class citizens, like the Jews, benefited from Napoleon. Like other governments after the French Revolution, the First Empire continued the rejection of discrimination on the grounds of class or religion. At the same time Napoleon did not in principle relax the grip of the state over society, even if his methods were less crude than those of his predecessors. The whole machinery of government was refined. Central control was everywhere strengthened and an efficient bureaucratic system was created to enforce the commands of the government. As a result partly of compulsion and partly of voluntary emulation, Napoleonic concepts took root in Germany. The bureaucratic system provided a means of creating coherence in the enlarged states of the Confederation of the Rhine, formed from a variety of territories both ecclesiastical and secular, which they would have otherwise found hard to achieve.

The intellectual basis of these French principles was purely rationalistic. Historic rights were not recognised. The institutions which were swept away were of many kinds, from dwarf principalities to assemblies of estates. The rights which were affected were thus not only those of individuals, but also those of groups which lost their representation. While some representative assemblies, such as at Hamburg, had become oligarchic, the example of England in this period shows that even outdated institutions could be adapted and given new life. French rationalism, which did not settle the issue between individual and state, did, however, prejudice the future in making an 'English' solution based on the gradual development of estates into parliaments more difficult. There were still those among the liberals in 1848, for instance the historian Dahlmann,[1] who looked to England rather than to France as the great political example to be followed. But they were bound to find themselves at a disadvantage. Only in Wurtemberg did the historic estates remain viable. Furthermore, as the Free Towns show, the estates often took a narrow view of their position, becoming oligarchic. There was, with the possible exception of Wurtemberg, little popular enthusiasm for the adaptation of historic institutions. From a national point of view, too, the danger was that the development of institutions in the states would only aggravate divisions within Germany as a whole. However, individual states were the only units to which reforms could be applied.

In 1815 the 'sovereign' states could no longer be ignored. They owed

[1] See below, p. 41.

their origin to quite a different conception than the one which they now assumed. Napoleon had intended them as satellites following French orders. Most of them had been members of the Confederation of the Rhine under French protectorate. The Kings of Bavaria, Wurtemberg and Saxony were not the only ones who had to fend for themselves after the withdrawal of French control and now had to think out problems for themselves. The first instinct of these princes and of their ministers was understandably that of self-preservation, and this became a factor in the peace-settlement. Historians have sometimes wondered why the Allies did not make a *tabula rasa* of the German map. This question ignores the basic disunity of the Allies, the usefulness of individual states to one or other of the European Powers and the patent un-desirability – nay impossibility – of destroying and altering more than was absolutely essential. Once the fact of the survival of the 'medium states' like Bavaria and Saxony was accepted, organic German unity had become impossible. The intervention of the Powers in German affairs was bound to continue as long as a unified Germany had not been created. This interest of the Powers was quite legitimate. The great European states could not allow the existence of a power vacuum in the heart of Europe. Russia, Austria, Prussia and Great Britain had helped, directly or indirectly, to free Germany from French control and they were bound to have a say in the future, particularly as long as the German states were not agreed among themselves. Just as the German princes had been quite ready to use Napoleon's support against each other, they now participated avidly in the European game of chess.

In the circumstances, a loose association of the German states was the obvious solution. Any other plan was quite unrealistic. The German Confederation was made an integral part of the Vienna settlement and the interests of the European Powers were preserved. This apparent foreign 'tutelage' of Germany was later resented by advocates of national unification. But in 1815 and during the following decades Germany benefited from the arrangement. The knowledge that all the European Powers would consider themselves affected by any changes in the position in Germany was a deterrent to aggression on the part of one of their number. As France was the most likely potential aggressor, this was one more reason for integrating the German confederation instrument into the Vienna Treaty, whose prime object was to prevent another French threat to the peace of Europe. The half-century during which the German Confederation was in existence happened to be free from any violation of purely German territory by a foreign power. While this is not proof of the efficacy of the German Confederation, yet one of its leading aims was in fact fulfilled. Russia and France had only such influence over German affairs as the German princes permitted. On balance, the arrangement helped rather than hindered Germany diplomatically for a time.

ii. *Student movements*

Another reason for a 'European' solution of the German question in 1815 was the direct interest of two major powers in Germany. Although Metternich was quite prepared to give up Austrian claims to German lands in order to achieve a more rounded territory, he regarded the preservation of Austrian influence over Germany as essential for the maintenance of the integrity and European position of the Habsburg Empire.

With Austria determined to hold on to Germany, and Prussia becoming more extensively engaged over the whole breadth of the country than previously through her acquisition of the Rhineland, there were two major powers involved in the future of the country, neither of which was prepared to subordinate itself to the other. Furthermore, neither Prussia nor Austria wanted to become submerged in the new German arrangements any more than they had been prepared to give up their separate existence outside the Holy Roman Empire. They insisted on remaining Great Powers quite apart from their position in Germany and did not join the Confederation with all their territories. Thus the ties binding together the German states, including the 'German' parts of Austria and Prussia, were bound to remain rather loose. This suited the German medium states like Bavaria and Wurtemberg, too.

The German Confederation provided a framework which could be developed in the future. The treaty establishing the Confederation did not attempt to settle questions in 1815 for the solution of which the time was not ripe. The clause about the granting of constitutions (*Landständische Verfassung*) was vague. After the removal of French direction, the country did not easily find a solution to its problems. This was bound to take time. For a quarter of a century the map of

Germany had not assumed a stable appearance. Some territories changed hands several times during this period. The country, its states and individual regions needed time to settle down once more. They had to find a fresh balance between the forces of change and stability. The new states needed time to establish their existence, to discover their own potentialities and then to work together to give the Confederation content.

The road to German national unity passed through the capitals of the member-states, certainly the larger ones. Yet there was a danger in this. For the strengthening of the individual states through the development of their institutions, for instance towards parliamentary representation, might in fact make eventual unification more difficult. It was an irony of this period that the advocates of national unity made their task more difficult by building up parliamentary institutions in their states. And yet their strongest motive for wishing to liberalise the political institutions of their state was to bring all the German states closer together. There was indeed a justified feeling that German unification could only be brought about by the weight of public opinion and that strong pressure would have to be put on the princes to make them give up even part of their sovereignty. Still, the critics in the opposition in the years before 1848 did not perhaps realise sufficiently clearly that the princes were not the sole obstacle to national unity and that there were many other forces of particularism.

The period from 1815 to 1848 was not a time of steadily growing awareness of belonging to Germany. There were certain landmarks, such as the fear of a French invasion in 1840 during the Eastern crisis. After the enthusiasm of the Wars of Liberation, which did not affect all regions in the same way, there was a certain cooling off, except for the younger generation which had fought the French, many of whom studied at the universities after the war. The newly formed states kept a watchful eye on the political tendencies manifesting themselves in the universities. These states represented the reality of the present as opposed to the dreams of a distant future. The rulers and governments had a duty to maintain law and order against further attempts at subversion. They and the German Confederation tackled this task with considerable energy when all the practical difficulties are taken into account. The Carlsbad decrees of 1819 are evidence that the German Confederation provided an organ for action if needed. At the same time the multiplicity of sovereign states helped to alleviate the situation of those in trouble with authority. The opposition was of many different kinds, without one clear guiding principle, ranging from the very radical to the quite moderate. In view of the restrictions on free political life, the exact aims and groupings within the opposition are difficult to recognise clearly. With the development of parliamentary life, particularly after 1830, the opposition came increasingly into the open, but even in the years just before 1848 the demarcation between moderates and radicals was not always easy to make.

Historians have tended to see the conflict in the years before 1848 more from the point of view of the opposition than from that of the governments. This is due to a natural sympathy for the underdog, for the weaker side (at any rate in the short run). There is the feeling that these men who stood out against authority fought for freedom. The governments between 1815 and 1848 are too easily equated in our minds, consciously or unconsciously, with the totalitarianism of our time. Thus the opposition seem to be always right and the governments wrong.

Considering all the difficulties, most of the German governments did not make a bad start after 1815. On the whole there was an effort to solve problems pragmatically, without too much reference to ideological principles. There was no general dismissal of ministers and officials who had been associated with the period of French influence. In Bavaria, the leading minister von Montgelas was retained for a time. At first in Prussia reformers like Boyen and Wilhelm von Humboldt were kept on. Governments were settling down to a vague authoritarianism as far removed from the excesses of the French occupation as from the safe-guards of a constitutional state. After 1815 there was no longer any-body like Napoleon who could with a stroke of the pen remove long established rights, either on the side of princes or on that of the estates. There were many internal administrative acts which governments could carry out without consulting anybody. But the preservation of the 'Rhenish law' of the Code Napoléon in several German states shows that there was a limit to the power of the governments. They were often foiled in their natural wish to achieve institutional uniformity in their state and were thus less free to sweep away established rights than their democratic successors. Generally, the approval of the estates had to be obtained for legislation. Also, these German governments of the post-1815 period which were not based on parliamentary support did have – with notable exceptions, like Hanover under the Duke of Cumberland –

greater respect for established rights than those of their successors with popular backing. After the end of French rule officialdom moved much more slowly and circumspectly again.

French bureaucratic methods could only be successfully applied in the larger states. Prussian officialdom certainly entered on a period of greater efficiency. In the smaller states French bureaucratic methods were hardly applicable to what was far more like a family business. This variety of government must be taken into account in assessing the severity of measures of repression, for instance from 1819 onwards.

The slow-moving patriarchal governments of this period did not want to have to take energetic political action. They were far too busy putting their own houses in order. They were forced to do so by the madness of a political assassination. In 1819 the student Sand murdered the playwright Kotzebue, who had at one time been in the pay of the Russians. Sand may have been a maniac acting on his own. But he had imbibed his dangerous ideas in one of the student movements, the *Deutsche Burschenschaft*. This association was founded at the University of Jena in 1816 to unite all Germans and to combat the particularist tendencies of the *Landsmannschaften* which were grouped round the old German tribes and the existing states. Sand acted on his own, taking seriously the vague talk he had heard about tyrannicide. He did not act on behalf of the *Burschenschaft*. But many students approved of the murder or at least did not regard it as a crime.

The assassination of 1819, like the plot to conquer the seat of the German Confederation by force in 1833 (*Frankfurter Wachensturm*), shook rulers and ministers out of their complacency. Obviously many minds were seething with revolutionary ideas. The measures taken by the governments, particularly after 1819, were extensive and often harsh. The universities were put under stricter control. Many university teachers were dismissed after investigation. Students were arrested and in some cases sentenced to terms of imprisonment in a fortress, the more honourable and less severe form of detention used for political offences. A vast system of reporting on suspicious individuals was built up. There is something degrading about fighting ideas by repression, and the methods used by the Confederation and by the governments were often crude. But those in authority could not remain passive. The conspirators might be amateurs, but that made them all the more dangerous, for in their fanaticism they were quite prepared to risk their own lives as well as those of others in ventures without the slightest prospect of success. The responsibility of the governments could not be abrogated because a number of university teachers and students, who were quite unrepresentative of the people generally, toyed with the idea of imposing their incompletely thought-out schemes of reform on Germany. The governments took very seriously what they regarded as the political aberrations of university students, as they had to draw future members of the administrative service and judges from this source. Usually the political indiscretions of the young were soon forgotten. There was some unnecessary brutality, but many detained students also received great kindness from their prison governors. However they fared during their investigations, most of them were eventually able to enter the civil service and the professions. Many of those who had served terms of imprisonment for their connection with the *Deutsche Burschenschaft* rose to high positions in the government service. The state in those days was not generally vindictive, less so than the democratic institutions in our day. Also the existence of so many inter-state frontiers alleviated persecution. The memoirs of members of the Frankfurt Parliament are full of escapes from arrest or impending arrest and of flights to other German states or abroad. Divided sovereignty often offered refuge and a chance of employment to those who had got into difficulty in their own state. The imperfections of government organisation of which the liberals complained had their good points.

Generally, the princes and ministers of the day were not cruel. There were some exceptions. King Louis I of Bavaria, not the worst of rulers, was at times personally vindictive. Two members of the Frankfurt Parliament, the Würzburg university teacher W. J. Behr and the medical writer J. G. Eisenmann, owed long periods of imprisonment for political reasons mainly to their king. There was also the long incarceration of the Marburg professor of law Sylvester Jordan – another member of the Frankfurt Parliament – in the Electorate of Hesse-Cassel, one of the worst governed of all German territories. These cases are no better because they were rather exceptional in the period between 1815 and 1848. They can hardly be considered part of the system of government in the sense of being approved by the other rulers. In judging the situation as a whole, it ought to be remembered that interference in the universities and the difficulties put in the way of free dissemination of information affected primarily the well-educated. The mass of the people was not touched by these measures of repression.

The extreme political tendencies of some members of the *Deutsche Burschenschaft* showed that youth had not yet discovered equilibrium after the heady period of the Wars of Liberation. The princes, including the King of Prussia, had been reluctant to fight an ideological war in 1812 and 1813, not only because that conflicted with their conception of their status as rulers, but also because they had seen the excesses of popular movements during the French Revolution. There was a potentially disruptive dynamism about a Prussian general like Gneisenau, about the propagandist Ernst Moritz Arndt and the admittedly much more complex personality of Baron Stein, the former Prime Minister of Prussia. These reformers were not necessarily more peace-loving or more tolerant than the rather dull men who occupied most of the thrones. They had an idealistic faith in their ability to carry out extensive changes, regardless of obstacles. They were advocates of the ruthless exploitation of military victory. As they were very gifted they were all the more dangerous. The prosaic Frederick William III has often been blamed for not finding room for these men in his government. His sober appreciation of the situation may have been more conducive to peace and stability. But the ideas represented by these men in varying degrees could not be eradicated from the minds of the young, and they form one of the starting points of the many ideological strands which were to have such far-reaching effects in 1848.

Basically, these Prussian reformers were impatient with the lethargy of government. Certainly in the period between 1812 and 1815 they wanted to be able to make far-reaching changes quickly, both internally and externally. In the case of Baron Stein, analysis is complicated by the difficulty of finding any basic principles underlying his policy both as Prime Minister of Prussia and as Russian representative on the council of occupation in Germany from 1813 to 1815. As chief minister in Prussia from 1807 to 1808 he took the first steps for a reform of the state. He raised the status of ministers, who had previously merely been instruments of the king. He helped to create the post of Prime Minister and to lay down a definite procedure within which the king agreed to operate. Thus the rudiments of the constitutional state, as distinct from constitutional monarchy with a government based on parliamentary support, were created. All this was clearly indispensable to the modernisation of government, whichever particular constitutional form was eventually adopted. A more difficult problem of interpretation arises with Stein's application of the representative principle to municipal government. As he was soon dismissed at Napoleon's instigation, we do not know what part this reorganisation would have played in a complete scheme of reform. Did Stein generally want to strengthen local rather than central institutions? There is a certain conservatism, seen for instance in his attempt to cling to his rights as an imperial knight (*Reichsfreiherr*) of the Holy Roman Empire, which is difficult to reconcile with his reforming zeal and with his later radicalism. The ruthlessness with which Stein imposed his orders on German princes as Russian governor during the final stages of the Napoleonic wars, and his insistence on tough terms for the French, made him unacceptable in the compromise atmosphere of 1815 and the following years.

Gneisenau, Blücher's highly effective chief of staff at Waterloo, shared many of Stein's ideas, particularly his wish for a stern peace. The writer Ernst Moritz Arndt, who was employed by Stein as his propaganda chief during the campaign of 1812–13 and who was to be a member of the Frankfurt Parliament, represents a different type of politician. Both Stein and Gneisenau were only to a limited extent German nationalists of the new dispensation. But in Arndt's emphasis on the superiority of the Germans and in his hate for the French new undertones were already noticeable. Like Fichte, Arndt was developing a theory on which a radical concept of German nationalism could be based.

iii. The roots of German nationalism – Romanticism – Religious questions – The Catholic Church

The impulse to German nationalism was given by the French, but the German brand was quite indigenous. In the first instance there were the international elements left over from the Holy Roman Empire which gave the Germans a singular position. While not equating the Holy Roman Empire in any way with a German state, it is nevertheless true to say that of all nations the Germans played the most important part in it over the centuries. The Germans could thus claim a special position in the Christian and the European world. The concept of *Weltbürgertum* (cosmopolitanism) had a certain reality in the Germany of the first half of the nineteenth century even apart from this historical basis. The absence of a national or even a proper territorial state for the whole area had left the field free for universalism. Perhaps more than the English and the French, German writers and thinkers regarded the whole world with its history and learning as their province, as the example of Goethe shows. This attitude rightly earned the German people the title of the people of poets and thinkers. The achievement of German scholarship was prodigious. In historiography, the great German historians of the nineteenth century laid the foundations on which successors in many countries were to build. These German historians might see their own problems in the history of other nations, this might and did colour their outlook, but no other nation in Europe took the same interest in foreign countries. The breadth of this scholarship is of particular interest in connection with the Frankfurt Parliament, as many branches of learning were represented in the assembly.

It is much more difficult to write about the Germans in this vein now than it would have been in the last century. For we know to what purpose the claims of the German people to a special position could be put. But in the nineteenth century, these supra-national ideas could only become dangerous if used to strengthen national claims. This certainly never occurred to Goethe, who was taken to task by German nationalists for not concerning himself with the establishment of German political unity. A great gulf divided the old internationalists from the new nationalists, and their abhorrence was mutual. At the same time, elements of *Weltbürgertum* were present in the nationalist doctrines of Fichte, Jahn and Arndt.

In the era of the European Concert and the Congressional System, German supra-nationalism could have played a useful role. The German Confederation was well placed for that. But there was not sufficient support, especially in the younger generation. The Wars of Liberation of 1813 to 1815, which could have been interpreted as part of a European movement to free the continent from foreign tyranny, appeared to public opinion in Germany primarily as a national war with the French. The germ of the French concept of nationality was beginning to take root in the German mind. Supra-nationalism lost its central position and became an occasional and potentially dangerous adjunct to German nationalism.

In this study the term nationalism is employed in a neutral sense, qualified where necessary by an adjective. The word is used to describe the movement to create a German national state in whatever form.

There was confusion or at least lack of agreement as to what the basis of this new German state was to be. The specifically German contribution to this complex problem was the emphasis on language, first effectively propagated by Herder. This linguistic criterion was to find favour with other national movements, but it had its limitations. The fact that they spoke German or something like German did not necessarily mean that the inhabitants of a certain region wanted to join Germany. The population of Strasbourg in the Alsace which spoke a German dialect hardly wanted to leave French rule. Indeed, there were problems of definition as to what precisely constituted the German language. Did it cover German dialects, and, indeed, could Flemish be regarded as a form of German? Again, to have drawn political inferences from the fact that a language akin to German was spoken in the Low Countries would have been inadmissible. There were some further difficulties about this linguistic criterion. Were all those who spoke German as their main language, wherever they lived, to be claimed for the new German state? Moreover in border territories this principle was an invitation to interference in the linguistic teaching in schools for political purposes. People were forced to give up their traditional language and to learn a new one. An unhappy chapter in European history which has not yet been concluded had begun.

German scholars – like the Grimm brothers, one of whom sat in the Frankfurt Parliament – played a leading part in systematising the study of language. In this, as in so many other fields of learning, the line between scholarship and politics could not be clearly drawn. This interconnection between academic and political life which characterised the Frankfurt Parliament was mainly due to the lack of a national state and to the restrictions placed on the diffusion of political information. The energies of many of the ablest men were diverted into learning as a substitute for political action which was not open to them at the time. But the political implications of their scholastic activities were never far from their minds. The conferences of scholars of German literature and linguistics, the *Germanistentage*, which were held during the years before 1848, became a breeding ground for German parliamentary life in the revolutionary year.

In a wider sense, the study of language was part of a revived interest in the past which replaced the more static eighteenth-century approach to history. The Romantic movement became a powerful influence after the decline in the belief in rationality as a universal principle. The histories of nations were seen to be very different from each other and the predominant eighteenth-century philosopher's attitude to man was found to be premature, to say the least. There was no standard reasonable man, as some of the philosophers of the Enlightenment had assumed. The French revolutionary era had shown that simple philosophical remedies, like the removal of kings, did not necessarily turn people into more rational individuals. General principles fell somewhat out of fashion and the interest in variety and distinction revived.

The Romantic movement which reached the peak of its influence in Europe in the first half of the nineteenth century covered many aspects of life and had a variety of consequences. In the context of this book, Romanticism was initially of importance in reviving interest in Germany's past. The collection of popular fairy tales by the Grimm brothers played its part in this respect. Peoples were beginning to see their history and their language as a national heritage and as the basis for a common culture. In Germany, Romanticism in one way reinforced a certain tendency to shun the unpleasant realities of life. Romanticism was not bound to have this effect. For neither did the past have to be irrelevant to the present and the future, nor did a study of the past necessarily have to lead to escapism. In Germany there was certainly an idealisation of the past which appeared as so much better than the wayward present. This attitude did not instil a sense of reality into those who were influenced by the Romantics.

In constitutional theory, the contribution of the Romantics to the national movement was the discovery of democratic elements in the remote Teutonic past, such as the jury and also an elective political system. This Teutonic freedom was contrasted with 'French absolutism'. It is not for a modern historian to comment on the controversies of medieval history, except to wonder whether historians with political objectives do not sometimes overdo the parallels of the past with the present day. Stein was influenced by these theories and by the English example in his municipal reforms. There were some Hanoverian thinkers close to Stein who thought along the same lines.

In Wurtemberg, the discoveries of the Romantic period strengthened those like the poet Uhland – another member of the Frankfurt Parliament – who were fighting for *das gute alte Recht*, for the ancient rights of the estates. On the whole, however, this German antidote to French ideas had little future owing to the lack of historic continuity in Germany.

In religion, the Romantic movement had two contradictory effects.

In one respect, in the German national student movements, the *Deutsche Burschenschaft* for example, Romanticism certainly did not lead to a return of anything like orthodox religion. There the glorification of German institutions and the emphasis on German superiority kept students away from the churches and led to a substitute religion compounded of all sorts of elements, like the worship of nature. This does not mean that the *Burschenschaft* failed to raise the standards of students. Morals were certainly taken seriously and formed part of the code of association. The Puritan approach comes to mind. But immorality seems to have been condemned mainly for its *worldly* consequences, so that the Puritan parallel does not quite work, except for the intolerance which both shared. In the *Burschenschaft* the fall from grace was irretrievable. There was no road back. Christian charity was missing and all this makes the code, however honourable in parts, somewhat stilted. The gods were of this earth.

Romanticism, however, also proved for many to be a bridge to the churches. To Friedrich Schlegel and his circle the renewed interest in the Middle Ages opened up the vision of a moral order based on a universal church. Like other Romantics, he was converted to Roman Catholicism. The Romantic movement led to a revival in the German Catholic Church which had for so long been passive. The moment was opportune as Napoleonic rearrangements had removed clerical rule and as the Church in Germany was now able to concentrate on the care of souls unfettered by worldly responsibilities. A new type of Catholic priest and prelate putting religion first, but not unaware of political realities, was coming to the fore, represented for instance by Wilhelm von Ketteler, who sat in the Frankfurt Parliament. This generation was deeply religious and determined to put relations between church and state on a basis which would permit the widest possible extension of the Catholic faith. These men were only gradually making their appearance in the period after 1815. There were many disagreements among them about the internal organisation of their church – such as over the position of the bishops – and about their duty towards the state. As in the state, there was a contest between democratic and authoritarian principles. There was also the whole question of the relationship with the Papacy, but the term 'ultramontane' has only confused the issue without leading to any clarification.

In a Catholic state like Bavaria, Catholic ministers and politicians were common in the years before 1848, particularly after the removal of the rationalist minister Count Montgelas in 1817. In Germany generally, however, Roman Catholics were very slow to take an active part in politics. In Prussia, they were roused by the arrest of the Archbishop of Cologne, von Droste-Vischering, on the orders of Frederick William III in 1837. The issue at stake between the Archbishop and the Prussian government was connected with the question of marriages between Catholics and Protestants. The Archbishop's stand was no doubt part of the general Catholic attempt after all the political compromises of the past to reassert the position of the church. In this sense, Droste-Vischering belonged to the new movement which was denigrated by its opponents as ultramontane or clerical. What the ageing archbishop lacked was the political suppleness of many rising clerics. Apart from religious conflicts of this kind, however, before 1848 Catholic participation in political life in Germany generally was much smaller than that of Protestants. Fundamentally, Catholics were put off – more than Protestants – by the almost religious zeal with which the necessity of German national unification was often advocated. To some, German nationalism was a substitute religion. This does not mean that all those who led this movement were irreligious. There were many devout Protestants among them. But even some of these joined the chorus of those to whom there was no higher aim at all than the achievement of German national aspirations. As they were used to a state church, the Protestants may have found this easier to accept than the Catholics. In addition, the universalist Catholic Church had to overcome objections to pursuing a purely national object.

There was a fundamental difference of opinion between the German liberals and the Catholics which could not be ignored in the long run. The German liberals were powerfully influenced by French rationalism. They often called themselves *fortschrittlich* (progressive) or *freisinnig* which could be rendered as 'free thinking'. One implication of these labels was that the liberals were overcoming old prejudices, including that which allowed people to be deceived by priests into believing in religion. As there could not be any organised political parties before 1848 all these terms are imprecise. But there are many in the varied ranks of the pre-1848 opposition who were religious freethinkers, like the Rhenish industrialist Gustav Mevissen who served in the Frankfurt Parliament and in the Reich Government.

The attitude of Roman Catholics to German unification became a crucial factor in 1848 and 1849. In many regions of Germany, quite

B

apart from Austria, Roman Catholics were in a majority, for instance in the South-East and the West. Yet the leading opposition spokesmen from the mainly Catholic Rhineland at the Prussian United Diet of 1847 were Protestants, including Mevissen, who then antagonised Catholics – and indeed all Christians – by a speech in the chamber in which he mentioned Jesus Christ in the same breath with Socrates and Huss as men who had come into conflict with the moral code of their time. All through the period after 1815, the broad alliance of liberalism and nationalism in Germany took little account of the future weight which the Catholics might have. The first great demonstration of the national student movement, the *Deutsche Burschenschaft*, was the celebration of the third centenary of Luther's affixation of the 95 theses at the Wartburgfest of 1817. The choice of this anniversary showed indifference to what Catholics might feel about German unification, in spite of all the phrases about Germany being one, including Austria with its millions of Catholics. Indifference is often too weak a word to describe the attitude of the liberals to the Catholics. The renewal of Catholicism was viewed with much more hostility than the pietistical revival on the Protestant side. This liberal unfriendliness to Catholicism was not due mainly to the freethinking element represented by a man like Mevissen. The attitude of the main body of the liberals to the Catholic Church is seen most clearly in the movement of *Deutschkatholizismus*.

iv. Deutschkatholizismus – *Increasing differences between the moderate liberals and the radicals*

The *Deutschkatholiken* are far less well known than the Old Catholics of the 1870s. But in many ways the earlier movement is the more interesting as it sprang from many sources beyond the purely religious. As in England at the same time, political and religious movements were closely interconnected. *Deutschkatholizismus* was a protest against the particular form the religious revival was taking in the Catholic Church in Germany in the 1840s. In Prussia, the accession of Frederick William IV had strengthened the position of the Catholics. The new king, a deeply religious man, leaning towards Protestant pietism, was determined to heal the wounds left by his father's treatment of both churches. Like Bismarck in the *Kulturkampf*, Frederick William III interfered not only with the Catholic but also with the Protestant Church. The forcible foundation of the Prussian United Evangelical Church in 1817 by Frederick William III was not achieved without persecution of tender consciences. The new king was sympathetic to both his Protestant and his Catholic subjects, including those who had clashed with the crown. He eased the position of Protestant dissenters. The situation of Catholics during the first years of his reign was at least as good as that in any Catholic German state. In looking after his millions of subjects belonging to another religion the King was not only responding to the dictates of justice and to his own wish for reconciliation between the Christian churches. He was also strengthening Prussia's political position in Germany.

Broadly speaking, the Prussian liberals were not entirely happy about the new key position accorded to the Catholics in the kingdom. To them, these moves at the Court of Berlin had a sinister ring. They seemed to forebode a new alliance between throne and altar directed against the liberal movement. In spite of some relaxation of government pressure, the new reign was, indeed, marked by greater severity towards religious unorthodoxy at the universities than before. Under Frederick William III, a rationalist indifference on the part of the authorities had on the whole prevailed towards religious deviation and indifference. Many university teachers, like the Hegelians Ruge[1] and Nauwerck[2] – both later members of the Frankfurt Parliament – were to feel the effects of this. 'Liberal' theology seemed to be in danger. These religious issues had political undertones.

Those who were afraid of being crushed by the alliance of throne and altar thought that their chance had come in the middle of the 1840s. A protest movement then developed in the Catholic Church against the exhibition of relics at Trier, which had taken place at the behest of the Bishop, Arnoldi. The leader was an excommunicated priest, Johannes Ronge. Undoubtedly the exhibition of these relics as well as the reaction against it reflected deep feelings which became crystallised in these events. Presumably, some of those Catholics who did not like the greater activity of the bishops and their tightening of discipline regarded the events at Trier as a signal. Looking back, the claim to represent the true Catholic Church by a comparatively small number of men who seceded and formed the movement of *Deutschkatholizismus* seems empty

[1] See below, p. 81.   [2] See below, p. 220.

of meaning. Not even all of those who seceded were in fact motivated entirely by their religious faith. The movement was partly one of discontent against authority with which every church, like every other organisation, is occasionally faced. Indeed, the whole secession movement would have collapsed within a very short time it if had not received help from outside. The liberals were interested in *Deutschkatholizismus* for two reasons. Many of them, including the men who in 1847 founded the newspaper of the German national movement, the *Deutsche Zeitung*, were thinking in terms of a German national church comprising both Protestants and Catholics. It is very surprising that some of the most eminent and shrewdest liberals of this period, including Mathy,[1] Mittermaier,[2] Bassermann[3] and Gervinus[4] – all later members of the Frankfurt Parliament – made so elementary a miscalculation. How could they imagine that the few congregations of the *Deutschkatholiken* which sprang up in parts like Saxony and Silesia represented any significant part of German Catholics? If these men now woke up to the importance of securing the co-operation of Catholics for their schemes of national unity, they set about it in a curious way. For surely there could hardly be anything which was going to antagonise the German Catholics against the circle of the *Deutsche Zeitung* as much as this – entirely vain – attempt to undermine their church.

The more radical elements in the opposition also wanted to use *Deutschkatholizismus* for their purposes, but in a much more logical way – from their point of view – than the moderate liberals. For Robert Blum[5] in Saxony, soon to become the leader of the Left in the Frankfurt Parliament, here was a chance to strike at the established order generally. This does not mean that Blum was indifferent to the religious side of *Deutschkatholizismus*. Indeed, Blum's radicalism, which was partly the consequence of his experience of social and economic misery, also received a strong impulse from his clash with the Catholic clergy who taught him during his childhood. For years he had ceased to be a practising Catholic. The new movement seemed to offer him a chance of being a Catholic without having to tolerate those aspects of the church which he disliked. Blum helped to found the *Deutschkatholische Gemeinde* in Leipzig. He was certainly anti-clerical and opposed to the dictation of dogma to the individual. He probably believed in a general Christian religion with a minimum of church organisation, something in

---

[1] See below, p. 54 f.   [2] See below, p. 44.   [3] See below, p. 41.
[4] See below, p. 41.   [5] See below, p. 134 ff.

the English 'independent' tradition, with a similar political connotation.

Taking account of the close link between politics and religion, three great forces are discernible in Germany by 1847. These were the governments, backed by the conservative forces in state and church. Then there was the Catholic Church, sometimes a pillar of the established order, but sometimes – as for a time in Bavaria just before 1848 – in opposition. Thirdly, there was the 'liberal' opposition. The term 'liberal' cannot be applied precisely, because in this era of press censorship and of authoritarian curbs on free movement, political parties were unknown. Indeed, members of the opposition were at pains to repudiate any suggestion of party and to emphasise that they had the public interest as much at heart as the government had. Members of the various assemblies of estates played an increasingly prominent part in the period between 1830 and 1848. Their actual powers were limited mainly to the legislative function of agreeing to new laws. But in a more subtle way, not having a chance of coming into office themselves before 1848, the leaders of the opposition in the various states had tremendous prestige in the country as *Volksmänner* and as spokesmen for the German cause. They could always tell the ministers that they, the opposition, represented the people. This claim, reiterated for many years, bore fruit in 1848 by demoralising the old ministers. It was soon found to be a somewhat empty boast.

During the gradual transition towards more effective parliaments, which received a great impulse after the 1830 revolution in France, one great difficulty proved to be the recruitment of members of sufficient calibre. This problem was due not only to the comparative political inexperience of the mass of the people, but also to an artificial restriction of those interested in serving as members of the estates, through property and residence qualifications. One constant source of friction was the right of the government to refuse to its officials leave to serve in parliament. As officials, versed in political affairs, always formed a high proportion of those who stood for parliament, this problem assumed considerable dimensions. There were dangers in the government being able to 'pack' parliament with dependent officials, or having the power to veto the admission of elected members of the legislature. The government could, however, fairly claim that officials who were elected to parliament should opt between their two positions. Also no government could be overjoyed at having officials – frequently of junior rank – challenging its policy in parliament. In many cases, officials refused leave to take up their seats in the estates resigned from the civil service, often making considerable financial sacrifices. Heinrich von Gagern, an official in the Grand-Duchy of Hesse-Darmstadt and later to be president of the Frankfurt Parliament, resigned his official position because the Prime Minister, von Du Thil, who disliked him, made difficulties about his leave. Gagern had means of his own, but none the less he put himself to considerable inconvenience for his political views. For others, the loss of income was much more crippling. Since university professors, too, were officials of the state, the area of those subject to government approval was very considerable.

On the whole it suited governments to regard the whole of the opposition as hostile to the régime and to make little attempt to distinguish between various elements. Generally, the opposition were written off as dangerous, on the grounds of being 'liberal'. The cracks within the rather mixed oppositions were pasted over again and again because governments persecuted indiscriminately and thus forced those in opposition to stick together. The coming division of the opposition into a moderate liberal and a radical group is seen most clearly in the state whose government was beginning to respond to liberal influences and even taking moderate liberals into the government, the Grand-Duchy of Baden.

The Chamber of Deputies in Baden attracted attention all over Germany because of the high standard of its debates, of a somewhat more relaxed atmosphere than was the case elsewhere and of the interest in affairs beyond the Grand-Duchy. Many leading personalities of the Frankfurt Parliament, like Welcker,[1] Mittermaier, Mathy and Bassermann, gained their experience at Karlsruhe. Besides these men, who formed the core of the Centre in the Frankfurt Parliament, others sat in the Baden Chamber who had more radical tendencies, above all Friedrich Hecker, who led two risings in 1848. Hecker was an out-and-out revolutionary, determined to carry out wholesale changes in society, though he did not in any way belong to the following of Karl Marx. During 1847, the moderate liberals in Baden found themselves coming increasingly under attack from the radicals. This development foreshadowed part of the great liberal problem for the future, their central position between Left and Right, offering certain tactical advantages, but also bringing with it the danger of being ground to pieces between extremes. It was an unwelcome change for the moderate liberals to find

[1] See below, p. 38.

themselves reprimanded for not sufficiently representing the people; so far they had been able to bask in popular glory. The split in the opposition found expression in the Offenburg manifesto of the radicals in September 1847 and the reply of the moderate liberals at Heppenheim the following month.[1] It would however be wrong to exaggerate the formality and clarity of the division. Some, like the leader of the Baden opposition, Adam von Itzstein, hovered uneasily between the two wings. Not all the politicians were clearly aligned, and even by the time of the elections for the Frankfurt Parliament in May 1848, the electors often could not tell to which section a particular politician belonged. Indeed the position of many parliamentarians was only gradually clarified with the unfolding of events. In the dramatic days of 1848 and the following years this confusion is not surprising.

In Prussia, 1847 also saw important developments, with the meeting of the first United Diet. Though the liberals had reason to feel disappointed with the extent of the King's constitutional concessions, the Diet gave a tremendous impulse to political life. Many leading personalities of the Frankfurt Parliament of all shades first attracted public attention at the Diet in Berlin.

Before the revolutionary events of February and March 1848, there was little evidence in Germany of things stirring. Even if the political front was quiet, Germany was in the middle of great economic and social changes, connected with increasing industrialisation. Many gained from this development, but more lost in the short run. The days of fairly easy movement up and down the social scale within a broad middle class – below the aristocracy and above the paupers – were gradually vanishing. How recent these changes were is seen from the lives of members of the Frankfurt Parliament who largely grew up in the days of pre-industrialisation; many had worked their way up from humble backgrounds and poverty. This was to be much more difficult during the following generations. To set up in business now needed far more capital than the journeyman who became a master required in the era before industrialisation. These developments in turn led to a more rigid class structure. Naturally, it would be idle to pretend that the old guild society did not also encourage immobility. Up to the reforms of the Napoleonic period, there had been some impediments to movement from one occupational class (*Stand*) to another. But the first decades of the nineteenth century saw the sweeping away of strong barriers, some

[1] Huber, *Dokumente* I 261 ff.

of which – in a different way – industrialisation was to restore. Many were afraid of being consigned to the proletariat without means of escape, even if they had ability, because they would not have the capital to found their own businesses. Men of the journeyman class who could no longer become masters because the smaller businesses were going badly constituted a strong element of discontent. Their outlook tended to be conservative in the sense of wishing to prevent industrial innovation and of demanding a return to a guild structure. Politically, they could, however, be revolutionary. There were many economic and social grievances at this time of change. This discontent provided varied and often contradictory backing for the German revolution when it came. But the main demands in the German revolution of 1848 was primarily political: constitutional, radical and national.

While there was not before the revolution a serious threat to the continued existence of the German Confederation, this did not mean that the political balance in Germany could be maintained for ever. After the French revolution of July 1830, which had profound effects in Germany, the standstill of the 1820s became much harder to maintain. More constitutions were granted, more parliaments started functioning in the various states, finally even in 1847 in a certain form in Prussia. The Metternich system of the status quo had broken down and, as the Chancellor himself realised, these changes would lead to further ones. The Swiss *Sonderbundkrieg* in 1847 also stirred German public opinion.

The question was really in which direction these changes were going to lead. Obviously the trend was away from autocracy to increasing control of the executive by the legislature. Was there going to be a 'mixed' form of government as in contemporary England? Or something like the Belgian constitutional monarchy? Or a republic like in Switzerland or the United States of America, two great examples? Or was Germany going to evolve its own form of government? On the national plane the question was whether the German Confederation could be adapted to meet current needs, for instance by the creation of a national parliament alongside the existing *Bundestag* which consisted of government representatives. How were all the problems involved in bringing together states with so different a history, rent by religious division, going to be solved? Many looked to Prussia, which had shown by the formation of the *Zollverein*, and the establishment of a large customs area in Germany by 1848, that she was capable of taking the initiative. But others looked askance at this Protestant militaristic and bureaucratic state.

The political forces which were going to settle these issues were gradually forming, though often imperceptibly. There were the governments, united by a common interest in their own preservation but by little else. There was the opposition, gradually splitting into a moderate and a radical or democratic section. There were the so far uncommitted masses of the Catholics and of the less well-to-do, identical in many cases. If manhood suffrage were introduced, how would these two mass groups vote? The democrats were increasingly active in mobilising mass support. This radical agitation was very worrying to the moderate liberals by the end of 1847 and they were well aware of the danger, for instance in Baden. The liberals were less conscious of the importance of the Catholic mass vote. They probably thought they could do without it somehow, an unfortunate miscalculation. Otherwise one could hardly have imagined that they were prepared to launch a newspaper for the German cause – the *Deutsche Zeitung* – with little or no Catholic support and that many of them were prepared to toy with the idea of *Deutschkatholizismus*. Or did they have a mainly Protestant Germany in mind, without Austria? One gets the impression that the moderate liberals had not thought out their ideas fully and that they were prepared to sit back in the hope that time was with them.

The test of power was to come only too soon for the liberals.

2 Revolution and Pre-Parliament

i. The Paris revolution – A French invasion? – Social riots in Germany – Liberal ministers – The radicals

THE Frankfurt Parliament met only in the middle of May, but its foundations were laid in the preceding three eventful months. It is generally agreed that the overthrow of King Louis Philippe on 24 February 1848 set off the chain of events which transformed Germany. But there is disagreement as to whether this impulse from outside was essential to get things moving. In the circumstances the burden of proof must be on those who claim that the Germans could have started on reform without the signal from abroad. It is true that there was not complete stagnation, as Radowitz's proposal for a reform of the German Confederation of 20 November 1847[1] shows. However, one of the Rhenish liberal leaders was complaining of a lack of public interest in political issues on 11 February 1848.[2] To believe, as the present author does, that an outside impulse was necessary, is no reflection on the Germans of 1848. In times of peace and quiet, the European Powers were quite strong enough to prevent fundamental changes in Germany. The German Confederation was a pillar of the European order, and far-reaching changes there involved a threat to the Vienna settlement which at any rate the three Eastern Powers were not prepared to tolerate; the support of Britain and France for change could not be assumed by any means. Prime responsibility for the status quo in Germany lay with the three Eastern Powers, two of whose rulers were members of the German Confederation. Though the military might of Prussia was considerable, the Prussian Government was bound to look over its shoulder to St Petersburg and to Vienna. Russia and Austria were thus the chief props of the conservative order in Germany. It was only when these powers were preoccupied with their own problems or with other vital issues that their hold over Germany was relaxed. This was well understood both by opposition politicians, who were constantly

---

[1] Meinecke, *Radowitz* 50.   [2] Hansen, *Mevissen* II 330.

inveighing against Russian influence in Germany, and by the princes
who relied on the support of St Petersburg and Vienna. In normal times,
many of the German courts would get a lead from these two capitals
almost from day to day. But after the French February revolution,
rulers like the King of Wurtemberg and the Grand-Duke of Oldenburg
realised that they could not count on Russian or Austrian backing.
They faced up to the fact that for the time being they were thrown on
their own devices, even before the revolutions in Vienna and Berlin in
the middle of March. These German princes were aware that the authorities at St Petersburg and at Vienna were more concerned with the
general European situation created by the setting up of a republic in
France than with what was going to happen in one of the smaller German states. They realised that the Russians were worried about the
Poles, and the Austrians about the Italians and some of the other
nationalities under their rule, quite apart from general unrest even
among their own people. From a pure power point of view, the Germans
were for most of the time until about November 1848 able to do as they
pleased within non-Habsburg Germany without fear of Austria or
Russia. Until Prince Schwarzenberg had made his influence felt as
chief minister in Austria, the Habsburg Empire, rent by revolution
and internal dissension, was in no position to interfere in Germany.
Russian intervention was hardly possible politically, quite apart from
any military difficulties: as long as the Habsburgs had not restored
order completely in their territories, Russian troops had to stand by
for the Austrian Empire. Indeed, in 1849, the Russians helped to quell
the Hungarian revolution. British intervention was unlikely, except
over Schleswig-Holstein. Thus, after any danger from France was seen
to be over by about June, the Germans were for nearly half a year
their own masters outside the limits of the Habsburg Empire.

It is no coincidence that the French revolutions of both 1830 and of
1848 had profound effects on Germany. France, defeated in 1815, was
the only one of the five Great European Powers which could possibly
have an interest in overthrowing the Vienna settlement. A change of
régime in Paris, particularly a violent one, was bound to stir up
nightmare memories of the French Revolutionary and Napoleonic era.
The substitution of the Orleanist Louis Philippe for the Bourbon
Charles X in July 1830 had been bad enough for European legitimists
and had led to a certain liberalisation in Germany. The abolition of the
monarchy on the abdication of Louis Philippe and the proclamation of

the Second Republic was an even graver blow. Not only was there uncertainty as to whether the new French government was going to
respect the European order, but for the first time since the Vienna
settlement a major European power had not only rid itself of its ruler,
but also established a republic. There were very few republics in Europe
at the time and those that existed could not all be considered very politically advanced, particularly when one thinks of the fossilised oligarchical
régimes in the German Free Towns. If a republican régime was synony-
mous to many of the governments and of the well-to-do with a threat to
the existing political and social order, this was due mainly to memories
of the First French Republic which were bound to be evoked. Besides,
there were, however, two republics which were very much on people's
minds in the 1848 period, both of their enemies and of their admirers.

The upholders of monarchical legitimism regarded the Swiss Republic and the United States of America as unpleasant examples of revolts
which had paid off. As recently as 1847, the wishes of the Eastern
Powers had been thwarted when the Swiss Confederation crushed the
revolt of the *Sonderbund*. What made Switzerland irksome to Metternich
endeared it to German liberals and radicals. Many of these found
refuge in Switzerland in the years before 1848. Germans of the pre-1848
opposition admired the way the Swiss applied democratic processes to
public life. Some of them hoped to emulate the Swiss by abolishing
the monarchy and caste distinctions in Germany. The existence of an
island of comparative political freedom and egalitarianism in the heart
of Europe had been a thorn in the flesh of the legitimist powers. The
Swiss Republic was bad enough. A French Republic would be worse.
For nobody could say exactly of what radical policies the new French
régime might be capable both at home and abroad. France might again
become a revolutionary centre which could infect the whole of Europe,
overthrowing thrones and property rights once more. As no other event,
the February revolution both stimulated and frightened the Germans,
was half welcomed and half feared. The whole ambivalence of the
German attitude to France was once more brought into the open. The
Germans could not have it both ways, they could not go on enjoying
the same external security they had possessed under the Metternich
system when they now rejoiced at the end of the European tutelage of
their country. French ideas at this time, however, were not always quite
logical. Political messianism might lead to oppression, and the line of
division between liberators and conquerors is notoriously a thin one.

A France which for the time being did not recognise European obligations might take it into her head to achieve once more her 'natural' frontier on the Rhine. A fresh French invasion of German territory could not be discounted.

It was this threat of a French invasion, no less than all the political and ideological implications of the February revolution, which impressed itself on governments and governed alike in Germany. For the princes there was the double worry that they might find themselves exposed simultaneously to a fresh invasion and to revolution at home, all this at a time when they could not reckon on any Russian or Austrian support. They could do little to prevent a French invasion from being attempted. But they could do something about their relationship with their subjects. They realised that in case of a French invasion domestic disunity was something the German states could ill afford.

Outside government circles, only the extreme Left had an unmixed joy about events in France. They were pleased about the radical turn of events in France and undaunted by the prospect of a possible French invasion of German territory. They would have been prepared at this stage to have welcomed the French as liberators. The more moderate opponents of the pre-March governments, however, did not regard developments in France as an unmixed blessing. They welcomed the political thaw in Germany, but they were full of misgivings and disquiet at the extremism and brutality which had marked the outbreak in Paris. Beckerath, one of the Rhenish liberals, in a letter on 27 February 1848 expressed his fear that constitutional development in Germany would be hampered by events in Paris which would discredit the opposition in the eyes of the governments. Political reform was going to take second place in the face of the danger from abroad.[1] While Beckerath misinterpreted the consequences of French militancy on the attitude of the governments, he correctly sensed the great danger for a steady political development in Germany which arose from the use of violence. In this respect the February revolution was an unfortunate beginning to reform in Germany.

The success of violence in Paris was not lost on the aggrieved social classes in Germany. In many parts of Western Germany, peasants rose up against the privileged classes, notably against the *Standesherren*, tearing up records of seigneurial claims and ravaging property. Others attacked Jewish creditors. These movements were spontaneous and

[1] Hansen, *Mevissen* II 332.

unorganised, reflecting deep popular feelings, but were outside the main stream of political development. The political radicals or democrats might at times use this social discontent, but they are not to be identified with these social revolutionary tendencies.

The social riots were, after the threat of a French invasion, the second *short-term* clause which inclined the princes to make concessions. The attacks on property showed the princes and many members of the bourgeois opposition how necessary it was for them to join forces. Suddenly, the *long-term* liberal demands for bringing government closer together with public opinion made sense to the princes. With external and internal danger ahead, this scheme now appeared as inevitable and commonsensical. Later on, the sudden surrender of rulers to liberal demands was given a sinister interpretation. It was argued on the radical Left that the princes had never been sincere in their co-operation with the liberals, that they simply used the liberal ministers for their own purposes, always intending to revert to their old 're-actionary' methods as soon as they could. While this stratagem was undoubtedly in the minds of some of the princes, the theory ignores the genuine feeling of relief which the decision to liberalise their govern-ments gave to most of the princes. In the ten days beginning on 4 March 1848, when the dozen main rulers outside Prussia and Austria conceded the liberal demands, the resolve to accept reform was usually quite straightforward and genuine, the only way out of a complete political impasse. It takes some believing to credit these princes with complex long-term plans during exciting days when nobody ever quite knew what the next hour was going to bring. The monarchs were only the first of successive groups in 1848 and 1849 to be caught up in rapidly moving events whose final outcome they could hardly predict.

Generally, apart from the social outbreaks, the transition to liberalisation was achieved with little bloodshed in the medium and small states. On the whole, it was sufficient to threaten violence, without actually resorting to it. These crude methods of coercing the authorities were presumably inevitable at a time when the machinery for bringing government policy into harmony with public opinion was insufficiently developed. The princes were no longer free agents. They recognised the strong popular backing for the liberal demands and hoped to benefit from their new alliance.

There were, however, certain flaws in the liberal takeover. The moderate liberals of the Rhineland and of the South-West of Germany had never anticipated being swept into power on the crest of a popular outbreak. Believing as they did in gradualism, they had aimed at increasingly stepping up their following and at making the most of their parliamentary position. They were unprepared for being lifted into power on the shoulders of the populace. They were not yet ready, their theories were only half worked out. Their theory of government was too static. They considered themselves the representatives of the people *par excellence*, in perpetuity; they could hardly envisage a time when somebody else would have a better claim to represent the people. In this respect, they were far behind the Whigs or Liberals of Great Britain, or similar political parties in, say, France or the United States of America. Indeed, the moderate liberals made their concept of representative government sound far too easy. They convinced the princes that the liberal system was workable, but they did not point out the difficulties, as they were only slowly beginning to find them out themselves in these hectic weeks. To this extent, the princes could afterwards claim that they had not been treated quite fairly by the liberals.

The main worry of the liberals during the ensuing political struggles was that from now on they would have to wage war on two fronts. The electoral contests in Baden during 1847 had already given them a foretaste of this, but only in a comparatively mild form. With the intensification of political life in 1848, competition for the claim to represent the people increased. The old liberal scheme of distinguishing between a government unrepresentative of the people and an opposition representing the people boomeranged on them when liberals became ministers. Liberals in position of authority, having at times to do unpopular things, were now to have a taste of their own medicine. They were to find themselves pilloried as enemies of the people by politicians to their Left unfettered by the responsibilities of power. The democrats or radicals were far more damaging to the liberals than the old 'reactionary' governments had ever been. The pre-1848 régimes had been able to hurt the liberals physically, they had been able to persecute them, but persecution only made the opposition more popular. The power of the radicals to attack the liberals physically was far more limited, though terrorism and at times even violence were used. The radicals could castigate the liberals and by threatening to discredit them with the electors could blackmail them at times into courses of action which the moderates disliked. The liberals were in a dilemma from February onwards. They wanted to preserve the unity of the old liberal-democrat coalition of bygone opposition days. They required the maximum support they could muster in order to impress the rulers. Only by maintaining their coalition with the democrats could they avoid having to lean too heavily on the help of the princes. The democrats naturally realised how essential their alliance was to the liberals, and they were determined – quite rightly from their point of view – to exact a price for their assistance. In March, the liberals could not but try and keep the door to the left open. They had no alternative at that time. But to do so they had to accept points of a political programme which did not suit them and to engage in ambiguities which did them and their cause no good.

The moderate liberals were quite prepared to co-operate with the princes. They could see many advantages in constitutional monarchy. But the democrats forced them, as the price for their support, to swallow something of the doctrine of the sovereignty of the people which was anathema to the princes. According to this theory, 'the people' could decree a new order of things for Germany, without reference to the princes. This purely rationalist approach was contemptuous of the apparently rather odd manifestations of historical growth. Starting from these premises, the radicals were not prepared to face up to the fact that the princes had power and even some popularity. The democrats could only break the position of the princes by a second revolution. The moderate liberals had a far truer appreciation of the strength of the princes. Even those of them who were *personally* inclined to the republican form of government, like Mathy, who had lived and worked in Switzerland, and Römer from Wurtemberg with its egalitarian tradition, were rightly convinced that any attempt to remove the princes – which some of the democrats desired – would lead to bitter and prolonged civil war. Theory apart, the liberals in order to maintain democrat support were afraid of coming out into the open over the necessity of negotiating with the princes, for instance about the reorganisation of Germany. They allowed an atmosphere of unreality to grow up over this question of the relations with the princes which was to prove a severe handicap later on.

While the line of division between the moderate liberals and the democrats was not always clear (and there were intermediate groups), a basic difference was that the liberals were prepared to be more pragmatic than the rather doctrinaire democrats. Thus the liberals were ready to accept the historical situation as their starting point and to try and modify it in details, whereas the democrats wanted to create an entirely new order. In turn, this was the difference between those who looked to English gradualism as against those who wanted to emulate French wholesale change. While most of the moderate liberals paid great attention to historical roots, for this very reason they were often opposed to transplanting English institutions to Germany. Once several of the moderate liberals had been entrusted with government responsibility, the rationalist proclamation of basic rights, irrespective of circumstances, also became a useful stick with which to beat the liberal ministers. For the latter had to suspend the basic rights at times against illegal acts on the part of these very democrats.

The liberals and the democrats had common roots and thus there were a number of agreed aims which could be pressed in the first half of March 1848. Both groups were united on the need for the strengthening of parliamentary institutions, for the dismissal of 'reactionary' ministers and for their replacement by men more in touch with public opinion. They abhorred the censorship of publications and the many curbs put on the expression and dissemination of political information. They wanted to encourage democratic decision-making. Similarly they were agreed on the desirability of creating a German national state, though disagreed on the methods. They meant something different by 'general armament of the people' (*allgemeine Volksbewaffnung*), the liberals thinking mainly of external danger and the democrats primarily of forging a weapon to aid their domestic plans. The two groups disagreed on the desirable extent of the franchise, and here the liberals initially capitulated, accepting universal manhood suffrage, although they would have preferred a more restricted electorate in the first instance. During the next year the liberals saw increasingly how unwise they had been to concede manhood suffrage. They had given up their gradualism in this important respect and thus undermined their whole position. They tried to undo their concession, but had to do this in adverse circumstances and in the end were forced to reverse their position once more.[1] They were to learn that a moderate party was unlikely to benefit from a sudden general extension of the franchise. One wonders whether the radicals were really in a position to exact this pound of flesh in March 1848 from the liberals. The explanation of the liberal concession is probably that the moderates did not want to fall behind in the general popularity contest and did not then realise

[1] See below, p. 382.

sufficiently how much they were giving away. Altogether, the radicals ensured that far more was spelled out than the liberals wished, restricting not only the princes, but also limiting the area for manoeuvre of liberal ministers. Basically, the liberals were prepared to trust the princes, if not absolutely, then certainly to a greater extent than the democrats. They were ready to leave quite a considerable position to the princes, confiding in their ability to handle them. The democrats basically mistrusted the monarchs and wanted to reduce them to the position of ciphers, as long as they could not abolish them altogether.

ii. The Heidelberg assembly – Revolution in Vienna and Berlin – The Pre-Parliament

In March, the alliance between liberals and democrats was still maintained, if with some difficulty. On 5 March 1848, at the Heidelberg assembly of fifty-one public figures from most parts of Germany, though mainly from the West and South-West, leaders of both groups, ranging from Bassermann to Hecker, issued a joint programme, demanding a German national parliament.[1] The Heidelberg assembly was the first of many bodies – unofficial and official – which were to be established in Germany in great numbers during the next few weeks, making the transaction of business more difficult, rather than easier. Some of these gatherings owed their origin to habits acquired during the pre-1848 period when various unofficial meetings made up for the lack of official representative institutions, particularly for Germany as a whole. In the new era, when liberal ministers took up leading positions in the state governments, these bodies weakened not only the princes but also these very governments. A German national parliament was in the air and was desired by both the liberals and the democrats. But its form was determined in important respects by the initiative which came from the Heidelberg meeting and would have been quite different if the calling of the parliament had been left to the state governments through their ministers at the German Confederation. Once more, the democrats lost no time and the Heidelberg assembly met just before the ten-day period when most states appointed former moderate opposition politicians to ministerial posts. Several of these

[1] Declaration in Huber, *Dokumente* i 264.

were present at Heidelberg. Had these men already been in office, they would hardly have supported at this meeting an extra-governmental initiative for calling a German national parliament. The Heidelberg assembly regarded arrangements for this parliament as its most important business. The meeting tackled this task with considerable energy, setting off a chain of events which led to the Pre-Parliament (*Vorparlament*) and to the Committee of Fifty (*Fünfziger-Ausschuss*). In effect, this development brought in its train the supersession of the Federal Assembly (*Bundesversammlung*) which might have still played a useful part[1] and aggravated the obstacles in the way of an understanding with the princes. These results were not intended by the liberals, and made their plans more difficult to carry out. They were, however, in the minds of the democrats and show their superior tactical skill at this stage. The same determination, bordering on unscrupulousness, marked the use made by the democrats of the Committee of Seven (*Siebenerausschuss*) entrusted by the Heidelberg assembly with the task of issuing invitations to a further meeting to prepare for a Constituent Assembly, the body which was later called briefly *Vorparlament* (Pre-Parliament). The Pre-Parliament was to consist mainly of men who had served in legislative assemblies, but the Committee of Seven was given discretion to summon a number of others whose presence would be valuable. Adam von Itzstein, a member of the Committee of Seven, who had led the opposition in Baden before the split into moderates and democrats, was suspected by the moderates of having packed the Pre-Parliament with radicals.[2] The Pre-Parliament was to meet on 31 March, by which time the general situation had altered again.

The ten days which followed the meeting of the Heidelberg assembly saw the change to liberal régimes in practically all the states apart from Prussia and Austria. In Hesse-Darmstadt, the conservative minister Du Thil made way for Heinrich von Gagern,[3] a member of the moderate Heppenheim assembly[4] and of the Heidelberg meeting, who was to play a central part in the Frankfurt Parliament. King William I of Wurtemberg, one of the most determined rulers, made the revealing statement

[1] For instance in the opinion of Jürgens, a member of the Right Centre in the Frankfurt Parliament (see his *Zur Geschichte* I (1850), in the first chapters). For Jürgens see *ADB* xiv; *BSTH*.

[2] See Jürgens, *Zur Geschichte* I 25.

[3] *ADB* xlix; Wentzcke and Klötzer, *Deutscher Liberalismus*.　　　[4] See above, p. 25.

that one could not mount on horseback against ideas.[1] Friedrich Römer, another opposition politician, balanced nicely between the liberal and the democrat wings, who had also been at Heppenheim and Heidelberg, became the leading minister. This forceful personality was not to act to the satisfaction of either the liberals or the democrats. Though in a key position in the government at Stuttgart, he had enough energy to spare to make a significant contribution to the Frankfurt Parliament.[2] In Baden, another participant of the Heppenheim and Heidelberg assemblies, the famous liberal theorist and propagandist Welcker,[3] succeeded the conservative Blittersdorf as minister to the German Confederation. In Saxony, Ludwig von der Pfordten, who had been penalised in Bavaria because of his liberal views some years previously, became a minister. In Hanover, even King Ernest Augustus (Duke of Cumberland), who had on his accession in 1837 involved himself in a bitter constitutional conflict, gave in and appointed a stalwart of the opposition, Stüve, to a leading position in the government. Stüve, one of the most interesting statesmen of the period, does not fit into any pattern, least into that of liberalism.[4] In all these states, constitutional reform was well under way. Usually the decision to change course was taken before the news of the sweeping changes in Vienna had come through. With the Austrian revolution a new phase began in which violence was not only threatened to achieve political changes, but was actually used. Only in the two major states, Austria and Prussia, a full armed clash took place before the régime surrendered fully to the liberal demands.

All over the Habsburg Empire, developments in France and Germany were followed with spellbound attention by those who were politically interested. There were a great many issues awaiting solution which had not been given the public ventilation they deserved owing to Metternich's heavy hand. The doyen statesman of Europe had been appointed foreign minister nearly forty years before. For most of this time he had been the leading minister. There were many, not only among the liberals or the radicals, who regarded as essential the appointment of a younger man with a fresh approach to the many problems which needed attention. The Habsburg Empire was con-

---

[1] To the Russian minister at Stuttgart, Prince Gorchakov (see Valentin, *Geschichte* I 352).

[2] *ADB* xxix; Köhler, *Römer*; *BSTH*.   [3] *ADB* xli; Wild, *K. T. Welcker*; *BSTH*.

[4] Stüve, *J. C. B. Stüve*; Stüve, *Briefwechsel*.

siderably behind the German states in constitutional development. Political interest was widespread, but owing to repression discontent had been bottled up in a dangerous way, instead of finding open expression. On 13 March 1848, the outbreak came with the storming of the house in which the Estates were sitting in Vienna. Students, mainly radical, were prominent in this act of violence. Metternich resigned and subsequently fled. This was the end of an era in Europe. The new liberal governments could now breathe more easily. Soon afterwards, the Habsburg Monarchy conceded under pressure the calling of an Austrian parliament.

The constitutional promises of the Habsburg Monarchy in the middle of March 1848 did not restore peace to the Empire. The Empire continued in a state of intermittent war through most of 1848 and even beyond. Two quite separate issues became mixed up in the civil war in the Habsburg Empire. There was the struggle between the dynastic party and the democrats. But there was also the increasing antipathy between the nationalities, notably between the Germans and the Slavs. The Austrian members of the Frankfurt Parliament were drawn from many combinations and permutations of this ideological-national tangle. The attitude at Frankfurt to the inclusion or exclusion of Austria in the future German state fluctuated with the news of who was on top in Vienna, as did, indeed, the weight to be attached to Austrian opinion, both governmental and parliamentary. For most of 1848, Austrian objections could be ignored, because they could not be enforced. But even those who wanted to do their best for Austria were in a dilemma. For where was the authentic voice of Austria to be found in this time of civil war? While on the one hand Austrian internal difficulties offered a chance for non-Austrian Germany to go ahead, on the other the final form of German unity could not be found until the Austrian position had been clarified.

The Viennese revolution had its own repercussions, in Berlin. Even before the news of Metternich's resignation arrived, there had been clashes between civilians and troops. These were intensified after receipt of the news from Vienna. King Frederick William IV promised a constitution, but refused to accede to the demand that the troops should be withdrawn from Berlin. On 18 March, the troops fired on demonstrators outside the royal palace, causing numerous casualties, many of them fatal. But now the King, who shrank from a period of prolonged street fighting, gave in. Most of the troops were withdrawn from Berlin. The King took on the German colours and bared his head to the dead of 18 March. The government was re-formed on 19 March, but inadequately. The King's belated concession to the cause of constitutionalism and German unity only caused contempt outside Prussia. Thus the advocates of Prussian leadership in Germany had to wait for a more auspicious opening for their plans. On 29 March one Rhenish Liberal, Ludolph Camphausen, became Prime Minister and another, David Hansemann, Minister of Finance. It was the declared task of this government to support Frederick William IV in the policy of constitutional reform and of activity in the German question, including the pursuit of the war against Denmark over Schleswig-Holstein, to which the King was already committed. The interests of the King and of the liberal ministers were identical in their determination to end the anarchic conditions in Berlin and to restore order. Neither Camphausen nor Hansemann, who had made their reputation as business men in the Rhineland, could be expected to have much sympathy with the almost fanatical determination of the radical groups in Berlin which were prepared, in the last resort, to appeal to the verdict of a civil war.

Thus, when the Pre-Parliament met on 31 March 1848, liberal ministers were installed in most of the German states outside Austria. Constitutional reform was everywhere promised. But from a radical point of view all this had merely been a partial success. For only rarely did democrats take office, like Oberländer in Saxony. On the whole, the moderate liberals had made all the running. The radicals were therefore all the more determined to use the Pre-Parliament for their purposes.

Unlike the Frankfurt Parliament, which was duly elected under the authority of the German Confederation, the Pre-Parliament was an unofficial – though very powerful – body. At the turn of March to April 1848, the Pre-Parliament was, indeed, considered more representative than any other body in Germany, in view of the discredited position of the Federal Assembly. But whilst the Pre-Parliament possessed great popular prestige, it was not representative of the country as a whole in any strict sense. Austria only had two representatives, although according to the official calculations of the German Confederation, the *Bundesmatrikel*, it was entitled to nearly one third of the seats in parliament. The representation of Prussia, which according to the *Bundesmatrikel* came second to Austria, was better. Prussia had 141 members in the Pre-Parliament, but these were drawn mainly from the Western part of the monarchy. As the Prussian United Diet met in

Berlin at this very time, many Prussian deputies were unable to attend the Pre-Parliament. Members of municipal assemblies in Prussia were therefore also admitted, thus making selection even more arbitrary. It was ironical that of the 574 members, the second biggest contingent – of 84 – should come from Hesse-Darmstadt, whereas the much larger and more important Bavaria only had 44 representatives. Altogether, the West and South-West were over-represented at the expense of the other regions.

The Pre-Parliament only had a limited task and authority. It had to prepare for the meeting of the actual parliament, though even in this respect its deliberations were not essential. Constitutionally, it was up to the Federal Assembly of the German Confederation to arrange for the elections to the German parliament. The Federal Assembly was going through a rapid process of rejuvenation as the liberal state governments appointed new ministers resident to the Confederation. Often these ministers were men well known throughout Germany owing to their steadfastness in opposition. Even where there had not yet been a change of minister resident, the current holder of the post was subject to the instructions of whichever government was in power in his home state. In addition, seventeen men of public confidence (*Männer des öffentlichen Vertrauens*) were attached to the Federal Assembly by the state governments. These included Dahlmann,[1] one of the seven Göttingen professors dismissed in 1837, for Prussia, the poet and former opposition politician Uhland[2] for Wurtemberg, the advocate of German unity in the Baden parliament, Bassermann,[3] for his Grand-Duchy, and the editor of the *Deutsche Zeitung*, Gervinus,[4] for the Free Towns. Thus many of the moderate liberals, as well as some, like Uhland, who were to move towards the Left, were then associated with the Federal Assembly they had attacked for so long. The Federal Assembly was now a pliable instrument in their hands, doing exactly what they wanted to such an extent that it rather unfairly lost even more prestige. But unless one condemned the German Confederation and the Federal Assembly altogether, there was nothing strange in the *Bundes-versammlung* obeying Metternich one day, and Heinrich von Gagern

---

[1] *ADB* iv, v; Springer, *F. C. Dahlmann*; Christern, *Dahlmanns . . . Entwicklung*; *NDB*; *BSTH*.

[2] *ADB* xxxix; Reinöhl, *Uhland*; *BSTH*; etc.

[3] *ADB* ii; Bassermann, *Denkwürdigkeiten*; Harnack, *Bassermann*; *NDB*; *BSTH*.

[4] *ADB* ix; Gervinus, *Hinterlassene Schriften*; *BSTH*.

the next. This was inevitable in the central body of a confederation.

The extreme Left was convinced that the Federal Assembly was iniquitous in itself and that no reform would make it any better. The leader of this group, the Baden oppositionist Friedrich Hecker,[1] was basically opposed to the moderate liberal policy of preserving continuity and of making do with traditional organs of government. Hecker and his collaborator Gustav von Struve,[2] also from Baden, wanted to create a republic as soon as possible, at whatever cost. Inspired by Danton and Robespierre, these men wanted to set up a ruthless convention and a revolutionary committee to carry out the far-reaching political and social changes in which they believed. Fundamentally this extreme Left was undemocratic in the sense that it was quite prepared to disregard even the freest elections held on the basis of a wide franchise if the results proved disappointing. Any assembly received the co-operation of the radicals only as long as they were able to manipulate its deliberations. Similarly, civil liberties meant very little to the extreme Left, which was only sincere in demanding them as long as they were denied to it. Once in power, the extreme Left was not prepared to allow freedom of speech and freedom from arrest whenever these interfered with its far-reaching plans.

Hecker and his associates made up their minds that the Pre-Parliament would mark their final attempt to achieve their ends by peaceful means. They did not really very much care whether they did so with or without violence, as long as they could get what they wanted. They soon realised that the Pre-Parliament would not accede to their wishes. However, if the unlikely happened and they had their way, they would be in a stronger position. Indeed, for part of their programme they could count on quite a respectable following, including many of those who were not ordinarily their supporters. There were many less radical members of the Left who were dissatisfied with the moderation of the liberal ministers.

iii. Directives for the elections to the National Assembly – The position of Schleswig

The day before the Pre-Parliament began its deliberations in the Paulskirche at Frankfurt, the Federal Assembly resolved to ask the

[1] *ADB* l; *BSTH.*   [2] *BSTH.*

state governments to hold elections for national representatives (*Nationalvertreter*) in those of their territories which belonged to the 'German state system'. To prevent delay, the Federal Assembly allocated seats on the basis of the official population statistics, the *Bundesmatrikel*.[1] The arrangement was hopelessly out of date, not having been materially altered since 1819. In general the population had grown by about 50 per cent. While this would not have mattered if the increase had been on the same scale everywhere, naturally some parts had greater population rises than others. Each area of 70,000 inhabitants (men, women and children) was to be represented by one member. The sixteen states with less than 70,000 souls according to the *Bundesmatrikel* were conceded one member each. The national representatives were to meet in Frankfurt, the seat of the Federal Assembly, a decision of far-reaching importance, not necessarily entirely salutary for the task to be carried out, but a natural one for the Federal Assembly to take. The elections were to take place with all possible speed. The Federal Assembly refrained from prescribing to the state governments the mode of election and merely stipulated that these elections were to be held in accordance with the law of the state concerned at the time of the election. This allowed for modifications to existing franchise laws as long as they were carried out constitutionally in time for the elections. While the decree of the Federal Assembly was marked by much practical common sense in its refusal to confuse matters by trying to amend the *Bundesmatrikel* or to issue detailed instructions to the member states, nothing was done to ensure any uniformity in the franchise.

Thus the Pre-Parliament could carry out a useful task by proclaiming general principles for the elections all over the country. The most far-reaching of these matters which the Federal Assembly had left undetermined was the question of how wide the franchise was to be. Here the Left, both extreme and moderate, took the Pre-Parliament by storm and almost completely had its way. In the end it was resolved that every subject of a state in the German Confederation was to be entitled to vote if he was of age and not a dependant.[2] Only men were meant: the exclusion of women from the franchise was taken so much for granted by the Pre-Parliament that it was not even mentioned. The

---

[1] Roth and Merck, *Quellensammlung* I 188 ff.

[2] *selbstständig*, i.e. independent, for instance not a domestic servant, see also below, p. 60, or somebody in receipt of poor relief.

sole defeat suffered by the Left in this connection related to the insertion of a stipulation about 'independence'. This restriction was, indeed, challenged in the Committee of Fifty which was left by the Pre-Parliament as a watchdog until the meeting of the Frankfurt Parliament.[1] Objection was raised on the grounds that the shorthand reports did not record this part of the vote. The secretaries of the Pre-Parliament, who included several members of the Left, were, however, able to prove by means of the official minutes that the Pre-Parliament had decided to limit the franchise to those who were independent. This still left the question of definition unsolved. As with all the other ambiguities, interpretation here rested with the state governments which differed widely in their application.

The moderate liberals later tried to introduce a restricted franchise in the Frankfurt Parliament. Why did they accept something at any rate in theory very near to manhood suffrage so easily in the Pre-Parliament? There were several reasons for this passive behaviour. The Pre-Parliament was not distinguished by the orderliness of its proceedings. The President, a distinguished jurist from Baden, Mittermaier,[2] who had presided over the Second Chamber there, allowed himself to be intimidated by the gallery, which mainly supported the Left. Any speech or vote which appeared to 'the people' as a betrayal of their rights was greeted with violent demonstrations of disapproval. Often speakers failed to make themselves heard. In this atmosphere, the leaders of the moderate liberals concentrated on what they regarded as the key issues, particularly on that of 'permanence'. They were determined to prevent an attempt to keep the Pre-Parliament in permanent session until the meeting of the Frankfurt Parliament and to use it as a Convention of the French Revolutionary type. They simply did not have the energy to make a fight over everything. The factor of personal fatigue which was to make itself increasingly felt during the next year or so was already beginning to show. Many of the moderate liberals could only spare a short time from their other activities. Heinrich von Gagern, who first established his ascendancy at the Pre-Parliament thanks to the confidence inspired by his personality and to the sincerity of his efforts to mediate between radicals and moderates, had to get back to Darmstadt, where he was Premier, as soon as possible. A moderate liberal from Baden, like Mathy,[3] was

---

[1] For the Pre-Parliament and the Committee of Fifty, see Jucho, *Verhandlungen.*
[2] *ADB* xxii; *BSTH.*   [3] *ADB* xx; Freytag, *K. Mathy*; Mathy, *K. Mathy*; *BSTH*

concerned about the future attitude of the radicals in his state and was eager to return. Apart from this, however, leaders of the moderate liberals like Bassermann do not seem to have recognised at this stage the danger to themselves of too quick an extension of the franchise. They failed to realise that in the changed circumstances they could no longer take their pre-March popularity for granted. In their endeavours to carry the masses with them they hoped to avert a final split between liberals and radicals which would have been brought nearer by acrimony over the franchise. Finally, they had a feeling that perhaps the Pre-Parliament would not have to be taken so seriously, as long as it could be packed off quickly. Why worry about a vote for manhood suffrage which might not mean very much anyway? If this was the reasoning, it was based on a miscalculation. For the Federal Assembly accepted most of the resolutions of the Pre-Parliament and it became very difficult for a parliament elected almost on the theoretical basis of manhood suffrage – whatever the practical shortcomings – to amend the electoral principle to which it owed its existence. Many moderate liberals lost faith in manhood suffrage during their bitter struggle with the radicals in the Frankfurt Parliament. But they could only afford the luxury of sponsoring a restricted franchise at those times when their relations with the radicals were so strained that they did not lose by antagonising them. This helps to account for their wavering attitude.

The Left failed to get the Pre-Parliament to stipulate direct elections. The democrats believed that they would gain from direct elections just as the moderates thought that they would benefit from indirect elections. This issue was somewhat technical and the moderates had their way without much difficulty, ostensibly conceding the principle of direct elections, while in fact leaving everything to the state governments. Normally election to the Frankfurt Parliament was, in fact, indirect. The voters elected electors who in turn elected the member.

An attempt to move the revision of the *Bundesmatrikel* failed. This would have delayed the elections. In compensation, it was resolved that constituencies should be reduced from 70,000 to 50,000 souls. Each smaller state and any excess of 25,000 souls was to qualify for one member.

The Pre-Parliament was truly united in laying down that there was to be no discrimination on account of religion or of social estate and that political refugees who had returned to resume their rights as citizens were entitled to vote and eligible to serve as members of parliament. Election by estates was ruled out. Furthermore, nobody was to be disqualified from sitting in parliament on the grounds that he had been elected in a state of which he was not a subject. The Federal Assembly on 7 April adopted all these decisions of the Pre-Parliament as the basis for the elections to the German National Assembly.[1]

The Pre-Parliament did not debate these matters only for Germans or for inhabitants of territories which belonged to the German Confederation. This assembly, which only sat for five days and had to deal with many questions, without adequate papers, demanded the admission of Schleswig,[2] as well as of East Prussia and West Prussia, into the German Confederation.

While the Federal Assembly was willing to meet the wishes of the Pre-Parliament wherever it could, the issue of Schleswig was not a purely domestic one and had to be treated with circumspection. The Schleswig-Holstein question was to occupy the attention of the Great Powers for many years and was one of the thorniest questions with which the Frankfurt Parliament had to deal. The problems of the Duchies were typical of the troubles caused by the transition from dynastic territorial to modern national states. The ambiguous status of the Duchies, partly belonging to Denmark and partly to Germany, did not become irksome until both Denmark and Germany found it necessary to streamline their administration and to base their states largely on the principle of nationality. Under this more rigorous dispensation, it was no longer feasible to belong to two state systems simultaneously, as Holstein did (though not Schleswig). For the King of Denmark was Duke of Holstein and as such was a member of the German Confederation. Soon after the foundation of the German Confederation, the Duchies, which were both in personal union with the Kingdom of Denmark, started increasingly to assert their rights, partly in accordance with the constitutional principle of emphasising the traditional claim of the Estates to be consulted, but partly also in order to claim German status. Neither the Germans nor the Danes were quite consistent. The flaw in the German argument was that while Holstein was indeed ethnically German, Schleswig was only partly so. North Schleswig was mainly Danish. Those who propagated the German cause, like Dahlmann, Droysen and the Beseler brothers, did not,

---

[1] Decree in Huber, *Dokumente* i 274.

[2] The German spelling of Schleswig is not meant to prejudice the national issue, which is considered in the text.

however, base their case entirely on self-determination. They claimed
that the Duchies had been guaranteed that they would never be separated from each other and that both were subject to the Salic succession
law which only allowed males in the male line to inherit them. As the
male line of the Danish royal family was about to die out, this would
have meant the separation of both Duchies from the Danish crown, to
which descendants of the female line were entitled to succeed. The
advantage of this reasoning from the German point of view was that it
allowed both Duchies to be claimed completely for Germany on the
extinction of the male Danish line, and that in the meantime any attempt
by the Danes to make any move whatsoever in relation to the Duchies
could be frustrated. In effect the argument used established historical
rights to support the new nationalism, without giving up positions not
covered by national claims. Only for a fleeting moment in March was
any consideration given by the Germans to the question of ensuring for
the Danes in North Schleswig their right of self-determination.

To the Danes, the whole question appeared in a completely different
light. They wanted to create a more viable state by reducing as far as
possible the distinctions between the various territories making up the
Danish monarchy. The Eider Danish party of Orla Lehmann which
came to power in Copenhagen on 21 March 1848 was quite prepared
to sacrifice Holstein, as long as Schleswig could be fully integrated in
the Danish monarchy. The same day the Danish government decreed
the incorporation of Schleswig into the Danish state, without consulting the Schleswig estates. The request of German notables in the
Duchies that Schleswig should join the German Confederation was
refused. With the incorporation of the duchy of Schleswig into Denmark, the Danish government was entering a path of questionable
legality. Denmark was also ignoring where inconvenient the new
principle of self-determination which was the real driving power of
change. An attempt was made to turn into full Danish citizens South
Schleswigers who had hitherto had a special position and who were
loyal to the German rather than to the Danish cause. In reply, the
leaders of the German movement in the Duchies declared that their
duke – the King of Denmark – had surrendered his freedom of action
by subordinating himself to the Eider Danish party. They formed a
provisional government for the Duchies, which included Wilhelm
Beseler[1] (who was later to serve in the Frankfurt Parliament) and the

[1] *ADB* xlvi; Schweickhardt, *W. Beseler*; *NDB*; *BSTH*.

son of the Duke of Augustenburg, who was considered by the German party as the rightful heir of the Duchies on the extinction of the male Danish line. The Provisional Government claimed that in this emergency the population of the Duchies was entitled to resist the Danish troops and officials sent over from Copenhagen. While the Provisional Government regarded the struggle in fact as one between German and Dane, it was careful to present its case in traditional legal terms and not to rely exclusively on the right of self-determination.

The cause of the Germans in the Duchies was one of the few issues on which several German governments, including that of Prussia, had some sympathy with the liberal national movement, even before March 1848. When matters came to a head in the Duchies during the second half of March, there was probably more agreement on the need to help their fellow Germans among all sections of the population than on any other question. Over Schleswig-Holstein there was no division between moderate liberals and radicals. Even some rulers felt sympathy for the rebellious subjects of their fellow-monarch. The Duchies became a test-question for the German national movement. Many Germans believed that unless German claims could be made good in the Duchies, the whole movement would come to nothing. They regarded their determination to see the Duchies through as an indication of their attachment to the German cause. The Pre-Parliament looked on the incorporation of Schleswig in the German Confederation as right and proper, and voted accordingly without any hesitation. Members saw only the wrong which had been done to their fellow Germans in the Duchies. They failed to see the Danish side, just as the Danes failed to see the German side. But in certain respects the Danes were in a better position. Diplomatically they had far more support than the Germans. In Germany, many people refused to face up to the bitter diplomatic and economic implications of a question which affected some regions more than others.[1]

The shortcomings of the Pre-Parliament were revealed quite starkly in its handling of the Schleswig question. During a very brief session this body did not hesitate to pontificate on what was one of the most complicated international problems, without even setting up a committee to study the matter. The vote did not lead to the incorporation of Schleswig in the German Confederation, since the Federal Assembly did not – and probably could not – take any action. However, the

[1] See below, p. 295 f.

attitude of the Pre-Parliament strengthened the position of the Provisional Government in the Duchies. It also helped to ensure that Schleswig would be represented in the Frankfurt Parliament.

The Federal Assembly did not incorporate Schleswig in the German Confederation, as it did East and West Prussia and parts of Posen. Even Posen was not entirely a domestic issue as the Polish question was bound to bring in Russia. But compared with Schleswig, the problem of Posen was child's play, for the Elbe Duchies affected Great Powers not only in the East but also in the West. One of the few issues on which Great Britain and Russia were agreed was to restrain the German northward advance and to buttress the Danish monarchy. The Federal Assembly feared the Great Powers more than public opinion in Germany. In order to avoid a European war, the Federal Assembly went as far as it could short of incorporating Schleswig.

The most pressing matter was military help for the Provisional Government. For unless this was given, Danish troops were going to overrun both Duchies. Already before the meeting of the Pre-Parliament, the King of Prussia had promised to help with troops, but at first these kept to Holstein, thus remaining within the confines of the German Confederation. In April, after an attempt to settle the conflict peacefully, Prussian troops crossed into Schleswig and eventually even entered Jutland. The Federal Assembly supported intervention in the Duchies and took various other steps to help the German movement, including allowing representatives of the Provisional Government to take over certain functions in the Federal Assembly previously exercised by the Danish minister resident. On 25 May, Prussian and other German troops withdrew to the northern border of the German ethnic territory, vacating Jutland and North Schleswig, obviously for diplomatic reasons, to allow mediation proposals to proceed. This was the complicated and unsettled state of affairs which faced the Frankfurt Parliament soon after it met.

iv. The incorporation of East and West Prussia and parts of Posen in the German Confederation – The Committee of Fifty – Hecker's rising in Baden

The Pre-Parliament also did not shirk diplomatic complications in other questions. The partition of Poland was declared to be a 'shameful injustice'. A resolution passed by the Pre-Parliament spoke of the 'sacred duty of the German people to co-operate in the restoration of Poland'. The German governments were asked to allow the unhindered transit of unarmed Poles returning home and to give them any necessary help. These feelings undoubtedly reflected a genuine concern for the Poles at the time, though they sprang to some extent from a dislike of Russia – the greatest enemy of the Poles – which had incurred intense hostility among the erstwhile opposition owing to the Tsar's support of the Metternich system. However, this resolution was coupled with others not entirely consonant with it. The Pre-Parliament voted for the incorporation of East Prussia and West Prussia into the German Confederation, without asking whether the Poles in West Prussia wanted to be so transferred. These provinces and Posen had hitherto been left out of the German Confederation, although they belonged to the Kingdom of Prussia, partly out of respect for the position of peoples which had not belonged to the Holy Roman Empire and partly because the King of Prussia wanted to mark his independence by having territories outside the German Confederation. The Federal Assembly acceded to the request concerning the embodiment of East and West Prussia. In April, the Prussian government also asked for most of the province of Posen to be incorporated, which was done.[1] By this time tension between Germans and Poles increased to the point of open fighting. The unilateral drawing of an ethnic boundary line by the Germans in a province with as mixed a population as Posen could not be regarded as a particularly friendly act to the Poles.

Prussia's position was completely altered by the incorporation of these territories. The Kingdom of Prussia now hardly had any territories outside the German Confederation, whereas Austria still did. According to the revised *Bundesmatrikel* (to allow for the incorporation of East and West Prussia and parts of Posen) Prussia now moved up to first place, just ahead of Austria. Prussia exchanged her comparative freedom as a European Great Power outside the German Confederation for a potentially leading position exclusively inside Germany. The timing of this move was not propitious, as it occurred at a period during which Prussian prestige in Germany had reached a low ebb following Frederick William IV's apparent lack of determination and volte-face during the Berlin revolution. In effect, Prussia was now compelled to follow up her lead in Germany if her moves meant anything

[1] See also below, p. 57.

at all. But a more forward German policy was fraught with great dangers. Was Austria going to stand by while Prussia deprived her of her leading position in Germany? Would Prussia be able to find a new ally to compensate for Russia which she had antagonised by her Polish and Danish policy? Britain was the only possibility, but this country, too, had been put off by German actions particularly in relation to Schleswig-Holstein.

There was not the same measure of agreement when it came to issues of a more domestic nature. A motion by Hecker that the Pre-Parliament should sit 'permanently' until the meeting of the Frankfurt Parliament was defeated by 368 to 148 votes. Though Hecker received support from many members of the Left outside his own circle of extremists, the assembly was clearly in no mood to play the part of a convention. The vast moderate majority saw no need for this in view of liberal state governments and of a responsive Federal Assembly. As a compromise, a committee of the Pre-Parliament was left behind, the *Fünfziger-Ausschuss* (Committee of Fifty).

Hecker now saw that the assembly was determined to confine itself to what he considered half-measures. He and his group decided to walk out of the assembly when a motion directed against the Federal Assembly failed in its original extreme form. This demanded that the Federal Assembly should renounce its unconstitutional decisions and expel all those from its midst who had participated in making and executing them. From an immediate practical point of view, a resolution of this kind was quite unnecessary, as the Federal Assembly was now quite amenable to public opinion. The motives for putting the motion were purely tactical. It was part of a campaign of the Left to weaken existing institutions in order to obtain a maximum of change. When Hecker walked out, he was only followed by a handful. Many of those who had voted with him remained in the assembly hall, putting on record that they regarded it as their duty to submit to the majority. Hecker thus split the Left. Though he and his followers returned once more to the floor of the Paulskirche, Hecker and Struve had made up their minds that the time for talking was over. Through absence, they prejudiced their chances of election to the Committee of Fifty.

While Hecker boycotted the Pre-Parliament, before he returned once more, the meeting debated a confused motion put forward by Alexander von Soiron,[1] a lawyer from Baden who was to become chairman of the

---

[1] *ADB* xxxiv; G. Mohr, *A. v. Soiron*.

C

Committee of Fifty and to play some part in the Frankfurt Parliament. His motion included a passage that 'the decision about the future constitution of Germany was to be left solely and exclusively to the popularly elected National Assembly',[1] that is to say to the Frankfurt Parliament. As was pointed out in the lengthy debate which followed, the motion had two aspects. It limited the competence of the Pre-Parliament, by implication because so unrepresentative a body was not entitled to prejudge the action of a properly elected parliament. In general, this reasoning was adopted by the moderate liberals, whereas many on the Left were quite prepared to go ahead letting the Pre-Parliament decide things, however unrepresentative it might be. The other aspect of the motion concerned the future relationship between the Frankfurt Parliament and the governments when it came to settling the terms of the German constitution. The motion could be read as a denial of any influence on the constitution to the princes and the state governments. When called upon to explain his meaning, Soiron, during one of his attempts to do so, supported the principle of the sovereignty of the people. In view of another passage it seems that Soiron wanted to show that even without Hecker's prompting the Pre-Parliament was quite prepared to back this theory. Welcker, who was emerging as one of the leading politicians of 1848–9, forcefully expressed his objections to the theory of the sovereignty of the people. The motion was passed after Soiron had declared that as the National Assembly would be solely in charge, it could do what it liked, which included consulting the governments.

The vote on permanence had been the first great alignment into moderates and radicals, although Raveaux,[2] a radical and an advocate of permanence, pointed out that some of his political friends voted against him on this occasion. The Pre-Parliament certainly taught parliamentarians the importance of meeting outside the chamber in smaller groups to decide tactics and thus helped to start the development of German political parties, a process which was carried much further in the Frankfurt Parliament. Private meetings to decide on candidates for the Committee of Fifty which was being left behind by the Pre-Parliament are well documented. There were even references to

---

[1] 'dass die Beschlussfassung über die künftige Verfassung Deutschlands einzig und allein der vom Volke zu wählenden Nationalversammlung zu überlassen sei.' Jucho, *Verhandlungen* I 132.

[2] *ADB* xxvii; *BSTH*.

these conclaves during the debates of the Pre-Parliament, some highly critical. The Pre-Parliament decided, curiously enough on the motion of the radical Robert Blum,[1] that each member of the Pre-Parliament should have the right to record fifty votes for the Committee. While this was in many ways the obvious method, it allowed the majority, if it wished, to get a block of fifty moderates elected and to exclude the radical minority altogether. As a member of the minority, one would have expected Robert Blum to have taken a different line. In fact, the danger was averted. After considerable discussion at a private meeting of the moderates, it was decided to include a number of radicals in their list, though not the most extreme ones. Among those elected were Robert Blum himself, Adam von Itzstein, Johann Jacoby from Königs-berg, Heinrich Simon from Breslau and Raveaux from Cologne, all men who were to play leading roles on the Left during the following period, mainly in the Frankfurt Parliament. They headed the poll. The moderate majority had little difficulty in getting their leading per-sonalities elected.

The functions of the Committee of Fifty were not clearly defined, which led to considerable friction later. There was general agreement that the Committee should make sure that the elections to the Frankfurt Parliament took place expeditiously and according to the standards laid down by the Pre-Parliament.

The net result of the Pre-Parliament might appear as stalemate between the moderates and the radicals. But this would presuppose a clarity of political alignments which did not exist at the time. The Pre-Parliament met at the end of four exciting weeks, the like of which had not been seen in Germany. There were few men, except among the doctrinaires, whose views had not been affected by constantly changing circumstances which were stronger than the political leaders. Rudi-mentary political groups were being formed, but the time had not generally come for men to determine for long periods ahead where they stood politically and with whom they wanted to collaborate. Thus the preconditions for the creation of political parties did not yet exist. For every member of the Pre-Parliament whose political attitude was fairly certain at the time, there was another who might drift from one group to another. Hecker and Struve found it impossible to work with the rest of the assembly, not only because they were more extreme, but

---

[1] *ADB* ii; H. Blum, *R. Blum*; Bergsträsser, *Frankfurter Parlament*. See also above, p. 22.

because they were more doctrinaire. They despised the tactical considerations of other members of the radical Left who were prepared to wait.

As March turned to April, it was not yet clear to what extent practical politics would in fact be influenced by those differences in theoretical outlook which divided the Pre-Parliament into moderates and radicals. At the end of the debate on Soiron's motion about the functions of the forthcoming parliament, there could be grave doubts whether acceptance or rejection of the sovereignty of the people made any practical difference at all. Politicians starting from opposite premises, such as those who wanted a maximum of change and those who wanted the least possible change, might in the end reach similar conclusions on a policy feasible in the circumstances. Some, like Mathy, who theoretically wanted a republic, had already realised that the preservation of monarchical institutions would divide Germans least.

In this continually changing situation, the balance achieved between radicalism and moderation reflected accurately the feeling in the Pre-Parliament and probably of public opinion generally. This was early days. The elections to the actual parliament were still to come. Everything remained fluid, except that Hecker and his associates became convinced that the time for parleying was over.

Baden, bordering on France and Switzerland, had long led the way politically. Now, mainly thanks to Hecker, this progressive Grand-Duchy was to become the scene of civil war. The preparations of Hecker and Struve were only lightly camouflaged and gave ample warning to those in the Grand-Duchy who were not prepared to tolerate the forcible overthrow of law and order by an unrepresentative minority. It was in Baden, under the threat of a Hecker Putsch, that the moderate liberals began their thankless struggle on two fronts, against the radicals on their left and the 'reactionaries' on their right. The claim of the moderate liberals on coming into power that they represented 'the people' was now being undermined by their more radical rivals. Potentially even more damaging to the moderate liberals was the accusation of their radical critics that they had betrayed common ideals by allying with the forces of 'reaction'. Finally, Hecker forced the liberals to do things they had condemned in their period in opposition and which they would rather not have done.

It was Mathy, as a deputy and a citizen – not yet as a minister – in Baden, who took the dramatic step against the Hecker conspiracy which led to the rising taking place prematurely. Mathy was a man of great force of character and convictions, who had for many years chosen to live abroad in Switzerland and to earn his livelihood as a schoolteacher. He was very popular there and was offered local citizenship. Even later he seriously considered returning to a country whose democratic institutions he and many liberals and radicals of the time admired. As there was no formal separation as yet between the moderate liberals and the radicals, Mathy was well aware of the intentions of the extreme radicals. He tried to dissuade one of these, Fickler, a Constance journalist, from going ahead with a rising which was not only illegal, but politically absurd, as the Grand-Duke had made far-reaching concessions. When Fickler adhered to his intentions, he arrested him on 8 April at the railway station in Karlsruhe. Mathy's deed was never forgotten by the Left, even by those who did not approve of the Hecker rising. Mathy's intervention, by throwing the plans of the insurgents into disarray, may well have contributed to the comparatively easy crushing of the revolt at Kandern. In this action the commander of the troops, General Friedrich von Gagern, probably the outstanding of the brothers, was killed.

Hecker decided to emigrate to the United States soon after the failure of his rising and was absent from the Frankfurt Parliament. He was elected for the Baden constituency of Thiengen, but the election was declared invalid by the Frankfurt Parliament in August.[1] Of his following, only Ignaz Peter, whom he appointed 'governor' in Constance, was a member of the parliament. He played a part in parliament as a subject for debate, whether his immunity should be lifted to permit his arrest, rather than as a speaker.[2] Thus the Hecker group was virtually missing from the Frankfurt Parliament. This almost complete elimination of the most extreme faction from parliament was a help to its proceedings. But it also meant that some of the actual opposition was not to be found in parliament, but outside. Those of the radical Left who were inside the assembly were certainly sobered by Hecker's failure. They saw that the time was not ripe for a successful rebellion.

The Committee of Fifty, which elected Soiron as its chairman, did not make an important positive contribution. In many ways, by adding yet another body to all those already in existence, the committee if anything tended to delay matters. One of its actions deserves mention, as it served as a precedent for the Frankfurt Parliament. Following

---

[1] See below, p. 252.　　　　[2] See below, p. 247.

some excesses of the military against the liberals at Cassel, in the Electorate of Hesse, early in April, the committee sent commissioners there to express its disapproval of what had taken place and to seek assurances for the future. The liberal government which had been in power since March satisfied the commissioners that it was taking stern measures against any reactionary attempts to upset constitutional progress.

In the main the committee dealt with problems arising out of the forthcoming elections for the Frankfurt Parliament, which are discussed in the following chapter.

3 The Composition of the Frankfurt Parliament

i. State management of elections – The obsolete federal population table
(Bundesmatrikel) *– Limitations on the franchise – Direct and indirect elections*

ACCORDING to the amended *Bundesmatrikel* of the German Confederation, 649 members were to be elected to the German National Assembly by the various territories of the Confederation. Although Schleswig was not incorporated in the Confederation, elections for the National Assembly did in fact take place there for five members. Also, the tiny lordship of Kniphausen claimed separate representation from the Grand-Duchy of Oldenburg in which it was situated, adding one additional member to the Oldenburg entitlement. While the running of the elections was in the hands of the individual states, the National Assembly itself determined who was entitled to sit and it accepted the six additional members, bringing the total up to 655.

The individual states acted as agents (*im Auftrage*) for the Confederation in organising the elections. This was the correct method for the implementation of the decisions of the Federal Assembly. The states had to keep within the general directive which allocated the number of seats to each state and also laid down some general principles.[1] The drawing of the requisite number of constituencies by each state presented considerable difficulties. Constituencies, which were invariably single-member seats, were normally supposed to represent 50,000 souls each. The basis was not, however, the current population, but that which was laid down in the *Bundesmatrikel*, dating from 1818 and based on the population of 1816. In the thirty years since then there had been a considerable increase in population, although the rate varied from state to state and region to region. In the case of territories added to the Confederation, such as East and West Prussia, as well as of parts of Posen, the seat entitlement was calculated by reducing the actual population by just above one third (about 35 per cent) in order to bring them into line with the provinces of the Kingdom of Prussia which

[1] See above, p. 43 ff.

already belonged to the German Confederation. The population of the areas covered by the *Bundesmatrikel* as a whole went up from just under 32 millions in 1818 to about 42 millions in 1847, so that a deduction based on the national average would have been rather less, about 24 per cent.[1] While the population of Prussia increased in these thirty years by about 54 per cent and that of Saxony by about 53 per cent, that of the Austrian parts of the German Confederation only went up by about 27 per cent and that of Bavaria by about 26 per cent. Thus in Prussia a constituency averaged about 77,000 inhabitants, but in Austria only about 63,000. These variations were of some importance, as the states concerned had divergent interests in the question of German unification and tended to differ in their ideological representation.

There were two further distortions of the arithmetical balance. It was left to the state governments to break up their quota of seats into constituencies. Even if the statisticians succeeded in establishing how many *actual* inhabitants the average constituency should contain, it was obviously impossible to make them all exactly equal, even in the bigger states. Naturally some account was taken of historical and administrative boundaries in drawing up constituencies. The Austrian Empire provided some glaring inequalities. In Styria, constituencies varied between 85,000 and 38,000 inhabitants. The two smallest constituencies together contained fewer inhabitants than the largest one.[2] It is of some consolation to the historian picking his way through the jungle of differing regulations in the various states to find that some of them were bewildering even to the men of 1848. In Tirol, 17 members were elected instead of the 14 to which this territory was entitled. Apparently the Tirolese got confused by the discrepancy between the size of the actual population and the entry in the *Bundesmatrikel*. This *may*, however, have been a deliberate error, to strengthen the representation of the German parts, although when the matter was debated in the Frankfurt Parliament the Italian members, too, defended the arrangement,[3] for everybody would have lost from a reduction of Tirolese representation. Apart from Kniphausen, this is the only case of *over*-representation. *Under*-representation was more frequent.

---

[1] The electoral statistics are based primarily on Dieterici, *Mitteilungen*, mainly i 14 ff.; Repgen, *Märzbewegung*, including 138.   [2] Ibler, 'Wahlen'.

[3] Wigard, *Stenographischer Bericht* v 3482. Hereafter cited by volume and page number only.

These Austrian muddles were not typical – at any rate in extent – of the elections in the German states generally. In Prussia, as detailed investigations for the Rhineland show,[1] an efficient statistical service worked out the entitlement of the various provinces in proportion to actual population, and the *Oberpräsidenten* of the provinces generally tried to apportion constituencies fairly. Thus in the Rhine Province, the variation in the population of constituencies was only between 89,000 and 68,000.

There were discrepancies in the size not only of the constituencies, but also in those of the electoral sub-districts in which the voters (*Urwähler*) elected one elector (*Wahlmann*). In Prussia one elector normally represented at least 300, but at most 999 voters.[2] The fixing of electoral sub-districts for the election of electors in the first stage of the process could have a considerable effect on the outcome of the elections. This was a matter which did not escape official interest.

The general principles laid down by the Federal Assembly were too vague to fetter the administrative discretion of the state authorities in drawing the boundaries of constituencies and electoral sub-districts. The states were less free in dealing with the question as to who had a vote, but even here their hands were not entirely tied. One basic difficulty was the absence of a national German citizenship. Not unnaturally, states confined the right to vote to their own citizens. This was hard on the many who were citizens of one state and residents of another, unable to reach their home state on election day, but dual voting was made more difficult. To prevent abuse, most states stipulated that the vote had to be recorded in the district of residence. The building up of accurate electoral registers, which often had to be done in two or three weeks, obviously required strict stipulations of this kind. There was no time to have cross-checked registers even within the province of a large state. Again this virtually meant some disfranchisement, for not everybody could get to his legal residence at the required time.

The law of the state concerned determined the minimum age for voting, but owing to the different law codes in existence, this was not always uniform within a state or even a province. In the Prussian Rhine Province, men came of age in various parts at 21, 24 and 25 years. Less difficulty was presented by definitions of who was in possession of the full civic rights necessary for voting, though these, too, varied from state to state.

[1] Repgen, *Märzbewegung*, e.g. 137 ff.   [2] Roth and Merck, *Quellensammlung* i 267 f.

The greatest loophole was left to the discretion of the state governments by the vagueness of the term 'independence' (*Selbstständigkeit*)
formulated by the Pre-Parliament.[1] This concept could be interpreted
with equal justice both comprehensively and restrictively. In Prussia,
everybody was considered independent in this sense and therefore
qualified to vote unless he received poor relief from the public purse.
In Austria, those who were in service (*im Dienstverhältnisse stehende
Personen*) were deemed to be dependent. Practice varied from province
to province as it was left to the provincial governors to interpret the
principles in the light of provincial conditions. In Styria, day-workers,
domestic servants and journeymen (*Taglöhner, Dienstboten, Hand-
werksgesellen*) were denied the vote.[2] In Bavaria, only those were allowed
to vote who paid direct taxes to the state. These restrictions occupied
much of the attention of the Committee of Fifty which was left behind
in Frankfurt by the Pre-Parliament,[3] though without avail. Thus, while
in Prussia there was almost general manhood suffrage, important
sections of the population were excluded in states like Austria and
Bavaria.[4]

In most states the vote was secret. But in Austria there was public
voting. In Styria, for instance, the voter had to record his vote orally in
public. In Lower Austria, signed ballot papers had to be handed in.

Two further matters had to be laid down, relating to eligibility, both
as an elector and for a member of parliament. Generally, only those
could become electors who were voters in the electoral sub-district and
thus resided there. On the latter point the Federal Assembly had
spoken quite clearly: the member of parliament elected did not have
to be a citizen of the state he represented. The various state electoral
laws were simply left with the job of finding suitable phrases to cover
this point.

There is another aspect of the elections which needs some explanation. Usually, in addition to the member (*Abgeordneter*), a substitute
(*Stellvertreter, Ersatzmann*) was elected.[5] In some territories, for instance in parts of Austria and Bavaria, two substitutes were elected.
Normally, such as in Prussia, the substitute was elected at the same

[1] See above, p. 43.
[2] Some of the main electoral laws are given in Roth and Merck, *Quellensammlung* I
267 ff. For Austria, see Ibler, 'Wahlen'.
[3] Jucho, *Verhandlungen*, II.
[4] See also Hamerow, 'Elections'; *cf.* Repgen, *Hitlers Machtergreifung* 10 n15.
[5] To avoid ambiguity, the term 'substitute' is preferred to that of deputy.

time as the member. But in Bavaria the substitutes were elected separately. The mode of election was important, as it *could* determine whether the substitute reflected views similar to the member or the very opposite. The substitute has been called by one member 'the counterpart of the member' (*der Widerpart des Abgeordneten*).[1] In many cases the substitute of a moderate member was a radical, as was seen following the resignations of centre members towards the end of the Frankfurt Parliament.[2] But in many others, member and substitute represented similar views. Often, whatever the exact mode of election, the two choices were regarded as related to each other. It was not uncommon for an aspirant to full membership becoming a substitute as a consolation prize.

There was something to be said for the simultaneous election of a substitute. The necessity of a by-election on the resignation or death of the member would thus be avoided. But the automatic moving up of a substitute could lead to minority representation.[3] Matters were not improved by the confusion which prevailed about this system of substitutes and the discrepancies in its application. The ambiguity of the term *Stellvertreter*, which *could* suggest a temporary relief, did not help, nor did the curious limitation of the role of the substitutes in Prussia, where they did not automatically move up, but where in many cases fresh elections had to be held. It was left to the National Assembly to sort out some of the difficulties which arose from the election of substitutes.

In view of the handling of the elections by the state governments, there was thus considerable variety in the arrangements. Perhaps the most serious discrepancies concerned limitations in the suffrage and in the mode of election. Direct elections only took place in Wurtemberg, the Electorate of Hesse, Schleswig, Holstein, Frankfurt, Hamburg and Bremen.[4] In all other states the electorate voted for electors who in turn chose the parliamentary representatives. Many other matters of procedure could also affect the result, for instance whether the majority principle was firmly applied. In most states an absolute majority was required in early ballots. It is, however, very difficult to generalise about the effect of procedural matters of this kind on the results.

---

[1] Arneth, *Aus meinem Leben*, I 206.   [2] See below, p. 386.

[3] The Committee of Fifty prevented this practice in Saxony (see Jucho, *Verhandlungen* II 109 ff.; Philippson, *Über den Ursprung* 50 ff.).

[4] Huber, *Deutsche Verfassungsgeschichte* II 608.

ii. Elections in the Habsburg Empire – Czech and Slovene opposition to participation – German pressure for elections in Bohemia and the Slovene districts

The elections took place mainly at the end of April and at the beginning of May, but the electoral process went on for a considerable part of May. Even after that, for various reasons fresh elections were held in a number of constituencies. The timing of the original elections affected the outcome in a variety of ways. The haste with which the elections were fixed allowed little time for an election campaign, even in the rudimentary sense in which it was possible in Germany in 1848. It might appear at first sight that the absence of national party machines and national slogans allowed a particularly faithful reflection of local opinion. Whatever feelings one might have about a modern election campaign on the scale of the 1960s, an attempt is at least made to state the various approaches to key issues, and candidates have to declare their attitude. Different political parties to which candidates belong debate the questions of the day with each other in public and are forced to give their views. For the elections to the Frankfurt Parliament there were no formal political parties, only vague associations of people of similar outlook on the state, regional or local level, but not for the country as a whole. To infer constituency public opinion from a successful candidature, the local background has to be carefully studied. For it cannot be taken for granted that the election of a 'liberal', for instance, meant the same thing in each state, or even within the same large state, such as Prussia. Furthermore, candidates did not always have to commit themselves before the constituency poll. Many prominent figures were elected without having stood in any formal sense, in some instances they were not even consulted beforehand. It might be argued that the political programme of these men who were 'invited' to become members of parliament was so well known to the electors that there was no harm in this procedure. This is not tenable. The only way to find out the views of a candidate was by questioning him. Those who did not personally contest their seat had not all publicly stated their precise views on the political problems of the day. Some were basically 'unpolitical', but had become involuntarily involved in clashes with authority. Those from whose minds political problems were never very far had not necessarily had a chance of formulating a political programme or of making it widely known. Even if they could publicise their views under the pre-1848 censorship, they now had to declare positions on the issues which had become crystallised in the weeks since the revolution. For all these activities, time had been rather short. Most people had not yet had the opportunity and leisure to rethink their position. Events were moving too fast for them to do so. Thus there was a considerable element of error in the choice of candidates. Except in certain areas of intensive political activity, such as the Rhineland,[1] there was often abysmal ignorance of the ideas for which candidates stood.

What generalisations, if any, can then be made about this political labyrinth? Three issues were of such importance that all or some of them affected the whole country, the national, the ideological and the religious.

The most general issue was certainly the national one. The elections were for the first German national parliament and it was clear to everybody that the main task of this body – whatever else was in dispute – was to unify the country. However, the acceptance of a seat in the Frankfurt Parliament did not necessarily involve sympathy with the necessity of German unification. The non-German nationalities which did not want to see the creation of a German national state, such as the Czechs, the Italians and the Poles of the Prussian province of Posen, were faced with the alternative of either staying away from Frankfurt, thus remaining without influence on the course of events there, or of finding themselves in a minority in the German national assembly. The Czechs decided to boycott Frankfurt. The Italians of the Austrian province of Tirol as well as the Poles of the constituency of Buck and Samter in the Prussian province of Posen went to Frankfurt. They were opposed to the incorporation of the territories they represented in a German national state, but the position of some of the other non-Germans, such as those from Luxemburg and Limburg, was less clear-cut. Not even all members of the Frankfurt Parliament of German stock were enthusiastic about German unification. Many Prussians were worried about the role of their state, with its history and tradition, in a unified Germany. In some of the medium-sized states, such as the kingdoms of Hanover and Bavaria, particularism was strongly entrenched. For the Austrians acceptance of German unification presented considerable problems, as they already belonged

[1] See Repgen, *Märzbewegung.*

to an important state system, the Habsburg Empire. The Germans in Austria could not really give a clear answer about their attitude to German unification in late April or early May 1848. They were bound to take into account two factors which had not yet been settled. First, they were likely to be antagonistic to a Germany led by Prussia, whereas they might be more favourably inclined towards the project under Austrian hegemony, on the assumption that the relationship between the two state systems could be satisfactorily arranged. Secondly, a great deal was going to depend on the whole future of the Habsburg Empire which was at times in doubt during 1848. The Western half of the Monarchy had not yet had time to understand fully the problems it had to face, let alone to solve them. The hectic pace of events since Metternich's fall in the middle of March was not conducive to calm consideration. The elections for Frankfurt mainly took place before the Vienna rising of 15 May which radicalised Austrian political life and sealed the division between moderate liberals and radicals, whereas the elections for the Austrian parliament were held in June. The results for Frankfurt were ideologically more moderate than those for Vienna, which was similar to the development in Prussia where the elections were actually simultaneous.

There were certain fundamental differences between the elections in the Habsburg Empire and elsewhere. All other states, with the exception of Prussia, were represented in the German National Assembly with all their territories. In the case of Prussia, only part of one province – Posen – was excluded. Thus for better or for worse, the other states had to take part, whereas the Habsburg Empire, with so much of its population outside the election area, did not necessarily have to throw its lot in with Frankfurt. The Habsburg Empire had an independent international existence apart from Germany, whatever its stake in Germany might be. It was the only state electing to Frankfurt which did not have to look up to Germany as a greater entity. Unlike even Prussia, the Austrian Empire could expect to be treated by Germany at the very least on terms of equality.

Furthermore, the Habsburg Empire and Prussia were the only states electing to Frankfurt which contained substantial non-German populations. But whereas Prussia had a preponderantly German population, the Germans did not find themselves in a majority in the Habsburg Empire. Even in the territories electing to Frankfurt there were substantial non-German populations, the Czechs in Bohemia and

Moravia, the Slovenes in Styria, Carinthia-Carniola, Görz, Trieste and Istria, and the Italians in South Tirol. Nationality statistics are notoriously difficult to compile objectively, but a careful analysis of the relevant statistics shows that the German lead, if any, over the non-Germans was slight.[1]

These two factors – the partial adherence of the Habsburg Empire to the German Confederation and the prominence of non-German nationalities – mark off Austria sharply from the other states electing to Frankfurt. They explain the totally different attitude taken up to the Frankfurt elections by its electorate, ranging from considerable interest to indifference and even to hostility. In the multi-national state which only partly belonged to the German Confederation, the question of participation in the elections became an issue, whereas elsewhere – with marginal exceptions – the contest took place within the election arena. The Czechs and most Slovenes made their position towards German unification clear by not voting. The authorities could not *make* the electorate vote, even if they wished to do so. In fact, officialdom in the Habsburg Empire was even less enthusiastic about elections to Frankfurt than that in the other states. The Austrian Court and Government were well aware of the potential usefulness of other nationalities against their German subjects. In Vienna, the authorities were particularly exposed to the pressure of the Germans, both ideologically and nationally. The radicals whom Court and Government saw at close quarters were German. In many ways, the German national movement presented an even graver threat to the survival of the Habsburg Empire than the Magyars. The Magyars were at least all within the Habsburg Empire and there was some justification for the hope that a solution might be found for them without disrupting the Monarchy. The danger of the German national movement to the Habsburg Empire was that there was no easy answer to the German demand for a special relationship of the German parts of the Habsburg Empire with a unified Germany. To the rulers of the Habsburg Monarchy a national movement drawing support from outside the frontiers – like the Italian then or the South Slav later – was bound to be particularly worrying. The German descent of the dynasty and the German background of so many of the leading men did not make any difference to this. For in their positions of responsibility all these men

---

[1] Sources include Hain, *Handbuch*; *Gegenwart*, III 1 ff.; Burian, *Nationalitäten*; Grafenauer, *Ethnic Conditions*.

and a woman like the Archduchess Sophia, the mother of the future
Emperor Francis Joseph, had as their overriding aim the maintenance
of the integrity of the Habsburg Empire. This was a natural – almost
inevitable – reaction to the dangers in which the Empire found itself
in the early weeks after the resignation of Metternich. It was feared
that any weakness in the face of the attack from outside (by Sardinia
in Lombardy) or from inside (in Venice by the Italian nationalists or
elsewhere by radical elements) might have grave consequences for the
very survival of the Empire. Though some verbal concessions were
made, and petitions demanding constitutional privileges granted, there
were clear limits to the policy of conciliation, even for the moderate
ministers in power after Metternich's fall. Actually it was easier for the
ministers to resist national German than general radical demands.
There was a veritable constitutionalist-cum-radical stampede after the
fall of the Metternich régime, with the two elements not yet clearly
divided. Open resistance to this movement was almost impossible,
though tactical shrewdness might divert it to zones where it could not
do vital harm. Opposition to the German national movement was far
less dangerous to the ministers, particularly as it did not have to be
done overtly. Court and Government were accustomed to being under
pressure from various groups. They would take the path of least resistance as long as feasible. Ideologically, they were usually being pushed
in one direction – the radical – and further than they liked to be. On
the nationality question, they were in the much happier position of
being under pressures which neutralised each other so that they could
assure everybody of their desire to help if only they were allowed to do
what they liked. The Germans wanted elections in the Czech districts
of Bohemia and Moravia, the Czechs did not. The Government did not
do anything, but left it to the local officials and electorate. The
German national movement was hoist with its own liberal petard.
Similar situations occurred in the Slovene districts in the south. Court
and Government in Vienna did not see why they should help a German
national movement in Austria which might possibly disrupt the Habsburg Empire. Czech and Slovene protests allowed ministers to refuse
their help to the Germans without incurring the slightest risk. The
German campaign in the Habsburg Empire thus began with a defeat.

   In the serious situation in which the Empire found itself, the
German argument about the importance of maintaining Habsburg
influence in Germany was bound to carry little weight. In a deeper sense

A sitting of the Frankfurt Parliament in the Paulskirche. Heinrich von Gagern is presiding and Robert Blum is speaking from the rostrum. Some of the more privileged members of the public, including the press, are seen in the background close to the deputies. The general public watched from the gallery.

Friedrich Daniel Bassermann

Georg Beseler

Karl Biedermann

Robert Blum

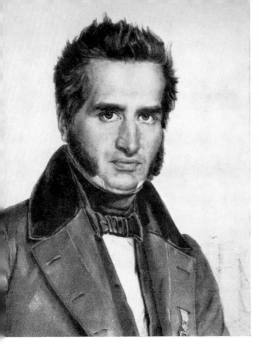

Friedrich Christoph Dahlmann

Johann Hermann Detmold

*Ignaz Döllinger. Etching by A. Bichard
from a drawing by F. Lenbach.*

Bernhard Eisenstuck

Heinrich von Gagern

Johann Gustav Heckscher

Archduke John, Vicar of the Empire

Wilhelm Jordan

Felix, Prince Lichnowsky

Karl Mathy

Robert Mohl

Joseph Maria von Radowitz

Franz Raveaux

Gabriel Riesser

Arnold Ruge

Anton von Schmerling

Heinrich Simon

Ludwig Simon

Eduard von Simson

Alexander von Soiron

Georg von Vincke

Carl Vogt

Karl Theodor Welcker

Franz Heinrich Zitz

the Government reflected a widely felt preoccupation with the problems of the Empire. The emphasis on strengthening German influence was only likely to create a negative impression on a supra-national government. Ministers could also, with a certain amount of justification feel some doubt as to whether the Germans in Austria had thought out properly the future relationship between the Habsburg Monarchy and the proposed new German state.

The political protagonists realised vaguely that the degree of union between the two state systems would have to be settled. This was crystallized into the question 'federal state or confederation' (*Bundesstaat oder Staatenbund*), though that formulation took for granted the desirability of a close association between Austria and Germany. Electors were asked to enter themselves in lists as to which of these two solutions they favoured.[1] What this alternative did not make clear was what territories would be included in the proposed confederation or federal state. Was the whole of the Habsburg Monarchy going to belong to a German-Austrian Confederation, including for instance the Kingdom of Hungary which did not send members to Frankfurt?[2] In the spring and early summer of 1848 there was still too much of the intoxication which came from the sudden crumbling of resistance to reform to allow for a sober assessment of practical difficulties. Those who wanted Austria to join Germany saw only their own problems. Before mid-May no expectation existed, even among these advocates of close ties with Germany, that the Habsburg Empire would disintegrate. They certainly did not want to break up the Habsburg Empire. Yet most of them do not seem to have thought out the problems involved in joining a German national state while keeping the Habsburg Empire intact.

The hostility of the Slavs to the Frankfurt elections needs less explanation than the interest taken in them by the Germans. The vital issues affecting the Habsburg Empire could only be decided by a body or bodies representing the whole Empire and dealing exclusively with the affairs of the Empire. Even if the Czechs and the Slovenes could be

---

[1] Ibler, 'Wahlen' 108.

[2] One of the few Austrians who had clear ideas on this subject was Johann Perthaler, who later served in the Frankfurt Parliament; see Kuranda, *Grossdeutschland* 106 ff. Perthaler wanted the whole of the Habsburg Monarchy to come to an arrangement with Germany, preferably on the basis of a confederative union between the two states, but under Austrian leadership. For Perthaler, see also *ADB* xxv; *NÖB* v; *BSTH*.

persuaded to participate, merely a rump of the Habsburg Empire would be represented in Frankfurt where the Austrian members could easily be out-voted by the non-Austrians. The state parliaments of Austria and Hungary were bound to be more important for the Habsburg Empire than the German National Assembly at Frankfurt. In spite of that, however, the Germans in the Habsburg Monarchy showed considerable interest in the elections for Frankfurt and devoted great energy to ensuring that they were held as widely as possible. As the Austrian authorities could not be expected to show great zeal for the German National Assembly, the number of members sent to Frankfurt was going to depend very much on voluntary and unofficial effort. To fill this need, a central committee for the elections to the German National Assembly in Frankfurt (*Zentralkomitee für die Wahlen zur deutschen Nationalversammlung in Frankfurt*) was set up in Vienna. Sub-committees were formed in the larger places.

While the non-Germans in the Habsburg Empire were bound to see the question of the Frankfurt elections purely with reference to the Habsburg Empire, many Germans in Austria regarded the future of Germany and that of the Habsburg Monarchy as two aspects of the same problem. They wanted to maintain at the same time the preponderant German influence in the leadership of the Habsburg Empire and to preserve Austrian influence in Germany. In the critical state of the Habsburg Empire in the spring and summer, attention is likely to have been focused mainly on the former. Indeed the Germans in the Habsburg Monarchy saw the preservation of Austrian influence in Germany as a means of bolstering up their position in Austria. As the nationality question was the over-riding problem of the Habsburg Empire, both the importance attached by the German Austrians to representation at Frankfurt and the opposition of the Czechs and Slovenes to this were quite logical. Both sides followed the dictates of their national interests as they saw them with the usual intolerance and one-sidedness of national movements at this time.

Not surprisingly, the German enthusiasm of the Vienna population took some time to develop. While primarily directed against the other nationalities, it was stimulated by the not entirely welcome news of the Prussian initiative in the German question which emerged from the Berlin rising in March. By early April, the German colours of black, red and gold were to be seen widely in Vienna. Whereas Anton Springer, who was later to win equal distinction as an art and political historian, regarded the attachment to Germany as shallow,[1] another Austrian contemporary of these events, the scholar and politician Josef Alexander von Helfert, noticed among the educated circles a serious shift of loyalty from Vienna to Frankfurt.[2] According to Helfert, only the German part of Tirol was entirely loyal to Austria. The conflict between these assessments by two expert – though not unprejudiced – observers of the political scene is not surprising when their involvement in the struggle is considered. Springer's scepticism about the strength of German feeling in Austria is understandable in the Great German Austrian from Bohemia who settled in Germany after the revolutionary period. Helfert's doubts about the loyalty of the German Austrians to the Habsburg Monarchy in a work published in his old age at the beginning of the twentieth century fits in with the fervent belief of a faithful follower of the Habsburg Monarchy in the broad multi-national base of the Empire. On the whole the Germans in Austria supported the German cause in order to strengthen the position of their national group in Austria.

Pressure from leading German organisations, like the *Politisch-Juridische Leseverein*[3] and the *Zentralkomitee*[4] in Vienna, to some extent at the prompting of the Committee of Fifty in Frankfurt, was required to make the Austrian authorities arrange for elections to the German National Assembly. The government of Austria was not the only one to need a reminder. The holding of elections in the German-inhabited parts of Austria was never really in doubt, as the administrations of Ficquelmont and Pillersdorf took the line of least resistance. It was a different matter when pressure in opposite directions was exerted on the Austrian ministers. The powerful National Committee in Prague decided to boycott the elections for the Frankfurt Parliament in Bohemia and if possible in Moravia. The Czech leader Palacky in a famous letter to the Committee of Fifty declined an invitation to join.[5] The National Committee in Prague was a predominantly Czech body, but initially contained a number of Germans in the early days after the March revolution. Although the committee did not have any official standing, it exercised considerable power in view of the weakness of the authorities. The Committee of Fifty in Frankfurt was very worried about the position in Bohemia and sent a deputation there consisting

---

[1] Anton Springer, *Geschichte Österreichs* II 254 ff.   [2] Helfert, *Geschichte* I 448 ff.
[3] Before 1848 the meeting-place of the liberal opposition.   [4] See above, p. 68.
[5] Jucho, *Verhandlungen* II 82.

of the distinguished Wurtemberg official Wächter and of Kuranda, a well-known journalist and a native Bohemian of Jewish faith. These two comparatively moderate supporters of the German cause were unofficially joined in Prague by another member of the Committee of Fifty, Schilling. This Viennese medical practitioner, later a member of the Moderate Left in the Frankfurt Parliament, was violently pro-German and anti-Slav. The two official delegates soon realised that they were badly served by their unofficial help-mate. The Czech leaders repeated the arguments put forward so persuasively in Palacky's earlier letter. For them the Czechs had a place within the Habsburg Empire, but apart from Germany. After all, it was quite illogical to assume from Bohemian membership of the German Confederation that Bohemia would join a German *national state*. If the Germans wanted to put their affairs on a national basis, the Czechs were entitled to do the same. Schilling countered the Czech arguments by threatening force and not unnaturally the discussions broke up in disorder.[1] By this time the Prague National Committee had already received assurances from the government in Vienna that Bohemia would not be forced to elect to Frankfurt. A German approach to countermand these pledges was unsuccessful, though in characteristic fashion the authorities in Vienna assured each delegation that they were on its side. Thus the government left the matter to individual action. The *Zentralkomitee* in Vienna and the German Committee in Prague[2] sponsored German candidatures in Bohemia and Moravia, one of the comparatively few examples of electoral organisation on a wide regional basis. Whereas the vast majority of members in the Frankfurt Parliament were elected in the constituencies where they lived or at least in the same comparatively small territorial or geographical region, the importation of non-residents into Bohemia and Moravia exceeded the norm.

The reports of the emissaries to the Committee of Fifty on their return from Prague included two complaints.[3] There were accusations of Czech terrorism. Threats to minorities were the order of the day because law and order had been undermined. Here the victims were

---

[1] Jucho, *Verhandlungen* II 298 ff.

[2] For the German Committee in Prague, see the account by the radical writer Moritz Hartmann, a German Bohemian of Jewish parentage, who took a leading part in organising the elections and himself won a seat. His autobiographical sketch covering this period appeared under the title 'Bruchstücke revolutionärer Erinnerungen' and is listed in the Sources below.

[3] Jucho, *Verhandlungen* II 283 ff.

not the 'reactionaries' or even moderates, but members of another national movement. The fronts were not ideological. It is doubtful whether the Czechs in Bohemia behaved worse than other nationalists at this time, including the Germans. The other complaint concerned the lack of support given to the German cause by so many in Bohemia who could be classed as Germans. But the ethnic definition in itself was not an easy one, as the names of some of the leaders of the Czech movement, such as Rieger, show. No doubt many Germans did not consider it wise to wear their German hearts on their sleeves at this time any more than national minorities in border areas during times of trouble usually do. The major inference to be drawn from the charges of disloyalty is that the Germans in the Habsburg Empire were caught unawares by the progress the Czech national movement had made during the Metternich era and that they overrated support for the German cause in Bohemia.

In the Czech areas and in some mixed districts of Bohemia, elections did not take place at all. In other parts of Bohemia inhabited both by Czechs and by Germans, a high proportion of electors refused to take part in the election. Thus in the town of Kaplitz, 82 out of 100 electors appeared for the poll, but 78 out of the 82 refused to vote. Only 4 electors elected the member and his substitute,[1] which made a mockery of the democratic process. The member, Wilhelm Huber, a surgeon from Linz, and a native of Bohemia, only took his seat in August 1848, as he was not aware of his election owing to the failure of the Austrian authorities to make it known to him.[2] The Assembly allowed him to sit and vote, which he did until his resignation in April 1849.

Some of the elections in Bohemia were delayed by the opposition of the Czechs. In Prague an announcement was put up on the afternoon of 22 May – when the Frankfurt Parliament was already sitting – stating that two members and two substitutes for Frankfurt were to be elected the following day. The posters containing details about the poll arrangements were torn down. Apparently only three votes were recorded,[3] though this may have been partly due to a printers' pay strike preventing the production of additional instructions by the government. All these arrangements show a lack of determination on the part of the authorities alternating with sudden bursts of energy. Presumably the shortness of the notice given was due to fear of Czech

[1] Helfert, *Geschichte* II 55.   [2] *Umrisse* 193.
[3] This rather weakens the claim made in *Gegenwart* I 69, that the population of Prague was two-thirds German!

opposition. The authorities hoped to rush through a matter which in its very nature required plenty of preparation and thought.[1]

The informality of the election arrrangements in Bohemia is reflected in the account of his own election given by the Bohemian-German writer Josef Rank[2] in his autobiography:

> . . . in August 1848 I received quite unexpectedly a letter from my father in which he informed me that my native place was no longer prepared to put off the election of a member, that I should get the government to call an election and that I could be confident that I would be elected, as only the Germans in the frontier districts were determined to vote. I went to the minister Pillersdorf, explained the situation in my native place to him, said that the Germans must not be prevented from holding elections because of the resistance of the Czechs and requested him to segregate a German election district and to have the election held as quickly as possible. The minister . . . said . . . he was gladly prepared to respond to the wish of my native place in the *Böhmerwald*. He kept word; to the governor of Bohemia went forth by telegraph the order to find out the constituency of my native place and to promulgate the election at once – and 12 days later I received news that I had emerged from the election in Bischof-teinitz as member of parliament . . .[3]

Thus, owing to pressure and counter-pressure, the initial elections to the Frankfurt Parliament continued into August, by which time many of the original members had already been replaced. Rank, too, may well have been elected by a minority of the constituency owing to the Czech boycott, or at least by a sadly reduced electorate. He himself reports that he had previously been beaten in the election for the Austrian Reichstag in his native place, as his Czech opponent had got four more votes.[4]

The Czechs certainly managed to prevent or impede a considerable number of elections in Bohemia. They were less successful in their efforts in this direction in Moravia.

Like the Czechs, the Slovenes objected to joining the new Germany, while wishing to remain in the Habsburg Empire. The Slovene national movement aimed at the creation of a Kingdom of Slovenia consisting of mainly Slovene districts in Carniola, Carinthia, South Styria and the Adriatic region within the Habsburg Empire. Not all Slovenes did,

---

[1] Helfert, *Geschichte* II 272 ff.   [2] Wurzbach XXIV 336; *ADB* LIII.
[3] Rank, *Erinnerungen* 333 ff. translated.   [4] Rank, *Erinnerungen* 333.

however, obey the instructions of their national movement to boycott the elections. The Slovenes were not nearly as successful as the Czechs in their prevention of elections for Frankfurt. This is not surprising as the Slovenes were much more scattered than the Czechs and only had a clear superiority over all other nationalities in the case of Carniola. In the *Gubernium Küstenland,* the Adriatic region, the Italians were strong rivals, particularly in the Trieste district, even if the Germans only represented a minute fraction of the population. In Carinthia and Styria, the Slovenes, though they only constituted about one-third of the population, formed solid blocks in the southern parts; in these provinces the Germans clearly prevailed. In Carinthia, Slovene opposition to the elections for Frankfurt achieved very little. The Slovenes were slightly more successful in Lower Styria. In some constituencies elections were prevented, in others the majority boycotted the polls and a minority election took place. In the two other provinces where the Slovenes were strongest, Carniola and *Küstenland,* minority elections were common. In other cases, elections were prevented or Slovenes were chosen who never went to Frankfurt. But there were also some instances of German candidates, such as Alexander von Auersperg (the poet Anastasius Grün)[1] getting elected with Slovene support. The authorities exercised little control.[2]

The Czechs and the Slovenes – as well as the Poles – were represented at the Slav Congress which opened in Prague on 2 June 1848.[3] In the teaching of Herder German and Slav nationalism had one of their many common roots[4] and the awakening of German consciousness was bound to strengthen that of the Slavs. Nearly all the initial elections for the Frankfurt Parliament were over by the time the Congress started, but the preparations for the meeting certainly increased the tension between German and Slav. Actually the Congress was not an unmitigated blessing for the Slavs, as it brought out important differences in the attitude of the various national groups to the problems of the day.

[1] *ADB* x; *BSTH*; *NDB.*
[2] Apih, 'Slovenische Bewegung'; Helfert, *Geschichte* I 467 ff.
[3] Namier, *1848 : Revolution,* particularly 91 ff.   [4] Kohn, *Pan-Slavism* 1 ff.

iii. The elections in South Tirol – General factors in the elections to the Frankfurt Parliament – Election committees

Sixty constituencies in the Habsburg Monarchy were not represented in the Frankfurt Parliament. The number of elected representatives who took up their seats was only 133, out of a possible total of 193 (allowing for the over-representation of Tirol). The missing sixty constituencies were situated in the Czech and Slovene districts, the majority – 45 – in Bohemia. In Bohemia only 23 out of 68 seats, that is just above one-third, were taken up. As the Germans in Bohemia constituted according to official statistics about 39 per cent of the population, this is a poor showing even if the authorities somewhat exaggerated the German element. In many districts the population was mixed and if the German element had really had its heart in the election for Frankfurt many more seats would have been filled. Undoubtedly many ethnic Germans were quite uninterested in the unification of Germany.

Matters took a different turn in the parts of South Tirol inhabited by Italians. Originally feeling ran high against any representation in Frankfurt, but the Catholic priest and theologian Baron Giovanni a Prato from Roveredo, who became the leading figure in the Trentino in 1848, persuaded the population to take part.[1] The Italians in the South Tirol, however hostile to Habsburg rule, could certainly afford less than the Czechs and the Slovenes to follow an independent line. Whereas these Slav groups were found mainly or entirely within the confines of the Habsburg Empire and saw their future within it, the majority of the Italians was outside it and the population of the Trentino looked to these Italian brethren for their future. Thus the Slovenes and the Czechs could make their influence far more felt in the Habsburg Monarchy than the Italians, as their loyalty was unquestioned. The choice of the Italians in South Tirol lay between revolt and co-operation. They realised after an abortive rising in April at Tione[2] that they had little chance of a successful rebellion against Habsburg rule. The authorities were determined to hold the Austrian hereditary lands, whatever happened in Lombardy and Venetia. Four leading noblemen of the Trentino, including Count Giuseppe Festi, who was elected to Frankfurt in May and served in the assembly, were arrested

---

[1] Marchetti, *Trentino* I 183 ff. See also Wurzbach xxiii.   [2] *Gegenwart* IV 94.

early in April.[1] In the whole Habsburg Empire there was no province more loyal to the dynasty and to the German connection than Tirol. Sir Lewis Namier believed that the Italians took part in the elections to the German National Assembly 'in the hope of having the national claims of the Trentino endorsed by it'.[2] Political realists in the spring and early summer of 1848 could hardly count this prospect among the practical possibilities. A more likely reason for participation was that as the inhabitants of the Trentino could not free themselves from the rule of the Habsburgs, they had to take advantage of any opportunity which was offered to them of making their voice heard. Six constituencies were represented by Italians.

Thus not all the 133 members from the Habsburg Monarchy were supporters of German unification or even of the German character of their constituencies. The six Italians reduce the figure to 127. Furthermore of the remainder some were elected in dubious circumstances, against the wishes of the majority in the constituency. Thus there were probably between 125 and 120 constituencies with German representatives, or roughly two-thirds of the total of possible seats in the Habsburg Empire. As only the Western part of the Habsburg Monarchy, where the bulk of the German population was found, was concerned in the elections for Frankfurt, this shows up the emptiness of the claim of regarding the Habsburg Empire as German even better than any population statistics, which are bound to be subjective.

The Slav boycott in the Habsburg Empire accounts for nearly all the seats which were not taken up. In the Kingdom of Prussia, the province of East and West Prussia was short of one seat, presumably in a non-German constituency. The remaining deficiency did not have anything to do with questions of nationality. The constituency of Thiengen in Baden was not represented because it insisted, rather *à la* Wilkes, on re-electing the ineligible Hecker. Here the non-representation of a constituency was not due to the unwillingness of the electorate to participate, but to the refusal of the Frankfurt Parliament to recognise Hecker as a member.[3] Normally the recognition of members was left to the assembly itself, but in one case the authorities stepped in to nullify an election on grounds similar to those for which the National Assembly rejected Hecker. In South Tirol the electors of Riva on Lake Garda at first elected a Dr Giacomo Marchetti who had set up a

[1] Marchetti, *Trentino* i 107.
[2] Namier, 'Nationality and Liberty' 178.   [3] See below, p. 252.

revolutionary régime not far away at Tione in April, but had soon had
to flee to Milan, then in the hands of the Italian national movement.
The Austrian Government simply declared the election null and void
and arranged for a fresh one. In spite of a protest, the Italians in the
constituency accepted the refusal of the Government and elected at
first Giovanni a Prato (who accepted for Roveredo) and then Francesco
Antonio Marsilli who took the seat.[1]

Both Germans and non-Germans had to make difficult decisions
quickly in connection with the elections to the Frankfurt Parliament.
Among the Germans, the dilemma of the ones in Austria can be most
easily understood. In varying degrees many Germans from other states,
too, who were *in principle* in favour of German unity, could rightly
claim that their eventual vote in the Assembly would depend on the
exact conditions proposed. They were bound to view German unity not
only from a state or regional angle, but to ask themselves what sort of
a Germany they were being invited to help to create. In the first
instance this was a matter of ideology.

Politicians and electorate were only gradually getting used to the
idea of the split between moderate liberals and radicals, after their
long years of co-operation in opposition before 1848, though in some
states, such as Baden, the cracks had already begun to show before the
Revolution. In this Grand-Duchy, owing to the Hecker rising in April,
the fronts for the election were more clearly drawn than in most other
parts of Germany. But even here, the position of many politicians was
not clearly defined by the time of the elections, which, owing to the
disturbed situation, would only have their first round between 13 and
18 May.[2] After the crushing of the rebellion any sympathisers with
Hecker who were at large were going to move very carefully, in order
to avoid arrest and trial. Those who wanted radical changes without
going as far as open rebellion were unlikely to risk being identified
with Hecker.

Ideological considerations were bound to have an effect on attitudes
to unity. All sides, from moderates to radicals and from federalists to
centralists, were only going to press hard for a German state which
corresponded to their ideological and constitutional ideas. Conversely,
they might be bitterly opposed to German unification on terms which
conflicted with what they regarded as their basic interests. At the time
of the election the exact manner in which attitudes to unity and to

[1] Marchetti, *Trentino* i 185.   [2] Philippson, *Über den Ursprung*, 62.

ideology were going to affect each other could not yet be measured, for this was going to depend largely on events which had not yet unfolded themselves and could hardly be foretold.

There was a further angle from which the new Germany could be regarded, from the religious point of view. A Roman Catholic would naturally want to know whether his church would be secure in the new state. He would be attracted by Roman Catholic leadership and by the prospect of a Germany in which his co-religionists were in the majority. Protestant leadership and the likelihood of being outnumbered by the other principal denomination would tend to repel him. Thus the three questions of unity, ideology and religion were closely inter-related.

Normally, the German members of the Frankfurt Parliament were elected on the assumption of their willingness to work for German unification. On the whole, regions not in the forefront of the unification movement, such as Hanover and Old Bavaria, did not choose members particularly enthusiastic for the German cause. Ideologically, there was a contrast between certain traditionally radical areas, such as the Rhenish Palatinate, the Grand-Duchy of Baden, parts of the Kingdoms of Wurtemberg and Saxony and of the Prussian province of Silesia on the one hand, and the comparatively moderate rest of the country on the other. Even in preponderantly moderate regions, such as the Prussian Rhine Province, some of the towns were radical. But as the other examples show, radicalism was not confined to the towns. It would certainly be wrong to contrast radical towns with a moderate countryside. Radicalism was strong in areas with grievances, in parts, such as Silesia, where changes in modes of production were causing great human distress, in places where the old crafts were being replaced by industry, and in rural areas where seigneurial privileges were resented. There were Socialist and Communist elements, but hardly of a Marxist type. Finally, there was the religious factor. In some of the Roman Catholic strongholds, such as the Prussian Rhine Province and Old Bavaria, Protestants were only elected with difficulty. Similarly Roman Catholics were rarely elected in preponderantly Protestant territories, such as Brandenburg.

Broadly speaking, at the time of the elections there was a rough division into conservatives of various shades, moderate liberals, and democrats of greater and lesser radical leanings. In addition, cutting across the ideological division, there were Catholic and to a far smaller extent Protestant groups.

Many candidates would have found it very hard to fit themselves into one of these categories which, though vaguely known at the time, did not have the precision which the historian tends to give them. Not only nominally – as there were no party labels to which candidates could attach themselves – but often in fact, men rather than measures were chosen. This is seen clearly in the high number of local men of distinction who won seats, sometimes with little reference to their political views, if these were known. It was felt to be more important to choose professional men of distinction for Frankfurt, where weighty constitutional issues were going to be debated at length, than for state parliaments. This helps to explain the high proportion of people of rank (*Honoratioren*) in the Frankfurt Parliament. Many men were mainly elected, one feels, because of the reputation they had made for themselves in their professions, in scholarship, in the law, in the civil service. There is here something of the German preference for the established expert, as opposed to the English attraction to the amateur with common sense. However, the personal choice took place within certain limitations. Normally only those were elected who came within the – admittedly rather wide – range of political views regarded as desirable. A radical Saxon constituency would hardly have chosen a conservative, and a typical moderate liberal constituency hardly a radical. The *Honoratioren* were a sufficiently big group from which somebody of the right political colour and the appropriate religion could be selected. The personal element also comes in with the preference for men who had suffered under the pre-1848 régime. A large number of these were elected. The choice was thus a combination of personal with political and religious factors.

At this time, when the authority of governments stood very low, the co-operation of the public in elections could not be taken for granted. Elections could not simply be decreed by the authorities. To take place effectively and successfully, some voluntary effort on the part of the population was also required. This was provided by election committees (*Wahlausschüsse*) which were set up in many constituencies. They had no official standing, but considerable influence. Originally, some of them had been formed as action committees to ensure that the governments would actually make arrangements for elections and to take over for them if they did not do so.[1] They put pressure on the Prussian government when the Prussian Chamber itself nominated members for

---

[1] Repgen, *Märzbewegung* 131 ff.

Frankfurt and forced the annulment of these 'elections'. The election committees consisted simply of those who were most active politically in a constituency at that time and were thus reasonably representative of the activists. Their composition tended to favour the Left, to the disadvantage of the moderates, who were much slower in organising themselves. The committees arranged public meetings for discussion of current problems and the selection of candidates. In some cases they even voted for a list of candidates, which the official proceedings afterwards sometimes, but not invariably, ratified. The committees undertook essential jobs such as writing round to possible candidates to ask them to stand and sometimes to interrogate them as to their political views. To capture the committee for one's political views was a considerable advance towards electoral victory.

On the whole the committees worked independently on a local basis, without being able to co-ordinate elections in a bigger area, as the large number of double and treble candidatures shows. But there were already a number of regional bodies working on a national, ideological or religious basis. The first kind operated mainly in non-German and border areas, for instance in Bohemia and Moravia,[1] as well as in Schleswig-Holstein. The struggle between the ideologies within the German camp was fought out in a different fashion. Representatives of various groups, for instance of the moderate liberals and the radicals, might serve together on local election committees, each trying to gain an advantage over the others. But at the same time there were informal contacts between men of similar views over a bigger area, for instance between the Rhenish liberals and between the Baden radicals. These efforts were usually confined to a region. Thus they hardly extended to co-ordinating activities in the Western and Eastern parts of the Prussian monarchy or of the Bavarian kingdom. Even within a state, co-ordination was often poor. Otherwise the Baden radicals would hardly have risked the loss of seats through the multiple election of Itzstein.[2] It is very doubtful whether other political movements besides the moderate liberals and the radicals went in for organised activity on a bigger scale. The conservatives were too dazed by the recent experience of the revolution to make themselves very much felt.

[1] See above, p. 68 ff.

[2] Itzstein was elected seven times. See Philippson, *Über den Ursprung* 62. For Itzstein, see *ADB* xiv; *Umrisse* 199; *BSTH*.

iv. Roman Catholicism

The new development in the life of the political groupings in the spring of 1848 was the emergence of an organised Roman Catholic movement. This does not imply that Roman Catholics all over the election area for Frankfurt took the same line on all political or even on all religious questions. That was not to be expected over so large a territory, with so big a population involved. In the lands included in the German Confederation at the end of 1848, the Catholics were still preponderant owing to the inclusion of parts of the Habsburg Empire. There were about 24 million Roman Catholics to roughly 21 million Protestants and half a million Jews. The remaining groups – Mennonites, gipsies, Greek Orthodox and Mohammedans – only accounted for a few thousand. In the Austrian parts of the German Confederation, the 12 million Catholics were an overwhelming majority, as there were only just over a quarter of a million Protestants and 120,000 Jews.[1] Without Austria, the Catholics in Germany were bound to be in a minority. This was only one reason for a general preference of Catholics for Austrian rather than Prussian leadership, other things being equal. The Catholics both inside and outside Prussia could hardly be expected to feel very enthusiastic about the Hohenzollern state. Although there had been a great improvement in the condition of Catholics since the accession of Frederick William IV, the memories of the Cologne church conflict still rankled. Even though a Catholic division had now been established in the Prussian *Kultusministerium* which dealt with religious and educational matters, Catholics in Prussia could never forget that they were a minority of about 6 to 10 in a state ruled by a Protestant. At this time not a single minister of the Prussian government was a Catholic.[2] In the civil service and in the administration of the law, the Catholics were nowhere represented in proportion to their actual strength. Though the fault was mainly that of the Protestant majority, sometimes the Catholics played into their hands by a certain detachment from the actual world and by a numerically less strong interest in education. To Catholics outside the Hohenzollern dominions, Protestant Prussia could hardly offer as strong

[1] *Gegenwart* III 17; Dieterici, *Mitteilungen* III 1 ff.
[2] See the quotation from a letter of Archbishop Geissel of Cologne in 1845 given in Bachem, *Vorgeschichte* I 151–2.

an attraction as Catholic Austria under a ruler of their faith.
The Catholic approach was bound to be basically different from that
of the moderate liberals or the radicals. These ideological movements
thought in terms of a mainly political solution. To the Catholic party,
matters of faith were bound to come first. The prime objective to the
Catholic was to ensure freedom to practise his own religion unfettered
by secular interference, while wishing to maintain the Christian nature
of the state. In order to try and harmonise these two aims which were to
some extent in conflict with each other, Catholic opinion veered from a
demand for the separation of church and state to the goal of the
independence of the church.[1] An active Catholic was bound to be more
interested in these aims than in anything else. Changes in political
structure were viewed from this angle. The shock of revolution brought
Catholics face to face with the necessity of entering the political arena
to gain their spiritual ends. They were not enamoured with the way the
pre-1848 régimes had run things. Their criticisms were not confined to
Protestant states, for it was King Louis I of Bavaria,[2] a Catholic, who
during the Lola Montez affair had one of the most severe clashes with
the Catholic clerical movement in this period. Catholics knew the
shortcomings of these states, but on the other hand the monarchies
had a certain Christian basis. The complete uncertainty about the
future must have shown to Catholics that they had been too prone to
take for granted a measure of state support for Christianity. They
were bound to wonder what would happen to the established position
of the Christian churches in Germany if philosophical radicals like
Hecker or even like Ruge[3] or Blum (an apostate Catholic and a *Deutschkatholik*) ran things. They could no longer stand apart. But as their
principal objectives were not those of the chief political ideological
movements, they were in a strong bargaining position. There are many
examples of Catholic committees seeking assurances on matters of
faith from political groups.[4] In 1848–9 the Catholics were not a political
party. They were prepared to co-operate with any group ready to grant
their requests. Perhaps this is one of the reasons why in spite of the
activities of the Catholic groups the number of their co-religionists
elected was not as big as might have been expected.[5] While it was
desirable to get a member of the faith elected if possible, Catholics

---

[1] See below, p. 230 ff.   [2] See above, p. 12.
[3] *ADB* xxix; Nerrlich, *Ruges Briefwechsel*; Neher, *Arnold Ruge*; *BSTH*.
[4] For instance in the Rhineland.   [5] See below, p. 99.

were prepared to deal with members of other denominations who gave the necessary undertakings. These assurances were frequently granted with great readiness as Catholic support was attractive, particularly to the moderate liberals against their political enemies on either side. Thus many mutually advantageous and certainly quite legitimate bargains were struck. Just as the Catholics were prepared to deal with any political group ready to meet their terms, so they were also scattered over all the political groupings, though they were more strongly represented on the Right and in the Centre than on the Left. During this period of transition for the Catholic Church under Pope Pius IX, while the exact balance between democratic and autocratic elements in ecclesiastical organisation was still in doubt, many religious and political issues still had to be settled for Catholics. Those Catholics who participated in public affairs were not necessarily all of one religious or political persuasion. In matters of faith, they ranged from what was called 'ultramontane' or 'clerical' to 'liberal Catholics' and even those with views considered doctrinally dubious by the hierarchy. Some of the prominent Catholics in the Frankfurt Parliament had been involved – like the Bonn professor Knoodt[1] – in heterodoxy. Others – notably Döllinger[2] – were to break with the Church over infallibility. Perhaps this was not surprising at a time of rapid political and religious change, with all their – often subtle – effects on each other. Similarly, the Catholic members were not all of one mind politically. The two strongest groups among them were first those who refused to associate themselves exclusively with any political grouping, an attitude adopted by many of the church dignitaries elected to Frankfurt, and secondly those who were broadly speaking in the Centre. But even those Catholics inclined to the Centre would not necessarily go with the liberals, and as Catholics they might see many matters – such as Prussian leadership in Germany or the exclusion of Austria – in a different light. In the Frankfurt Parliament, there were some Catholics on the Right, but comparatively few connected with political Catholicism on the Left. There was, however, considerable support for the radicals among the Catholic masses, as the successes of strong left-wingers in parts of the Rhineland show.[3] Even where there was a local electoral arrangement, radical representation indicated popular support.

---

[1] See Schnabel, *Zusammenschluss* 78; *ADB*; Repgen, *Märzbewegung* 261.
[2] *ADB* xlviii; Friedrich, *Döllinger*; *NDB*; *BSTH*.
[3] Ludwig Simon in Trier, Raveaux in Cologne and Wesendonck in Düsseldorf.

The Catholics had always fought over *ad hoc* issues which arose. But now they took the initiative over a much wider field. They learned a great deal from the liberals and the radicals in political theory, but they soon outstripped certainly the moderate liberals in the extent of their political organisation. One of the most striking things was that the church, which had a strong autocratic side and which had between 1815 and 1848 preferred to deal with governments, was now prepared to enter the democratic arena. Suddenly, after the revolutions of 1848, from the spring onwards, the greatest reservoir of mass support, the flocks of the Catholic faithful, was tapped for political life.

There was thus a certain turning-away from other-worldliness in the German Catholic Church, while spiritual aims were kept firmly in mind. One limitation still remained because this was inherent in the whole spiritual approach. A political party could never come first to a believing Catholic in the same way as it did to an agnostic radical or even to some of the Protestant liberals. But a Catholic could be an active supporter of a political party. The spiritual reservations of the Catholics were more noticeable in their attitude to German unification. Many of them like the Tirolese theologian Beda Weber[1] did not hide their contempt for the idolatry of nationalism. Both internationalism and a spiritual sense of values continued to impede whole-hearted Catholic participation in the German unity movement. No doubt here, too, considerations of religious statistics played their part. But the main reason lay deeper.

No statistical table of election results for the whole country would, even if it could be drawn up, accurately reflect this intricate combination of political, religious, regional and national factors. Liberalism meant something different in the Western part of the Prussian monarchy from what it did in the East, just as the Frankfurt and Berlin ministers and Parliaments were to diverge,[2] even if originally drawn from the same political stock. Besides, there is a technical objection to a tabulation of 'general election' results, even where members could be neatly classified in some category or other. There was no clear break between a 'general election' and by-elections in constituencies. The initial elections in the constituencies did not always determine who was going to serve in Parliament, as so many of those elected declined to sit for one reason or other. Some could not accept for one particular constituency as they were also elected elsewhere and had to choose between

[1] *ADB* xli; Weber, *Charakterbilder*; Wurzbach liii.   [2] See below, p. 171 f.

D

several seats. Others were unable to serve in the Frankfurt Parliament
as they were elected to state parliaments or appointed state ministers
and felt that they could not do justice to their duties in the German
National Assembly. Others again had not been consulted before being
elected and simply turned down a seat. Unless the law of the state
allowed the substitute to move up in the particular circumstances and
the substitute was still available, a fresh election had to be held, and
this process went on for some time until the seats were filled. What is
attempted here is an impressionistic sketch of results in the three parts
of the election area, in Prussia, in the smaller states and in the Habsburg Empire.

v. Election results in Prussia

In *Prussia,* elections for the German and Prussian National Assemblies were made initially by the same electors, though not necessarily
with the same ideological or religious result. This apparent inconsistency is not as surprising as it looks at first sight. Often *one* local
election committee (*Wahlausschuss*) provided candidates for the elections. Where there were several strong groupings, care would be taken
to reflect the main shades of local opinion. As four men had to be elected
(including the substitutes), this provided an opportunity for representing several points of view. There cannot, however, be a question of
inferring a 'deal' or 'alliance' between the groups from these arrangements. What took place was a preliminary sifting of candidatures in
the unofficial associations which flourished in the early weeks after the
revolution. Thus in the Rhineland, conditions allowed plenty of scope
to the three main groups, the Catholics, the liberals and the radicals.[1]
A give and take was all the easier as there was no general preference for
Berlin or Frankfurt. In the Rhineland, Frankfurt was on the whole
considered as more important than Berlin, but the Archbishop of
Cologne, Geissel, took a different view and got himself elected for the
Prussian National Assembly. In Prussia generally, both Frankfurt and
Berlin got their share of able men. As in the case of Austria, the local
parliament was more radical than the representatives of the state in the
Frankfurt Parliament. On the one hand, this was due to the different

[1] For instance in Cologne, see Repgen, *Märzbewegung* 245 ff.

tasks of the parliamentary bodies, to the friction which resulted from the closer contact of the Austrian and Prussian parliaments with their state government. On the other hand, partly because of the difference in tasks, the parliaments in Berlin and Vienna attracted a tougher kind of person, interested mainly in the practical tasks of government, whereas the more academic or theorising type of representative – not necessarily less determined in his field – was more attracted to Frankfurt. The preference of the electors in each case was just as important and served to reinforce that of the candidates. In the elections for Frankfurt, the electors certainly looked for men who were sufficiently well educated to understand the complex constitutional problems the German National Assembly was going to be called upon to solve. This accounts for certain characteristics of the Frankfurt Parliament reflected in its composition.[1] The educational requirements which flowed from this excluded – where strictly applied – many members of occupations such as master craftsmen, inn-keepers, brewers, butchers and primary school teachers, which hardly figured at Frankfurt, but were noticeable in Berlin. As radicalism drew a great part of its strength from these groups, the Left was weaker at Frankfurt than at Berlin. Also, the radicals, bent on achieving something at once, were more interested in the state parliaments, where they could see more scope for realising their immediate aims than in the long-term work at Frankfurt.

As elsewhere in Germany, generalisation is difficult as personality on the one hand and political and religious views on the other played their part in varying proportions. But there were certain regional differences in political confrontation and in the outcome of the elections.

As was to be expected, religious questions played a prominent part in the electoral battle, mainly in the predominantly Roman Catholic regions and not so much in areas inhabited principally by Protestants, except where Protestantism was regarded as being on the defensive. The Protestants, by virtue of their leading numerical and political position, had usually been able to make their voice heard. For the Roman Catholics, the new constitutional machinery provided in the elections the first opportunity to give an adequate political airing to their religious requirements which they used to the full.

In *Prussia*, the change which came over the fortunes of the various groups even since the elections to the United Diet the year before was

---

[1] See below, p. 93 ff.

quite astounding and cannot be explained simply in terms of an alteration in the law. Certainly the Catholics had suffered from censorship
and they claimed that the authorities discriminated against them,
playing havoc with their case while allowing their opponents, for instance the *Deutschkatholiken*, to put theirs.[1] The liberals had suffered
from the censorship, too, but the blue-pencil did not benefit any of
their rivals. Indeed, the liberals gained sympathy thanks to their
tussles with the censor, who also shielded them to some extent from
their more extreme allies on the Left. While the liberals before 1848
basked in popular glory, the Roman Catholics were inhibited in their
political activity by the feeling that not only the authorities but most
of the population were against them. This impression, a tendency to
other-worldliness, and a negative attitude to education and to new
ideas, account for the comparative political inactivity of the Catholics
before 1848. The abolition of censorship and the depressed position of
authority in 1848 allowed the Catholics to feel suddenly that it was
worth their while to join the political battle. They were quite prepared
to make use of the liberal achievements, but the net effect was to
threaten the key liberal position. The liberals were taken aback by a
consequence inherent in their ideas, that the people might transfer its
trust any time to another political group. In the Rhineland, on which
the best and fullest election study has been done,[2] the overshadowing
of the moderate liberals by the Roman Catholics can be most clearly
seen.

If the moderate liberals were often at the mercy of Roman Catholics,
they also had to contend with radical competitors, mainly in urban
areas, particularly in those which were being industrialised, with all
the economic and social disturbance involved. Radical successes were
gained in both halves of the Monarchy, in the East for instance in the
Berlin area itself and in Silesia. On the whole the agrarian areas in the
East held out against radicalism, mainly thanks to the entrenched
position of the landed gentry. In these districts there were even some
conservative elections, probably best understood in personal terms.

In Prussia, four main groupings thus emerged in the elections for
the Frankfurt Parliament, if only in an embryonic form. Over the
Monarchy as a whole the moderate liberals were the strongest group.
In parliament they were at first to receive the support of many Catholics.
These liberals were generally the forerunners of the National Liberals

---

[1] Bachem, *J. Bachem*, I 153 ff.   [2] Repgen, *Märzbewegung*.

of the 1860s. The Catholics came out of the elections as the second strongest group, but in the Frankfurt Parliament they became submerged in political groupings. They foreshadowed the Centre Party.

The radicals did worse than either the moderate liberals or the Catholics. They were a heterogeneous group even then. The most moderate of their flock eventually became members of the Progress Party (*Fortschrittspartei*) in the 1860s. The non-Marxist Communist movement of Dr Gottschalk in Cologne boycotted the elections.[1] In spite of the presence of Marx and Engels on Prussian soil, there was little evidence of their influence on the polling in the direction of their own peculiar views. The Frankfurt Parliament only contained one member of their closer circle, the writer Wilhelm Wolff[2] of Breslau, though others had collaborated with Marx in his earlier less radical phases.

The conservatives did worst. They were too much associated with the unpopular régime of pre-1848 days and were certainly under-represented in the Frankfurt Parliament in terms of public opinion in the country. In the weeks after the revolution, the tide ran too heavily against conservatism to encourage people to avow support. But there were more quiet conservatives in Prussia even in the spring of 1848 than is apparent from the polls, just as the vociferousness of the radicals exaggerated the extent of their support. For the time being, many conservatives voted for moderate liberals, unless they were Catholics and had a suitable candidate of their faith. Conservative under-representation meant not only that the liberals were over-represented in the long run, but also that many prominent liberal members of parliament were men with conservative leanings, who in times more favourable to conservatism might have been found more to the Right. Some falling off in liberal support to both political neighbours was almost inevitable in the not too distant future: to the Right at any rate in the agrarian East of the Monarchy with its hereditary ruling class, and to the Left in the areas which were being industrialised.

The initial elections were mainly fought on religion and political ideology. Though there were specific references to German unification in many election manifestos, the exact nature of the decisions required from the Frankfurt Parliament could hardly be predicted in April and May. On the whole German unity was a non-party matter, except for dogmatic opponents on the Right. The old Prussian territories, par-

---

[1] Repgen, *Märzbewegung* 245 ff.   [2] *BSTH.*

ticularly in the East, attached considerable importance to keeping Prussian institutions in being. The newly acquired Rhineland hardly had any loyalty to the Prussian state, and Catholic interests demanded a retention of Austria which would have made Prussian leadership impossible. Main support for Prussian hegemony in Germany inside the Monarchy certainly came from the Protestants in the old Prussian territories. Catholics, even in eighteenth-century acquisitions like Silesia, were certainly reserved towards Hohenzollern leadership in Germany.

vi. Election results in the 'Third Germany'

The question of German unification was viewed more sharply and urgently in the smaller states. Prussia and the Habsburg Empire could stand on their own, but perhaps not even Bavaria or Hanover would be able to do so. For the *Third Germany* (the third member of the Trias)[1] definite ideas about the future shape of Germany seemed essential in the spring of 1848. Thus more than in Prussia, attitudes to German unification were a factor in the elections along with religion and ideology, especially in Bavaria and Hanover, two of the biggest medium-sized states. There was little enthusiasm for German unity in Hanover and in Catholic Old Bavaria. These parts were comparatively resistant to radicalism, for in the spring and summer of 1848 the Left had scant sympathy for the differing interests of the various states, regarding them as anachronistic survivals and identifying them entirely with the princes whom they abhorred. In Catholic Old *Bavaria*, the conservatives were able to do comparatively well, as the clerical party benefited from its political martyrdom at the time of the Lola Montez influence at court.[2] The outcome of the election was different in the newer parts of Bavaria where the Catholic Church had less of a following. In Franconia, with its varied political and religious origins, the results were mixed. The mainly Protestant Rhenish Palatinate, for long a centre of radicalism, voted extreme Left.

Like Bavaria, *Hanover* was a stronghold of particularism. Under the

[1] *Trialism*, some form of co-operation between the rest of Germany, was advocated by some statesmen in Southern Germany as a means of overcoming Austro-Prussian dualism.
[2] See above, p. 81.

guidance of Stüve[1] Hanover went very much its own way. Particularism did comparatively well there and representation was mainly in the hands of Hanoverians who wanted to see the interests of their state preserved, though not necessarily to the same extent as Stüve. In the main moderates were elected, with some conservatives.

In most of the other medium-sized states, the emergence of strong *radical* representation prevented an insistence on state rights. Besides the Rhenish Palatinate, *Baden* and the kingdom of *Saxony*, were stoutly radical, as were parts of *Wurtemberg*, of the *Hesses* and of *Nassau*. In *Wurtemberg* with its democratic and even republican tradition, the line between moderate liberalism and radicalism was difficult to draw. The leading minister Römer, who eventually disbanded the Rump Parliament in Stuttgart by force in June 1849, both as a minister in Wurtemberg and as a member of the Frankfurt Parliament preserved a somewhat intermediate position, with perhaps a slight preference *in practice* for the more moderate point of view, though he was *in theory a republican*.[2] The majority of those elected initially had a similar outlook to Römer, but there was some representation of radicals, though not anywhere on the scale of that in the neighbouring Baden. Similarly in the *Hesses* and in *Nassau* the radicals were in a minority. These states voted mainly for moderate men, like Heinrich von Gagern, the leading minister, in Hesse-Darmstadt. *Schleswig-Holstein*, the *Hanseatic* cities, *Mecklenburg*, *Oldenburg* and *Brunswick* voted largely moderate.

In the non-German duchies of *Luxemburg* and *Limburg*, representatives of local national groups were elected. In *Schleswig-Holstein*, representation was naturally confined to Germans.

vii. Election results in the Habsburg Empire

In the *Habsburg Monarchy*, the national issue was in the forefront. The outcome can be largely read in terms of the numbers of constituencies either accepting or refusing representation in Frankfurt.[3] Apart from the Italians who sat for constituencies in South Tirol, the Austrian representatives elected to Frankfurt believed in the main-

---

[1] See above, p. 38.
[2] Bassermann, *Denkwürdigkeiten* 67.   [3] See above, p. 71ff.

tenance of the ties between the Habsburg Monarchy and Germany.[1] The radical minority viewed the possibility of the formation of a federal state (*Bundesstaat*) including Austria with more sympathy than the moderate majority who preferred a confederation of states (*Staatenbund*). Not too much should be read into the proportion of moderates to radicals among the Austrians in the Frankfurt Parliament, as the ideological issue was secondary before the Vienna rising of 15 May. The fronts were not yet clearly drawn before the elections and considerations of personality were often uppermost. Radical representation was stronger in the towns than in the countryside. Only Tirol returned a strong *clerical* delegation.

In spite of the competition of the Austrian Reichstag, a large number of men distinguished in various walks of life was elected initially. Clearly personal reputation – rather than ideology – marked out those among the German Austrians who were considered the right men for Frankfurt. In the towns some hard-fought elections took place. In the Viennese constituency of Josephstadt the poet Friedrich Hebbel succumbed to the prominent lawyer and official Joseph von Würth,[2] perhaps mainly because he was born outside Austria and had only settled there a few years previously. Würth was better known and better connected. He was also a member of the Central Committee for the elections to Frankfurt. There was some representation of the pre-1848 'opposition' to Metternich, including Anton Ritter von Schmerling[3] (the later minister), the poet Anton Alexander von Auersperg ('Anastasius Grün')[4] and Franz Philipp von Somaruga[5] (who was to hold important offices in Austria).

viii. Turn-over of representatives during course of assembly

Long before the last constituency had elected a representative for Frankfurt, in August,[6] a considerable number of members had already resigned. There was thus a fluctuating membership during the first two or three months and the situation did not improve later. For this reason

---

[1] For a time in the autumn the Left followed a somewhat different line. See below, p. 234 f.

[2] *ADB* lv; Wurzbach lviii. [3] *ADB* lvi; Arneth, *Schmerling*; *BSTH*.

[4] See above, p. 73 . [5] Wurzbach xxxv. [6] See above, p. 72.

the most convenient method of analysing the composition of the parliament is to take as the basis the nearly 800 members who actually sat at some stage in the German National Assembly at Frankfurt.[1] Members who only belonged to the Rump Parliament at Stuttgart are ignored in this context.

In the majority of constituencies, representation did not change. But many constituencies were represented successively by two, three and in one case even by four members.

Constituencies represented by the same member throughout					..	418
,,	,,	,,	successively by 2 members		..	156
,,	,,	,,	,,	,, 3 ,,	..	22
,,	,,	,,	,,	,, 4 ,,	..	1
Total number of constituencies represented					..	596

These figures do not quite add up because Heinrich Henkel[2] resigned from one constituency in the Electorate of Hesse in July, as he did not consider the assembly fruitful enough, but rejoined for another constituency in the same state early in March 1849. He had presumably changed his mind about the Frankfurt Parliament and was now – unlike most people – better satisfied with it.

In view of the novelty of the whole situation, the high turn-over in the parliament is not surprising in as short a period as one year. It was hard to predict at the time of the elections exactly how arduous the duties of representatives would be or how long Parliament would take over its task. Many members certainly expected or hoped for a short session. Few could foresee the intense activity which developed in Frankfurt both in and out of the chamber. The majority of the members had not had enough political experience, for instance in state parliaments, to judge whether they were temperamentally suited to the parliamentary arena. Often they had not been consulted about their candidatures at all. Many members, particularly those with homes outside a small radius of Frankfurt, soon found that they had to make

[1] Analysis of the members of the Frankfurt Parliament is mainly based on the following sources: Franz Wigard, *Inhalts-Verzeichniss*; *Parlaments-Kalender*; *ADB*; *BSTH*; *NDB*; *ÖBL*; *Biographisches Jahrbuch und Deutscher Nekrolog*; the short biographies by H. Niebour of the representatives of various regions; *MdR*; random biographical information gleaned from the literature of and on the period; the files of the German Federal Archives (Bundesarchiv); etc.

[2] *ADB* xi; *BSTH*.

a choice between their professional and their parliamentary occupation. Also some members were elected for their state parliaments as well and, though not legally forced to do so, often found that they had to resign one of their seats. Here again, members from neighbouring states were more happily placed. Even some ministers in state governments, like Römer in Stuttgart and Hergenhahn in Nassau, kept their seats in the Frankfurt Parliament. Römer managed to play a considerable part both at Stuttgart and at Frankfurt. Other members of the Frankfurt Parliament had to resign for health or family reasons. In the end those stayed the course who were most interested in the political task at Frankfurt, among them some of the great names of the parliament. While sitting at Frankfurt, the parliament lost several members through death, five through normal causes,[1] and three others by assassination and execution. Felix, Prince Lichnowsky[2] and Hans von Auerswald[3] were murdered in the September disturbances in Frankfurt, and Robert Blum was executed by the Austrian authorities in November for his part in the Viennese revolt. During the last two months, in April and May, there was a mass exodus of members, only some of whom were still replaced at Frankfurt. The method of filling up seats varied. Sometimes the substitute moved up, but often a new election was held. Where the substitute succeeded, he frequently represented the opposite point of view to that of the member he replaced.[4]

Whatever may have divided the members in politics and religion, what did they have in common? Except for foreigners like the Italians and the succession of Polish members for a constituency in Posen, most of them had a more or less passionate belief in the future of Germany. In the great moments of the parliament, this strong political and even more cultural bond could bridge intense party differences. Few Germans deliberately came to Frankfurt to *prevent* German unification altogether. The Germans who did not believe in it – like Bismarck at the time – normally did not go to Frankfurt. There were many opponents of German unification then and their absence must be considered in determining how representative the Frankfurt Parliament was and what weight was attached to it. Just as the Frankfurt Parliament consisted in large measure of men who considered the German Confederation to be in need of reform, so the vast majority quite generally regarded a return to the conditions before the March

---

[1] Baur, Brunck, Smets, Wiebker and Wirth.   [2] *ADB* xviii; *BSTH*.
[3] *ADB* i.   [4] See above, p. 61.

revolutions as quite out of the question. The men who were identified in the public mind with the Metternich era were automatically excluded from the Frankfurt Parliament. The Right was very weak. As identification with the pre-1848 régimes was a bar to election, so resistance to them was a positive qualification. At least one-sixth of the members had suffered a greater or lesser degree of political persecution, ranging from the long periods in prison spent by Behr, Sylvester Jordan and Eisenmann[1] to the petty restrictions on liberty and on the exercise of a profession suffered by many. At least 18 of the members had emigrated for political reasons, many of them only returning to Germany after the revolution. More than one-fifth of the members had served in state, provincial or municipal assemblies before 1848, mainly in opposition. A small number of ministers who served in state governments before 1848 was elected to the Frankfurt Parliament, but they were those who had made their opposition to oppression clear, like the late Saxon minister Bernhard von Lindenau[2] or the former Prussian minister Maximilian von Schwerin-Putzar.[3] The disqualification rather surprisingly did not extend to civil servants, even senior ones, to judges and to public prosecutors, who were represented in large numbers.[4]

ix. Local factors – 'Honoratioren'

342 out of the 799 members of the parliament, i.e. about 43 per cent, were elected in the locality in which they were resident, that is to say either in the same constituency or very close to it. Of these 342 members, 101 or nearly 30 per cent were local *Honoratioren*, men who had a recognised leading position in the locality by virtue of their social or professional eminence, such as the owner of a big estate in the district, the leading local official or the major businessman in the place. While in many cases the classification is obvious, it must remain a matter of opinion to what extent it should be extended downwards. In this survey the criterion is whether the member is likely to have owed his election mainly to being a personality highly respected in the locality by virtue of his position in it. With about one hundred members

---

[1] See above, p. 12. [2] *ADB* xviii; *BSTH*.
[3] *ADB* xxxiii; *BSTH*. [4] See below, p. 95.

this seems to have been so. The *Honoratioren*, in the sense of the leading men in society, business and professional life, were altogether well represented in this parliament, over and above the hundred or so to whom reference has been made. The *Honoratior* elected in the constituency where he lived or worked or owned property or did all this was certainly a characteristic type of member.

Representation was still largely a local, state or regional matter. Where members were elected far from their place of residence, there was often a special reason for it, for instance in Schleswig-Holstein which returned a man like Dahlmann to show that the struggle of the Germans in the Duchies was a national German matter and in order to enlist the support of one of the most powerful members of the parliament. Dahlmann, one of the Göttingen Seven, was then a professor at Bonn, where, as a Protestant, he could not get elected easily.

The importation of non-residents into Bohemia and Moravia also exceeded the national average. These Bohemian representatives include the only example in the whole of the Habsburg Monarchy of a member of the Frankfurt Parliament who was not a subject of the Habsburgs. The connection of this pillar of the 'Young Germany' movement, the poet Heinrich Laube, who then lived in Leipzig, with Bohemia was a rather tenuous one. Laube had taken the waters at Karlsbad on several occasions and was elected for the constituency in which the famous resort lay. In many cases, however, the members concerned had been born in the territory where they were elected or had worked there. Dahlmann had been a professor in Kiel and secretary of the Holstein estates.

x. Professional composition of parliament – The clergy

When the parliament is broken up into ten main professional groups, always classifying a member by his principal occupation in 1848 (apart from politics), the following result emerges[1] in order of size:

[1] Cf. the composition of the British House of Commons in this period in William O. Aydelotte, 'The House of Commons in the 1840s', *History*, xxxix (Oct. 1954).

TABLE 1

	Number of Members	Per cent of total
*Civil servants, including local government (apart from other groups in state employment marked *)	157	19·7
Lawyers (apart from judges and public prosecutors)	130	16·3
*University or school teachers	123	15·4
*Judges and public prosecutors	119	14·9
Businessmen	75	9·4
Landowners	68	8·5
Clergy (unless mainly teachers)	45	5·6
Writers, journalists	36	4·5
Medical practitioners (apart from university teachers)	25	3·1
*Army officers	15	1·9
Not yet in profession	2	0·2
Not known	4	0·5
Total	799	100

* In public employment

It will be readily seen that the occupations which did not require a higher education were poorly represented. At least 764, or 95·5 per cent of the total, had attended a *Gymnasium* (secondary school). At least 653, or 81·6 per cent of the total, had a university education. The educational background of the members had a considerable effect on the character of the parliament and indeed on the whole German national and liberal movement. For the members of the parliament the cultural values which they had imbibed at the *Gymnasium* and at the university were a strong bond.

Not only did the vast majority of the representatives share the experience of having been to a university, but most of them had studied the law. 249 members, or 31·1 per cent of the total, practised the law either as judges, public prosecutors or lawyers, quite apart from the university teachers who professed the law. In addition, a law course at the university was the normal requirement for higher civil servants. Above all, the Frankfurt Parliament was a lawyers' parliament. The presence of so many men trained in the law was certainly useful. It helped for instance with the drafting of complex legislation. On the other hand, there may have been an excessive concern with words and procedure. It would be unfair to blame the legal profession for this. Good lawyers may maintain with some justification that an obsession with comparatively unimportant matter is not inherent in the lawyer's way of thought, indeed that the capable lawyer will at once get to the heart of a problem.

Similarly, the majority of members were employed by state or local government. For a parliament which wanted to break with the past, the high proportion of men who were in the service of the state is somewhat curious. Even ignoring the university and school teachers who were not necessarily identified with the pre-1848 régimes and were often known to have been opposed to them, three groups represented in the Frankfurt Parliament had helped to carry out the orders of the governments: the civil servants, the judges and public prosecutors and the army officers, altogether 291 members or about 36 per cent of the membership. Naturally they were neither all employed by governments or local authorities which came under public criticism, nor did they all commit acts which were condemned. Some were comparatively young or junior men, but others had held senior positions in the civil service and in the administration of the law. Among those elected there were two censors, the Austrian Karl Eduard Bauernschmid[1] and the Bavarian Sebastian Daxenberger.[2] Considering that censorship was one of the main targets of the erstwhile opposition, it is odd to find men like that in the Frankfurt Parliament.

The extent to which officials were elected to the Frankfurt Parliament is evidence that the pre-1848 régimes were not as *universally* bad as the opposition tried to make out. Indisputably there had been grave abuses and many cases of unjust imprisonment. But the opposition also focused its criticism on matters which could be viewed in more than one way and on which the critics of the government were not necessarily right. Because of the rigidity of the pre-1848 governments, and owing to the limited possibilities of peaceful change, all these questions tended to be lumped together as a package indictment of the governments and almost of government as such. Historians who have to select their material carefully have tended to add to the distortion by emphasising certain aspects, and in more recent times by writing about the 1815–1848 period against the background of totalitarianism. The electors of 1848 were not taken in quite so much by the exaggerations of liberal and radical propaganda.

Actually, the political system before 1848 in Austria and in many other states was indirectly responsible by stifling *public* criticism for the government service becoming one of the centres of opposition. The civil servants were less hampered in the old type of *autocratic*, as opposed

---

[1] Speidel, *Bauernschmid* (1910) i; *ÖBL*; *BSTH*.
[2] *ADB* xlvii; Schärl, *Zusammensetzung* 313.

to the later type of *totalitarian*, state by restrictions on the flow of news and on the expression of opinion than the general public. This explains the existence of a group of civil servants which, while bound to carry out the orders of the government, had certain reservations about many of them and was hoping for change. Also, the qualifications laid down for eligibility to state parliaments before 1848 favoured civil servants.

Legal background and state employment stand out as the predominant characteristics of members of the Frankfurt Parliament. The designation *Professorenparlament* is less convincing. Many of those who had the title of professor among the 123 teachers were not university professors but masters in the more senior forms of the *Gymnasium*, though often scholars of note. The numbers do not measure up to the two leading groups.

Of the smaller categories, both the businessmen and landowners range considerably in scale of activity and ownership. The line between great and small is not always easy to draw. But the majority in both groups were men of some substance. There were no peasants and only a few small shop-keepers. The master-locksmith (*Schlossermeister*) Nägele from Wurtemberg was exceptional in that his main occupation was a manual one. Even he had had a very good school education.[1] The 'labouring class' in the sense of an uneducated, propertyless working class, as represented for instance by the industrial proletariat, was not to be found in the parliament.

A different picture emerges when the social origin of members is analysed. A considerable proportion, perhaps as high as 20 per cent, rose from comparatively humble origins to professional positions, to wealth and to higher social status. The vast majority of members had fathers practising the professions mainly represented in the parliament. 130 members prefixed their surname with *von* as a sign of belonging to the nobility, but many of these were of recent creation.

52, or just under 6·5 per cent of the members, had been ordained.[2] Of these 34 were Catholics, including 4 bishops. 14 Protestant ministers served in the parliament. One minister was a *Deutschkatholik*. The religion of 3 ministers could not be established. Not all the Catholic priests went into parliament with the blessing of their ecclesiastical

[1] See Niebour, 'Biographisches'.
[2] 7 of these are classed as university teachers (their main occupation) in the table of professions (see above, p. 95).

superiors. At least 6 of the Catholic priests were in difficulties with the church authorities, mainly because of attachment to the teaching of men like Wessenberg, Hermes and Günther which had been condemned by the Church. Johanun Wilhelm Joseph Braun,[1] a follower of Hermes, was suspended from his teaching duties as a professor of Catholic theology at Bonn by the Prussian Government at the instigation of the Roman Church; Braun remained a believing Catholic. Another Bonn professor, Peter Knoodt, a disciple of Günther, engaged in the age-old exercise of keeping Christianity up-to-date by trying to reconcile religious teaching with philosophy. Rather dubiously he likened the freedom won in the March revolution to that gained for his flock by Jesus Christ.[2] Knoodt was a member of the Catholic Association in the Frankfurt Parliament.[3] Somewhat curiously the 'liberal' encyclopaedia *Die Gegenwart* calls him 'ultramontane'.[4] The four other priests were in much more serious conflict with the Church. Joseph Sprissler, a priest in the principality of Hohenzollern (an enclave in Wurtemberg), was suspended in 1849 after conducting a campaign against celibacy and publicly praising Luther.[5] Another priest from Hohenzollern in the Frankfurt Parliament, Joseph Blumenstetter, was a close associate of Sprissler. The priest from the Rhenish Palatinate Franz Tafel applied to the *Deutschkatholiken* for a ministry in 1845,[6] but nothing came of it. He was deprived of his living by the Catholic Church in 1851 following his participation in the revolutionary Stuttgart Rump Parliament of 1849.[7] The priest Dominikus Kuenzer from Constance, who served from 1830 to 1842 in the Baden parliament, drew the censure of the church authorities on himself by his persistent, though unsuccessful, efforts to curb the authority of the bishops through the establishment of synods containing a proportion of laymen. Kuenzer was a radical both in religion and politics. He served in the Rump Parliament.[8]

Knoodt – like Döllinger – later broke with the Catholic Church over the proclamation of the infallibility dogma. Another prominent Catholic clergyman in the Frankfurt Parliament, the professor of Catholic Theology at Bonn, Franz Xaver Dieringer, objected to the

[1] *ADB* iv; *BSTH*.   [2] Article on Knoodt in *ADB* li.
[3] Repgen, *Märzbewegung* 261.   [4] *Gegenwart* v 180.
[5] Information from the file on Sprissler in Bundesarchiv.
[6] Krautkrämer, *Kolb* 112 ff., 178.   [7] H. Niebour, 'Vertreter der Rheinpfalz' 101.
[8] Articles on Kuenzer in *ADB* xvii; Weech, *Badische Biographien* i 482 ff.; *BSTH* ii.
According to Pfülf, *Ketteler* i 159, Kuenzer was excommunicated in August 1848.

proclamation of the dogma, but eventually submitted, though he resigned his chair.[1]

xi. Deutschkatholiken *and Jews in the assembly*

Although in the area covered by the elections the Catholic inhabitants were slightly in the lead, the Protestants – including a small number of members of independent congregations (*Freie Gemeinden*) – had a majority in the parliament. This was mainly the result of the mass abstentions of preponderantly Catholic constituencies in the Habsburg Empire, but it also shows that the political pressure of the Catholic parish priest on the electorate in this case was not as great as Protestant critics often suspect.

A small number of members did not belong either to the Protestant or to the Catholic Church. There were 8 *Deutschkatholiken*, 5 Jews, 2 Mennonites and 1 member of the Greek Orthodox Church. The leading Prussian liberal Beckerath,[2] who became Reich Minister of Finance in the Provisional Central Power, was one of the two Mennonites; the other was the merchant Brons from Emden. The *Deutschkatholiken* included the leader of the Moderate Left, Robert Blum. Among the Jews there was Gabriel Riesser,[3] the champion of Jewish rights, who was a popular Vice-President of the parliament; Ignaz Kuranda,[4] the editor of the journal *Grenzboten*, who strove hard to maintain German influence in Bohemia; the publisher Moritz Veit[5] from Berlin; and (towards the end) the famous radical politician and medical practitioner Johann Jacoby[6] from Königsberg. A further 11 members came from Jewish stock but had been baptised. These include Heinrich von Gagern's widely respected successor as President of the parliament, Eduard Simson;[7] Moritz Heckscher,[8] who was for a time Reich Foreign Minister in 1848; Johann Hermann Detmold,[9] the great satirist of the parliament and later Reich minister; Heinrich Simon,[10] the leader of *Westendhall*, the right wing of the Left; and the poet Moritz Hartmann,[11]

[1] Article on Dieringer, *ADB* v. See also *NDB*   [2] *ADB* ii; *NDB*; *BSTH*.
[3] Isler, *Riessers Schriften*; *BSTH*.   [4] *ADB* li; *BSTH*.
[5] *ADB* xxxix; Geiger, *Briefwechsel*; *GJNB*.   [6] *ADB* xiii; *BSTH*.
[7] *ADB* liv; Simson, *E. v. Simson*; *BSTH*.   [8] *ADB* xi; *BSTH*.
[9] *ADB* v; Stüve, *Briefwechsel*; *NDB*; *BSTH*; Detmold, *Taten und Meinungen*.
[10] *ADB* xxxiv; Jacoby, *H. Simon*.   [11] *ADB* x; Wittner, *M. Hartmann*; *BSTH*; *NDB*.

who – like Kuranda – defended German interests in Bohemia.[1] The high honours accorded by the parliament to Riesser, a pronounced Jew, and to Eduard Simson, a baptised Jew, show an absence of religious and racial prejudice.

A few members were either non-religious or anti-religious. Mevissen, who had been brought up as a Catholic, had broken with religion.[2] But it would be difficult to measure statistically how many members were irreligious – something no outsider can determine.

xii. Age groupings – Participation of former members of Burschen-schaft

The age grouping is of some interest. The oldest member of the parliament, the writer Arndt, was born in 1769, and the youngest members in 1825. The vast majority of members, about 75 per cent, were born between 1796 and 1815. Rather more were born before 1796 than after 1815. Thus in the biggest age-group the oldest members were in their early fifties in 1848 and the youngest in their early thirties. Yet what a difference there was in the political experience which had formed them. Those born between 1796 and 1800 could still well remember Napoleon at the height of his power, unlike those born later. Those born around 1796 would already be old enough to take part in the liberation of Germany from Napoleonic rule. One of the youngest of these was Heinrich von Gagern, born in 1799, who served at Water-loo. Most of those who rallied against Napoleon between 1813 and 1815 were somewhat older, belonging to earlier age-groups which were sparsely represented in the Frankfurt Parliament. This explains why only about 41 members, or about 5 per cent, are known to have served in the Wars of Liberation against France.

The age composition of the Frankfurt Parliament was more favour-able to the *Burschenschaft*,[3] which was founded in 1815, as most of the

---

[1] Cf. the not entirely reliable publication which came out during the National Socialist régime in Germany: Siegfried Erasmus, *Die Juden in der ersten deutschen Nationalver-sammlung 1848/9*. See *GJNB*. At least two members of the parliament, the later Austrian minister Johann Nepomuk Berger and the historian Max Duncker, had Jewish mothers. The first wife of the historian and secretary of the Constitutional Committee in the parliament, Johann Gustav Droysen, came from an originally Jewish family. The radical Oskar v. Reichenbach married a Jewess.

[2] *Umrisse* 213 ff; *ADB* LIII; Hansen, *Mevissen*; *BSTH*.   [3] See above, p. 11 ff.

members of the parliament born after 1795 would have studied after the war. The *Burschenschaft* was, however, prohibited in 1819, though clandestine membership continued. In view of the need for secrecy, records are not always available. There are 92 known cases of membership of the *Burschenschaft*, or 11·5 per cent of the total. Even among these there were several who turned eventually against the movement, having been disappointed by some of its tendencies, like Alexander Pagenstecher[1] who served in the Frankfurt Parliament. There was a sprinkling of members of other student movements based more on particular regions (*Landsmannschaften* or *Corps*).

Another movement which was well represented in the assembly was that which propagated gymnastics (*Turnen*), mainly to create a feeling of solidarity in order to strengthen the national cause. Both the founder in Napoleonic days, Friedrich Ludwig Jahn,[2] and the much younger Otto Leonhard Heubner,[3] who launched the idea in the kingdom of Saxony in 1833, were members of the Assembly. Many other members were *Turner*. The movement was liable to the political restrictions similar to those imposed on the *Burschenschaft*.

There is little reference to the Freemasons (*Freimaurer*) in the biographies of the parliament.[4] Owing to the secrecy surrounding the Freemasons paucity of information does not necessarily prove a small membership.

This was the composition of the Assembly which for the better part of a year held the centre of the German stage.

---

[1] Pagenstecher, *Lebenserinnerungen* i 51 ff.; *ADB* xxv; *BSTH*.
[2] *ADB* xiii; *BSTH*.   [3] See *ADB* l; Meinel, *Heubner*.
[4] One of the few instances where membership of the Freemasons is mentioned is in the case of the Halle bookseller, publisher and writer Schwetschke. He had also belonged to the *Burschenschaft*. Schwetschke was one of a number of members of the parliament who resigned from the official Protestant Church to join an independent congregation (*Freie Gemeinde*). See *ADB* xxxiii.

4 Beginnings

i. Heinrich von Gagern

IN spite of the preparatory work of the Committee of Fifty, the first days of the Frankfurt Parliament were a testing time. This is not surprising, as the National Assembly had to create its own organisation and procedure. No binding decisions could be taken before the assembly had been duly constituted. As soon as the parliament began formal sittings, the transaction of business required rules. Understandably, the assembly did not permanently accept at once without further study any of the proposed codes of procedure and a very slow start was thus made.

Early in May, a committee consisting of the distinguished Heidelberg professor of law Robert Mohl[1] and two others[2] had been entrusted by members of the parliament already present with working out rules of procedure.[3] In a section on preparatory measures (I. *Einleitende Massregeln*), Mohl and his colleagues had wisely recommended that as soon as 350 members had arrived in Frankfurt a meeting should be held under the president of the Committee of Fifty to elect a provisional president of the assembly. This would have saved time by providing an ex officio chairman right at the beginning and indeed somebody, in the person of the Baden lawyer Alexander von Soiron, well versed in handling debates. In the explanatory notes which accompanied the draft rules the authors had warned specifically against putting the father of the house (*Alterspräsident*) in the chair. They pointed out that the oldest member was less likely to be able to handle a big and unorganised assembly than his younger colleagues. In their opinion, whenever any of the smaller state assemblies had called on the *Alterspräsident* to

---

[1] *ADB* xxii; Mohl, *Lebenserinnerungen*; *BSTH*.

[2] Murschel and Schwarzenberg, presumably Ludwig.

[3] *Entwurf einer Geschäfts-Ordnung*. Archivrat Dr R. Moldenhauer of the Bundesarchiv, Aussenstelle Frankfurt am Main, was kind enough to supply the author with a manuscript copy of his essay 'Geschäftsverfahren der Frankfurter Nationalversammlung', and the author is greatly in his debt.

preside, the result had been chaos and loss of time.[1] They could hardly have been more prescient in the case of the Frankfurt Parliament, which ignored their advice. The earlier hope of opening the National Assembly on 1 May 1848 had not been fulfilled. Only after the middle of the month a sufficient number of members had arrived in Frankfurt to make a start. A gathering of more than three hundred members held in the *Kaisersaal* of the famous *Römer* building (the old town hall) on 17 May decided to convene members for a more formal meeting on the following day. In spite of the warning of Mohl and his colleagues on the procedural rules committee, the decision was taken to put an *Alterspräsident* in the chair on 18 May. In accordance with these arrangements, about 380 men who had been elected to serve in the first German parliament assembled in the *Kaisersaal* of the *Römer* at 3 o'clock in the afternoon of 18 May and elected an *Alterspräsident*. The most senior member in years of age willing to serve was the lawyer and judge from Hanover, Friedrich Lang,[2] who had not only belonged to the state parliament, but had also for a time been president. However, Lang's political services dated back mainly to the period up to the Hanoverian *coup d'état* of 1837. He was by now a gentleman of seventy, no longer quite up to the strain of conducting parliamentary proceedings, though his compatriots in the Guelph kingdom took a different view of his ability when they restored him to the parliamentary presidency on his return home. Under his chairmanship, during the remainder of the day the Frankfurt Parliament had an unnecessarily rough start which some members felt did not augur well for the future.

The slightly younger Bernhard von Lindenau, who as a minister had helped to create the constitution of the Kingdom of Saxony in 1830–1, was elected deputy to the *Alterspräsident*. The eight youngest members were appointed secretaries. After the elections members moved in solemn procession to the neighbouring St Paul's Church (Paulskirche), where the Pre-Parliament had met earlier and where the National Assembly was to sit for most of its time in Frankfurt.[3] This was a solemn moment which remained imprinted on the memories of members

---

[1] *Entwurf einer Geschäfts-Ordnung* 12 f.
[2] Niebour, 'Die Hannoverschen Abgeordneten' 146 f.; Bundesarchiv.
[3] From 6 November 1848 to 9 January 1849, the National Assembly sat in the German Reformed Church (Deutsch-Reformierte Kirche) while heating was – rather belatedly – being installed in the Paulskirche.

as long as they lived. The wealth of black-red-gold flags which fluttered from most buildings symbolised the main task of the assembly, the creation of a united Germany. For a short time, the belief in the common goal silenced the very real differences of opinion as to its attainment.

In the Paulskirche, members began their deliberations under the chairmanship of the *Alterspräsident*. When Lang after a short introduction wanted to read a message from the Federal Assembly after declaring the assembly constituted, he was curtly interrupted by another lawyer from Hanover, Freudentheil,[1] who moved that the assembly should solemnly declare itself constituted. In response to the chairman's question as to the wishes of the assembly, all members rose from their seats, raised their right hands and called three times: 'The assembly is constituted! Three cheers for the assembly!' (*Die Versammlung ist constituiert! Sie lebe hoch!*), or at least so say the shorthand reports issued under the direction of Franz Wigard, a teacher of stenography from Dresden.[2] Ominously the reports refer to tempestuous applause not only from the house but also from the gallery,[3] thus already on the first day pointing to one of the major difficulties of the assembly, which was outside pressure. When the *Alterspräsident* then tried to resume reading the message from the Federal Assembly, he did not get very far and eventually asked one of the *Alterssekretäre*, actually the later Austrian Minister of Education Stremayr,[4] to read it for him. The Federal Assembly in this message greeted the National Assembly and wished it success. Feeling against the Federal Assembly ran so high in many quarters, however, that no reply was made after a hostile speech by the Mainz lawyer and extreme radical Zitz,[5] of whom more will be heard.

The disorderly proceedings had underlined the need for rules of procedure. The next speaker moved that the assembly should use the rules drawn up by Robert Mohl and his colleagues. Another extreme radical, the lawyer Wesendonck[6] from Düsseldorf, proposed instead some short provisional standing orders drafted by himself.[7] The debate which ensued for a time seemed unable to resolve the issue, but in the end a compromise was found. To save time, the standing orders drafted

---

[1] *ADB* vii; *Umrisse* 17; *BSTH*.
[2] Wigard, *Stenographischer Bericht,* quoted in future simply by the volume and page number, without any title. For Wigard, see *ADB* xlii.
[3] i 4.   [4] Wurzbach xl; Stremayr, *Erinnerungen.*   [5] *ADB* xlv.
[6] Klötzer, 'Abgeordnete' in Wentzcke, *Ideale* 305; Wesendonck, 'Erinnerungen'; *Deutscher Nekrolog,* v (1900), col. 125; Zucker, *Forty-Eighters* 354; Bundesarchiv.
[7] i 5.

by Mohl and his colleagues were provisionally accepted *en bloc*. A committee of fifteen members was to be elected to report on the rules.[1] This saved the assembly the necessity of going through the numerous clauses of the draft one by one. From now on the chair could at least appeal to a body of regulations, even if the transitional period still offered considerable problems and if the rights of members were so extensive that the speedy transaction of business was endangered.

There was now an increasing awareness – particularly among the moderates – that the assembly needed firmer chairmanship. With the adoption of the provisional rules the way had been cleared for the election of a president. Unfortunately the assembly got bogged down in the question as to who should chair the election of a provisional president. The *Alterspräsident* was in fact in the chair. But according to the Mohl draft which had just been passed, the election had to take place under the President of the Committee of Fifty.[2] In the end it was decided to proceed to the election of the officers in accordance with provisional standing orders, but to leave the *Alterspräsident* in the chair.[3] The elections were arranged for the following day. Before adjourning, the assembly took the important step of authorising the publication of short-hand reports, though these were not to have any official standing,[4] like the protocols.[5] A motion by the Roman Catholic Bishop of Münster, Johann Georg Müller,[6] that the assembly should arrange services to invoke divine blessing for its work was rejected.[7]

Behind the scenes there was considerable activity. Both the Left and the moderates were making great efforts to organise themselves and to exert influence on the parliamentary proceedings. The election of the provisional president naturally became a focus of their attention. The Protestant minister Jürgens from Brunswick had ever since the sittings of the Committee of Fifty formed a circle of men around himself who believed broadly speaking in the establishment of constitutional monarchy,[8] most of them members of the later Right Centre (*Casino*), but including also some who were to sit on the Right and in the Left Centre. As Jürgens points out in his work on the Frankfurt Parliament, the group considered collaboration among the moderates as quite essential in order to oppose the activities of the radicals.[9] Although the moderates were to claim that the Left was ahead in organisation, in

---

[1] I 9. [2] *Entwurf einer Geschäfts-Ordnung*, I 2. [3] I 11. [4] I 12.
[5] Hassler, *Verhandlungen*. [6] *ADB* LII. [7] I 14.
[8] Biedermann, *Erinnerungen* 3. [9] Jürgens, *Zur Geschichte* I 115.

the initial moves they themselves showed great determination and no mean canvassing talent. They were agreed that Heinrich von Gagern was the only man who could preside with dignity over the parliamentary proceedings and at the same time curb the influence of the radicals. Gagern's ascendancy dates back to the days of the Pre-Parliament.[1] He was probably the most popular constitutional minister in the South-west, the heart of the liberal movement. There was great sympathy with him over the death in action of his brother Friedrich,[2] with whom he had been united not only by close family ties, but also by a common belief in the future of Germany.

Heinrich von Gagern was to play the leading part in the Frankfurt Parliament, first as President and then from December as Minister-President of the Provisional Central Power. He represented in an unusual degree the qualities which were regarded as the most important in that parliament and to some extent in wide sections of the German people at the time.

Gagern came from a distinguished family. His father, the *Reichs-freiherr* Hans von Gagern, rose from the service of the Nassau dominions to become Netherlands representative at the Congress of Vienna. After retiring from his official positions, he devoted himself to writing books on a wide range of political and social topics, and to furthering the cause of moderation in the upper house of the estates at Darmstadt in the Hessian Grand-Duchy. A friend of Stein and an enemy of Napoleon, he clung to many of the traditions of the past while recognising the necessity for some change. Heinrich von Gagern, with his brothers and sisters, benefited greatly from the cultured atmosphere of the parental home and from the father's wide national and inter-national contacts.[3] The eldest son of Hans von Gagern, Friedrich, joined the army of the Netherlands, serving for some years in the East Indies, and was on secondment to the Grand-Duchy of Baden when he was killed at Kandern in April 1848.[4] The youngest, Max, who sat with his brother Heinrich in the Frankfurt Parliament and also joined the Reich government, for a time served in the Netherlands army, but then tried his hand at an academic career in Bonn. In 1840 he joined the service of the duchy of Nassau and was for several years minister of

---

[1] See above, p. 44.   [2] See above, p. 55.

[3] Treitschke, *Historische und Politische Aufsätze* I 153–206; Rössler, *Zwischen Revolution und Reaktion.*

[4] Heinrich wrote his brother's biography *Das Leben des Generals Friedrich v. Gagern* (3 vols., 1856–7).

Nassau to the Netherlands. Born of a Protestant father and a Catholic mother, Max, like the other sons, was educated as a Protestant, while the daughters were brought up as Catholics. Friedrich and Heinrich were decided Protestants, but Max, to the annoyance particularly of Heinrich, became a Catholic in 1843.

Heinrich, with whom this study is particularly concerned, was born in 1799 and was just old enough to serve in the battle of Waterloo. He studied law after the war and took a prominent part in the formation of the *Burschenschaft*. After completion of his training, he entered the service of the Grand-Duchy of Hesse, and, like so many other officials, in 1832 became a member of the state parliament. Largely under the influence of his brother Friedrich, Heinrich became highly critical of conditions in Germany. This did not make any easier his dual position as a comparatively subordinate official and as a member of the legislature, already strained by his poor relations with the leading minister, von Du Thil and by Heinrich's strong temperament. In 1833, Heinrich decided to secure political freedom by resigning from the service of the state. While he did not suffer in any way like the political martyrs of the pre-1848 period, Heinrich von Gagern's decision was nevertheless a courageous one. The Gagern family was well-off, but not rich. Heinrich lost some income and independence. The father, although he regarded Heinrich as hot-tempered and as a political firebrand, allowed the son to take over one of the family estates, Monsheim, in Rhenish Hesse, still in the Grand-Duchy. Heinrich threw himself into farming with great zest and eventually became president of the local farmers' union (*Landwirtschaftlicher Verein der Provinz Rheinhessen*). For some years he was absent from the state parliament, but returned early in 1847 and at once established his position as a leading constitutionalist parliamentarian. A year later, on 5 March 1848 he took over the government of Hesse-Darmstadt from Du Thil. Although Heinrich von Gagern had visited Western Europe, including France, he was not familiar with the North and East of Germany. However effective Heinrich might be on his home ground in Hesse-Darmstadt, he subordinated himself willingly to his elder brother's greater vision and experience of the wide world. It was understood in the Gagern family that any leading place in the future conduct of affairs in Germany was reserved to Friedrich rather than to Heinrich. The ageing father, though he might at times be worried by Friedrich's and Heinrich's views, was proud of his sons, particularly of the eldest, and shared the admiration shown to the Dutch general. After the battle of Kandern, Heinrich, who did not possess Friedrich's strength of personality – whatever his other qualities – had to fill the void. He did so with some' sincere diffidence, certainly without undue personal ambition and in response to the call of his political friends and to the memory of his brother.

Although Heinrich had been overshadowed by the elder brother, his parliamentary experience – entirely lacked by Friedrich – helped to fit him for the presidency of the Frankfurt Parliament, and thus, pending the formation of a German government, for the most important post in connection with the unification of Germany. There were other members of the Frankfurt Parliament who had similarly proved themselves both in opposition before the revolution and in office since. But men like the Wurtemberg minister Römer or the Nassau minister Hergenhahn[1] never had the same following. In May 1848, Heinrich von Gagern seemed to possess more than any other member of the parliament the qualities needed to bring matters to a successful conclusion. The ascendancy of Heinrich von Gagern in a parliament containing many great names in the main professions certainly needs an explanation. He was not a highly intelligent man, often slow in getting to the heart of the matter, sometimes awkward in his formulations as a speaker from the floor. But he commanded a natural respect as few other members did.

In trying to secure the election of Heinrich von Gagern as provisional president, the moderates left as little to chance as possible. They printed ballot papers with Gagern for president and Soiron, the chairman of the Committee of Fifty, for vice-president.[2] This procedure was resented by the Left who wanted to secure the election of their leader, Robert Blum. The moderates did, however, slip up on one important point of organisation. There were two members of the assembly called Gagern, Heinrich and his brother Max. A member moved at once that all ballot papers containing simply the surname Gagern should be annulled. Eventually Venedey,[3] a radical writer from Cologne, made the helpful suggestion that unless anybody rose to say that he meant Max and reclaimed his ballot paper, all votes should be credited to Heinrich von Gagern.[4] Nobody rose to say that he had meant Max. Heinrich von Gagern was elected provisional president by an overwhelming majority. He received 305 out of 397 votes. 85 votes were cast for Soiron and only 3 for Blum. Obviously the Left had decided

---

[1] *ADB* xii; *BSTH.*
[2] Jürgens, *Zur Geschichte* i 115.   [3] *ADB* xxxix.   [4] i 16 f.

that it would be useless to launch a Blum candidature and supported Soiron instead. Though Soiron was also a moderate and joined the Right Centre (*Casino*), both his famous speech in the Pre-Parliament[1] and the fact that he had presided over a body which had kept the activities of the German governments under a watchful eye made him acceptable to the Left.

All observers are agreed that the atmosphere in the Paulskirche was suddenly transformed when Gagern ascended the presidential chair. The scholar Rudolf Haym of the Right Centre, who as one of the youngest was an *Alterssekretär*, in his report on the assembly wrote of the fresh hope which came over the assembly at this moment.[2] Haym's testimony is of particular interest as he was the author of an outstanding summary of the recent meeting of the Prussian United Diet.[3] This impression of the effect of Gagern's assumption of the presidency is confirmed by the man who not only served as a vice-president under him but also succeeded him in the chair, the distinguished jurist Eduard Simson. As Eduard von Simson's son, Bernhard von Simson, relates, his father often paid tribute to the change in atmosphere due to Gagern expertly assuming the reins which had been dragging along the floor (*es war, als wenn ein des Fahrens Kundiger am Boden schleifende Zügel ergriffen hätte*).[4] Both Haym and Eduard Simson belonged to the Right Centre. That the impression about this change in atmosphere on 19 May is not confined to Gagern's political friends is shown by the favourable, if somewhat ironical description of the scene given by a political opponent, the Protestant minister and teacher Wilhelm Zimmermann from Stuttgart, who belonged to the Extreme Left.[5]

The clearest explanation of Gagern's success in the Frankfurt Parliament comes from the Viennese archivist and official Alfred Arneth,[6] even though the testimony relates to a later period. Arneth only joined the assembly in November 1848 when Gagern's presidency was nearing its end. The Austrian member had been able to observe the Vienna Reichstag at close quarters. After having seen Gagern preside at Frankfurt, he came to the conclusion that the president of the Austrian assembly, Anton Strobach, could hardly be mentioned in the

---

[1] See above, p. 51 f.

[2] Haym, *Deutsche Nationalversammlung* i 10. For Haym see his autobiography *Aus meinem Leben*; Rosenberg, *R. Haym*; *BSTH*.

[3] Haym, *Reden und Redner*.   [4] Simson, *E. v. Simson* 100.

[5] Zimmermann, *Deutsche Revolution* 599. For Zimmermann see *ADB* xlv; *BSTH*.

[6] *ADB* xl; Arneth, *Aus meinem Leben*; *ÖBL*; *NDB*; *BSTH*.

same breath with him.[1] Arneth admits that Strobach's sensible chairmanship indeed deserved recognition, but then refers to the unfavourable impression created by his unappealing appearance (*sein wenig gewinnendes Äusseres*), his slender narrow-chested personality (*seine schmächtige, engbrüstige Persönlichkeit*) and his Bohemian accent. He contrasted with that Gagern's 'high and vigorous figure' (*hohe und kraftvolle Gestalt*) and his 'really imposing personality' (*wirklich imposante Persönlichkeit*). 'With what majestic earnestness he knew how to discharge the duties of his office, and how pure sounded his deep and sonorous organ through the . . . Paulskirche!' (*Mit welch majestätischem Ernste wusste er seines Amtes zu walten, und wie glockenrein klang sein tiefes und sonores Organ durch die . . . Paulskirche!*)[2]

Arneth is certainly a typical member of the Frankfurt Parliament in his receptiveness to form. Gagern's success in the Paulskirche would have been impossible without his expressing widespread sentiments on the future of Germany. But that he rather than any other of the supporters of constitutional development and of German unification became the symbol of these endeavours was due as much to such outward things like his looks and his voice as to his political qualifications. Arneth's reference to the chairman of the Austrian Reichstag demonstrates that it was not sufficient to be a good chairman, but that he also had to look the part.

One word runs right through the comments on Heinrich von Gagern. His 'nobility' is frequently emphasised. Eduard Simson was impressed by his 'grand, noble appearance' (*stattliche, edle Erscheinung*),[3] and even the medical practitioner Pagenstecher from Elberfeld, a critic from his ranks, refers to 'the truly noble' (*der wahrhaft edle*) Gagern.[4] The Tübingen philosopher Vischer, somewhat to the Left of Gagern, wrote about the first speech of the new president: 'there was nobility, there was masculine worth and dignity, there was consolation, now my soul is again easy.'[5] Haym speaks of Gagern's presidency 'surrounded by the splendour of moral dignity' (*umgeben von dem Glanz sittlicher Würde*).[6]

---

[1] Anton Strobach, though nominally one of the vice-presidents, had to bear the brunt of the chairmanship with a Pole, Smolka. See Springer, *Geschichte Österreichs*, ii 405.

[2] Arneth, *Aus meinem Leben* i 207 f.   [3] Simson, *E. v. Simson* 100.

[4] Pagenstecher, *Lebenserinnerungen* ii 48.

[5] 'Da war Adel, da war Männerwert und Männerwürde, da war Trost, jetzt ist mir die Seele wieder leicht.' Rapp, *F. T. Vischer* 17. For Vischer see *ADB* xl; Vischer, 'Mein Lebensgang'; *BSTH*.

[6] Haym, *Deutsche Nationalversammlung* i 10.

Ludwig Bamberger, a liberal member of the Reichstag during Bismarck's chancellorship, then a revolutionary radical, for a time reported on the Frankfurt Parliament for his Mainz newspaper. In his memoirs he wrote that he only knew two men who understood how to represent the parliamentary presidency in the dignity of their appearance (*Würde des Auftretens*). They were Gagern in the Frankfurt Parliament and Eduard Simson in the Reichstag in Berlin. Bamberger emphasised this point as he felt that the Reichstag in the Bismarckian Empire paid too little attention to form.[1] While German impressionability certainly continued beyond the turn of the nineteenth century, Bamberger's remarks seem to show that the kind of atmosphere to be found in the Paulskirche only lasted a comparatively short time.

Nobility, masculinity, vigour, majesty, earnestness, morality, these are Gagern's apparent attributes which evoke so much admiration. There was danger for the future in this idealisation or idolisation of their president. Would he be able to live up to what was expected from him? Indeed, was not too much being expected from one man? Many members of the Frankfurt Parliament applied this idealisation not only to their leader but to the German people as such, a people which was noble, courageous, without guile, as compared with other nations which were not. Gagern became the impersonation of this idealised German. The highly educated men of the Paulskirche probably formed these ideas mainly from a curious combination of two sources, a partially Christian Romanticism and a pagan antiquity. The search for the ideal is apparently vindicated by the Romantics' discovery of a better, more chivalrous and also more Christian world in the Middle Ages. There is also the pagan ideal of the perfect or near-perfect hero of Greece and Rome seen through German nineteenth-century spectacles. Non-Christian elements predominate. The idolisation of fellow human beings put off Roman Catholics more than Protestants and it may not be sheer coincidence that only one of the authorities quoted, Arneth, was a Roman Catholic.

Heinrich von Gagern himself maintained his modesty, in spite of all the adoration. Whatever his defects, arrogance or even conceit were not among them. Gagern continued to realise his own limitations. His great gift lay, occasional personal brusqueness apart, in his ability to echo and crystallise the ideas of his day which he had already proved before 1848 by his championship of the cause of constitutional progress

[1] Bamberger, *Erinnerungen* 85.

and that of German unification. In the Frankfurt Parliament he sometimes managed to achieve a surprising degree of unity by coining a
phrase which combined the advantage of satisfying all shades of
opinion with the disadvantage of shelving the actual problem. This
tendency was illustrated in his first speech as provisional president.
Gagern said that the authority for the task of the assembly, the creation
of a constitution for the whole of Germany, lay in the 'sovereignty of
the nation' (*Souveränität der Nation*). At this point the short-hand
reports note tempestuous cheers (*Stürmisches Bravo*).[1] Gagern's
formulation was just enough to satisfy the Left, who supported the
theory of popular sovereignty, while sufficiently weak to reassure the
opponents of the doctrine in the Centre. But no answer was given to
the practical question of the extent to which there would have to be
negotiations between the Frankfurt Parliament and the state governments.

Gagern's runner-up for the presidency, Alexander von Soiron, was
elected vice-president. As he was acceptable to some of the Left, he
received even more votes than Gagern had got for the presidency, 341
out of 392. Blum obtained 26 votes, Dahlmann 10 and various others 15.
While Soiron did not possess Gagern's dignity in the chair, he had a
certain geniality and bonhomie which were at times quite useful. The
presidium was completed by the appointment of two of the *Alterssekretäre*, von Stremayr, the later Austrian minister, and Riehl, an
Austrian lawyer, as provisional secretaries.

The provisional standing orders in section 2 dealt in some detail with
the examination of credentials. While the elections were in the hands
of the state governments, the assembly claimed the sole right of deciding
who was entitled to sit in parliament. The Mohl draft[2] proposed that the
president of the assembly should satisfy himself that the quota of
representatives laid down for each state had not been exceeded. Any
excess of members was to be eliminated by lot. This procedure was
deferred in order to speed up the process of admission. Two clauses in
the standing orders relating to the election of sections (*Abteilungen*)
were combined. These sections were modelled on those found in the
French and Baden chambers and they were designed to speed up the
business of the plenary assembly. The same sections, fifteen in number,
were to be used both for examining the credentials of members and for
electing to parliamentary committees. The historian Johann Gustav

[1] i 17.   [2] Mohl, ii 1.

Droysen was one of those who had supported the creation of sections during the preparations for the Frankfurt Parliament. As he put down in his diary on 12 May, otherwise the assembly would never gain ground (*wir kommen sonst ins Bodenlose*).[1] Each member of the assembly was to be allocated to a section by lot. It was also decided to have the credentials of a section examined by the following one, the first by the second, and so forth. In accordance with the Mohl draft (II, 6), disputed elections were to be referred to a central committee (*Zentralausschuss*) consisting of the chairmen of the sections. The assembly decided that any exclusion proposed by the central committee was to be referred to plenum.[2]

The advantage accruing to the transaction of business from the creation of sections is clear. The problem of examining credentials or of electing to a committee would be reduced to manageable proportions. For a parliamentary committee of fifteen, one member would be put up per section. Thus each member would only cast one vote, whereas if the election of the committee took place in the plenary assembly, fifteen times the number of names of candidates would have to be counted. In the absence of organised political parties, the sections played a useful and indeed necessary part. They were not meant to be pure voting machines. In order to elect wisely, their members obviously had to know each other. Their first act, that of electing their chairmen and secretaries as well as the members of the committee for the drawing up of standing orders (*Ausschuss für die Geschäftsordnung*), was rather a hit and miss affair, as most members of sections had only recently met. Initially, the sections, or at least some of them, had preliminary discussions about points on the agenda for the following sitting. However, as soon as the assembly got under way, the sections were overshadowed by the political clubs and the parliamentary committees. They were purely accidental groupings and could not stand up to the competition of bodies consisting either of like-minded people or of men set a common task.

ii. Raveaux's motion

It was not long before the assembly, having begun to organise itself, was called on to settle several matters of principle. One of these arose

[1] See Hübner, *Droysen* 807.   [2] I 27.

from a motion by a radical member from Cologne, Franz Raveaux. His father, born a Frenchman and at one time a republican, later became a good Prussian official in the Rhineland, though he – apparently unconsciously – continued humming revolutionary songs even in his new position, from which his son claimed to have imbibed his radical political sentiments.[1] Franz Raveaux was born in Cologne in 1810, deserted from the Prussian army after a tussle with a major of the *Landwehr* (territorial army), fought in the Belgian army as a volunteer in 1830 and on the 'constitutionalist' side in Spain in 1834, being captured by the Carlists. In 1836 he returned to Cologne, where he received some close if unfriendly attention from the authorities. Raveaux does not seem to have made any attempt to merge with the landscape. The official report said:

> On his arrival he wore a red cap, the base of which was black and the braid golden, but otherwise mufti. His passport was in the name of François Raveaux, capitaine au service de S.M. la reine constitutionelle d'Espagne. He boasts that he received two decorations in Spain . . . and attracts attention by his tales.[2]

After serving the sentence for his earlier desertion, Raveaux engaged in various activities, ranging from politics and journalism to the rather successful ownership of a cigar factory. He stood up for the rights of the citizens during the disturbances in Cologne in 1846 at the time of the *Martinskirmess* (church fair) and received a short prison term for reprimanding an army lieutenant. He was thereupon elected to the Cologne town council and, what may have been just as important as a sign of the approval of his fellow-citizens, he became chairman of a carnival society. In the Rhineland, the carnival societies played a political role in the period before 1848. This is not surprising as it was safer to say a serious word about affairs of state in jest than to do so openly. The societies fulfilled the part of the fool at the court of a despot.[3] In the spring of 1848, Raveaux became Deputy Commandant of the Cologne *Bürgerwehr* (citizens' defence force). Raveaux is an interesting example of a radical who alternated between extremist and more moderate phases. In the Pre-Parliament, Raveaux, though a

[1] See Bergsträsser, *Frankfurter Parlament* 224, quotation from the Meissen lawyer Hallbauer.

[2] Translation of extract from the files of the Geheime Staatsarchiv (Secret State Archives) in Hansen, *Rheinische Briefe* II 77.

[3] See Bamberger, *Erinnerungen* 29.

radical, broke with Hecker and bowed to the majority decision rejecting permanence.[1] His adventures did not cease with the Frankfurt Parliament.[2]

During the second sitting, on 19 May, Raveaux moved that those members of the assembly from Prussia who had been also elected to the Prussian National Assembly in Berlin should have the right to accept both seats. The Prussian parliament had been called for 22 May and according to Raveaux the Prussian authorities had demanded that members should choose between Frankfurt and Berlin.[3] In speaking to his motion Raveaux went even further and demanded that no state legislatures should be called anywhere in Germany while the German National Assembly was sitting in Frankfurt. The gloss on his motion revealed nakedly the far-reaching nature of Raveaux's propositions. He asked for an immediate vote by the assembly without reference to a committee as normally prescribed by standing orders, ostensibly on the grounds that the matter could brook no delay. In actual fact, Raveaux was not being particularly helpful in sorting out the problem of dual elections in Prussia. The members concerned were meeting the same evening, as Raveaux is likely to have known, to discuss the question. The matter might well be sorted out without the help of the Frankfurt Parliament. As to urgency, very little would be settled to influence the situation in Berlin on 22 May anyway. When Raveaux failed to rush the assembly, he readily agreed to a more leisurely treatment of the question, concentrating on the constitutional principle, the actual reason why he had raised the matter.

Although Raveaux was not acting officially on behalf of the Left, in many ways his strategy and tactics were to be characteristic of the attitude of the Left in the Frankfurt Parliament. From the first the attainment of popular sovereignty was the main aim. The logical end of the road was the establishment of a German republic. In the meantime every opportunity was to be used to weaken the princes and, above all, the King of Prussia as the leading representative of the monarchical system in Germany outside the Habsburg Empire. For the Left, one of the main uses of the Frankfurt Parliament was as a ram to shake the foundations of the monarchical order. The method of achieving these aims in the assembly was to apply shock tactics, to attempt overawing parliament. Time and again members of the Left put forward emergency motions which they tried to get accepted on grounds of urgency without

---

[1] See above, p. 51.   [2] *ADB* xxvii.   [3] i 18.

E

full discussion, through by-passing the normal procedure of investigation by a committee. The Left welcomed the support of the gallery to frighten the undecided. All this may sound harsh, but it would not necessarily have been considered unfair comment by members of the Left. The radicals in the Frankfurt Parliament were mainly an action group who believed they knew what the people wanted. They regarded themselves as the true representatives of the people, even if outvoted in the assembly. To substantiate this claim they relied on the stream of petitions pouring into the Frankfurt Parliament, mainly of a radical nature.[1] The local 'democratic' associations (*Volksvereine, Demokratische Vereine*, etc.) were certainly very active, only too eager to withdraw confidence from moderate members of parliament, and to demand their 'recall', though in vain. The Left had a sense of mission. Its leaders believed that they knew what the situation demanded and that they were supported by the mass of the people. They increasingly despaired of the moderate majority of the Frankfurt Parliament who – they judged – in their gradualness misrepresented the popular will and doomed the revolution to failure. The radicals claimed to be 'democrats'. Yet they were so little troubled by the theoretical weakness of their position that they were soon to advocate using force, no longer against unrepresentative tyrants, but against duly elected parliaments and constitutional governments supported by representative assemblies. Where persuasion no longer worked, they were prepared to mount the barricades. Similarly, the Left was ready to revise its theories about the evils of particularism when it failed to dominate the centre. All this is not criticism of the Left, but a statement of the consequences of its principles. The moderate liberals might be surprised about the crumbling of their popularity, but they were at least prepared to submit to an adverse vote. The messianic Left saw itself as the interpreter of a vague 'general will' in Rousseau's sense. If parliamentary elections and divisions conformed to this general will as interpreted by the Left, then it could be respected. If not, the Left was free to adopt whatever means in its power to ensure that the true general will which was revealed to them alone should prevail.

Raveaux arrogated to the Frankfurt Parliament the sole right to hold constitutional deliberations for the time being. He had a sound reason for doing so, for otherwise the Frankfurt Parliament and the state assemblies might pass mutually exclusive legislation. There were,

---

[1] These are noted in Wigard, *Stenographischer Bericht*, beginning I 15.

however, some dangers in his proposal. Many urgent tasks were awaiting parliamentary attention in the states. If constituent assemblies
were not allowed to meet in the state capitals, the constitutional
development of the states would to some extent be frozen largely in its
pre-March condition, leaving the liberal ministers exposed to the whims
and fancies of the rulers without full parliamentary support. The population of the states would thus be denied certain democratic rights for
the time being. These apparent inconsistencies did not worry the Left.
They had very little tenderness for the new liberal members of the
state governments. They sincerely believed that these ministers, in
Prussia, in Baden, in Wurtemberg and elsewhere, had allowed themselves to be placed in a false position. They regarded them as mere
temporary props of the old order for which they were not going to
receive any thanks. They believed that the princes, as soon as they had
recovered their grip, would ruthlessly rid themselves of the liberal
ministers. The Left rejected liberal constitutional compromises and
strove for a radical alteration in the political situation. In the opinion
of its leaders, the collaboration between liberal ministers and their rulers
could not last. The sooner what appeared to them as a sham solution
was exposed, the better. The Left was convinced that a second revolution was necessary in Germany, to complete the first. Unfortunately
Hecker's rising in Baden – which many of its members might have
joined and in which some were implicated[1] – had failed. But in the early
days of the Frankfurt Parliament reports were coming in of the successful Vienna rising of 15 May, as a result of which the Austrian authorities
agreed to the election of a uni-cameral Reichstag on the basis of
manhood suffrage. Members of the Left in the Frankfurt Parliament
believed that public feeling in Germany was with them and that
however the voting in the elections to the German National Assembly
had gone, the masses in the country as a whole were solidly radical and
tired of liberal half-measures. Events proved that the Left took too
rosy a view of radical support in the country. The democrats were also
of the opinion – at least at the beginning – that particularism stood
and fell with the princes, that the individual states had no place in the
hearts of their citizens. They failed to see that many states, princes and
dynasties had over the years developed strong roots.

[1] For instance Ignaz Peter, lately Hecker's *Statthalter* in Constance, who sat throughout the Frankfurt Parliament although criminal proceedings against him were pending
in Baden.

To the Left, if a choice had to be made, attainment of their ideological objectives was more important than the establishment of German unity. During the early days of the Frankfurt Parliament, the radicals still worked on the assumption that the two aims could be harmonised. They wanted to unite Germany so that the democratic institutions which they favoured could be established.

Germans in 1848 were bound to look largely abroad for political inspiration, which may appear a strange thing for a national movement to do. However, for years all but the most determined defenders of the old order had followed constitutional developments in other countries with intense interest, especially owing to the lack of an active political life at home. In a curious and presumably completely unintended manner, censorship had reinforced this tendency to look abroad. It was less dangerous to write about constitutional demands in foreign countries than about what was happening at home. Also, a number of those most politically active had been forced to seek refuge abroad and they came back in 1848 full of what they had seen abroad, some of them to take up seats in the Frankfurt Parliament. Here too, repression, though generally a hindrance, had helped political education. The countries to which political refugees had been able to flee were those among the neighbours which took a kindly or at least not a hostile view of radical dissent, Switzerland, Belgium and France. Neither the Netherlands nor Denmark were attractive to the radicals, who naturally opted mainly for France or Switzerland, often going from the one to the other, like the philosopher Ruge. The revolutionary tradition of the French and the republican institutions of Switzerland were closer to the hearts of the radicals than the constitutional monarchy of Belgium, or of England for that matter. Similarly, the United States of America, which proved more suitable to the extremists as a field for permanent emigration following the defeat of the 1848 revolutions rather than as what was hoped would be a temporary asylum before 1848, interested the German radicals, though somewhat remotely.

In the Frankfurt Parliament the attraction of members of the Left to the French revolutionary tradition helped to divide them from their more moderate opponents who believed more in something like English or Belgian constitutional monarchy. Whereas the radicals wished to redraw the political map of Germany according to rational principles without paying attention to historical tradition and boundaries, as was done in France following the 1789 revolution, the more moderate sections wanted to preserve and adapt the historical past. At the beginning of the Frankfurt Parliament the radicals aimed at setting up a unitary state on the French revolutionary model. Though vaguely in sympathy with the constitution of the United States of America, they certainly did not want to copy federalism. It was only when the radicals despaired of dominating the centre – Frankfurt – that they began to take a different view of state rights. By then they had begun to switch their attention to some of the state capitals, such as Dresden, in the hope of being given a second chance to achieve their aims.

Raveaux's motion was central to the thinking of the Left. Popular sovereignty was the basis. The national parliament, as the elected representation of the people, was entitled to issue decrees to all, including governments and princes. There was no limit to the power of the assembly. As the representatives of the people the assembly could determine how widely its competence over the affairs of the nation extended. The parliament possessed what the Germans call *Kompetenz-Kompetenz*. Whatever the Federal Assembly (*Bundesversammlung*) might have said about the task of the Frankfurt Parliament, the latter was entitled to decide any matter it wished. The Left wanted government by parliament for the time being, it wished to set up the Frankfurt Parliament as a Convention of the French revolutionary type. The Federal Assembly was going to be ignored. The state governments and rulers simply had to carry out what the Frankfurt Parliament decreed. The radicals urged the assembly to speak to the rulers in the only language they believed them to understand, that of the lash. Nothing was further from the minds of the democrats than to woo the rulers. No love was lost on either side. The rulers had made quite clear what they thought of the democrats when they had almost invariably appointed liberal rather than radical ministers following the March revolution. This attitude of the rulers only confirmed the radicals in their view of the princes. The two sides did not have any common ground and they realised it. The Left suspected that the princes were trying to sabotage the work of the Frankfurt Parliament by calling state parliaments, which would hamper unification by passing legislation incompatible with a Reich constitution. The constitutional rights of the state parliaments and of the governments based on them were ignored by the Left whenever they proved inconvenient.

If the Left wanted to rush through important matters, this negative attitude to *form* and procedure was not only due to their hope of being successful in their tactics. The whole matter went much deeper than that. The Left was more interested in a response to the needs of the moment, echoing public opinion outside the parliament chamber, than in the strict observance of procedural rules. The public gallery for the radicals was a necessary link with the people represented by the assembly. The democrats did not believe in insulating members from the outside world to ensure undisturbed and impartial discussion. They welcomed petitions from bodies and individuals. They wanted the minimum of interposition between members of parliament and their constituents. We do not know what attitude radical members would have adopted at this time if mass pressure had been on the other side.

Raveaux failed to get his way in obtaining an immediate decision, which he probably hardly expected. The case for a deviation from reference to a committee had not been made out. Readily, Raveaux agreed to postpone a debate on further action regarding his motion to Monday, 22 May, the very day on which the Prussian National Assembly was due to meet, thus sacrificing his main argument for urgency.[1] When the debate was reopened on 22 May, 17 amendments were already in the President's hands, representing various attitudes to Raveaux's motion ranging from support to straight rejection.[2] After a short debate, the assembly decided by a clear if not overwhelming majority that the motion should be referred to a committee. At this stage, the Left still had some support from members who were to join the moderate side of the house, including the vice-president Soiron.[3] A committee was thereupon elected by the sections to report on Raveaux's motion. Before the report could be debated, the assembly had to deal with another radical move, this time on the part of the member for Mainz, Zitz.

iii. Disorder in Mainz

Franz Heinrich Zitz, a lawyer from Mainz in his mid-forties, had, like Raveaux, been helped in his rise to popularity by holding the presidency of a carnival society. In the early days of the revolution Zitz was, with Hecker, Struve and Blum, one of the handful of radical heroes known all over Germany. A member of the Hesse-Darmstadt

---

[1] I 30.   [2] I 39 ff.   [3] I 44.

state Parliament, he had taken an active part in securing concessions from the government in March. Zitz was one of the many fluent speakers who bloomed into sudden prominence in 1848 without possessing any higher political ability. Ludwig Bamberger, who knew him well and had some influence over him, called him a typical *Mainzer*, combining a lively and gay temperament with good and strong character. Zitz had been blackmailed by the suicide threat of a highly-strung Mainz writer, Kathinka Halein, into agreeing to marry her. He left her after the marriage ceremony, never to see her again, although – much to his disgust – the roses of the infatuated woman were rarely missing among the tributes offered to the popular politician. Zitz joined the Extreme Left (*Donnersberg*) in the Frankfurt Parliament and took part in the Palatinate rising of June 1849. Bamberger believed that he would have liked to have seen a compromise with the princes. But he could not resist the temptation of saying what was likely to bring him applause. This was one of the factors which drove him into more extreme courses.[1]

Ever since the days of the French Revolution of 1789, Mainz had been one of the radical centres in Germany, deeply influenced by French republican ideas. Though part of the Grand-Duchy of Hesse-Darmstadt, the city was a fortress of the German Confederation, manned by Prussian and Austrian troops. For a long time, relations between the Prussian troops and the citizens of Mainz had been strained, while the Austrian soldiers had got on quite well with the local population. Tension between the Prussian troops and the population was increased by the formation of a citizens' force (*Bürgergarde*) in March. The Prussian soldiers ridiculed the drilling of the amateurs. On 21 May, matters came to a head with fighting between the citizens and the Prussian soldiers in which four of the troops were killed, while civilians were only wounded. The first casualties occurred, however, among the civilians. The Austrian and Prussian military commandants thereupon issued an ultimatum to the civilian population, demanding that all weapons be surrendered within two hours and the armed citizens' force (*Bürgergarde*) be dissolved. Otherwise the town would be bombarded. The town gave in after an extension of the time limit.[2]

Early during the sitting of the Frankfurt Parliament on 23 May Zitz asked to be allowed to speak about the position in Mainz as a matter of urgency and to put forward an emergency motion. He gave a

---

[1] Bamberger, *Erinnerungen* incl. 27 ff., 75 ff.; *ADB* xlv.
[2] i 53 ff., particularly 93 ff.; Bamberger, *Erinnerungen* 74 ff., 98 ff.

long and detailed account of the whole background which had led to
the dramatic events in Mainz. As may be expected, Zitz, who was chief
of the *Bürgergarde*, was not quite objective about happenings in his
home town. To him his fellow-citizens were innocent lambs who had
done nothing to provoke the wrath of the Prussian wolves. Zitz made
the most of his opportunity. In castigating the action of the commandants and their men, he was able to hit two of the main targets of
radical aversion, the military and Prussia. The Austrians got off lightly
to increase the effect, in spite of the fact that the Austrian commandant
had signed the ultimatum together with his Prussian colleague. The
Prussian officers and soldiers were represented as beasts.

Zitz moved that the German National Assembly should intervene
in order to secure a number of changes at Mainz. The Commandants
should be instructed to revoke all special measures they had recently
taken, privates and non-commissioned officers[1] should not be allowed
to wear uniform off duty, and Prussian troops should camp outside the
town until relieved. Zitz followed Raveaux's example in asking the
assembly to come to a decision without reference to a committee. As he
was leaving the speaker's rostrum he was given letters which he said
indicated that the situation in Mainz had deteriorated again. If these
letters had, in fact, just come in at that moment, then they were excel-
lently timed. Here once more was an attempt to rush the parliament.

The happenings in Mainz were certainly a matter of public concern.
But was the German Constituent National Assembly the right body to
deal with them? The Federal Assembly (*Bundesversammlung*) which
controlled the federal fortresses was still in being. So were the state
governments. Nothing had yet been decided about the exact functions
of the German National Assembly and about its relationship with the
Federal Assembly (*Bundesversammlung*) and with the state governments. The objections which had been raised against Raveaux's motion
applied equally to that put forward by Zitz, except that affairs at
Mainz were of more *immediate* practical importance. If Zitz was right,
the citizens of Mainz were still in danger.

Whatever the rights and wrongs at Mainz, Zitz like Raveaux
certainly intended the assembly to commit itself to an active role beyond pure constitution-making. The two radical members wanted the
assembly to supervise and instruct the existing authorities where necessary. Was the assembly entitled and able to do so? There were con-

[1] The omission of any mention of commissioned officers by this 'democrat' is interesting.

siderable doubts as to whether interfering with the actions of the executive was really part of the brief of the assembly. It was even less certain that the state governments, particularly the large ones, like that of Prussia, would carry out the orders of the German National Assembly. The radicals were quite prepared to accept a challenge from the state governments, for they believed they would prevail in a show-down. The historian must wonder whether they did not misjudge their prospects. Certainly there was one definite inconsistency in the radical position. The democrats might inveigh against Prussian militarism, but like the rest of the German national movement they relied mainly on Prussian troops to fight the Danes in Schleswig-Holstein. Though the Left might in the early days emphasise the rights of other nationali-ties, it was on the whole uncompromising over the Elbe Duchies. Zitz also showed little awareness of the strategic significance of Mainz in the defence of Germany against a possible threat from France.

After a procedural wrangle, Zitz' motion was referred to a committee.[1] There was certainly little support for confining discussion to the plenary assembly, even among the Left. The moderates were quite insistent that the matter, now that it had been raised, should be fully investi-gated. The radical member Carl Vogt,[2] who took a conciliatory line on this occasion, had moved that a committee of enquiry should be sent to Mainz. It was left to the committee to decide whether to carry out local investigations.

The committee at once sent several members to Mainz. On 26 May, the report was debated by the assembly.[3] Though the military were not exonerated, the difficulties of the fortress authorities, with their obligation for the defence of Germany, were given full weight. The description given a few days earlier by Zitz was seen to be biased. Whoever was to blame for what had happened, the committee regarded preventive measures for the future as quite essential. There was to be some change of garrison units, though the withdrawal of Prussian troops was not specifically mentioned. Furthermore, the citizens' armed force was to be revived when proper arrangements could be made, yet only within the limits prescribed by the fortress regulations. The recommendations were moderate and certainly did not favour the anti-Prussian side. A minority on the committee recommended that no action be taken.

Zitz was not satisfied with the report of the committee, but Blum,

[1] I 62.   [2] *ADB* xl; Vogt, *Aus meinem Leben*; Misteli, *C. Vogt: BSTH.*   [3] I 93 ff.

E2

who as one of its members went to Mainz to investigate, realised by
now that the recommendations were the best that could be achieved
from the point of view of the Left. For as the debate was to show, many
moderates felt that even the somewhat mild proposals of the committee
went too far. The point of view of these sections of the assembly was
put forcibly by a member who was to influence the Frankfurt Parliament deeply, both positively and negatively, Anton von Schmerling.[1]
This scion of the minor Austrian nobility was born in 1805, studied law
and entered the judicial service, but resigned in 1847 as a liberal
opponent of the Metternich régime. He had recently assumed the
position of Austrian presidial delegate at the German Confederation
in Frankfurt, but this was no bar to his taking up his seat in the German
National Assembly for which he had been elected by a constituency in
Lower Austria. By his first speech in the assembly during the debate
on the motion by Zitz he established himself in the front rank of the
Frankfurt Parliament. In view of popular hostility to the Federal
Assembly (*Bundesversammlung*), it certainly cannot be maintained that
he owed his success to his official post. Welcker, the delegate of Baden
in the Federal Assembly, was if anything impeded in his role in the
Frankfurt Parliament by his dual position. Schmerling rejected the
doubtful indirect compliment paid to the Austrian troops in Mainz,
which he regarded as an attempt to sow dissension between different
parts of the garrison. He defended the right of the Prussian soldiers to
retaliate against provocation, and put the blame for the disturbances
squarely on the shoulders of the Mainz citizens. He regarded the further
disposition of troops as a matter for the military authorities. He therefore moved 'next business' (*Übergang zur Tagesordnung*). Schmerling
was one of the few members at this time courageous enough to try and
stem what appeared to be the popular tide. He was certainly a man of
great determination, as he was to show during the September disturbances in Frankfurt. He spoke sharply, without any attempt to
bridge differences. He may well have lacked the subtlety and suppleness
of higher statesmanship. In one way he showed remarkable prescience,
when he referred to the importance of the federal fortress at Mainz for
the defence of Frankfurt and of the assembly against attack, the very
situation which was to arise in September.

    There was another man on the anti-radical side of the assembly who
was also quite fearless, Felix von Lichnowsky. Not yet in his mid-

[1] I 102 ff.

thirties, this Catholic magnate from Silesia had already crammed as
much excitement into a decade and a half of adult life as most of us do
not get even into a lifetime. After serving in the Prussian army, he went
to Spain to fight for Don Carlos on the anti-constitutional side. He was
wounded, and after adventures of various kinds returned to Prussia
following the accession of King Frederick William IV. He was a successful author of memoirs and served in the Prussian United Diet of 1847 as
a member of the Right.[1] Like Schmerling, Lichnowsky did nothing in his
speeches in the assembly to lower the temperature and his barbed formulations earned him the hatred of the radicals both inside and outside the
chamber for which he was to pay so dearly in September. But unlike
Schmerling, Lichnowsky spoke with a certain elegance and with the
natural self-assurance of the person of rank and wealth. He was too
big a man and too experienced in politics to see salvation simply in the
defence of every inch of ground. For a time he deliberately joined the
Right Centre (*Casino*) rather than the Right. He was extreme in form
rather than in substance. He added colour to the assembly, and all but
his most intolerant opponents will have appreciated his rhetorical
talents. He was able to capture the attention of the house and could
certainly not complain about lack of interest on the part of the gallery.
He is one of the few speakers of the Frankfurt Parliament whose
rhetorical gifts are apparent from the shorthand reports. Prince
Lichnowsky mercilessly attacked Zitz and his circle in Mainz.[2] He
called on members from Schleswig to vindicate the honour of the Prussian
army, whereupon two representatives of the Elbe Duchies expressed
their thanks for the fine achievements and bearing of the Prussian
troops. After this, even the timid recommendations of the committee of
investigation were lost. A considerable majority voted 'next business',[3]
though a number of moderates divided with the minority.[4]

iv. Vincke – Vote on Raveaux's motion

The way was now clear for a decision on Raveaux's motion, the
debate on which was postponed owing to the greater urgency of the
situation in Mainz. The report of the committee and the debate[5]

---

[1] See Haym, *Reden und Redner* 5 ff.   [2] I 105 ff.
[3] I 114.   [4] I 115 f.   [5] I 121 ff.

concentrated on the major issue of the relations between the German National Assembly and other constituent assemblies. The question whether members should be allowed to serve at Frankfurt and Berlin, which Raveaux had originally put first, was relegated to the background, a procedure against which the mover did not protest. Undoubtedly Raveaux had the overriding constitutional issue in mind from the very beginning. The committee was unable to agree and formulated four different motions, as usual ranging from Extreme Right to Extreme Left. This body was a very strong one, containing a number of dominant – including some domineering – personalities. The strength of the membership may well have been the weakness of the committee. It took the Frankfurt Parliament some time to develop the perfect committee man. Whatever the effect of personality, four main possible views about the constitutional position emerged, corresponding to Right, Right Centre, Left Centre and Left. These were to be the main groups in the assembly, with the additional triple sub-division of the Left. Although the quadruple division emerged during the debate on Raveaux's motion, many members had not yet reached the position in the chamber which really suited them. This is clear from the signatures of the four motions to emerge from the committee.[1]

As was to be expected, the Right objected to the Frankfurt Parliament laying down unilaterally the relationship between the constitution to be drawn up by the assembly for the whole of Germany and that of the states. The Right had a great respect for the institutions hallowed by history. The rationalistic approach of dictating the political future of Germany from Frankfurt was anathema to the Right. When the Frankfurt Parliament had drawn up a constitution, then would be the time to come to terms with the states, by negotiation. Four members of the committee, therefore, in the confidence that the states would take the necessary steps in due course, moved 'next business'.[2] They were Vincke, Eduard Simson, Somaruga and Neuwall.[3] Only Vincke was to remain on the Right, to become its leader in due course. Eduard Simson and Somaruga joined the Right Centre, Simson to become one of its leading personalities. Neuwall even became a member of the Left Centre. Vincke made one of the main speeches in the debate when proposing his motion.[4]

[1] I 124 f.
[2] *Motivierte Tagesordnung.* This was less abrupt than the simple motion of 'next business'.
[3] Erasmus, *Die Juden*; Bundesarchiv.   [4] I 135 ff.

Georg von Vincke was one of the outstanding German parliamentarians in the middle of the nineteenth century. A descendant of the old Westphalian nobility, born in 1810 as the son of the later well-known *Oberpräsident* (head of the provincial administration) of Westphalia, he studied the law and entered the service of the state. In 1837 he was elected *Landrat* (i.e. official in charge of a rural district) for Hagen in his home province. In 1843 he served as a member of the nobility (*Ritterschaft*) in the Westphalian provincial estates. Here he began his great campaign for the maintenance and if possible the revival of the rights of the estates, a battle which had been fought with great vigour in Wurtemberg some years earlier. Vincke became famous all over Germany during the Prussian United Diet of 1847, where he vigorously pressed for the preservation of constitutional rights against the crown. Both he and his father, who had fled to England during the Napoleonic wars, were strongly influenced by the English political example. Georg von Vincke was a Burkean in his insistence on historical continuity. His speeches were closely argued with the precision of the lawyer, and enlivened by formulations which combined brilliance with brevity. There was never a word too much or a phrase out of place. Vincke set out to convince intellectually, not to rouse by sentimental appeals. A born speaker in the best sense, he was able to present his point of view clearly and crisply. In the United Diet he spoke of the soil of the law (*Acker des Rechtes*) which his ancestors had ploughed for many centuries and from which they had won much costly fruit. In German this turn of phrase has an even richer meaning, as *Recht* is not only the law, but also justice, and as the word is the singular of rights (*Rechte*). Vincke's conservatism would have nothing to do with a shallow legitimism which always regarded the latest political upheaval – if carried out by autocratic monarchs – as hallowed by history and as divinely ordained. His historical interpretation had a much wider sweep, attempting to uncover those institutions which, while they might more recently have been neglected, could be fruitfully adapted for the future. Vincke's conservatism was selective, being quite ready to discard aberrations. As was the case with his master Burke, Vincke's political philosophy combined liberal with conservative elements. Thus during his political career from 1843 to 1870 he did not always occupy the same position in the Left-Right spectrum in the various assemblies to which he belonged. This was due to changing circumstances, rather than to any inconsistency. Vincke's principles remained constant. His main aim was to defend historical continuity and constitutional development against those trying to encroach on it. Before 1848 and from the end of 1850 these were mainly threatened by the monarchy, whereas during the revolutionary period the principal threat came from the Left. Thus it will be readily understood that Vincke sat on the Right in the Frankfurt Parliament, although he had been further to the Left in the Prussian United Diet and was to be Left of Centre again in the 1850's when the threat of revolution had passed. During all his political vicissitudes Vincke was forced to collaborate with many others who did not subscribe to his own brand of principles. In the Frankfurt Parliament, certainly, some of Vincke's fellow-members on the Right represented a rigid, barren conservatism which the Burkean from Westphalia never shared.[1]

In many ways, Vincke's parliamentary technique was the very opposite of Heinrich von Gagern's. While Gagern excelled in the evocative phrase which meant all things to all men and therefore found a wide body of support, Vincke was precise, almost meticulous in his argument, apparently not caring very much whether anybody was going to agree with him. Whereas Gagern was in all but name leader of the majority during the first months of the Frankfurt Parliament, Vincke's following in 1848 remained small. At that time, Vincke was resigned to representing a rather unpopular minority. He kept the flag of the Right flying with great tenacity. As in the United Diet, he knew in the Frankfurt Parliament how to make himself heard. He was one of the few speakers in the Right half of the house who succeeded in silencing even the gallery. Vincke achieved this by admitting that much of what he said would run counter to the opinions of many members, that his speech would probably come under strong criticism and that this could best be expressed forcefully at the end by manifestations of dissent. Even his opponents could not deny respect to a speaker who stated his views clearly and fearlessly, but without rancour.

The Right was the only part of the assembly which did not want any action whatever to be taken on Raveaux's motion. While even much of the Centre was prepared to assume for the assembly certain powers over the states, Vincke was not prepared to concede that the Frankfurt Parliament was more than one of the several organs which would have to decide on the future constitution of Germany. It was in the nature of the Centre to try and mediate between Right and Left. This allowed

[1] Haym, *Reden und Redner* 55 ff.; *ADB* xxxix.

Vincke to have a feast pointing out the inconsistencies in the motions emanating from the Centre asking the states to come into line with the German constitution in due course, without going the whole hog of popular sovereignty. Vincke said that if he had to choose between the motions of the Centre and of the Left, there was a great deal to be said for the Left, which was at least consistent in demanding that the German National Assembly should have the overriding power. He, however, sharply denied the claim of the Left that the Frankfurt Parliament was the sole organ concerned with the future German constitution. He asked the assembly to face facts, even unpleasant ones, something at which the Frankfurt Parliament was not to be particularly good. However sad it might be, there was not yet a German nation. There were still 38 different German nations. The German states had only surrendered a certain part of their sovereignty in the Federal Act (*Bundesakte*) of 1815, which was still the basic law of Germany. It was the task of the assembly to move away from this 'desperate' state of affairs, that was why members were here. But until a new solution had been found, the old powers still represented the German people. Vincke asked those who did not approve of his sentiments to state clearly how they defined the German people. What criterion was going to be used to decide who belonged to the German people and who did not? If Germany was to consist of all those who spoke German, as some desired,[1] then the Alsatians – who formed part of France – would have to be included and the Czechs and North Slesvigers would have to be excluded. Were members prepared to draw these conclusions? Vincke ended a speech, which gave much food for thought to all those who were prepared to do so afresh, with an appeal for unity.

Two different motions were put forward by the Centre, both from within the committee on Raveaux's motion. They were clearly distinguished from those emanating from Right and Left. They differed from the views of the Right in recognising that some action had to be taken. On the other hand they did not accept the interpretation of the Left which regarded the German National Assembly as the sole organ involved in the creating of a constitution. But the two motions proposed divergent methods for bringing the constitutions of the various states into line with that for the whole of Germany. A member who was to

[1] As in E. M. Arndt's poem '*Was ist des Deutschen Vaterlands*' (1813), with its '*Soweit die deutsche Zunge klingt*' (as far as the German tongue sounds) which Vincke quoted.

join the Left Centre, the advocate Johann Peter Werner from Koblenz, proposed the following motion:[1]

> The German National Assembly . . . declares: that all stipulations of individual German constitutions which do not agree with the general constitution to be founded by it are to be only considered valid in so far as they accord with the latter, notwithstanding their existing efficacy up to that time.

Seven other members of the committee also then ranged in the Centre proposed another method of proceeding. Their motion read:[2]

> The . . . National Assembly . . . declares that all stipulations of German constitutions which after completion of the general constitution do not agree with it are to be amended and to be brought into harmony with the German constitution.

This motion had the powerful backing of the *rapporteur* of the committee, the Wurtemberg minister Römer, a liberal who belonged to the Centre without being fully committed to any of the clubs. The other signatories, too, were mainly men of distinction: Hermann von Beckerath, a banker from Krefeld and an erstwhile member of the liberal opposition in the Prussian United Diet; the senior Prussian judge Adolf Lette[3] from Berlin; the Bavarian economist and civil servant Friedrich von Hermann;[4] the Hamburg lawyer Johann Gustav Heckscher; the famous author of the *Briefwechsel zweier Deutscher* (correspondence of two Germans) first published in 1831, the Wurtemberg liberal Paul Pfizer[5] and his fellow Swabian, the official Adolf Schoder.[6] At this distance of time, one may be pardoned for wondering why the seven and their fellow-member of the committee, Werner, could not agree on a common wording. It is even difficult to be sure which of the motions was the more radical or which the more moderate. Personality may well have played as much of a part in the differences as principle. There was also a motion of the Left[7] dealing with the subject Raveaux had raised. This emphasised that the German National Assembly had the exclusive right (*einzig und allein*) to decide about the German constitution and that the laws of the German states were valid only in so far as they agreed with the German constitution. As to the other point raised by Raveaux, the motion stipulated that members of the German National Assembly could only be relieved of the obligation to

[1] i 125.   [2] i 124.   [3] *ADB* xviii; Bergsträsser, 'Briefe'; *BSTH*.
[4] *ADB* xii; *BSTH*.   [5] *ADB* xxv; *BSTH*.   [6] *ADB* xxxii.   [7] i 125.

take part in its deliberations by the assembly itself. The signatories, all members of the committee to report on Raveaux's motion, were Wilhelm Michael Schaffrath,[1] a radical lawyer from Saxony; Georg Friedrich Kolb,[2] a journalist and publisher from Speyer, one of the best-known opposition personalities in the Bavarian Palatinate before 1848; and the young democratic writer Moritz Hartmann from Bohemia.[3] Both Schaffrath and Hartmann were to join the Extreme Left, whereas Kolb was generally a somewhat more moderate member of the Left.

Neither motion from the two extremes had any chance of success. The choice for the assembly lay between the other two motions which came from the committee. By now their sponsors had dug their toes in, each violently attacking the version of the other. Römer, the draftsman of the motion of the seven and *rapporteur* of the committee, regarded Werner's proposal as quite impracticable, as the National Assembly could not possibly, after drawing up a constitution, sit as a revision committee for all the constitutional states in Germany.[4] Werner retorted that it was not feasible, as Römer and his colleagues proposed, to allow thirty-eight chambers and governments to debate the clauses of the national constitution.[5] Behind the different remedies proposed lay the question as to whether German unification was to be achieved on federal or unitary lines. It so happened that the Left was at that time committed to the unitary principle, not only on general grounds of doctrine, but also because it still hoped to dominate the centre of the national state and to enforce its ideas that way. In this sense Werner's motion was closer to the heart of the Left than that of Römer and his friends, which left more say to the individual states. It was, however, debatable whether a curtailing of the functions of state parliaments was more 'democratic' than an admission of their right to co-operate. While four of the seven sponsors of the Römer motion – Beckerath, Pfizer, Lette and Heckscher – were to join the Right Centre, the other three – Römer, Schoder and Hermann – tended more to the Left Centre. Römer himself was theoretically a republican[6] though he recognised that this form of government was not then feasible for Germany. Werner was certainly no more to the Left than for instance Schoder. It is no coincidence that three of the seven came from Wurtemberg whose population was very strongly rooted in its history. This state

[1] *Umrisse* 61; Bundesarchiv; *MdR*.   [2] Krautkrämer, *Kolb*; *BSTH*.
[3] See above, p. 99 f.   [4] I 129.   [5] I 138 f.   [6] Bassermann, *Denkwürdigkeiten* 67.

provides the clearest illustration of the fact that particularism was not confined to the rulers, but had a strong popular, here even a partially republican, basis. Beckerath and Lette were Protestants from older parts of the Prussian monarchy and Heckscher – also a Protestant – came from the Free Town of Hamburg. All three were in greater or lesser degree attached to the traditions of their states. Hermann was a Bavarian particularist, though a Protestant and a native of the free Imperial city of Dinkelsbühl which was only incorporated into Bavaria after his birth. It is not without significance that the sponsor of the rival motion, Werner, was a Catholic from Koblenz, who had not become a subject of the King of Prussia until he was an adolescent[1] and was rather indifferent to the future of the Hohenzollern dynasty and of their dominions.

Raveaux had a feeling for atmosphere. Already in the Pre-Parliament he had demonstrated both his sense of timing and his readiness to adopt a more moderate position than the Extreme Left if he saw an advantage in this. He quite enjoyed himself in the role of bridge-builder between the Left and parts of the Centre. When Raveaux first opened the discussion on relations with state parliaments on 19 May, he had been petulant and relied on support mainly from the Left. But as he was denied quick success, he began to realise that more subtle tactics were required. He was put off by the crude methods of the more extreme members of the Left and tried to found a Left Centre in the *Holländischer Hof*, the original meeting place of the Left before it moved over to the *Deutscher Hof*. At first, this Left Centre in the *Holländischer Hof* under Raveaux's leadership seemed to flourish. On 26 May, a well-attended meeting held there agreed to support Werner's motion, which now received Raveaux's blessing.[2] The failure of Zitz may well have shown to many members, including Raveaux, that the Left was only liable to unite the remainder of the assembly against itself by an uncompromising attitude. Certainly on 27 May Raveaux's Left Centre could celebrate a triumph. Although the heavy guns of the seven of the committee and of their supporters tried to kill Werner's motion stone-dead, as the debate proceeded it became clear that Raveaux had set the tone by his speech at the beginning.[3] He at once dissociated himself

---

[1] Werner's life is badly documented. He was born at Koblenz in 1798 and died there in 1869 (Bundesarchiv).

[2] Biedermann, *Erinnerungen* 7 f.; Droysen, Tagebuch for 24 May 1848 in Hübner, *Droysen* 813.

[3] i 127 ff.

from the radical motion of Schaffrath and came out clearly for Werner's version. From his point of view, all he sacrificed was a reiteration of the sole right of the assembly to determine the constitution. But this right had already been claimed by the Pre-Parliament and did not have to be repeated, as he pointed out in his speech. Even if the two moderate motions did not resolve the question whether anybody else would have any say about the German constitution besides the Frankfurt Parliament, they insisted on state laws coming into line. This sufficed for Raveaux and he preferred Werner's version, because he believed that Römer's proposals would leave too much scope for mischief to the state parliaments. At the end of the debate, when the strong support for Werner's motion had become apparent, Raveaux appealed to the Left to withdraw its motion,[1] which Schaffrath did readily.[2] Römer, who had the last word as *rapporteur*, characteristically refused to budge.[3] But this obstinacy was of no avail, for when it came to a vote on Werner's motion it was carried nearly unanimously. Less than 10 members did not vote for it.[4] For a fleeting moment the assembly felt united, but it was not easy to see what tangible agreement had been achieved by the formula about state constitutions. The original practical issue ventilated by Raveaux concerning members with seats in the two national assemblies in Frankfurt and Berlin had been dropped altogether. Only the future would tell whether the Left Centre, which had just won its first victory, would be capable of showing sufficient coherence, and whether it could aspire to the leadership of the assembly.

v. *Party groupings on Left and Left Centre*

Although much time was wasted on procedural wrangles, the first ten days had enabled members to discover their political friends in finding a president and in taking up positions over the issues raised by Raveaux and Zitz. While Zitz had unwittingly effected a rallying of the moderates against the Left, Raveaux had succeeded in putting a Left Centre, in sympathy with many aims of the Left, on the political map. While later the difficulties of combining leftist tendencies with moderation became abundantly clear, during these early days of the Frankfurt

---

[1] i 152 f.   [2] i 153.   [3] i 153 f.   [4] i 155.

Parliament the Left Centre seemed to provide an ideal strategic position. Members could boast of some democratic principles, without being too extreme. If necessary they could move slightly to the Left, or more into the Centre. This was the present strength and future weakness of the Left Centre.

Raveaux was only one of several active members who tried to break out of restricted party political positions by creating a larger grouping round the kernel of their close political allies. He was not the first in the field in forming a parliamentary group, for Robert Blum (whose follower he was at first) had beaten him to it. Right up to his fatal departure for Vienna in October, Blum was the main leader of the Left. He was born in Cologne in 1807 during the rule of the French. His family, which was quite well educated, fell on hard times and during his childhood the future parliamentarian often experienced dire poverty. Catholic priests helped him with his education, but according to his son Hans[1] his father already as a boy became very critical of the Catholic Church. He allegedly discovered abuses for which he was punished.[2] After some time as a journeyman and factory worker, Blum became porter in a theatre and eventually rose to the position of cashier there. All the while he continued his education and began to write for publication. From 1840 he lived in Leipzig, where he took an active part in cultural and political life. He became renowned by his intervention during the clashes between troops and citizens in Leipzig during August 1845 which helped to bring the severe disorders to an end. The government gave him no thanks and indeed made an unsuccessful attempt to prosecute him, which only contributed to his popularity. Both as a former Catholic and as a political radical Blum welcomed the movement of *Deutschkatholizismus*[3] and helped to found a congregation of this denomination in Leipzig. He also set up as a bookseller, publisher and editor of political journals. He seems to have served a short prison sentence in connection with his journalistic activities. According to his son he often harboured Polish revolutionaries and was privy to their plots to take the citadel of Cracow by force.[4] As his son criticises these

---

[1] H. Blum, *R. Blum* 26 ff. See also *ADB* ii; Bergsträsser, *Frankfurter Parlament* 333 ff.

[2] Hans Blum was a boy of seven when his father was executed and therefore could not contribute personal impressions to a biography which is highly coloured owing to his attempt to reconcile his own attachment to Bismarck with his filial loyalty to the memory of his father.

[3] See above, p. 20 ff.   [4] H. Blum, *R. Blum* 234 f.

activities which hardly commended themselves to a nationalist member of the Reichstag in Bismarck's day, the information may well be correct. The debates of the Frankfurt Parliament were to show how complex the attitudes of various groups, including the Left, was to other nationalities. If Robert Blum aided some Poles before 1848 against the powers which had partitioned Poland, it would have never occurred to him that he might indirectly be weakening the hold of his fellow-Germans over parts of Posen. In those years the German radicals believed that there existed a fundamental unity of interests among those oppressed, whether by their own governments or by other nationalities, whether German, Slav, Magyar, French or whatever. Nationality appeared to the German radicals simply as an aspect of popular sovereignty. They had not worked out the possible complications. Even before the meeting of the Frankfurt Parliament some of them had already changed their attitude to other nationalities, as the example of Schilling in Prague during April 1848 shows.[1] In the Pre-Parliament Blum established himself as leader of the sections of the Left which were prepared to work within the parliamentary arena. Already well known in Saxony and in some parts of Germany before 1848, he now became a national figure. As a member of the Committee of Fifty he remained in Frankfurt after the end of the Pre-Parliament and was thus well placed to enrol members of the German National Assembly in his group as they began to arrive during May. Himself at heart an extremist, as his later career was to show, he was prepared to adopt a prudent attitude for the time being and to wait for his chance. Like Raveaux, though from a different point of view, Blum also wanted to form a major party of the Left extending as far as possible into the Centre. He therefore welcomed, first in the *Holländischer Hof* and then more permanently in the *Deutscher Hof*, more moderate members of the Left and aimed at detaching from the Right and the Centre as many deputies as he could. These basically sensible tactics could not satisfy both his two extreme wings and may well have contributed to Raveaux's decision to emancipate himself. Blum's close friendship with many of the extreme radicals in the Frankfurt Parliament, including his wife's brother, the writer Georg Günther[2] who also came from Leipzig, was well known. Those most disappointed by Blum's compromises were these extremists who eventually left the *Deutscher Hof* and set themselves up in the *Donners-*

[1] See above, p. 70.
[2] See p. 53, n. 1, on Blum. See also Fontane, 'Von Zwanzig bis Dreissig', 130 ff.

berg, rather an appropriate name for these thunderers. In spite of all the differences of opinion, Blum was recognised as the dominant personality on the Left in the Frankfurt Parliament as long as he lived. Whatever reservations his colleagues may have had about his personality, they admired his rhetorical gifts. Blum was one of the born orators of the Frankfurt Parliament and few on the Left touched him. He had an advantage over academics like Vogt and Ruge, in that he could speak about the lot of the working man from personal experience. This gave his interventions in parliament authenticity.

At the time of the division on Raveaux's motion, the number of those who regarded themselves as members of the Left is likely to have been well below one hundred in a house of about five hundred. Gustav Rümelin, the headmaster of a grammar school in Wurtemberg and a member of the Left Centre at that time, wrote a report for the newspaper *Schwäbischer Merkur* dated 30 May that Blum had a following of barely forty to fifty members, with about the same number of sympathisers.[1] The Left comprised a considerable spectrum of political attitudes, even without the presence of Hecker, ranging from outright revolutionists like Ruge to the judge Christian Schüler[2] from Jena, who according to the economist Wilhelm Stahl from Erlangen was 'no longer a republican'.[3] The line of division with the Centre was bound to be fluid. The Left was united by its hatred of the existing order and particularly of the Federal Assembly. Not surprisingly, it contained the highest proportion, both absolutely and relatively, of those who had suffered at the hands of authority before 1848 and of the political refugees who had returned to Germany after the revolution. Perhaps less expected is the finding that the Left contained in relation to its numbers a far higher proportion of former members of the *Burschenschaft* than the Centre.[4] According to Rümelin's report of 30 May 1848 most members of the Left came from the Rhineland and Southern Germany. Actually the Left did not conquer a very high proportion of the seats in the Rhineland in so far as it was Prussian, but some of the Left-wingers from there, like the advocates Ludwig Simon[5] from Trier and Hugo Wesendonck from Düsseldorf, were very well known and played a leading part in the deliberations of the Left. Numerically, the

---

[1] Rümelin, *Aus der Paulskirche* 4. For Rümelin see *ADB* LIII; *BSTH*; Schnizer, *Rümelins politische Ideen*.
[2] Niebour, 'Die Vertreter Thüringens' 403 f.
[3] Gerber, 'Briefe' 8, letter dated 21 May 1848.
[4] The representation of ex-*Burschenschafter* on the Right was minimal.
[5] *ADB* XXXIV.

contingents from Southern Germany were the strongest components of the Left, particularly if one includes the Rhine Palatinate, which belonged to Bavaria, in this category. Baden and Wurtemberg were mainly Left. Most representatives of the Left were Protestant, but there were also some Roman Catholics, even some priests. The majority of the *Deutschkatholiken* sat on the Left.

Professionally, the picture among the Left is very similar to that of the other sections of the assembly. There is the usual preponderance of lawyers, civil servants and teachers. As one would expect, the army officer representation is much weaker on the Left than elsewhere: indeed, there was no single serving army officer on the benches of the Left, though some members had held commissions.[1] The proportion of writers and journalists (without regular teaching appointments) and of medical practitioners who served on the Left is particularly high. The free-lance writer was a characteristic type of left-wing politician at this time. The prominence of the medical profession on the benches of the Left, on a comparatively small sample, may be coincidence. Possibly, though, these practitioners may reflect the attraction of the scientifically trained mind to the rationalist approach of the Left during the period. As to social origin, more members of labouring class origin both absolutely and relatively sat in the Centre than on the Left. Blum was a less typical representative of the Left in the assembly than the intellectuals and academics, the writers and poets, whose daily problems and education were rather remote from those of the industrial proletariat. As to age, it may be noted that the majority of those born after 1820 sat on the Left. This again is not unexpected. However, the older age groups were also represented on the Left, for instance the Baden opposition leader in the days before 1848, Adam von Itzstein, who was born in 1775.

For the Left, its ideological basis was both its strength and weakness. It gained power from a sense of mission, from a certainty of being correct in its political diagnosis and on the right lines in the remedies it proposed. But this very certainty in each individual was bound to lead to difficulties at times, for there were inevitably different opinions as to timing and tactics. An ideological party thus finds it more difficult to compromise on matters which in the nature of things cannot be viewed

---

[1] Thus the lawyer Wilhelm Schulz from Hesse-Darmstadt had been an officer in the Prussian army, but had been discharged in 1821 following imprisonment for political activities. *ADB* xxxii.

with any detachment, but become matters of faith. Thus the Left had its share of regrouping. By 28 May, Raveaux had taken his followers out of Blum's *Deutscher Hof* into the Left Centre. According to the professor of history and German literature at the Stuttgart Polytechnic, the extreme radical Wilhelm Zimmermann, the Left wing decided to secede from the *Deutscher Hof* at this very time, on the evening following Raveaux's triumph in the assembly.[1] Most observers believed that the foundation of the *Donnersberg* club by the Extreme Left only took place at the end of June.[2]

A penetration of the Left into the Centre was limited by the degree of radicalism on the Extreme Left. The more extreme the Left wing, the less likely was the Left to make proselytes among the Left Centre. This problem remained even after the secession of the Extreme Left, for an attempt was made to maintain some co-operation between the various groups on the Left by means of a loose association called *Die vereinigte Linke* (the united Left). This was facilitated by the fact that not all members of the Left joined the particular group which corresponded to the radicalism or moderation of their views. Thus the leader of the main body of the Left, Blum, in the *Deutscher Hof*, would have fitted in far better with the extremists. Similarly some members of the Leftist grouping closest to the Centre, particularly Raveaux and the Silesian former judge Heinrich Simon, were much more radical for most of the duration of the Frankfurt Parliament than their position in the assembly would suggest.

Although the Left was first in the field of party organisation, there were limits to its unity. To some extent the appearance of compactness and determination given to the outsider was deceptive. The Left was united in its negations and may have seemed sure of itself for this reason. Owing to its numerical weakness, it rarely had a chance of putting its coherence to a real test by the formulation of a positive programme of practical value. By itself the Left in the Frankfurt Parliament was in a frustrating position. That was why some members of the Extreme Left, like the philosopher Ruge, resigned from the assembly at an early date, in the hope of being able to fight the battle of the Left in more advantageous conditions elsewhere.[3] From the point of view of the Left,

[1] Zimmermann, *Deutsche Revolution* 641.
[2] E.g. Eisenmann, *Parteyen* 43; Biedermann, *Erinnerungen* 18.
[3] Ruge formally ceased to belong to the Frankfurt Parliament on 10 November 1848, but had already been absent for longer periods before that date. See Neher, *Arnold Ruge* 192 ff.

some of the state parliaments, for instance in Berlin or Dresden, offered a better chance.

There was bound to be a Left, though its extent and coherence could not be predicted at the start. The penetration of the Left into the Centre had repercussions on party constellations in the remainder of the chamber. This is one reason why Raveaux's attempt to create a strong Left Centre was important. For obviously, this group would draw off support from a formation based on the Right Centre. The Left Centre constituted itself at the end of May in the *Holländischer Hof*, following Raveaux's victory. Like Raveaux himself, many members of the Left Centre had come from the Left at the *Deutscher Hof*.[1] Others were presumably recruited from those not yet committed, for only the Left was at this stage reasonably organised. The group which flocked together in the *Holländischer Hof* was so mixed that in June the key troops moved over to the *Würtemberger Hof*.[1] The task which the Left Centre set itself was not an easy one to fulfil. While arrogating to the National Assembly the sole right to decide on the constitution, the Left Centre yet wanted to have something to distinguish itself from the Left. It aimed at providing a more moderate version of popular sovereignty. For only on this basis could radicals and moderates be brought together. There were on the one hand the radical antagonists of the pre-1848 régimes, men like Raveaux himself and the former judge and outspoken critic Heinrich Simon from Breslau, and on the other more moderate opponents like the university professor and journalist Karl Biedermann[2] from Leipzig and the lawyer and protagonist for Jewish rights from Hamburg, Gabriel Riesser. The former group demanded much more thorough-going changes than the latter. In view of the structure of this club, secessions continued and any agreement on a common policy was fraught with difficulty. Gabriel Riesser reported home on 10 June that the most active members of the Left Centre had not yet been able to agree on the policy the group would adopt towards the next major issue, the formation of a provisional central power.[3] In view of the mixture of various elements, generalisations about this club are difficult to make. The balanced regional composition and the considerable weight given to the Third Germany (the parts outside Prussia and the Habsburg Monarchy) are perhaps the most distinct characteristics.

[1] Biedermann, *Erinnerungen* 7.
[2] Biedermann, *Erinnerungen* and *Mein Leben*; Schneider, *Grossdeutsch oder Kleindeutsch*; *NDB*; *BSTH*.
[3] Isler, *G. Riessers Schriften* I 555.

vi. Regional groupings – Catholic Association – Radowitz – Right Centre – Right

For the Left a common ideology was the bond of unity, for the Left Centre a certain more complex attitude to political matters which is very hard to define. The parties based on the Right Centre and on the Right had the possibility of various principles of association besides that of political ideology.[1] They could also unite on the basis of a religion or group themselves by the regions from which they came, or combine both elements. The most successful regional gatherings were those of the Austrians in the *Sokratesloge* and of the Bavarians in the *Pariser Hof*. The latter, however, seem to have been mainly social, devoted to drinking Munich *Bock* provided by a fellow-member, the right-wing Bavarian Minister of Church and School Affairs, Hermann von Beisler.[2] The Austrian club in the *Sokratesloge* was politically of greater significance. Here the Austrian government provided an excellent centre for representatives from the Habsburg Monarchy to meet and to discuss their tactics. The *Sokratesloge* gave Schmerling, with his official position as Austrian presidial delegate at the German Confederation, his chance of assembling a core of followers and helped him to obtain a key position in parliament and government during the following months. The *Sokratesloge* appealed particularly to the more moderate members among the Austrians and not so much to the radicals. By opening itself to non-Austrians, it gradually became a focal point for the activities of the Right Centre.[3] The Prussians were scattered among the various groups (though particularly prominent in the Right Centre) and never succeeded in forming a club of their own. There were complaints that this reduced their influence. To try and remedy the situation, a meeting was held in the *Hirschgraben* on 31 May 1848 at which von Vincke called for a political programme openly aimed at bestowing the imperial German crown on the King of Prussia.[4]

Whether dispersal really hampered the Prussian cause was a matter of opinion and of judgment. Were the Prussians going to maximise their influence by banding together? This was not necessarily so at all.

[1] The party programmes are given in Eisenmann, *Parteyen*.
[2] Gerber, 'Briefe' 22, letter dated 30 May 1848. For Beisler, see *ADB* ii; *NDB*; *BSTH*.
[3] Pagenstecher, *Lebenserinnerungen* ii 61 f.; Biedermann, *Erinnerungen* 5 f.
[4] Raumer, *Briefe* i 35 ff.

Indeed the reverse might be the case. There was liable to be a reaction against a Prussian party, a 'ganging up' of the others. Those Prussian representatives who urged their state and dynasty to take a lead in unifying Germany were likely to be more influential mixing with members from other states and winning them over to their point of view. Certainly a purely Prussian party would have deprived Prussian members of the opportunity of lobbying other North Germans and those South Germans, for instance from the Baden and Wurtemberg contingents, who were favourably inclined to Prussian hegemony, such as Bassermann, Mathy and Pfizer. On balance the Prussian cause benefited from an initial dispersal.

Similar organisational problems arose in the religious sphere for the Roman Catholics. As the Prussian state parliament was more obviously important from a denominational point of view, the leading German Catholic prelate, Archbishop Geissel of Cologne, had himself elected to Berlin rather than to Frankfurt. It was in Berlin that the strategy to be followed by Catholics in Germany was settled. After initially favouring the formation of a Catholic party – such as was to come about later – Geissel and his associates decided it was better to let Catholic members follow their own political preference and to confine co-operation to religious matters. These tactics were also adopted at Frankfurt where the far less determined Prince-Bishop of Breslau, von Diepenbrock, acted on the prompting of his more vigorous fellow-prelate in the Prussian National Assembly. Diepenbrock had been in favour of turning the other cheek during the Cologne church conflict of 1837.[1] For his attitude the militants had accused him of being weak and of lacking a strong faith. The Prince-Bishop of Breslau, who came from an old noble patrician family in Westphalia, did not find the atmosphere in Frankfurt congenial and resigned from the assembly as soon as he could, like some of his clerical brethren. He did not possess the temperament of a parliamentarian and it required Geissel's prompting to make him act at all. Part of the explanation of Diepenbrock's passive attitude lies in his poor state of health. One of the youngest members of the Frankfurt Parliament to serve in the wars against Napoleon, he was only fifty years of age in 1848. While in Frankfurt he was very ill and he died in 1853.[2]

Diepenbrock held a meeting with leading Catholics in the Frankfurt

[1] See above, p. 19.
[2] *ADB* v; *NDB*; Reinkens, *M. v. Diepenbrock*; Lill, *Bischofskonferenzen* 55.

Parliament during the second week in June. On 14 June, the Prince-Bishop arranged a second gathering, jointly with two distinguished lay members of the assembly, the Prussian General Joseph Maria von Radowitz[1] and the judge August Reichensperger[2] from the Prussian Rhineland. The result was the founding of the *Katholische Vereinigung*, which Catholic members of the Frankfurt Parliament were free to join irrespective of their political affiliation. Radowitz was elected chairman and Reichensperger vice-chairman. As chairman, Radowitz saw to it that the association confined itself to the consideration of religious questions and did not venture into politics, though naturally the line of division between the two spheres was not always easy to draw.

The Catholic association eventually adopted the *Steinernes Haus* as its meeting place. By the middle of June this building was already the headquarters of the Right in the Frankfurt Parliament, which has led to some confusion among historians, particularly as Radowitz presided over both bodies. However, the two clubs were run quite separately and many members of the Catholic association, including August Reichensperger and Max von Gagern, belonged to the Right Centre. Both Radowitz' personality and his policy in the Catholic association caused some disquiet among his co-religionists.[3]

Radowitz was the son of a free-thinking originally Catholic father and of a Protestant mother, and was only introduced to the faith of his fathers during adolescence. In spite of the religious indifference in his home, he soon became a convinced Catholic, though he was never a 'clerical' or 'ultramontane'. He was the grandson of a Hungarian officer[4] who after his capture by the Prussians in 1745 decided to stay in Northern Germany. Our Joseph Maria von Radowitz was born in 1797 in the Harz region as a subject of the Duke of Brunswick. At the age of eleven he became a military cadet and in those days of Napoleonic rule received part of his training in France. He was wounded as a West-phalian artillery lieutenant on the Napoleonic side at Leipzig in 1813. He then took service in the army of the Electorate of Hesse, one of the politically most backward German states, but eventually fell into

---

[1] *ADB* xxvii; Radowitz, *Gesammelte Schriften*, particularly iii 353–496 (Berichte aus der Nationalversammlung); P. Hassel, *Radowitz* i (1905); Meinecke, *Radowitz*; *BSTH*.

[2] Pastor, *A. Reichensperger*; Wegener, *P. Reichensperger*; *BSTH*.

[3] Meinecke, *Radowitz* 154 ff.; Pastor, *Max v. Gagern* 267 f.; Schnabel, *Zusammenschluss* 57 ff.

[4] Thus Meinecke, *Radowitz* 3. According to the German Foreign Office official Friedrich v. Holstein, the Radowitz family was of Serbian origin. N. Rich and M. H. Fisher (eds.), *The Holstein Papers* i (1955) 98.

disgrace owing to his criticism of the Elector's mismanagement. In 1823 he transferred to the Prussian army and this proved a turning point in his career. Radowitz was an example of the highly cultured army officer so common in Germany in those days. To a man like that Prussia offered opportunities which would have never been open to him in a small state. Interestingly enough the Catholic Radowitz did not rather choose to enter the service of the Habsburg Monarchy. The 'Josephine' traditions of the Austrian Empire did not appeal to this deeply religious man. In Prussia he certainly found a group of other Christians, including many Protestants, who viewed the relationship between religion and politics much as he did. He felt at home in the conservative Protestant pietistical circles in Berlin where he became a close friend of the then Crown Prince, the later King Frederick William IV. The Cologne church conflict cast a shadow over the co-operation between the Catholic and the Protestant advocates of the Christian state, though Radowitz managed to keep up cordial relations with his Protestant friends without any undue spiritual concession. As Prussian military plenipotentiary to the Federal Assembly in Frankfurt Radowitz was deeply aware of the deficiencies of the German Confederation and on several occasions advocated reforms. He was at one time under the influence of Haller's theories on the Christian state based on the estates. But nothing could have been further from the truth than his widespread reputation as a bigoted Catholic and a political arch-conservative. Like Vincke he was a conservative, but not in the sense of standing still. He was too independent and cultured to fit into any neat category in this or any other period of his life.

By the beginning of 1848, nearly twenty-five years after entering Prussia as a stranger, General von Radowitz (as he had become), the trusted adviser of the King and a well-known writer, had certainly established himself in a leading position not only in the state of his adoption, but also in Germany generally. This must have exceeded any hopes and ambitions he might have had in 1823 when his fortunes were at a low ebb. His assimilation in Prussia, which is paralleled by that of many other leading men in the nineteenth century, including Baron Stein and von Hardenberg, was certainly rapid and far-reaching. But there were limits to this which are likely to have been due more to his Catholicism than to his birth outside Prussia or to his foreign descent. Radowitz yielded to none in his belief in Prussia's mission, but as a Catholic he could never feel fully at home in a state mainly adhering to another religion, in spite of his marriage to a Countess Voss, a member of one of the old Protestant families. He realised himself that for a number of reasons he could never be fully accepted. After the March revolution in 1848, Radowitz appreciated that he would have to make room for men with a more acceptable political past. At fifty he retired from the Prussian army. He would have liked a seat in the Prussian National Assembly, but this was not available. He was, however, elected to the German National Assembly by a Westphalian constituency. The electors, mainly Catholics, but some also conservative Protestants, knew him from his writings which they scrutinised carefully. They elected the orthodox Catholic, the political conservative and the friend of the King in preference to a less orthodox Catholic. This support from a Catholic majority and a Protestant minority suited Radowitz who had always felt close to the believing Protestant.[1]

Radowitz carried considerable weight in the Frankfurt Parliament, partly because of his close connection with Frederick William IV. But an air of mystery surrounded him and he never achieved the popularity of a Vincke, the other leading personality on the Right. The man with the fine facial features and the rather un-German appearance was respected, even feared, rather than loved.

Even among his co-religionists Radowitz encountered some reserve. Though Radowitz took his Catholicism very seriously, he was not prepared to devote himself entirely to the interests of his church and he also interpreted these far more widely and generously than many other members. With his subtle and refined mind Radowitz saw only too clearly the dangers inherent in the formation of a Catholic party. He feared that the gulf between the two denominations would be widened even further and that endless problems would be caused by basing a political party on a religious faith. Naturally Radowitz' firm line in refusing to allow the Catholic association to become a political party was not to the liking of all. One of his opponents in this question was Wilhelm von Ketteler, then a Catholic priest in Westphalia, later to become Bishop of Mainz and Bismarck's opponent in the *Kulturkampf*. Ketteler was like Diepenbrock a reluctant member of the Frankfurt Parliament. He had to be dragooned by his ecclesiastical superiors to stand. In an undated letter written from Frankfurt during the summer Ketteler reported to his brother:

---

[1] Meinecke, *Radowitz*, particularly 1–79; Treitschke, *Deutsche Geschichte*, particularly v 20 ff. in 1920 edition.

There is great excitement in our Catholic Club. Many are determined to convert it into a political party in order to gain more weight in the assembly. This could cause a great schism, as Radowitz would then resign without fail. I do not know what I should say about this, but I am more inclined for than against. Evidently Radowitz hinders us and ties us in the Prussian interest, and, however much I esteem and respect him, this is definitely of the greatest disadvantage. If the 'cleric' did not deter me, I would favour decidedly a political party of some Rhinelanders, Westphalians and Bavarians, for one can hardly stand our political indifferentism any more.[1]

From the Catholic point of view, the Frankfurt Parliament had to solve two – inter-connected – problems, in the first place to decide the extent of the proposed German state and then to settle the position of the churches in it. Logically the former had to be determined before the latter, though in fact the sequence was reversed in the parliamentary discussion. With reference to the major question, it was obviously in the Catholic interest to keep in as many co-religionists as possible. On the population figures, the Catholics could only achieve a majority with the inclusion of large parts of the Habsburg monarchy. In view of this, it is strange that Ketteler does not mention the Austrians at all. Indeed he seemed to have in mind the creation of a Prusso-Bavarian Catholic party, which would have been rather an uneasy partnership. Even from an exclusively Catholic point of view, Ketteler's prescription seems crude, as the association of members of his faith was not likely to be able to muster a parliamentary majority at Frankfurt.[2] Among Catholic members with reasonably orthodox views, Ketteler could not have counted on each one putting religion before everything else. Many Prussian Catholics, and not only Radowitz himself, would not have been keen on following out Catholic interests to the bitter end, for instance to the extent of helping to frustrate plans of Prussian hegemony. Not all Roman Catholics were prepared to look at the question of German unification primarily from the Catholic point of view.

The case for a Catholic political party was still less made out from the purely religious angle. As Radowitz saw it, there were certain common religious interests. In religious questions, the issue was not so much between Roman Catholics and others, as between Christians on the

---

[1] Pfülf, *Ketteler* I 158. The exact date of the letter is uncertain. See also *ADB* xv; *BSTH*.
[2] See above, p. 99.

one hand, and those who were non-religious or anti-religious or practised other religions (that is mainly the Jews) on the other. In purely Catholic concerns, in view of the balance of religious affiliations in the assembly, these were best achieved by co-operation with non-Catholics. In general, there was a strong pull towards party alignments based on common interests other than religion throughout the Frankfurt Parliament. The Catholics could not present a common political front, scattered as they were over all groupings, from Right to Extreme Left, even if the proportion of Catholics decreased in a leftward direction. As political and religious extremism often went hand-in-hand during this period, the wide spectrum of political ideology among the Catholics augured ill for religious unity. A representative like Dean Kuenzer from Constance who, if not actually excommunicated by his ecclesiastical superiors, was certainly not on good terms with them, could not be expected to co-operate with the bishops and orthodox laymen in the Catholic association, either in religion or in politics.[1] Even among Catholic members more orthodox in religion and more moderate in politics, there was hardly agreement on such questions as the position of the clergy and the powers of the Pope. This was inevitable in a time of re-interpretation which was bound to affect the religious sphere intensively.

Ketteler, who particularly during the last decade of his life following the Prusso-Austrian war of 1866 became one of the most determined leaders of the Catholic church in Germany, was at this period still handicapped by the impetuosity for which he was well known. Neither he nor those who came into contact with him were allowed to forget it, for they were reminded of his stormy youth by the missing tip of his nose, lost during a student duel as a member of the *Corps Westfalen*, one of the *Landsmannschaften*.[2] Ketteler's ideas developed in this letter about the Catholic association were half-baked and immature, but they are of interest as talking-points and show the opposition to the firm line advocated by Radowitz. It is not surprising that the better thought-out strategy proposed by Radowitz prevailed.

Radowitz may well have had another factor in mind. The core of a Catholic clerical party would have been members of the Right, or at least right-wing members of the Right Centre. This might have led to

[1] *ADB* xvii and Weech, *Badische Biographien* i 482–7, do not mention the excommunication of Kuenzer on 31 August 1848 which took place according to Pfülf, *Ketteler* i 159.

[2] See above, p. 11.

an identification of the political Right with the Catholic party and caused resignations of Protestants from the Right. Indeed, a Catholic party might have split the Right, a development very undesirable for Radowitz in his other role as chairman of the Right. Although both the Catholic association and the political Right for a period met at the *Steinernes Haus* and shared a leader, Radowitz could least afford to get the two organisations mixed up with each other.

As neither regional nor religious affiliations could form the main foundation of party alignment, the Right Centre and Right had to base themselves mainly on common attitudes to political ideology or to constitutional questions. The two groups could form either a united party or two separate parties. The pressure for a united party came from the Right. For nearly everybody in those days – even some on the Right – wanted to appear progressive. Therefore recruits from one's left were on the whole more attractive than those from one's right. The idea of a united party thus appealed far less to the Right Centre than to the Right. There was too much to be lost for the Right Centre by seeming to be reactionary. Potentially, the Right Centre could gain far more recruits from the Left Centre than from the small Right. It was not worth antagonising potential recruits from the Left Centre by including a handful of members from the Right. The efforts of some members of the Right to form a united party were therefore doomed to failure, though on certain occasions there was bound to be tactical co-operation to defeat the Left. Prince Lichnowsky and a Pomeranian representative, Alexander von Wartensleben,[1] were particularly active in trying to establish a large conservative party. But their names deterred rather than attracted.[2] The failure to create a united party cleared the way for the establishment of two separate groups.

Considerable difficulties had to be overcome before a Right Centre could be organised. No doubt many in the Right Centre would have liked to have seen the creation of a wider central grouping, but this had been forestalled by men like Raveaux. From the first the Right Centre aimed at becoming the dominant group in the assembly and at providing the major foundation for the support of a central German government. In view of these aims, the Right Centre was ready to sacrifice compact-

---

[1] Niebour, 'Die Abgeordneten Pommerns' 166–7; information from Deutsches Adelsarchiv, Marburg and from Bundesarchiv.

[2] Gerber, 'Briefe' 22, letter of 30 May 1848: 'Die Bildung eines konservativen Klubs will nicht gelingen. Überall drängen sich Wartensleben und Lichnowsky vorn an und von ihnen will man nichts wissen.'

F

ness and welcomed a certain breadth or range of views on the
assumption that no encouragement was given to ideas of starting a
second revolution or of trying to undo the first. The Right Centre
believed in a balance between the forces of revolution and reaction
such as the liberal 'March ministers' in states like Baden and
Wurtemberg were trying to maintain. The policy of the Right Centre
was the creation of a united Germany on the basis of constitutional
monarchy. The line of division with the two neighbouring groups was
not a sharp one. The Right allowed the princes a greater and the Left
Centre a smaller say in the drafting of the constitution than the Right
Centre. Movement backwards and forwards into the Right Centre and
out of it, particularly from and to the Left Centre, was quite frequent.

The Right Centre provided the majority of those who had voted for
Heinrich von Gagern as President of the assembly.[1] The core of the party
consisted of moderate liberals, mainly *Honoratioren* from various professions, particularly from the civil service, the law, commerce and the
universities. The Right Centre was made up not just of university
professors, but generally of leading men from many professions. They
were the pioneers who had the energy, common sense and ability to
put through innovations in their various walks of life which were due
or overdue, men like Mevissen who had taken a prominent part in the
building of railways, and scholars like Jacob Grimm, Dahlmann,
Johann Gustav Droysen and Georg Beseler who were applying new
scholastic techniques to their respective academic disciplines. They
were men who in politics wanted to develop and adapt what was already
existing, rather than to try and start on a completely new basis. They
were often those who had achieved great things in their professions,
who now wanted to try their hand at politics, some of them in the belief
that they would be equally successful. Others had already taken part in
government, as civil servants, like Adolf Lette who introduced new
economic and social ideas into agriculture. Except for those who found
sufficient scope for their talents within the framework of political
conditions before 1848, they were irritated and frustrated by the
inefficiency of the governmental system. In some ways this jarred as
much on them as restrictions on freedom of expression. The party was
in the nature of things attracted particularly by the English practice
of adapting existing institutions, rather than by the more radical
methods which had become associated in the public mind with France.

[1] See above, p. 106 ff.

Though many men of similar professional experience and even of not substantially different attitudes joined the Left Centre rather than the Right Centre, certainly greater weight was given to historical factors by the latter.

The Right Centre comprised all regions – even if representatives from Prussia were usually in a majority – and all the principal religions. This range gave it considerable weight, if at times weakening its coherence. Without the diversity of its membership, the Right Centre would have never achieved the numerical strength it did. What Stahl wrote at the beginning of the parliament, on 23 May, remained true throughout 1848:

> ... the moderate party ... has no consolidation. In the results we shall always come together, but we lack compactness, as always happens with a majority ... [1]

The main brains behind the creation of the Right Centre were the Protestant pastor from Brunswick, Karl Jürgens, and two leading business men from the Rhineland, Mevissen and Beckerath. From about 25 May, the formation of a *comité directeur* to spread the influence of the Right Centre in the assembly was discussed by them.[2] By the end of May, after many deliberations, the party was reasonably established, though it consisted of too many different elements to be able to commit itself publicly to a written programme. Eventually, by the end of June, the group moved to the headquarters by which it has become known, the *Casino*. Except for a handful of members on the Right and some independents, all those on the right of the Left Centre joined this party.

The Right was formed last. Radowitz was the founder and leader of this group which tried to avoid the term party. The club was formally constituted on 7 June in the *Steinernes Haus* which remained its headquarters until the re-formation of the Right in the autumn. Vincke did not join the *Steinernes Haus*.[3] Even though small, the Right had little coherence and was united only by common aversions and less by positive beliefs. The Prussian, Hanoverian and Bavarian particularists had little in common, one of the difficulties with which federalists and anti-centralist parties have always had to contend. The proportion of

[1] Gerber, 'Briefe' 15.
[2] Jürgens, *Zur Geschichte* I 115; Hansen, *Mevissen* II 379; Hübner, *Droysen* (Tagebuch) 808 ff., particularly entries for 22 and 29 May 1848.
[3] Jürgens, *Zur Geschichte* II 51.

Catholics, particularly those of 'clerical' views, was higher than in the other groups. But there were present equally the champions of Protestantism. The Right was a mainly Prussian, on the whole conservative, Christian grouping, which claimed for the states a say in the formation of a united Germany. One of its outstanding members was the lawyer Johann Hermann Detmold from Hanover, a close associate of the leading Hanoverian minister Stüve,[1] and like him determined to assert state rights against the National Assembly. Detmold wrote the satire *Thaten und Meinungen des Herrn Piepmeyer, Abgeordneten zur constituirenden National-Versammlung zu Frankfurt* (1848–9), which caricatured the popularity-seeking member who never ceased drifting in pursuit of an objective which always appeared on the horizon, but was only momentarily within his grasp. In spite of its small numbers, the Right commanded in Radowitz and Vincke some of the most effective speakers in the assembly.

Thus, by the middle of June, four of the five main groups of the assembly, which were to be maintained with fluctuating membership throughout the remainder of 1848, were in being. Only the Left had not yet fully split into two, a movement completed by the end of June with the secession of the extremist *Donnersberg*. Within the basic framework of five parties, there were, however, a number of intermediary groups.

vii. Standing orders

For its formal working the assembly now only needed permanent standing orders. The committee set up to report did its work promptly, basing its proposals on the Mohl draft.[2] There were some additions and deletions which generally tidied up the rules. When the debate on the committee's proposals began on 29 May,[3] it soon became clear that any attempt to discuss the draft clause by clause would be extremely time-consuming. In the end a motion was passed by a considerable majority which accepted the standing orders proposed by the committee *en bloc*,[4] but left it open to any fifty members to move the alteration of any particular clause whenever they wished.[5]

---

[1] Like Stüve, Detmold was unsympathetic to Catholicism. See Stüve, *Briefwechsel*.
[2] See above, p. 102 ff.   [3] I 163.   [4] I 163 ff.   [5] I 173 f.

Each member was to be allocated by lot to one of fifteen sections (*Abteilungen*) every four weeks.[1] Each section was to check the validity of the election of the members of another section.[2] Disputed elections were to be considered by a committee consisting of the chairmen of the fifteen sections (*Ausschuss für Prüfung der Legitimationen* or *Central-Wahlausschuss*). This committee was to report to the assembly which would take the final decision.[3] The chairman and other officers of the assembly were to be elected as soon as 350 members had been recognised.[4] The chairman (*Vorsitzender* or *Präsident*) and his two deputies (*Vice-präsidenten*) were to be elected by ballot every four weeks by an absolute majority of those taking part in the voting. The three chairmen were to be re-eligible.[5] The assembly was also to elect eight secretaries (*Schriftführer*, or *Sekretäre der Versammlung*).[6] In the light of recent experience, the position of the chairman was considerably strengthened in relation to visitors. He now received power to suspend sittings if order was disturbed, to expel individuals responsible and *in extremis* to have the galleries cleared.[7] Sittings were normally public, but could in certain cases be turned into secret sessions.[8] The assembly was to have a quorum of two hundred members.[9]

All subjects to be deliberated in the assembly were to be referred to the sections for preliminary discussion.[10] After due consideration of the subject and after ascertaining the opinion of its members by a vote, each section was to elect one of its number by absolute majority to the committee (*Ausschuss*) set up to report to the assembly.[11]

The position of the committees of the assembly was strictly regulated, as their importance was fully realised. The presence of half the – normally fifteen, but exceptionally more – members was to constitute a quorum. They were to elect a chairman (*Vorstand*), deputy chairman and secretary (*Schriftführer*) from their midst. Each member was to put the view of the majority and minority of his section (*Abteilung*) without, however, being bound in his own vote in committee by the opinions of those who had elected him. The results of the deliberations were to be reported to the assembly by a rapporteur (*Berichterstatter*) elected by a majority of the committee.[12] In view of the accidental composition of the sections, the assembly had power to allow them to elect representatives on committees from outside their number and

---

[1] *Entwurf einer Geschäfts-Ordnung* I 1. The following footnotes refer to the rules.
[2] I § 2.   [3] I § 5.   [4] I § 4.   [5] II § 10–11.   [6] II § 12.   [7] II § 14.
[8] II § 16–17.   [9] III § 18.   [10] IV § 19.   [11] IV § 20.   [12] IV § 21.

indeed to vary the whole manner of election by allowing each member
of a section to put down fifteen names for a committee.[1] This last
method amounted to election of committees by the whole assembly,
except that it was to be done in the sections to save time.

The clause to allow sections to elect to committees from outside their
number took into account the possibility that more than one expert in
a particular field might by chance belong to the same section. Any
exclusion of talent was liable to be all the more damaging in view of a
clause in the standing orders preventing committees from making
contact with governmental authorities or single persons unless specially
authorised to summon witnesses and experts, inside and outside
government.[2]

A minority of at least three on a committee was entitled to present a
minority report.[3] The reports or motions of a committee were to be
printed and to be in the hands of members of the assembly at least
twenty-four hours before a debate.[4]

All motions from the floor of the house were normally to be referred
to the relevant committee for consideration. Where no appropriate
committee existed, the motion had to be briefly explained, but failed
unless supported by at least twenty members.[5] If the motion survived
this hurdle, then the assembly could refer the matter to the sections for
preliminary discussion.[6] The debate in the assembly on a motion could
take place at the earliest twenty-four hours after the text had been
distributed to members.[7] Exceptions to this rule could only be made in
questions which concerned formal business or if the assembly considered the subject as a matter of grave urgency or as quite unimportant.[8] On the other hand amendments (*Verbesserungsanträge* or
Amendements) could be moved at any time during a debate. However,
the assembly was entitled to ask for investigation of an amendment and
to suspend the sitting until a report had been received.[9] The chairman
possessed the very considerable power of determining the agenda which
he had to announce at the end of one sitting for the next.[10] Similarly,
the president decided the order of questions to be put to the assembly
at the end of a debate.[11] Closure could be moved by twenty members.[12]

---

[1] IV § 22.   [2] IV § 24.   [3] IV § 25.   [4] IV § 26.   [5] V § 29.
[6] V § 30.   [7] V § 31.   [8] V § 32.   [9] V § 33.
[10] V § 34. The president of the assembly was assisted in the sifting of motions by members
and of petitions from outside by the *Ausschuss für die Priorität der Anträge und Petitionen*. I 67 ff.
[11] V § 40.   [12] V § 38.

Voting was normally by rising and remaining seated.[1] An insertion – obviously at the instigation of the Left – allowed for voting by name if moved by at least fifty members.[2] Deputations were not to be admitted to the assembly.[3]

No time was lost by the assembly in regularising itself. At the next sitting, on 31 May, more than five hundred members were formally recognised[4] and the regular presidium could now be elected. Heinrich von Gagern's election as chairman could be taken for granted, but his majority exceeded even the hopes of his followers. He polled 499 votes out of 518, thus receiving a well-deserved tribute from members for the fine leadership he had given the assembly during the difficult first ten days. He now resigned his premiership in Hesse-Darmstadt. Soiron, as the first deputy chairman, did somewhat worse than Gagern this time, but was still overwhelmingly elected by 408 votes out of 513. The well-known Austrian official and writer Victor von Andrian-Werburg,[5] who belonged to the Right Centre, was elected second vice-president by 310 votes out of 505. In this contest, Robert Blum of the Left received 116 votes and the Austrian army captain (the later field-marshal) Carl Möring,[6] who was not committed to a particular party but was sympathetic to the Left Centre, polled 66 votes.

The standing orders left open the whole question of the relationship of parliament with government. This was inevitable in view of the lack of agreement on the role of the assembly. For those brought up on the traditions of the British parliament, the absence from the assembly of the government – without which the British House of Commons is unthinkable – this state of affairs appears strange. If the Frankfurt Parliament restricted itself, as the Right and parts of the Right Centre wished, to the role of a constituent assembly, relations with the governments could be confined simply to discussion of the constitution. But the Left and parts of the Centre wanted the assembly to play a more active part, even in anticipation of the constitution. Now that the assembly had regularised itself, this question – which the Raveaux motion had touched but not solved – had to be settled.

A notable omission from the rules was any stipulation laying down that only members could speak in the assembly and that a seat in the chamber was incompatible with holding government office. Quite apart

[1] v § 41. [2] v § 42. [3] vi § 45. Thus far the references to the rules.
[4] i 184 ff. [5] *ADB* i; Andrian-Werburg, *Österreich*; *NDB*; *BSTH*.
[6] *ADB* xxii; Möring, *Sibyllinische Bücher*. See also Wigard i 433; Rössler and Franz, *Biographisches Wörterbuch* 592 f.

from the serving civil servants, judges, public prosecutors and army officers who sat in the Frankfurt Parliament, there were also ministers resident and 'men of public confidence' accredited to the Federal Assembly (*Bundesversammlung*), as well as ministers in state governments, who had been elected to the German National Assembly. Thus Schmerling as Austrian minister resident presided over the Federal Assembly and Welcker represented Baden there.[1] The ministers in state governments came mainly from the South-West, from Wurtemberg (Römer, Paul Pfizer), Nassau (Hergenhahn), Hesse-Darmstadt (Jaup),[2] but also from Prussia (Max von Schwerin-Putzar), Bavaria (Hermann von Beisler) and Saxe-Weimar (Wydenbrugk).[3]

At this stage, therefore, no decision was taken either in favour of any 'separation of powers' or of government mainly by parliamentarians. As the assembly did not have the focal point of a government and therefore of an opposition to the government, of the 'ins' and 'outs', the formation of parliamentary groupings as such was essential to the working of the assembly. Obviously it was quite impossible for all individuals to act simply on their own. This would have slowed down the work of parliament and increased the initial chaos. As the political groupings were quite unofficial, the absence of any reference to them in the rules was of little consequence. Certainly those who drafted standing orders accepted their formation as part of the parliamentary process.

The parliamentary committees (*Ausschüsse*) were held together by a common task, just as the political groupings were united by particular attitudes. This common bond was lacking in the sections (*Abteilungen*). They were useful at the beginning, for members to get to know each other and to make the checking of credentials more manageable. The election of parliamentary committees through the sections could certainly save time in the plenum. But even by the time the standing orders were drafted by the parliamentary committee, there was a realisation that this method of election might be harmful if two experts in a particular field happened to serve in the same section, or if one section – possibly for perfectly good reasons – barred the election to a committee of one of their members who might be considered suitable in wide circles of the assembly. The standing orders therefore allowed a

[1] Sylvester Jordan, another member of the Frankfurt Parliament, was the minister resident of the Electorate of Hesse at the seat of the Federal assembly. See *ADB* xiv; Wieber, *S. Jordan*; *ÖBL*; *BSTH*.

[2] *ADB* xiii.   [3] *ADB* xliv; Behrend-Rosenfeld, 'O. v. Wydenbrugk'.

variation of the normal method in some circumstances. Above all, if it was really intended to give the sections a part to play in the assembly, this was not encouraged by the reallocation of members to sections which was to take place every four weeks. For all these reasons, the sections remained an artificial creation and were gradually allowed to fall into disuse. The competition of political groupings and of parliamentary committees was too strong for them. Members simply did not have time to attend the sections in addition to the plenum and to these bodies. The decline of the sections left open the question of the relative influence of plenum, parliamentary committees and political groupings, which will be discussed with the progress of the work of the assembly.

Did the standing orders strike the correct balance between the ability of the majority to put through its programme and the right of the minority to criticise and to amend? Members could certainly not complain about lack of opportunities for raising issues. Indeed, if they all took advantage of this privilege, the assembly was bound to grind slowly to a standstill, for neither would the parliamentary committees be able to cope with all the work of preparation nor would the plenum ever have enough time to get through all its business. The rules encouraged collaboration by giving privileges to even small minorities, for instance on parliamentary committees. There was a modest requirement of support – on the part of twenty members – in case of motions for which there was no appropriate parliamentary committee. The question was far more whether it was not open to a minority to paralyse the work of the majority. On the whole, in so far as the matter could be settled by procedural rules, the balance was good, slightly tilted in favour of minorities, as was reasonable in an assembly of this kind, to prevent parliamentary tyranny.

It is known from the history of the English House of Commons what an important effect the shape of a meeting place can have on the development of parliamentary institutions. St Paul's Church (Paulskirche) at Frankfurt was chosen for the sittings of the German National Assembly because it had the greatest seating capacity. The church, which was completed in the 1830s, was quickly adapted for its new use and the president now sat where the altar had been. Pulpit and organ disappeared from view under flags and national emblems. The rostrum from which members addressed the house was erected below the table at which the presidents and secretaries sat. The floor of the church was so spacious that not only the five hundred or so members could be

F2

accommodated there in concentric semi-circles facing the presidium, but room was also found in close proximity to the members for diplomats and journalists, as well as visitors of both sexes. The arrangement had many advantages for the journalists who had an ease of access to members of the assembly which their successors to-day might envy. The benches of the members broke up into four parts divided by gangways, but as a surviving seating plan shows,[1] members did not necessarily choose the position in the chamber which corresponded to their ideology. According to the usual practice, all members of the Right should have sat on the president's right and all members of the Left on the president's left.

There was also a large public gallery, which seems to have been able to accommodate 1500 to 2000 spectators.[2] In principle, the opportunity given to comparatively large numbers of citizens to observe the proceedings in parliament (in addition to the more privileged ones down below) was to be welcomed. But as in the Pre-Parliament, the gallery disturbed the work of the house and caused constant trouble to the presidium. This was part of the atmosphere of 1848. It was difficult for an assembly which indirectly owed its birth to a revolution to forbid popular interference with its proceedings. The Left certainly did not want to curb the gallery, not only because it regarded the public as its ally, but also because it based itself on a doctrine of representation different from that of the Right Centre. Whereas the moderates regarded themselves as members of an elected assembly free to vote in the light of discussion and not as delegates, the Left demanded that members should obey the general will of the people. The vagueness of Rousseau's concept allowed the Left to set itself up as interpreter of this general will, but it was far more than simply a matter of furthering the aims of one's party. At other times the Left insisted that members should obey the instructions of their constituents. Any demands of the Left for the recall (*Abberufung*) of particular members who no longer pleased their constituents were firmly resisted by the moderates on the Burkean grounds that members were not delegates and that they had been elected for the duration of the parliament. Here again it was not simply a matter of self-interest. Naturally, all these moves were connected with a moderate political attitude of the parliament, against

---

[1] Bundesarchiv.

[2] G. Beseler, *Erlebtes* 59; Laube, *Das erste Parlament* I 38; Raumer, *Briefe* I 275 (letter of August 1848).

which vocal groups of radicals all over the country, who believed themselves sincerely to be much more strongly supported than they were, saw their only remedy in fresh elections in as many constituencies as possible. To the Left, their supporters in the gallery were a muchneeded and perfectly proper reminder to the assembly of feeling outside the chamber. For the moderates, these people had every right to hear, but none to be heard in the chamber, as has been the English custom. In the revolutionary assemblies in France after 1789, a less purist attitude was adopted to non-members. Though the situation was much worse in Berlin, there was some terrorisation of members by the gallery in Frankfurt. The other, less exceptionable, instrument of the Left to make representatives responsible to public opinion was the demand for voting by name. This swayed votes, according to some observers.

A less controversial defect of the Paulskirche from the point of view of parliamentary meetings was the absence of committee rooms. Members had to disperse for meetings of parliamentary committees and of their own political groups. They had to leave the building for refreshment, often not returning as quickly as they might. Much time was lost in this way and advantage could be taken of the dispersal of members to force a snap vote, as was occasionally done. The inns were not perhaps the best place for the meetings of parliamentary groups, and some members certainly made the most of the non-political attractions of the town in more senses than one. On the whole, however, members worked very hard. After hours in the plenum, possibly from 10 a.m. to 2 p.m., or even until 7 p.m., with a two-hour break in the early afternoon, assiduous members often continued until the late evening attending the meetings of parliamentary committees and of political groupings, sometimes going to more than one club to hear various views. As the clubs, in spite of a certain informality in some of them, often observed something like parliamentary procedure, members did not get much of a change once they had finished in the plenum.

The machinery of the assembly, both official and unofficial, was put to a test in June over the setting up of the Provisional Central Power.

5 Provisional Central Power and Vicar of the Empire

i. Slav Congress – Schleswig-Holstein

FROM the end of May, when the assembly had straightened out its organisational problems, it was able to give proper thought to the tasks for which it had been elected. Disagreement as to the exact functions of the parliament, which had been quite apparent in the debates on the motions put forward by Zitz and Raveaux, was bound to affect further proceedings. Many of the more moderate members of the assembly would have been quite happy if the assembly had confined itself to drawing up a constitution. But there was an increasing realisation that this was going to be a lengthy process. Ideology apart there arose the practical question whether the assembly could afford to disinterest itself in developments – both internal and external – in the meantime. The impetus given to events by the February and March revolutions had certainly not yet exhausted itself. However differently the various parliamentary groups might interpret such happenings as the May risings in Vienna or the military and diplomatic handling of the Schleswig-Holstein question by the Prussian government, they were agreed about their relevance to the constitutional issues with which the Frankfurt Parliament was faced.

The Habsburg Empire was particularly affected by events in 1848, because both constitutional and national problems – to some extent linked – became acute in that year. Matters were complicated by the fact that territorial and ethnic boundaries did not correspond within the Empire. At the end of May and during June the situation was certainly confused. The Kingdom of Hungary, which formed most of the Eastern part of the Monarchy and was inhabited by many other nationalities besides the Magyars, had achieved an increased measure of autonomy, and at times even continued Hungarian membership of the Habsburg Empire was in doubt.[1] In view of the many other urgent

[1] For the reception of Hungarian missionaries by the Frankfurt Parliament see below, p. 256.

problems which faced the Imperial family and the Austrian government, Hungary had to be left to its own devices for the time being. There were even more urgent and immediate matters, such as the rebellion of the Italian provinces and the war with Sardinia. The situation in Northern Italy looked gloomy for the Austrians until Radetzky captured Vicenza just before the middle of June, but victory was still a long way off. Not even the Austrian heartlands were at peace, because not only the nationalities, but also the political radicals – often in unison – made demands on the imperial authorities. The Vienna rising of 15 May was followed by the flight of the Emperor and the court to Innsbruck, the capital of the loyal Tirol, on the following day. The government under Pillersdorf was left behind in Vienna in an unenviable position, having been denied any advance information about the departure of the Austrian court. The ministers were powerless in face of the increasingly unrestrained elements in the city which carried out a further coup on 26 May. The departure of the court was a blow to Vienna, which benefited in influence and wealth from the presence of the imperial family. Vienna was easier to replace as a capital than Paris. There were many regional centres only too glad to provide a residence for the Emperor. The court was not so much at the mercy of the German and Viennese radicals as these had believed. Indeed, the citizens of the Austrian capital were unpleasantly reminded by the welcome given to the Emperor in Innsbruck that they were not politically representative of the Western part of the Monarchy or even of the German inhabitants. At the very time when Vienna radicals, mainly of German stock, put the monarchy under pressure, a Czech address of loyalty to the Habsburgs was received at Innsbruck. In the long run, the extremists in Vienna probably affected national even more than ideological issues, as they made the imperial family reappraise the reliance of the Monarchy on the Germans. With many of the Germans of Vienna in the radical camp, the Italians in open rebellion and the Magyars uncertain, the possibility of leaning more on the Slavs deserved serious consideration. All these matters had reached a delicate stage when the 'Slav Congress' began sitting in Prague on 2 June.[1]

An attempt by the Slavs to strengthen their position was quite natural at a time when the Germans were calling on Czechs, Slovenes and Poles to elect representatives to the Frankfurt Parliament and

---

[1] Springer, *Geschichte Österreichs* II 329 ff.; Kohn, *Pan-Slavism* 61 ff.; Namier, *1848: Revolution* 102 ff.; Münch, *Böhmische Tragödie* 190 ff.; Erickson, *Panslavism* 16 ff.

when the Magyars were asserting their authority over Slovaks, Croats and Serbs. There were, however, great difficulties in creating any kind of coherence among the Slavs scattered over the three empires. The nationality issue raised many hopes for the Slavs, but also some fears. The Poles wished to see the re-creation of a Polish state, but were reluctant to recognise the claims of other Slav races, like the Ruthenes, who had been their subjects. The differing historical experience of the various Slav peoples was bound to affect their attitudes to the European order and thus to help shape their ideological outlook. Whereas the Poles had been divided among three states, the Czechs remained together, even if the Kingdom of Bohemia became merged in the other dominions of the house of Habsburg. The Czechs, as those among the Slavs most exposed to German pressure in the spring and summer of 1848, welcomed support from their Slav brethren against the Germans. But most Czechs, certainly the moderate Palacky, did not want to become associated with the revolutionary plotting which had become almost second nature to the Poles in recent years. The Czechs were quite happy to work within the current political framework, which was an impossibility for the Poles. Most Czechs wished to avoid a clash with the authorities in Prague and Vienna. The local governor and the Austrian ministers could be, and often were, valuable allies. There was some community of interests between the Austrian authorities and the Czechs, for instance in their dislike of Austrian representation in the Frankfurt Parliament.

As they were to be hosts to the Slav Congress, the Czechs were for a time able to keep matters under some control. On 1 May the organisers of the congress issued a rather shrill summons to all Slavs to unite, incidentally protesting against elections to the Frankfurt Parliament being held in the Habsburg Empire. To reassure non-Slavs, the Czechs put out a manifesto on 5 May emphasising their loyalty to the Habsburg Empire. Certainly at no other time would the Austrian authorities have tolerated the publication of a political programme which – if it meant anything at all – was bound to call into question Austrian rule over Galicia. The cautious Czechs succeeded in formally confining full membership of the congress to subjects of the Habsburg Empire, but during the congress the dividing line between full participants and observers from outside the Monarchy soon became so thin as to be meaningless. Two pure insurrectionists, the Russian Bakunin and the Polish philosopher Libelt from Posen – a Prussian subject – dominated the conference. In spite of all his protests against the German National Assembly, Libelt[1] later replaced the theology professor Janiszewsky,[2] who also attended the congress, as member for a Posen constituency inhabited by Poles[3] in the Frankfurt Parliament.

After its formal opening on 2 June, the congress soon got bogged down over the official programme proposed by the organising committee. One of the main planks of the programme was the proposal for a Slav union within the Habsburg Empire, a vague concept not adequately explained. Libelt, who succeeded in obtaining the chairmanship of one of the three ethnic sections[4] into which the conference was divided, then suggested a manifesto to the European nations typical of the curious mixture of cosmopolitanism and nationalism based on the sovereignty of the people so fashionable in republican circles in 1848. After castigating the other races for depriving the Slavs of their liberty and demanding that the German governments should respect Slav rights and culture in Silesia, Posen, the Province of Prussia[5] and Lusatia (Lausitz), it called for a general European congress in the name of the liberty, equality and fraternity of European nations. Before the conference could adopt any further resolutions, it was brought to a sudden halt by the Prague rising of 12 June. While the congress provided the background to the rising with the excitement it generated, there is no evidence that the initiative for disturbances came from the participants. At the time, perhaps not unnaturally, a direct connection between the two events was often assumed, particularly in Germany. In fact, the moderate participants at least were horrified by the violent turn of events. Indeed, an abrupt end to their deliberations was about the last thing the organisers of the conference would have wished. What happened was that a comparatively small disturbance made by radical Czech university students, through clumsy or deliberate handling by the Commander-in-Chief, Prince Windischgrätz, became the prelude to the siege of the town by regular troops and to its reconquest. Thus Radetzky's victories over an enemy army coincided with Windischgrätz' defeat of a domestic rising. Three months after the Vienna March revolution which had overthrown Metternich, a weapon

---

[1] Niebour, 'Vertreter der Provinz Posen' 70 f.; Polish Archives.
[2] Niebour, 'Vertreter der Provinz Posen' 68 f.; Mollat, *Reden und Redner* 741; Polish Archives.
[3] Buck und Samter.
[4] The Polish-Ruthene section. The others were the Czechoslovak and Yugoslav sections.
[5] East Prussia and West Prussia.

seemed to have been forged at last for protecting the monaichy against
its external and internal enemies. The conflict in Prague was rightly
regarded by Windischgrätz as primarily ideological, between radical
youth and the upholders of law and order. It was not a racial struggle,
though many Germans elsewhere regarded it as such.

Many of these developments in the Habsburg Empire, particularly
the increased activity of the Slavs, caused concern at Frankfurt and
certainly played their part in strengthening the demand for a provisional
central power. Opinions varied in different parts of the assembly about
the merits and demerits of the Vienna risings of 15 and 26 May. Many
of the more moderate representatives in the assembly attributed a large
part of the blame for the troubles of the Habsburg Monarchy to sense-
less radicalism.

Similarly there could not be any agreement among the radicals and
moderates in the Frankfurt Parliament in their assessment of developments which were taking place in Prussia. For the radicals the disturbances in Berlin on 15 June, when the military arsenal (*Zeughaus*)
was stormed, was good news. In the eyes of the moderates at Frankfurt,
the lack of stability in Prussia, the state which might hold the key to
German unification, caused grave concern. It was not just a matter of
the help that Prussia might give in the future, for the brunt of the
Schleswig-Holstein war was actually borne by Prussian soldiers. As was
pointed out in the Mainz debate[1] it was an inconsistency in the radical
position that the Left did everything to weaken Prussia while relying
on the Hohenzollern monarchy to pull the Schleswig-Holstein chest-
nuts out of the fire.

Even among moderate members of the assembly not hostile to
Prussia, there was some criticism of the military and diplomatic con-
duct of the Schleswig-Holstein question[2] by the Prussian government.
More generally there was a feeling that this whole question was of such
considerable importance to Germany as a whole that it could not be
left to one state, even to one of the two largest. There was jubilation in
Frankfurt over the advance of the German troops – which were mainly
Prussian, with some Hanoverians and others – into Jutland, on 2 May,
thus entering Denmark proper. This was followed by anxiety when
Wrangel, the Prussian general in command, retreated into the Elbe

---

[1] See above, p. 121 ff.
[2] For a brief summary of the Schleswig-Holstein problem in 1848, see Eyck, *Prince Consort*.

Duchies on 25 May and even for a time abandoned North Schleswig to
Danish troops. Doubts about the determination of the Prussian government to pursue the war vigorously were reinforced by reports of armistice negotiations with the Danish government. These began seriously
in Malmö at the end of June with the help of the Swedish government
and fighting was virtually suspended pending the conclusion of an
armistice.

There were, on calm consideration, ample reasons, both internal and
external, for the desire of the Prussian government to end hostilities
with Denmark. Prussia could rightly feel that the rest of Germany was
not giving her enough support. The Danish blockade of the North Sea
and the Baltic was causing great economic harm to Northern Germany,
not least incidentally to the Elbe Duchies themselves, but there was no
agreement on counter-measures. A clamour now arose in Germany for
the creation of a fleet. The stream of donations, regularly recorded in
the parliamentary reports, testified to the real enthusiasm felt for the
cause. But a fleet could not be created from one day to another. From a
practical point of view the Prussian government could draw little
comfort from the agitation for a German navy. What was far more to
the point was the reluctance of other North German states to support
the war fully. Strong national support within Germany was all the more
important in view of the opposition of the Great Powers to German
designs against Denmark. The Prussian government risked estrange-
ment from two powers often in different camps, Russia and Britain.
There was a widespread feeling in the Frankfurt Parliament that
Prussia was not pulling her weight and that the assembly should
directly or indirectly play a more active part in the Schleswig-Holstein
question.[1]

Another aspect of Prussian policy was also watched very carefully at
Frankfurt. Under pressure from the German national movement, the
Prussian government had asked the Federal assembly to incorporate
part of the province of Posen in the German confederation.[2] This had
naturally been resented by the Polish inhabitants. There were constant
disturbances in the province and the Prussian government vacillated
between policies of conciliation and oppression. While the outcome of
the Schleswig-Holstein conflict was regarded by many Germans as the
crucial issue for their national movement, the attitude of the Germans

[1] For the events leading up to the Malmö armistice see below, p. 288 ff.
[2] See above, p. 50.

to the Poles was to be seen abroad as a test of German good faith to other nationalities.[1]

With all these internal and external strains, there were arguments for and against the assembly concentrating on the drawing up of the constitution. On the one hand, the National Assembly would be able to complete its one generally agreed task most quickly by confining its attention to it. On the other hand it was not easy for the Frankfurt Parliament to isolate itself from events at home and abroad. The merits of constitutional proposals in many cases depended on the outcome of developments – in the Habsburg Empire, in Prussia, in Schleswig-Holstein – which had not yet been concluded. At the very least the Frankfurt Parliament had to make an intelligent guess about these events. Some representatives went even further. They advocated that the assembly should not stand by idly while matters intimately affecting the future of Germany were being settled by others. Indeed, events moved so fast in 1848 that even within six months – and the constitution could hardly be ready more quickly at best – the situation might have changed sharply to the disadvantage of Germany and of the work of the assembly. Many representatives were of the opinion that the authority of government was so shaken that neither the states nor their organ, the Federal Assembly, were strong enough to cope with the many internal and external problems which faced them. Whereas the moderates wanted to strengthen government in order to root out anarchy and to prevent further attempts at revolution, some of the Left regarded the occasional erection of barricades as necessary in order to keep the princes and other 'reactionaries' in order. Yet Germany could not achieve any influence abroad unless its own internal problems were sorted out in one way or the other.

ii. Committee on the Central Power

From 23 May onwards a series of motions were tabled from nearly all quarters of the assembly asking for the establishment of some central authority. This prompted the committee dealing with the disposal of motions and petitions (*Ausschuss für Priorität und Petitionen*) to

---

[1] The changing attitude of sections of the Frankfurt Parliament to the Poles is analysed on p. 269 ff., below.

recommend to the assembly that the subject should be granted priority and that the relevant motion by Ludwig Simon should be considered first.[1] Simon had asked for the election of a committee of fifteen to examine all motions concerning the provisional establishment of a central power.[2]

Ludwig Simon, not to be confused with another prominent member of the parliament with the Christian name of Heinrich, had practised for nearly a decade as a lawyer in Trier. He was a native of the city which elected him to the National Assembly. He openly belonged to the Extreme Left, democratic, republican, possibly even anarchist. He was a ruthless exponent of the doctrine of popular sovereignty. On the Left, he was perhaps the only other great orator besides Blum, in the opinion of some even greater. Bamberger, who knew him well and liked him, remarked on his pleasing appearance, but criticised the shallowness of his knowledge and education. In the latter respect he was thus quite unrepresentative of the Left in the Frankfurt Parliament which could boast many men of the highest education among its leaders, parliamentarians who had arrived at their rather drastic ideas about necessary reforms of the political system as a result of wide erudition. If Bamberger is correct, Simon's rather simple political beliefs were based on dialectic rather than wide experience and knowledge.[3]

On 3 June Simon spoke to his motion.[4] While he gave his proposals a typically Leftist twist, in many ways he delivered the key-note speech for the lengthy debates that were to follow. Although his motion used the neutral term central power (*Centralgewalt*), in his speech Simon at once referred to the need to form an executive committee (*Vollziehungsausschuss*). The model was the special executive committee set up by the Paris Commune in 1792. The term which he used quite deliberately, though full of historical association, was in itself rather imprecise and added to the difficulties of debate. An executive committee could be more or less than a provisional government, such as some of the moderates had in mind. Simon based the need for a central authority first on internal reasons. 'We shall perhaps need the executive power against anarchy, but perhaps also against ... the old order, which does not know how to adapt itself to the new order.' In a speaker

[1] i 198 f.   [2] i 199.
[3] Bamberger, *Erinnerungen* 94 ff.; *ADB* xxxiv; Ludwig Simon's memoirs – rather disappointing for this period – *Aus dem Exil*, 2 vols., 1855; Lagbe, *Das erste Parlament* i 291 ff.
[4] i 199.

of the Extreme Left the earlier part of the sentence was remarkable, but it may have been merely a gesture. The second reason for the need to create a central power was the external position of Germany. He asked for 'strong action' (*kräftiges Handeln*) in relation to Italy, Poland, Bohemia and Moravia 'in the sense in which the good Tirolese have recently replied to the citizens of Prague.' Presumably this referred to the rejection of an appeal by a Bohemian delegate for common efforts to strengthen an independent Austria. The Tirolese told the Czechs that they regarded this suggestion simply as an attempt to sow dissension between the German tribes and that their own future lay with Germany. If the Czechs were not with Germany, then they would be regarded as the enemy of all the Germans, the Tirolese among them.[1] Simon also argued that the absence of a proper central German power weakened the country's war effort in Schleswig-Holstein. Stronger direction was needed to make the states honour their obligations to fill their troop quotas. Any separatist tendencies which showed themselves in Germany could be kept in check by a central authority. Indeed, any resistance to the will of the National Assembly could then be met with force and determination.

One senses how towards the end of his speech Simon found the restraints of moderation too much. The implied threat to the state governments was unlikely to find favour in many sections of the parliament. Quite intentionally, there was no mention of the Federal Assembly. The assumption on the Left was that it would have to go.

The short debate which followed showed that the need for some kind of a central power was widely accepted. Discussion revolved round the technical issue whether the matter should be investigated by a new or by an existing committee. As a speaker of the priority committee rightly pointed out, the Constitutional Committee[2] had enough to do with drawing up a constitution. Reference of this further problem to the committee would only delay both the drawing up of the constitution and the setting up of a central power. A clear majority of the assembly voted for the setting up of a special committee.[3]

12 out of the 15 members elected by the sections[4] belonged to the Centre – 8 were to belong to the *Casino* (Right Centre), 3 were aligned with the *Würtemberger Hof* (Left Centre) and one is difficult to place precisely; 2 were clearly on the Left and one on the Right. As the elections took place on 4 June when the Right Centre had not yet

---

[1] *Gegenwart* iv 99.   [2] See below, p. 206 ff.   [3] i 201.   [4] i 218.

properly constituted itself, the line of division within the Centre was not so precise as later and voting did not follow party allegiance so strictly. The Right Centre was probably over-represented, at the expense mainly of the Left Centre and remotely even of the Left.

The geographical representation on the committee was rather uneven. 5 of the members were elected for constituencies in Prussia, but only 2 came from Austria, a reflection of the smaller involvement of the Austrians in the issues at stake in Frankfurt. More serious was the poor representation of the medium states. There were 2 members from Bavaria, 2 from Saxony (both from the Left), but none from Hanover, Wurtemberg and Baden. The remaining 4 members of the committee came from the smaller states. The majority of the committee consisted of Protestants, but there were 4 Catholics.

The committee was a strong one and drew on wide administrative, judicial and academic experience. The outstanding member was Dahlmann, one of the Göttingen Seven,[1] a redoubtable constitutional expert who had already been mainly responsible for the abortive organisational proposals of the 'Seventeen Men of Public Confidence' for the future of Germany. Dahlmann was appointed *rapporteur*. As his patience was bound to have been strained by the failure of his previous plan, this choice was not an entirely happy one. The debate on the report of the committee[2] began on 19 June. The committee failed to reach agreement and no attempt was made to disguise the fundamental cleavage between those who wanted to innovate completely and those who wished to adapt existing institutions to current needs. The former were not deterred by the risks they were incurring in venturing out into the unknown. They regarded the foundations of the political and social order as so rotten that an entirely new basis had to be found. The Leftist minority on the committee consisted of two Saxon radicals, Robert Blum and Wilhelm von Trützschler, a judge from Dresden. Both men were gradually driven to more extreme courses, paying the supreme penalty for their daring. Blum and Trützschler looked on the National Assembly as the sole source of political power and therefore demanded an executive committee (*Vollziehungsausschuss*) appointed exclusively by parliament and bound to execute its decisions. These proposals quite deliberately ignored the rights of state governments and of the Federal Assembly. They would have established government by a committee of parliament, and in the opinion of the majority of the

[1] See above, p. 41.   [2] I 356 ff.

investigating committee the way to a republic would then have been
open. As the moderate members of the committee believed that most of
the population was attached to the monarchy, the recommendations of
the Left carried a grave risk of civil war and anarchy. In committee, the
proposals made by Blum and Trützschler were rejected by 13 votes to 2.

The majority on the committee found it easier to reject one solution
than to propose another. The committee examined ways of integrating
the Federal Assembly with a new and stronger central authority, but
came to the conclusion that the only methods of doing so, either by
removing all urgent business from the Federal Assembly or by allowing
the ministers resident to vote without instructions from their governments, would be reducing this body to a shadow of its former self. In
view of that, the committee did not find a place for the Federal Assembly
in its system. To the majority the only way out appeared to be to
establish a directory provisionally charged with the care of the general
safety of Germany, thus leaving to the state governments most of their
prerogatives. Bearing in mind Austro-Prussian rivalry and the existence
of the 'Third Germany', the committee rejected the more attractive
solution of a sole director in favour of three. The directors were to be
designated by the German governments and to be appointed by them
after the National Assembly had approved the names by a simple vote
without discussion. The directory in turn was to appoint ministers, who
were to be responsible to the National Assembly, and to settle matters
of peace and war, as well as treaties with foreign powers, in agreement
with parliament. The drafting of the constitution was to be excluded
from the functions of the directory, which would come to an end with
the adoption of a constitution. Nobody could be at the same time a
member of the directory and of the National Assembly.

These proposals were supported by 11 members of the committee.
They were rejected outright by the two Leftists. Lindenau (Left Centre)
proposed a mixed system under which a directory of seven would have
been appointed partly by the state governments and partly by the
National Assembly. The only right-winger on the committee, Flottwell,[1]
supported the majority proposals for the appointment of a directory
of three, but had some reservations about the other recommendations.

The majority of the committee had strong grounds for believing that
most of their fellow-citizens were attached to monarchical institutions.

[1] The senior Prussian official and former Minister of Finance. *ADB* viii; Laubert,
E. Flottwell; *BSTH*; *NDB*.

Some of the speakers on the Left denied during the debates which followed that the republican form of government was implicit in the minority recommendations. But the maintenance of monarchy along-side an all-powerful single chamber was unthinkable to monarchs and public opinion alike at the time. It is doubtful whether the denial made by the Left can be taken at its face value. Similarly the uncompromising centralism of the Left, based in the first instance on the prestige of the national parliament and on the support of public opinion, and *in extremis* on the force of revolution, was not a constructive solution to the intricate problems of Germany.

The moderates on the committee were quite right to take the states – at least the larger ones – and their governments very seriously and to try and discover a federal solution to the question within the framework of monarchy, which was bound to be an additional complication. For if the rulers of individual states were to continue to be more than mere rubber stamps for their elected chambers, a federal system would have to provide an organ reflecting the views of both rulers and state govern-ments. It was no coincidence that up to that time the federal system had been applied successfully only in republics like the United States of America and Switzerland. There was general agreement that a loose federation – such as the *Deutscher Bund*, which the princes had been able to join without too much difficulty – was no longer adequate and that the whole character of the Federal Assembly would, if retained, have to be changed to fit into the concept of one federal state.

iii. A triumvirate?

Certainly the adaptation of the Federal Assembly created problems. Members of the committee, even with the assistance of so shrewd an academic mind as Dahlmann, saw no way out except to abandon the Federal Assembly. They might with profit have taken the argument one stage further and asked themselves whether the difficulties over the Federal Assembly were not merely symptomatic of the underlying constitutional problems of the country for which no solution had yet been found. What was wrong with the Federal Assembly was not that the state delegates were originally only supposed to act on the instruc-tions of their governments. A liaison body of this kind could be very useful in certain respects. The defect lay primarily not in the institution, but in the attitude of the state governments. If there had been real unity of purpose, even with all the cumbrous machinery set up in 1815, any shortcomings could have been remedied. During the first weeks after the March revolutions, the Federal Assembly was able to function comparatively quickly and smoothly, because the state governments were too dazed to insist on their full rights, including that of instructing their delegates and delaying decisions until they had been consulted. All this was facilitated by the general and comparatively uniform nature of the first demands made following the overthrow of the old régimes. But this unity and uniformity ceased once the demands had been granted and put into practice. The concessions made to freedom and constitutional progress did not necessarily further the cause of unification. Particularism was strengthened and not weakened by the granting or extension of constitutions and by the establishment of constitutional ministers responsible to elected assemblies. The hostility which the Federal Assembly had incurred before 1848 deterred the moderates on the committee from evolving other methods for securing the co-operation of the state governments in the work of provisional central power. Under a federal system the very defect of the Federal Assembly – its close contact with the state governments – could be turned to advantage. The proposed central power was bound to need a liaison body with the states and to this function the Federal Assembly could have been easily adapted. The majority recommendations not only failed to deal effectively with this question of liaison with the state governments, but – by assuming that the Federal Assembly would be abolished – largely eliminated this body from discussion in connection with both provisional and permanent arrangements. A federal system required not only a federal government and a popular chamber but also some kind of a federal house or house of states (*Staatenhaus*). The abandonment of the Federal Assembly weakened the influence of the states. To the extent that the state governments were a bulwark against further radicalisation, the moderates on the committee thus played into the hands of the Left. Part of the answer for this may be due to representatives at Frankfurt, even if they did not belong to the Left, hardly being able to escape in some degree the general mood of belief in the omnipotence of the assembly. They thus, up to a point, unconsciously became converts to the doctrine of popular sovereignty. Helping to create this kind of atmosphere in the assembly was – from their point of view – perhaps the greatest achievement of the Left, all the more considerable in view of the numerical strength of the moderates.

Perhaps the conduct of Dahlmann and his colleagues also exposes a certain inconsistency in the liberal position. A hankering after centralisation and greater bureaucratic efficiency was difficult to harmonise with the professed wish of the moderates generally to maintain many of the existing states and to foster the principle of constitutional monarchy at federal and state level. These pulls in different directions were symptomatic of the more fundamental difficulty of reconciling liberty with efficiency.

Theory apart, the practical question was whether the Frankfurt Parliament could afford to do without the close co-operation of the governments. After the events of the spring it had become the fashion to believe that the state governments would always come into line. But since March there had been great changes. While in the spring the demand for liberty had been coupled with that for unity, practical progress had only been made with the former, not necessarily to the advantage of the latter. Thanks to constitutional development, the states were now more strongly entrenched than they had been for many years. The liberal leaders serving as ministers in state governments were often as enthusiastic for state rights as their colleagues in the Frankfurt Parliament were for those of the nation as a whole and of the assembly as its organ. This great new division can best be seen in the case of the four leading Rhenish liberals.

Mevissen and Beckerath – unlike Camphausen and Hansemann – served in Frankfurt. During 1848 Beckerath became increasingly convinced of the necessity of Prussian sacrifices on the altar of German unity. He certainly looked at political problems from the angle of German unity rather than of Prussian interests. If German unity demanded, Prussia had to be split up.[1] On the other hand Camphausen and Hansemann as ministers of the Prussian crown attached more importance to the survival of the Prussian state – as a constitutional monarchy – than to the achievement of German unity. The diverging paths of these two pairs of erstwhile collaborators illustrate the sensitivity to atmosphere – whether of a parliamentary assembly or of ministerial office – so typical of the educated German of 1848, which

---

[1] *ADB* ii; Oncken, *H. v. Beckerath*; Kopstadt, *H. v. Beckerath*; Siebourg, *H. v. Beckerath*; *BSTH*; *NDB*.

sprang from a particular interaction of classical and romantic ideals. Certainly these differing viewpoints proved damaging both to German unity and to constitutional development. The presence of several state ministers in the Frankfurt Parliament[1] only helped slightly to reconcile the interests of the assembly with those of the states.

If even liberal ministers like Camphausen and Hansemann in Prussia were reluctant in their striving for German unity and an old constitutionalist like Stüve in Hanover largely hostile, it was quite unrealistic to expect the rulers, above all those of the larger states, to be enthusiastic in this cause. The monarchs were not going to like any surrender of their powers to a central authority in Germany any more than to their own subjects. To an even greater extent than their liberal ministers they were opposed to what they regarded as the pretensions of the Frankfurt Parliament. The dislike of Frederick William IV of Prussia for the assembly was fed by every assertion of its omnipotence, and Gagern's substitution of the concept of 'the sovereignty of the nation' for the doctrine of 'the sovereignty of the people'[2] hardly helped. In view of all these circumstances the rebuff to the state governments which the majority recommendations constituted was politically unwise. The assembly could not afford to antagonise the governments if it wanted to achieve its ends by peaceful means.

No doubt the state governments also allowed their case to go by default. They were not united, jealous of each other, often mainly concerned to see what territorial gains they could get out of the troubles of the country. But they were also terrorised by the radical sections of public opinion which had been able to make some use of bodies like the Pre-Parliament and the Committee of Fifty. An earlier attempt sponsored by the minister resident of Hesse-Darmstadt at Frankfurt, von Lepel, to rescue something of the Federal Assembly was hastily disavowed by Heinrich von Gagern, Minister-President of the Grand-Duchy.[3] The rude treatment meted out to the Federal Assembly over its welcome to the Frankfurt Parliament[4] did not encourage the governments to make any proposals. As in the long run the assembly needed the governments rather than the other way round, their hesitation should not have made any difference.

Unlike the Left, the moderates, on the committee certainly did not want to affront the governments and it is a reflection on their political

[1] See above, p. 154.
[2] See above, p. 112.   [3] Valentin, *Geschichte* I 528 ff.   [4] See above, p. 104.

acumen that they did so all the same. It is true that they allowed them the right to appoint the directors. Though they tried to reduce interference with the sphere of the state governments to a minimum, they put all the state troops under the command of the directory, which would have deprived the states of what was perhaps their most highly prized possession. Handing over military command in these troubled times was tantamount to surrendering power. The pill was sweetened somewhat, but only slightly, by the attempt to have all the three parts of Germany represented. Though no names were mentioned in the report, rumours were current that the state governments had agreed on the choice of 'the three uncles', of the three princes who stood in this degree of family relationship respectively to the Austrian Emperor, the King of Prussia and the King of Bavaria – the Archduke John, Prince William (not the Prince of Prussia, who was a brother of Frederick William IV) and Prince Charles of Bavaria. Even then, some of the medium states were not going to be represented. There was also a doubt about the numbers of governors. Triumvirates did not have a very encouraging history, as was pointed out in the debate. In these circumstances, the states were only going to collaborate in the setting up of a provisional central power if they had no option. They were not going to like it.

iv. Parliament as the executive?

Debates on the setting up of a provisional central power, interspersed with other business, went on from 19 to 27 June. There was a multitude of motions and amendments, in many cases the signature of the same members appearing in two places, sometimes inconsistently. The list of representatives who put themselves down to speak grew at such an alarming rate that eventually the assembly had to try to limit numbers. This could only be done by political party organisation. The prolonged debate on the provisional central power, the first topic of prime importance with which the assembly had to deal, thus certainly hastened the trend towards the consolidation of parliamentary groups. In some ways the debate was the last before the establishment of stricter party organisation, but it was not the beginning of party tyranny and it did not – in spite of some observations to the contrary –

mark the end of the influence of the plenum. A considerable number
of representatives at any one time did not attach themselves firmly to
any grouping. Although there was ample discussion in the clubs, many
issues were so complex that members did not make up their minds until
they were about to vote following plenary debate. The parliamentary
groups were not straitjackets for the views of members. Decisions of the
parliamentary groups were not necessarily binding on members and
there was nothing like the British House of Commons system of whips.
Most of the groupings embraced a wide range of opinion. Finally, the
ideological division did not necessarily provide the key to the attitude of
members to all questions. Notably on religious questions there would
be quite a different alignment and on some matters regional loyalty
was decisive. In any case, in an assembly split into at least four or five
substantial groups nothing was ever a foregone conclusion before a
debate. During 1849, none of the three main groups – the Left, those
favouring Prussian hegemony and those opposing it – by itself had a
majority, which certainly heightened the suspense of the plenum. Right
through the life of the assembly, many vital divisions were so narrow
that they were unpredictable.

As only a handful of members was prepared to advocate the retention
of the Federal Assembly, the debate revolved round the kind of central
authority to be constituted, the method of appointment, and its
relationship with parliament and with the states. The Left denied the
state governments a say at any stage during the whole process, both
before the establishment of the provisional central power and after. The
new authority was to be a servant of parliament and to be obliged to
execute the resolutions (*Beschlüsse*) of the National Assembly. The
Left thus regarded the new central power, which it called *Vollziehungsausschuss*, simply as a committee of parliament, looking upon the
assembly as the real executive. The Right Centre wanted executive
powers to be handed over to the new authority, confining parliament to
control and legislative functions.

In putting forward their proposals, the Left made certain assumptions. Blum and Trützschler,[1] as well as other members of the
Left, presupposed that 'the people' was sufficiently powerful to force
the state governments into line if necessary. A contest with the old
powers was welcomed. On 20 June Trützschler claimed that it was
treason (*Hochverrat*) to deprive the people of its sovereignty as the

[1] *ADB* xxxviii.

majority report had recommended.[1] Along this line of argument any means were justified to make the state governments subservient to the will of the people. Such terms as lawful authority and mutiny were simply inverted in their meaning. The Left took it for granted that the people would act according to the ideas of the radical members of the Frankfurt Parliament, that the National Assembly would follow the lead of the Left in trying to force the state governments into line and that state legislatures and public opinion in the country at large would support the struggle against the state governments. These assumptions could be questioned. There were many doubts on the Left as to whether the National Assembly would play the part expected of it by the radicals. There were those on the Extreme Left, like the Düsseldorf lawyer Hugo Wesendonck, who were becoming increasingly disenchanted with the National Assembly and believed that the time for Blum's comparatively conciliatory tactics was past. Wesendonck therefore put forward a motion[2] taking the election of the executive committee (*Vollziehungsausschuss*) out of the hands of the assembly and putting it into those of the electorate. The assumption behind this scheme was that the country at large was more favourably inclined towards radicalism than the National Assembly. An executive committee of nine was to be elected by the people in nine different places from among members of the National Assembly. There is little evidence that unless the nine places had been very cleverly – and unrepresentatively – chosen, the results would have been any different from those for the assembly.

Wesendonck's motion is further evidence of a split on the Left. Though Blum may well at heart have been an extremist even at this stage, he was right in moderating his demands, for that was the only hope of enlisting the co-operation of the Left Centre and thus of securing a majority. These tactics were frustrated by Wesendonck's move, at least for the time being. For Blum this development must have been very galling, something like one month after the departure of Raveaux and his friends for the Left Centre. The end of any hope of creating a really large party of the Left was not made any easier for Blum by the suspicion – which to some extent was justified – that personal dislike of their leader played some part in this. Certainly Blum did not have the natural authority of a Radowitz, a Vincke, a Heinrich von Gagern or a Schmerling. That may have had something to

[1] I 415.   [2] I 359.

do with class, but also as much with the nature of political parties. The fact that all the four parliamentarians mentioned belonged to the nobility and that they were all drawn from the Right or the Right Centre is not entirely coincidence.

In spite of this weakening of Blum's position, he still retained some influence over his lost flock. The breach with those who moved towards the Left or the Right was not complete. Trützschler still collaborated with Blum during the committee and plenary proceedings in connection with the provisional central power, although he was to join the Extreme Left at the *Donnersberg* at the end of June.[1] In spite of the break-up, some co-operation between the two sections continued. Members of the *Deutscher Hof* were not necessarily more moderate than their neighbours in the *Donnersberg*. The distinction was perhaps mainly that the members of the *Donnersberg* had already travelled further on the road of disillusionment with the assembly and had nearly reached Hecker's position during the Pre-Parliament of regarding force as necessary for solving the problems of Germany.

Wesendonck withdrew his motion on 22 June as there was insufficient support for holding the election of a provisional central power outside the assembly, but that did not end the separatist efforts of the Extreme Left. The Saxon judge Julius von Dieskau,[2] an extremist, though he seems to have belonged to the *Deutscher Hof* for some time, even after the split, put down a motion as early as 25 May[3] which not only claimed the right of electing the new authority solely for the National Assembly, but also stated clearly that the proposed power was to take over the government of the whole of Germany. As Dieskau explained in the course of the debate on 22 June[4] the motion by Blum and Trützschler merely asked for an executive committee to carry out the resolutions of the National Assembly. Dieskau wanted to go further and to set up a government. In this sense, therefore, an executive committee (*Vollziehungsausschuss*) was less far-reaching than a government (*Regierung*). Dieskau moved that instead of the Federal Assembly the National Assembly was to elect from its midst a commission for the government of the whole of Germany. As he stated in his speech, he chose the term *Commission* in order to leave no doubt that the new authority was responsible to the National Assembly and had to carry

[1] According to Zimmermann, *Deutsche Revolution* 641, Trützschler had already lost confidence in Blum and was committed to secession by 27 May.

[2] Niebour, 'Plauener'; Deutsches Adelsarchiv, Marburg.

[3] Hassler, *Verhandlungen* v 63.   [4] I 456 f.

out the decrees of parliament. Dieskau thus succeeded in combining in his proposals the two aspects to which the Left attached the greatest importance – government elected and carried out by parliament, as well as the omnicompetence of the assembly. Dieskau's ideas were largely taken over in a motion by a number of members of the Extreme Left, including the Mainz representative Zitz and the philosopher Ruge.[1] In view of the more powerful support given to the latter, Dieskau's motion was dropped.

A substantial number of representatives connected with the Left Centre, including both the left and the right wing of the party, put down an amendment to the majority report.[2] In this Raveaux, the Stuttgart official Schoder and the later Reich Minister of Justice Robert Mohl (among others) largely accepted the argument of the Left that the new authority would have to carry out the resolutions (*Beschlüsse*) of the National Assembly, but restricted these to matters concerning the general safety and welfare of the German federal state. The motion, however, conceded to the governments the designation of the holder of the central power, a president. The Left Centre was not united on the question of the provisional central power, as is clear from the way signatures of members of the *Würtemberger Hof* were scattered over a number of motions.[3] Lindenau's proposals were not supported by the Left Centre, although they embodied the kind of compromise which it favoured and in spite of the fact that he not only belonged to their group but also was highly respected.

The Right Centre succeeded no more than the Left Centre in hammering out a policy on the subject. Those who were to join the Right Centre group which was formally constituted at the end of the month[4] gave their support to a wide range of motions from the Right to the Left Centre. As the moderates had not fully thought out their position on the series of intricate issues which were bound to be raised by the attempt to set up a central authority, they failed to oppose the demands of the Left with sufficient vigour. They had no agreed policy on the relationship between the centre and the governments. Indeed, the Right Centre may well have contained all shades of opinion from centralists to those whose ideal it was to preserve as much of a federation

[1] i 394.   [2] i 391 f.
[3] In a letter of 10 June the Hamburg lawyer Gabriel Riesser, who then belonged to the *Würtemberger Hof*, testified to the difficulty the Left Centre had in making up its mind on this question. See Isler, *G. Riessers Schriften* i 555.
[4] Eisenmann, *Parteyen* 13.

as possible, though the majority were probably advocates of the federal principle. There was more unity on the ideological aspects. But even here, in spite of widespread agreement for the principle of constitutional monarchy, there was more consensus on what was to be resisted than on what was to be achieved. As at this time the danger seemed to come mainly from the Left rather than from a 'reaction', its efforts were devoted to averting the establishment of a republic.

The majority proposals of the committee had the backing mainly of the Right Centre. But membership of the committee did not deter several of these representatives from supporting amendments to their recommendations. The views of many on the Right Centre were fluid during the first few weeks of the assembly. Dahlmann himself and some of his colleagues on the committee, like Max von Gagern, had travelled a long way since the end of May, when they had signed a motion asking the state governments to designate ministers for a central government through their delegates in the Federal Assembly.[1] While Dahlmann tried to hold fast at least to what he regarded as the essential recommendations of the committee, some of his co-signatories of the majority report were quite prepared to make further concessions to the Left. There was very little enthusiasm in the Right Centre for reviving the issue of whether the Federal Assembly should be retained. On the other hand there were doubts as to whether it was wise to give up any representation of the states altogether. One of the members of the committee, the Austrian army officer Franz von Mayern, as early as 21 June tabled an amendment which abandoned the triumvirate and instead asked for a *Reichsverweser* (Vicar of the Empire).[2]

v. The role of the states

It was the Right which was in the most serious disarray. On the committee Flottwell, who was admittedly its sole representative, had put up only a very tame resistance to the whittling down of the power of the state governments. Radowitz, who spoke on the first day of the debate,[3] abandoned the Federal Assembly without firing a shot. He said that he regretted the absence of a house of states (*Staatenhaus*), but quite saw that nothing could be done to fill the void until the

---

[1] Hassler, *Verhandlungen* v 17.   [2] Hassler, *Verhandlungen* v 148.   [3] i 375 f.

regular constitutional settlement. He thus discouraged plans to replace
the Federal Assembly during the transitional period. In these circumstances, however, he claimed it was all the more essential that the
governments should nominate the central power. If Radowitz thought
that this right would be more secure owing to the concessions he had
made, he was mistaken. He had given ground too early, thus restricting
his scope for manoeuvre and reducing his influence on this question.

There has been considerable speculation on the reasons for Radowitz' attitude. According to his great biographer Friedrich Meinecke,
he may well have been influenced by fears which the Prussian government had that it would be overruled in a Federal Assembly in which
delegates were not subject to instructions from their governments.[1]
This cannot be the whole explanation. It does not account for Radowitz' rejection of an alternative to the Federal Assembly. There is also
some danger of misjudging the situation by assuming that Prussia
really had *one* policy at this time. Ever since March a dichotomy had
existed between court and government. In addition, during June,
Prussia was in the throes of a cabinet crisis. Ludolph Camphausen, the
Prime Minister, finally resigned on 20 June after mounting tension
with the radical Prussian National Assembly. Radowitz and Vincke
received hints from Berlin during this period. But there was no person
who could throw the complete weight of the Prussian state into the
balance. Radowitz and Vincke may well have decided independently
of each other that the states were unlikely to agree on any effective
representation of their interests and that it was not worth fighting a
battle in parliament for this, as the governments would not in any case
take their cue from the assembly. Whether Radowitz represented his
master's voice or not, he was always believed to be the mouthpiece of
the King of Prussia and his words therefore carried added weight. In
view of his speech it was certainly widely believed that the Prussian
government was quite happy about the plan for a directory.

The extreme radical Wesendonck spoke[2] for the Blum–Trützschler
proposals, having decided that his own motion[3] was unlikely to get any
support. He made the valid point that the governments would, if their
past record was any guide, have difficulty in agreeing on the three
directors to be nominated by them.

---

[1] Meinecke, *Radowitz* 118; Jürgens, *Zur Geschichte* I 135 f.
[2] I 377 f.   [3] See above, p. 175.

Wesendonck was followed by a leading speaker of the Right Centre, Friedrich Bassermann.[1] Born in 1811 in Mannheim, Baden, as the son of a merchant, Bassermann studied history at Heidelberg and went into business in his native city, eventually setting up a successful firm of booksellers and publishers with his friend Karl Mathy. For a time the firm published the leading liberal national newspaper in Germany, *Deutsche Zeitung*. Bassermann entered the Baden state parliament in 1841 and soon became one of the most prominent members of the moderate opposition. On 12 February 1848 – well before the Paris revolution – he tabled a famous motion for the setting up of national German representation. He was Baden member and vice-chairman of the 'Seventeen Men of Public Confidence' attached to the German Federal Assembly, took part in the Pre-Parliament, but failed like Mathy to find a seat in his own state for the Frankfurt Parliament owing to the hostility of the radicals. Thanks to his nation-wide reputation this did not keep him out of the assembly, as he was elected by a constituency in the Franconian part of Bavaria. He became chairman of the Constitutional Committee of the assembly. Bassermann belonged to that group of liberals in the South-West of Germany which saw the only hope for the country under Prussian leadership. Like Mathy, he was a firm opponent of radicalism. Bassermann was one of the ablest members of the assembly and excelled in speaking and de-bating. Whenever the radicals appeared to be getting the upper hand, he was asked by the moderates to intervene. Bassermann was a highly sensitive person who entered the political arena with heart and soul, fully committing himself emotionally. He was indispensable to the Right Centre as he was, but may himself well have had to pay too dear a price for his political involvement.[2]

Bassermann at once carried the war into the enemy's camp. The proposals of the Left were impracticable, because they did not provide what was needed at the moment, a government able to act in a crisis, for instance an external one. Furthermore, the new authority could not be created without the co-operation of the states. Any attempt to impose the will of the assembly on the states could only lead to civil war. He warned against the dangers of radicalisation, for there might easily be a reaction on the part of public opinion. People might

---

[1] I 379 f.
[2] *ADB* II; Harnack, *Bassermann*; Bassermann, *Denkwürdigkeiten*; *NDB*; *BSTH*.

then prefer order without very much liberty to such liberty without order.

On the following day, 20 June, the mayor of a Pomeranian town in the Kingdom of Prussia, August Ernst Braun, spoke[1] to the amendment which he and two other members from his province also belonging to the Right Centre had tabled, that the provisional power should be entrusted to the Prussian crown. Braun's speech was interrupted by laughter. In this case the chairman was asked at once to test the support given to the amendment, which he did, with the shattering result that less than 20 members answered in the affirmative. The amendment therefore dropped. Undoubtedly many representatives, particularly from Prussia, wished the imperial crown to go to the Hohenzollern dynasty. But they did not regard the moment as propitious.

Welcker made an important contribution to the debate soon afterwards on the same day.[2] Karl Theodor Welcker was born in 1790 in Hesse as the son of a Lutheran pastor, studied law and became a university teacher. After short periods at the universities of Giessen, Kiel and Heidelberg, he received a chair at the Prussian university of Bonn in 1819, but was soon involved in accusations of conspiracy with the *Burschenschaft* against the state, together with Arndt, another professor at Bonn. Welcker was acquitted of the charges after a number of years and received a call to the university of Heidelberg in the Grand-Duchy of Baden, in which he now made his home. As a political theorist he helped to evolve the concept of the *Rechtsstaat*, the constitutional state based on law. He collaborated with Karl von Rotteck, the apostle of the older, more rationalist, liberalism, in the famous *Staatslexikon*, the voluminous political encyclopaedia which was the bible of the liberals in the middle decades of the century. He was elected to the Baden chamber in 1831 and in the following year was deprived of his university chair, thereafter devoting himself to writing and active political work. In March 1848 Welcker took part in the Pre-Parliament and became minister resident for Baden at the German Federal Assembly. Unlike Bassermann and Mathy, Welcker managed to obtain a seat for the Frankfurt Parliament in the Grand-Duchy as a moderate liberal. His duties as minister resident and later as plenipotentiary to the Provisional Central Power did not prevent Welcker from playing an active part in the work of the assembly, both in the plenum and in the Constitutional Committee. As is clear from Welcker's career, he was a man

[1] ɪ 397 f.   [2] ɪ 409 ff.

of great courage and he showed this again when he intervened during the debate on the provisional central power.

Welcker did not hesitate to defend the Federal Assembly, even going so far as to say that it had acquired some merits during the maligned period of reaction. He spoke of their country as being a partnership of prince and people.[1] Justice had to be done to the reality of the German situation which included princes and states. He therefore proposed an amendment to the majority recommendations:

> In connection with the executive measures (*Vollzugmassregeln*) the federal directory has as far as feasible (*so weit tunlich*) to come to an understanding with the plenipotentiaries of the individual state governments.

A speech of a different kind was made by Wilhelm Jordan on the following day, 21 June.[2] Wilhelm Jordan was born in 1819 in East Prussia, studied theology and philosophy, established himself as a writer in Leipzig in 1845, but was expelled in the following year for press offences. After that he worked as a teacher and journalist in Bremen, Paris and Berlin. He was elected to the Frankfurt Parliament by a Brandenburg constituency and began his activity in the assembly as an extreme radical. He took a particular interest in the establishment of a German navy, was elected secretary of the Naval Committee of the assembly (*Marineausschuss*) and at the end of 1848 became an official in the Reich department for the navy, even being retained until 1853, after the end of the Frankfurt Parliament.[3]

Wilhelm Jordan did not yield to anybody in the violence of his radicalism. He spoke without any restraint, trying to overawe rather than to persuade. A born orator, phrases came easily to him. 'The rule by the grace of God has come to an end through the power of the barricades.' Here Wigard, the editor of the short-hand reports, noted loud applause. A ghost (*ein Gespenst*) had dictated the majority recommendations: fear of the republic. This all started well for the Left, but Jordan already at this stage had some surprises in store for those there who counted on him. 'I, too, am of the opinion that the great majority of the German people does not want the republic.' Here the report records the exclamation 'Really?' (*So?*) on the Left. 'Cannot one openly, as I am doing, profess the principle of constitutional monarchy in the

---

[1] '*Das Vaterland sind Fürst und Volk ...*'   [2] i 426.   [3] *BSTH*; Bundesarchiv.

individual states if one wants to give the summit of the whole state a republican form?' (No! on the Right. Yes! in the Centre.) 'Certainly, one can.' Jordan proceeded to liken the directory to the Holy Trinity and condemned it as the manifestation of a one-sided party dogmatism. He then attacked those who had something good to say for the Federal Assembly. 'There are men who fly into passion because the present revolution claims not to be complete . . . , although the great moment in world history has already come when *they* have become ministers to the Federal Assembly!' (Unrest in the assembly.) As the remark was obviously personal, aimed particularly at Welcker, who had spoken on the previous day, the chairman, Heinrich von Gagern, called Jordan to order. This hardly made any impression on Jordan who replied that he was only thinking of a general category of people. Jordan concluded by claiming that the majority recommendations would only weaken Germany further and increase dissension. He prophesied that if the first German parliament failed in its task, there would eventually '. . . emerge . . . a man of force, who is perhaps already now somewhere in a barracks dreaming of future laurels, a man who will achieve unification by the power of the sword . . .' Though the report indicated applause at the end of the speech, many members of the Left must have felt uneasy about parts of the address. The radical tone was fine, but there was too much abandonment of what to the Left were articles of faith. The Left valued its idealism, its belief in the democratic feelings of the people, yet here was Jordan admitting that the majority of the German people was still loyal to the princes and forecasting not a democratic revolution, but some kind of a military coup if the assembly failed in its task. Jordan's realism was disturbing. He was to have even more unpleasant surprises in store for the Left.

Wilhelm Jordan was followed by a speaker of the Right, Flottwell,[1] who had served on the committee. Eduard Heinrich Flottwell was born at Insterburg in East Prussia in 1786 and entered the service of the Prussian state as a government official, heading the administration of several provinces as *Oberpräsident*, interspersed with a spell as Minister of Finance from 1844 to 1846. As *Oberpräsident* of the province of Posen in the decade following the Polish rising of 1830, he began a policy of Germanisation.

Flottwell withdrew most of the amendments he had tabled as a member of the committee. Instead, he came out strongly for the

[1] I 429 f.

preservation of at least some functions of the Federal Assembly. He supported Welcker's efforts to secure representation for the states, but went even further. Flottwell maintained that the complete dissolution of the Federal Assembly was inadmissible, as it was part of the whole settlement of 1815 regulating both the internal and external condition of the country.

A forceful and effective speech was soon after made by the Wurtemberg official Adolf Schoder[1] on behalf of the motion of the Left Centre.[2] With great skill and vigour Schoder applied tactics similar to those of his political collaborator Raveaux, though admixing rather more bellicosity to persuasiveness than the representative of Cologne. Schoder was trained as a lawyer and his speech was argued with the cogency of the advocate. There were plenty of references to the sovereignty of the people, but also appeals to the extremists to face reality and to preserve unity. The Left Centre rejected the proposals of Blum and Trützschler on the grounds that it was unrealistic to exclude the governments from a say in the appointment of the central power. But the states would have to be quick about making a nomination, otherwise they would forfeit their right to do so. Schoder insisted on the obligation of the central power to execute the resolutions of the assembly. He emphasised that his friends were quite happy about the sphere allotted to the central power, which was to be confined to matters concerning the general safety and welfare of the German federal state. He left it to his listeners to decide whether his motion meant that the central power would only be obliged to carry out those resolutions of the assembly which related to these matters. Schoder declared for a president, in preference to the directory proposed by the committee, to some extent because of the more democratic ring of the term, but also because a triumvirate could not provide real unity. He showed far more understanding for the position of the governments than the Left. He had a tender spot for those of the smaller states, including his own, Wurtemberg, which – though a medium state – was not likely to be able to appoint a triumvir. In his opinion, the triumvirate merely gave a privileged position to three governments. 'Has the committee considered what the smaller states are going to say to the directory?' Schoder concluded with an appeal to the Left on the one hand and to the Right Centre and the Right on the other to compromise. Rather incongruously after all this he exhorted the assembly

[1] *ADB* xxxii.   [2] i 436 ff.

not to shrink from a conflict with the governments. The states would have to do what the assembly agreed.

Vincke, who followed almost immediately,[1] agreed with Schoder in one respect, that the central power should be entrusted to one person. But there agreement between them ended. Vincke moved that a federal director should be appointed solely by the governments. He hinted that the governments were agreed on a nominee, the Archduke John. As he was believed to be in touch with the authorities in Berlin, this helped to sway many members when it came to taking a decision. Actually the governments were not of one accord and Vincke's references may have been misinterpreted.

vi. Gagern's intervention

Even on 22 June, the fourth day of the debate, the rate of speakers putting themselves down showed no sign of abating. At the same time, the number of motions and amendments was increasing. Considerable dissatisfaction with the lack of progress was felt in many quarters of the assembly. After some discussion, it was decided to test amendments for support and to limit to two each the number of speakers on the 9 motions which remained before parliament. The patience of the assembly was gradually running out and the repetition of argument putting a strain on attention. The billed speakers, too, often lacked freshness. Some of them had spoken before in the same debate. Of the speeches made under this arrangement the most notable was probably the last, that of Mathy on 24 June.[2] This politician from Baden had already, as we have seen, incurred the hostility of the Left by his arrest of one of Hecker's henchmen just before the April rising.[3] Mathy's defence of law and order was all the more galling to the radicals as they had at one time closely collaborated with him. Mathy had not always been a moderate. He was born in 1807 at Mannheim in the Grand-Duchy of Baden as the son of a former Roman Catholic clergyman. As a student in Heidelberg he belonged to the *Burschenschaft*. He became a civil servant in his home state in 1829, but at the same time engaged in journalistic activities in the radical interest and even attended the democrat Hambach festival of 1832. The government did

[1] i 439 ff.   [2] i 517 ff.   [3] See above, p. 55.

not like his outside activities, but tolerated them as long as there was a hope that they might be dropped. They did not want to lose the gifted young official. In the end he was asked to choose between his official and his unofficial career and opted for the latter. He was thereupon dismissed from the civil service in August 1832. The following year he helped participants in the unsuccessful Frankfurt Putsch (*Wachensturm*)[1] to escape from justice, and when this came to the notice of the authorities, he was himself arrested, but released after a month. The case against him was adjourned for further investigation and when he was warned that he might be arrested again he fled to Switzerland in 1835. There he worked as a translator on Mazzini's *Jeune Suisse*, was again detained in 1836, this time by the Swiss authorities, which were beginning to be seriously troubled by the activities of political refugees on the soil of the republic and were under pressure from other governments to control subversive activities. For Mathy this new detention was a much greater blow than his imprisonment in Baden, not only because he had in the meantime founded a family. He was fair enough to realise that he had infringed the law in Baden, but he had not done so in Switzerland, where he was careful not to get involved in Mazzini's extra-journalistic conspiratorial activities. His treatment in Baden had been correct and in many ways even generous. He had fought the authorities and had to be prepared for punishment. In Switzerland he was in a different position. He had sought refuge there. By arresting an innocent man the Swiss authorities violated the age-honoured usages of hospitality. The matter was aggravated by the cavalier treatment given to Mathy while a prisoner.

Since the Hambach festival in 1832, Mathy's views had undergone considerable change. Increasingly his sense of reality had corrected the idealism of his youth. He had been disgusted by some of the irresponsible and immature speeches he heard at Hambach and thoroughly disapproved of the Frankfurt *Putsch*, though prepared to help those involved in it to escape arrest. What he saw in Switzerland instead of strengthening weakened his republicanism, even before he was arrested. It became clear to him that republican authorities were not necessarily more tolerant or fair than the executive organs of a monarch. Gradually he began to wonder whether the evils of the political order in Germany could be ascribed primarily to the rulers, as he had at one time thought. Many matters now appeared to him in a different perspective. Though

---

[1] See above, p. 11.

he was released from imprisonment by the Swiss authorities after a
month thanks to the intervention of a friend, for a time he was still
under the threat of re-arrest and deportation. In spite of that he
managed to train as a schoolteacher and to qualify in this new profession, becoming schoolmaster in the small village of Grenchen in the
canton of Solothurn. Early in 1841 he returned to his homeland, where
he had in the meantime been acquitted *in absentia*. During the years of
absence his political views had notably become more moderate. He was
one of the few former political refugees in the Frankfurt Parliament
whose radicalism had not only been checked, but actually reversed by
his experiences abroad. Mathy had emerged from all his suffering, from
straitened circumstances, from the loss of some of his small children
through illness, with dignity and courage. His triumph over adversity
deepened his character and strengthened his personality. He was
quickly accepted at home, was elected to the Baden state parliament in
which he rose to the front rank of the moderate liberals, and became
Bassermann's partner as a bookseller and publisher in Mannheim. In
1847 their firm brought out the famous *Deutsche Zeitung*,[1] to which
Mathy also contributed articles. In 1848 he took part in the Heidelberg
assembly, the Pre-Parliament and the Committee of Fifty, before being
elected to the Frankfurt Parliament for a Wurtemberg constituency.
At the end of April 1848, three weeks after he had, as a private citizen,
arrested Fickler, he was appointed *Staatsrat* (literally state councillor,
roughly the equivalent of a secretary of state) and a member of the
Baden government.[2]

Mathy supported the amendment by von Mayern asking for the
appointment of a Vicar of the Empire by the German governments,
subject to the approval of the National Assembly. His main point was
that the Federal Assembly should be maintained until a permanent
solution for the problems of Germany had been found. He regarded a
body of this kind as quite indispensable for maintaining contact with
the governments. For the sake of speed and effectiveness, the Federal
Assembly could decide matters by a simple majority, without taking
up instructions from the governments.

Mathy did a great service to the assembly by raising the matter of
the Federal Assembly which had not had a proper hearing during the

---

[1] See above, p. 22.
[2] See particularly Gustav Freytag, *Karl Mathy* (1870), a wonderfully written biography by the leading German novelist who knew him well; L. Mathy, *K. Mathy*;
H. Treitschke, *Historische und politische Aufsätze*, 1886 ed., i 484–99; *ADB* xx; *BSTH*.

long debate. Whether his proposal to dispense with the taking up of instructions from the governments would have solved the problem is a difficult matter to judge. The decisions of the Federal Assembly were only going to be of practical consequence if supported by the governments. No Prussian minister resident in Frankfurt, even if well informed about the current political situation in Berlin, could be sure of casting his vote in accordance with the wishes of king and government. Indeed, the scheme embodied in Mathy's proposal may well have been the one of which the Prussian government was afraid and which discouraged the authorities in Berlin from taking any initiative to preserve the Federal Assembly.

With Mathy the debate from the floor should have been over, to be followed by an address from the *rapporteur*. But at this moment an unscheduled speaker mounted the rostrum, Heinrich von Gagern.[1] Some members had already noticed that on this day the vice-president, von Soiron, took the chair instead of the president. Others had heard from Gagern himself that he might wish to speak. The situation in which Gagern intervened, quite apart from his status in the assembly, was an extraordinary one. The assembly had decided to limit the number of speeches and procedurally there was not room for another. What was even more serious was the question of the admissibility of further motions. There had been acrimonious clashes on this. Certainly, whatever the exact technical position (about which there was some doubt), the assembly was liable to veto the bringing in of any further motions. The Left was determined to use this power to prevent second thoughts, for instance about the abolition of the Federal Assembly. It was therefore doubtful whether the assembly would be able to vote on any new motion put forward by Gagern.

When the president addressed the house from the speaker's rostrum, as an ordinary member, the sense of the assembly could not yet be fully judged, except for the preference of the majority for a single head of state. The clash between the Left and the moderates, with the Left Centre adopting an intermediate position, was still unresolved. The Left wanted an authority exclusively elected by and subservient to the assembly, the moderates a power nominated – at least in the first instance – by the governments, accountable to the assembly, but not its slave. In constitutional jargon, the question was partly whether the new authority would be directly responsible to parliament, or whether

[1] I 520 ff.

it should be 'irresponsible', with responsible ministers. The former conception, that of the Left, was fundamentally republican. Only the notion of constitutional responsibility confined to ministers would allow the appointment of a monarchical personage as provisional head of the new state. On this key question, the motion of the Left Centre was equivocal. The term president had a republican ring, but the only specific mention of responsibility related to the ministers appointed by him.

As was his wont, Gagern only slowly and gradually came to the heart of his speech. Unlike his political friend Mathy, he did not see how the Federal Assembly could possibly continue existing once the provisional central power had been established. The Federal Assembly had been the executive and legislature for the whole of Germany. The former function would be surrendered to the new authority, the latter was now in the hands of the National Assembly. But there was need for another body to represent the states. One of the first acts of the provisional central power would undoubtedly be to propose to the National Assembly the creation of such an organ. The provisional central power would have to act through the state governments and would require a liaison body. He did not see how the new authority could be committed to executing every resolution of the National Assembly. Gagern then moved on to the main proposal of his speech, the method for appointing the central power. From the point of view of principle, it could hardly be maintained that the governments had no say in this matter. But on practical grounds he dissented from the proposals of the committee and even from those of Schoder and the Left Centre. 'Gentlemen! I carry out a bold stroke and I say to you: we must create the provisional central power ourselves.'[1] (Long persistent impetuous acclamation.) That was the only way to proceed quickly. It might have been a different matter if the assembly had wished to appoint a triumvirate. But he agreed with the majority of the chamber who wished to entrust authority to one man, to a Vicar of the Empire, as he put it. The governments might have been able to agree on three directors, but hardly no one vicar. They would be spared considerable embarrassment if the assembly acted for them. The vicar would have to be taken from the highest sphere, he would have to be a prince (*ein Fürst*), not because, but although he was a prince. This

---

[1] '*Ich tue einen kühnen Griff... wir müssen die provisorische Centralgewalt selbst schaffen.*'

remark was greeted by 'a general repeated cry of bravo and clapping of the hands in the assembly and gallery.' He for his part could not share the bitter feelings which had been voiced about the princes. Love for other human beings was always nearer his heart than hatred. This was received with cheers by the Right, which in the terminology of the editor Wigard, who belonged to the Left, included the Right Centre. Gagern ended by appealing for unity.

Though no name was mentioned, Gagern made his proposals with a view to the appointment of the Archduke John as Vicar of the Empire. Indeed, at one time he had apparently considered asking for the Archduke to be elected at once by acclamation. Gagern had previously consulted individual members of the assembly,[1] but he only spoke for himself and not for any parliamentary group. Though clear in his mind about certain points before be began, he probably improvised parts of his speech. Many of his political friends in the Right Centre were taken aback by the unexpected turn the debate took with his address.[2] When Gagern descended from the rostrum the parliamentary situation was totally different from that of a few minutes before.

Some of the concessions Gagern made certainly pleased the Left, particularly his abandonment of the Federal Assembly and his dispensation with the co-operation of the governments in the appointment of the central power. On the other hand the substitution of one for three governors cleared the way for a monarchical solution and Gagern explicitly asked for the election of a prince as Vicar. This part of his programme was thus unpalatable for the Left, which still strove for a republican summit. The rest of his speech was overshadowed by these important points and hardly any attention was paid to his demand for representation of the state governments.

Gagern quite deliberately asked for concessions from all sides. He believed that the new power could only speak with authority if welcomed by the vast majority of the assembly and the sections of public opinion in the country represented by it. During the previous days of the debate he had been saddened by witnessing a spectacle of dissension which appeared to him unworthy of a people striving for nationhood. He regarded himself primarily not as leader of one section of the assembly but as the conscience of the parliament and indeed of the German

---

[1] For instance Detmold of the Right, who tried to dissuade him from this intention. See his letter to Stüve of 24 June in Stüve, *Briefwechsel* 50.

[2] E.g. Haym, *Deutsche Nationalversammlung* I 31 f.

people. Gagern was the only member of the chamber capable of playing this part. He carried some authority even with the Left. The moderates could hardly disavow him. Some of the Right Centre felt that he had taken advantage of them by combining in this manner the role of national leader above party with that of their political mentor. In this situation, the Left was much freer tactically than the Right Centre. The moderates were – on this view – hamstrung because Gagern was one of theirs.

The correctness of this reading depends on an assessment of the strength of the parties before Gagern's speech. Both sides saw themselves deprived of victory, but which had actually been winning? The situation in the assembly was still very confused, because the Right Centre was far less organised at this stage than all the other groups. Left and Left Centre knew on how many members they could count, the Right Centre did not. Two well-informed representatives came to different conclusions on the same day. Detmold, of the Right, wrote to the Hanoverian minister Stüve on 22 June that the majority report was sure of acceptance, though there would be a vicar – the Archduke John – instead of three directors.[1] On the other hand, the Wurtemberg representative Gustav Rümelin, at that time a member of the Left Centre, reported to the newspaper *Schwäbischer Merkur* on the same day[2] that the Left would on the whole be victorious in the issue of the provisional central power. He attributed this to the *Drang nach links*, the pressure towards the Left which was always predominant in the first period after a revolution. Whatever the actual balance in the chamber, there was certainly some truth in Rümelin's general observation. Leftist tendencies in the assembly were strengthened by the activists in the country. The question was whether the first post-revolutionary phase, so often followed by reaction, was coming to an end. In this connection developments in France, where a new Paris rising on 23 June was to be crushed by General Cavaignac during the following three days, were being closely followed at Frankfurt.

[1] Stüve, *Briefwechsel* 48. [2] Rümelin, *Aus der Paulskirche* 19.

vii. A Vicar of the Empire

Procedurally, Gagern's intervention came at an awkward moment. The debate had already been closed and further motions were difficult to table. Gagern's plan did not correspond closely to any motion already before the house, not even to that of the Left Centre, for he proposed a monarchical vicar instead of a possibly republican president. Also Gagern rejected the obligation on the provisional central power to execute all resolutions of the National Assembly, which would have fitted more into a republican form of government. On the other hand, Gagern went even further than the Left Centre in claiming the appoint- ment of the provisional central power solely for the National Assembly. He ingeniously combined elements of various motions. But this did not make the practical realisation of his proposals any easier, however much applause there might have been when he made his main suggestions.

Dahlmann, the *rapporteur* of the committee who followed immediately afterwards,[1] certainly did not see why he should accept Gagern's proposals. Indeed as spokesman for a body of people he could hardly do so without consulting his colleagues. The committee had met the previous evening to reconsider their report in the light of the debate and proposed certain modifications to their recommendations, in particular the substitution of a Vicar of the Empire for the three directors. According to Dahlmann, 9 out of the 15 members of the com- mittee were agreed on the amendments. With some justification, the Left challenged the way Dahlmann had suddenly sprung changes on the assembly without the printing of papers and due notice required by the rules of the house. How could anybody in fact be sure, without seeing something in writing, that the nine were agreed, as Dahlmann claimed? To raise this question is no reflection on Dahlmann's undoubted in- tegrity, but on the consistency of members at this time of constant change.

The next move on the parliamentary chessboard illustrated this difficulty of speaking for others. On 26 June, Schoder announced[2] the withdrawal of the Left Centre motion in favour of that of Blum and Trützschler. Almost at once 14 signatories of the Left Centre motion protested[3] against Schoder's statement and claimed that they had not authorised the withdrawal of the motion. This was the beginning of the

[1] i 522 ff.   [2] i 534 and 538.   [3] i 538.

break-up of the Left Centre. With one exception,[1] all the signatories of
the protest refused to follow the move of Schoder, Raveaux, Heinrich
Simon and other members of the *Würtemberger Hof* (Left Centre) to
the Left, which led them to form a club of their own at *Westendhall* in
July. Its nickname *die Linke im Frack* (the Left in a dress-coat) summed
up its position rather well. This distinguished but comparatively small
group of about three dozen members, of which a third came from Prussia,
tried to realise the broad aims of the Left without the fanaticism sometimes shown in attempting to achieve them. A typical representative of
Westendhall, the originally Catholic schoolteacher Theodor Paur[2] from
Prussian Silesia, a rationalist, was disgusted by the way some of the
Left exploited popular passion, for instance to overawe parliament.
For him one of the main purposes of the new club was to ensure the
dignity of deliberations in the Paulskirche.[3] Like several other members
of *Westendhall*, Paur was very critical of organised religion.

The most significant group among those who protested against
Schoder's withdrawal of the Left Centre motion included prominent
members of the Left Centre like the writer Biedermann from Leipzig,
the jurist Robert Mohl and the Hamburg lawyer Riesser, who were to
secede from the Left Centre in September after the Frankfurt disturbances and to form the club in the *Augsburger Hof* which collaborated with the Right Centre. Although the outcome of the vote in
the grand debate harmonised with the general aims of the Left Centre
in being a compromise, it was the last great victory for this group. The
seeds of decay were already visible.

Undeterred by the split in the Left Centre, Schoder and Blum aimed at
full victory. They were only encouraged by Gagern's concessions to aim at
the attainment of a maximum radical programme. Procedurally they were
in a strong position, as they could block the admission of any further
motions. They took full advantage of the disarray in the ranks of the Right
Centre after Gagern's speech and managed to prevent the tabling of
amendments introduced by the moderates to take account of Gagern's proposals. The chairman, the vice-president Soiron, did not have Gagern's
ability to handle the assembly. However, it must be admitted that many
of Soiron's procedural problems had been created by Gagern himself.

While the line to be followed by the Left was fairly clear, the Right

---

[1] The Kiel lawyer Hans Reimer Claussen, who was radical in both his German
nationalism and his general political views.

[2] See below, p. 235.

[3] See Paur, 'Briefe', for instance letters of 9 June and 12 August 1848 (9 f., 41).

Centre was deeply troubled. At an unofficial meeting held on the evening of 25 June, attended by nearly three hundred members,[1] apparently mainly moderates, the argument was used that Gagern, as president of the assembly, could not be disavowed. Dahlmann replied that the assembly was more important than the president and that everything ought to be done to maintain an understanding with the governments. Various possibilities were discussed of trying to harmonize the mode of election proposed by Gagern with some method of obtaining government approval. In view of the known determination of the Left to prevent further amendments from being moved, there was deep scepticism about the feasibility of any constructive action. The Left, believing that it had already had a foretaste of victory, did not see why the moderates should be allowed to escape from a dilemma into which they had been thrown by one of their number. After great acrimony, in which particularly the Hamburg lawyer Heckscher of the Right Centre figured prominently, the Left won the procedural battle. Only those points were included in the questions on which a vote was taken which had been raised before the closure of the debate on 22 June. The drafting of these questions for voting formed the last, long, hurdle of the protracted debate. On 27 June the assembly began a series of divisions.

It was not until the result of the first divisions was announced that the balance of opinion in the assembly became apparent. The historian must be grateful to the Left for often insisting on voting by name, for the division rolls provide an invaluable source for voting behaviour. At this time there was certainly much more consistency in voting among the Left and to a limited extent even among the Left Centre than among the Right Centre and the Right. The Right half of the house was thrown off balance and the greater degree of parliamentary group organisation in the Left Centre and the Left paid off. In the case of individuals, the voting record sometimes seems curious, but as there are mistakes in the division lists one can never be quite sure whether this is due to personal inconsistency or to the fallibility of the report. Still, there is enough evidence to show that members often found it very difficult to make up their minds, either because they had not found any general principles which they could apply to the issue in question, or because the particular problem was so complex. All these factors tend to emphasise the effect the plenum could have on voting and to discount the view that everything was settled beforehand.

[1] According to Haym, *Deutsche Nationalversammlung* i 31 f.

Total voting strength was around 550, though with absentees the house counted 587 members.[1] Vincke's amendment that the central power was to be set up on condition that the governments agreed (*vorbehaltlich des Einverständnisses mit den Regierungen*) was lost by 513 to 31 votes. The number of those who stood out for the rights of the state governments through thick and thin was thus about 30. These were made up of some members of the Right, like Vincke, Radowitz and the Hanoverian lawyer Detmold (the friend of the Hanoverian minister Stüve), a few Roman Catholics not attached to any grouping, like the bishop of Breslau, von Diepenbrock, and Döllinger, and a handful of members who were to join the Right Centre. The mass rejection of the amendment was certainly assisted by Gagern's speech. The minority might have been larger if allowed to remain anonymous.

The setting up of a provisional central power was accepted in principle by a large majority. So far the result was much as expected, but the next division was harder to predict. This was on a clause in the motion of the united Left (Zitz, Blum, Schoder, etc.) that the provisional central power was obliged to publish and execute the resolutions

TABLE 2

Motion by Zitz, Blum, Schoder etc.:

'*The Provisional Central Power has to publish and to execute the Resolutions of the National Assembly*'

	Yes*	No	Absent	Total	% (circa) All	% (circa) Parties only
Right	—	38	5	43	7	10
Right Centre†	20	126	10	156	27	37
Left Centre	100	16	5	121	21	29
Left	97	—	4	101	18	24
No party	41	101	13	155	27	—
Total:	258	281	37	576	100	100

* Figures based on *Parlaments-Kalender*. According to the official protocol (Hassler), 259 voted for and 285 against. The three sources for divisions, Wigard, Hassler and *Parlaments-Kalender*, often do not tally exactly. Hassler which gives only the bare figures for the ayes and the noes, though not always accurate, must be given preference as the official minutes.

† These figures include all belonging to or about to join the Right Centre which was formally constituted at the end of June and soon moved to the *Casino*, the inn by which it has become known.

[1] I 622.

of the national assembly. The clause was rejected by a narrow majority. As this division reveals the state of opinion in the assembly at the end of the debate better than any other, it is analysed in the table above.

The assembly accepted nearly unanimously the stipulation that the establishment of the constitution was to be excluded from the competence of the central power. The participation of the assembly in matters concerning peace and war and in ratifying treaties was agreed by 396 votes to 142. The noes included not only the Right but many of the Right Centre and even some further from the Left. The appointment of a president advocated by the Left was rejected by 355 votes to 170. The minority even included some of the Right Centre. A great majority voted for entrusting the provisional central power to a Vicar of the Empire (*Reichsverweser*). The principle that the Vicar should be elected by the National Assembly went through by 420 votes to 134. The minority consisted of the Right and of many of the Right Centre, including Dahlmann, Beckerath and Beseler. A considerable number of members who voted for election by the assembly issued a declaration that they did so trusting that the governments would agree.[1]

Great stir was caused by the proposal that the Vicar should (constitutionally) not be responsible. Biedermann asked Dahlmann as *rapporteur* of the committee for an explanation as to what exactly was involved in this matter, but Dahlmann – indignant about the way the work of the committee had been treated – brusquely refused. The clause was accepted by 373 votes to 175. Biedermann and his political friends in the Left Centre, like Riesser, voted against. After the result had been announced Riesser issued a declaration that he and his group had only voted against the motion because the committee refused to give any information. They had merely sought confirmation that the 'irresponsibility' of the Vicar only applied to acts of government, for which the counter-signature of a minister was necessary. They also believed that the Vicar was not constitutionally responsible for such acts.[2]

Only a small minority, in a vote by name, rejected the dissolution of the Federal Assembly on the establishment of the provisional central power. 510 voted for, 35 against. The result was similar to the first division. A clear majority agreed to the stipulation that the central power in so far as possible was to come to an understanding with the state governments with regard to executive measures. The whole law[3]

---

[1] I 602 ff.   [2] I 611, 642.   [3] I 621 f., 28 June; text also in Huber, *Dokumente* I 276 f.

was accepted by 450 votes to 100. The minority consisted mainly of the Left, who could not reconcile themselves to an irresponsible monarchical personage, but also of some of the Right, like Vincke, who considered that the rights of the governments had been violated.

viii. Election of Archduke John

The way was now clear for the election of the Vicar of the Empire and there was little doubt that the Archduke John would be elected by an overwhelming majority. After some discussion it was decided to have members voting individually by sections (*Abteilungen*) in alphabetical order. The Archduke John received 436 votes, Heinrich von Gagern (who did not agree to be a candidate and indeed supported the Archduke John) received 52 votes, Adam von Itzstein 32 and the Archduke Stephen, the 'Palatine' of Hungary, 1 vote. There were 25 abstentions and 33 absentees.[1] The Left voted for one of the defeated candidates or abstained. Heinrich von Gagern, who had resumed the chair, thereupon solemnly proclaimed the Archduke John of Austria as Vicar of the Empire over Germany.[2] Assembly and gallery – for once united – cheered three times. All the church bells in the town rang and guns were fired to mark the occasion. At this moment of great enthusiasm, the doubts even of many critics were stilled. A deputation was chosen to deliver the invitation of the assembly to the Archduke.

Not only had the assembly made its first major decision, but in the lengthy process of doing so had got to know itself much better. After the series of votes the Left had to realise that it could not sway the assembly unaided. On the other hand, the moderates could not be sure of a majority, unless they either organised themselves more effectively or made considerable inroads into the Left Centre. Both developments happened, the first at once, the second later. At the end of June, with the formation of the Right Centre and with the secession of the Extreme Left from the *Deutscher Hof* to their own headquarters in the *Donnersberg*, the strength of the parties was roughly:

---

[1] i 628 ff.   [2] i 638, 29 June.

TABLE 3

	Numbers	% (All)	% (Parties only)
Right (mainly in the *Steinernes Haus*, but many still without membership of parliamentary group)	43	7·5	10
Right Centre (in the *Hirschgraben*, but soon to move to the *Casino*, by which it became known)	156	27	37
Left Centre (*Würtemberger Hof*)	121	21	29
Main Left (*Deutscher Hof*)	55	9·5	13
Extreme Left (*Donnersberg*)	46	8	11
No party	155	27	—
Total:	576	100	100

The greatest difficulty in parliamentary management still lay in the large proportion of members not belonging to any grouping. This category consisted mainly of Catholics, particularly of church dignitaries, and of members who could not make up their minds and may well have favoured the kind of compromise the Left Centre advocated. Only a minority of the non-party members were close to the Left. The Catholics tended mainly to the Right Centre or to the Right.

Discounting the non-party members, the Right and Right Centre failed narrowly to command an overall majority. The key to the situation was held by the Left Centre which could swing power either to its right or to its left.

As members were not elected to parliament by clearly defined parties as we know them, only a very general indication of the election results could be given earlier.[1] The affiliation of most members to five groupings at the end of June for the first time allows the drawing of a political map of the country, though analysis of state parliaments would give different and generally more radical results. Certain generalisations can be made about parts of the country. In spite of the freedom of members to attach themselves to a parliamentary grouping of their choice, most representatives reflected, within fairly wide limits, opinion in their constituencies, not only – as one would expect – at the time of their election, but also later. They tried to keep in touch with their constituents, not simply contenting themselves with listening to their views, but also attempting to shape their opinions by correspondence, articles in the local press and as often as possible by meetings held in the constituency. These efforts to keep in step were

[1] See above, p. 84 ff.

not always successful, as the endeavours of some constituents to 'recall' their members and to hold fresh elections show, though the petitioners were not necessarily representative of their local fellow-citizens.

The following two tables indicate members' party affiliations under the state which they represented. The first lists members under 8 groups of states, the second under 20 headings to give a more detailed regional picture. See table 4A below, and table 4B on p. 200.

The proportion of members who did not belong to any parliamentary group was much higher among those from the Habsburg Empire than from the rest of Germany. The average percentage of non-party members throughout the assembly was 27 per cent of the total, but among representatives from the Habsburg Empire it was 55 per cent. The average percentage of non-party members in Germany apart from the Habsburg Empire was 20 per cent.

Discounting non-party members, there were considerable differences between the political complexion of the various states. In the *Habsburg Empire*, the Extreme Left was comparatively highly represented. In *Prussia* as a whole the Left did badly, with only 11 per cent (24 per cent).[1] The Left Centre was below average with 20 per cent (29 per cent). The Right Centre did particularly well with 53 per cent (37 per cent) and the Right comparatively well with 16 per cent (10 per cent). If Prussia is considered in three groups (see table 4B), the Left did best – though still badly – in the central area (Brandenburg, Pomerania, Silesia and Saxony) and worst in the Eastern territories (East and West

TABLE 4A

	Right	Right Centre	Left Centre	Main Left	Extreme Left	No Party	Total	% (circa)
Habsburg Empire	7	13	17	7	9	64	117	20
Prussia	25	85	33	6	12	39	200	35
Bavaria	7	15	20	6	4	17	69	12
Saxony (Kingdom)	—	1	2	12	7	2	24	4·3
Hanover	2	10	8	—	—	7	27	4·7
Baden	—	3	1	4	8	2	18	3·1
Wurtemberg	—	2	11	10	1	4	28	4·9
Small States	2	27	29	10	5	20	93	16
Total	43	156	121	55	46	155	576	100
Approx. % (all)	7·5	27	21	9·5	8	27	100	
Approx. % (parties only)	10	37	29	13	11	—	100	

[1] The percentages in brackets give the national average.

TABLE 4B

	Right	Right Centre	Left Centre	Main Left	Extreme Left	No Party	Total	% (circa)
A. Habsburg Empire								
i. Upper & Lower Austria, Tirol	4	9	7	4	2	29	55	9·6
ii. Styria, Carinthia, Carniola, Adriatic Littoral	3	1	2	1	3	18	28	4·9
iii. Bohemia, Moravia, Silesia	—	3	8	2	4	17	34	5·9
B. Prussia								
i. Brandenburg, Pomerania, Silesia, Saxony	14	44	16	5	8	16	103	18·0
ii. East & West Prussia, Posen	4	25	2	—	1	12	44	7·6
iii. Westphalia & Rhine Province	7	16	15	1	3	11	53	9·2
C. Bavaria								
i. Main part	7	15	19	—	1	17	59	10·2
ii. Rhine Palatinate	—	—	1	6	3	—	10	1·7
D. Other Medium States								
i. Saxony (Kingdom)	—	1	2	12	7	2	24	4·2
ii. Hanover	2	10	8	—	—	7	27	4·7
iii. Baden	—	3	1	4	8	2	18	3·1
iv. Wurtemberg	—	2	11	10	1	4	28	4·9
E. Small States								
i. Schleswig-Holstein & Lauenburg	—	5	4	—	—	2	11	1·9
ii. Hamburg, Bremen, Lübeck	2	2	—	—	—	1	5	0·9
iii. Mecklenburg	—	1	4	—	1	2	8	1·4
iv. Oldenburg, Brunswick, Lippe, Anhalt	—	7	2	1	—	4	14	2·5
v. Thuringian Territories*	—	3	6	3	1	1	14	2·5
vi. Hesse Region†	—	8	12	5	3	4	32	5·5
vii. Hohenzollern & Lichtenstein	—	—	—	1	—	2	3	0·5
viii. Luxemburg & Limburg	—	1	1	—	—	4	6	1·0
Total	43	156	121	55	46	155	576	100
Approx. % (all)	7·5	27	21	9·5	8	27	100	
Approx. % (parties only)	10	37	29	13	11	—	100	

* Saxon Duchies, Schwarzburg, Reuss.

† Cassel, Darmstadt, Nassau, Homburg, Waldeck, Frankfurt.

Prussia, Posen). The Left Centre exceeded its national average only in the West (Westphalia and Rhineland), did rather badly in the central area and dreadfully in the East. The Right Centre did brilliantly in the East, was well above the average in the central area and at the norm in the West, where the greatest concentration of Catholics lived. The Right did best in the West (owing to its Westphalian gains) and in the central area. Even in the East, where its performance was worst, the Right was still above its national average.

For *Bavaria*, the second table brings out the contrast between the main part of the state and the isolated Rhine Palatinate. The Rhine Palatinate was almost solidly Left, whereas in the main part of Bavaria the Left only secured one representative. The Left Centre was well above average, with 45 per cent (29 per cent), the Right Centre up to norm, and the Right well above with 17 per cent (10 per cent).

In *Saxony*, 87 per cent of the seats were in the hands of the Left, compared with the national average of 24 per cent. This left little room for the Left Centre which secured 9 per cent (29 per cent). The Right Centre was even more catastrophically defeated, with only 4·5 per cent (27 per cent). The Right was not represented at all.

Hanover did not count a single member of the Left among its number in the assembly. Both the Right Centre and the Left Centre did better than average and the Right was up to the norm.

In *Baden*, the Left did nearly as brilliantly as in Saxony, with 75 per cent of representation. The Right Centre secured half of its average strength, the Left Centre again did very badly in view of competition from the Left; the Right was absent.

In *Wurtemberg*, the Left and the Left Centre each secured 46 per cent of seats. The remainder, about 8 per cent, fell to the Right Centre. There was only one member of the Extreme Left, so that the vast majority of the seats were in the hands of the Left Centre in the *Würtemberger Hof* and of the Main Left in the *Deutscher Hof* led by Blum, with a slight advantage to the former.

The rest of the country, the smaller states, conform to the national average only in the case of the Main Left and of the Right Centre. The Left Centre was up from 29 per cent to 40 per cent; the Extreme Left with 7 per cent (11 per cent) and the Right with 2·7 per cent (10 per cent) considerably down.

The regional strength and weakness of each party is clear from reference to the tables, especially 4A. The Left relied particularly on its contingents from Saxony (19), Prussia (18), the Habsburg Empire (16), Baden (12), Wurtemberg (11), the Rhine Palatinate (9), the Hesse region (8) and the Thuringian territories (4). Comparative dependence on the smaller states was bound to have some influence on the policy of the Left. For those states which could not aspire to leadership, submission to the authority of a central organ was easier than for the large powers. The balance of regions in the parliamentary groups of the Left reinforced an existing tendency to centralism inherent in the doctrine of the Left and widened the gulf with the Prussian monarchy even further.

In the Left Centre, the representatives from Prussia (33) formed *absolutely* by far the largest group, but *relatively* to other parties the Left Centre did best in Wurtemberg, Bavaria and Hanover (in that order), that is in parts in which particularist feeling was very strong. The Left Centre had a good regional spread in all parts except those in which the Left was too strong a competitor, Baden and Saxony.

The Right Centre had relatively and therefore absolutely (because of the strength of Prussian representation) its best performance in Prussia. The 85 representatives from Prussia formed 55 per cent of all the members of the Right Centre. The Right Centre also did very well in Hanover, but badly in Baden, worse in Wurtemberg and worst in Saxony. Prussian predominance made the Right Centre the obvious base for launching Prussian hegemony.

The Right also drew the majority of its members from Prussian constituencies, an even higher proportion, 58 per cent. Relatively, the Right did slightly better in Bavaria than in Prussia. The only other strong contingent came from the Habsburg Empire. In the states in which the Left was predominant, such as Saxony, Baden and Wurtemberg, the Right was not represented at all. Apart from small numbers, the Right was weakened by a lack of coherence.

This was the state of the assembly which called on the Archduke John[1] to take on the office of Vicar of the Empire. For a variety of reasons wide sections found the Archduke John an attractive choice. He was a member of the revered Habsburg dynasty which had so long had in its possession the imperial crown of the Holy Roman Empire, but he was not associated with the Metternich régime. Indeed, the Archduke had often put forward liberal and national German ideas. He had been an opponent both of the Emperor Napoleon and of Metternich. His popularity was increased by his marriage to the daughter of a village postmaster. In May 1848, at the age of 66, he was appointed deputy in Vienna of his mentally feeble nephew the Emperor Ferdinand, making him virtually regent there. He was needed both in Austria and Germany, but when he received the invitation from the

---

[1] *ADB* xiv; Theiss, *Erzherzog Johann*; *BSTH.*

German National Assembly he accepted and arrived in Frankfurt on 11 July.

The Vicar's first official act in Frankfurt was a visit to the National Assembly where he was addressed by the president, Heinrich von Gagern, who welcomed him on behalf of the parliament, asked him to give the new task his undivided attention and promised him the full support of the assembly. The law on the setting up of the provisional central power was formally read to the Archduke who promised to act according to it and to take steps to be relieved of his duties in Austria.[1] Significantly, only the second call was made on the Federal Assembly which had already, on the day of his election as Vicar, encouraged him to take over the office. At this ceremony, the Austrian presidial delegate, von Schmerling, in the name of the German governments transferred the exercise of the constitutional duties of the Federal Assembly to the Provisional Central Power. The wording of the declaration[2] is capable of several interpretations. The continued existence of the German Confederation, as distinct from the Federal Assembly, may well have been reserved. Also, the eventual revival of the Federal Assembly may have been kept open. These matters concerned the future. For the present the Federal Assembly had ceased to exist.

Although the Federal Assembly played the game, this did not necessarily mean that the state governments were in practice prepared to do what the Central Power ordered. The decisive question was the attitude of the two Great Powers. The election of a Habsburg prince was a gesture even more to the ideas of the *Grossdeutsche*, that is to say of those who wanted the Danube Empire (or at least the German provinces) to be included in the new Germany, than to Austria itself. For the Austrians it was certainly better than the choice of a Prussian, but it was too much to expect them to be enthusiastic about it and in any case the difficulties inherent in the relationship of the Habsburg Empire with Germany were as great as ever. The Austrian court and government were certain to resist attempts by the German Central Power to treat the Austrian territories belonging to the German Confederation as subject to the authority at Frankfurt.

The Prussian king and government liked the Austrian Vicar even less. It is true that Frederick William IV had some hankering after the Holy Roman Empire with a Habsburg head, but an Austrian prince elected by a democratic assembly was a different proposition. An

[1] II 844.   [2] Huber, *Dokumente* I 277.

Austrian Vicar of the Empire was not incompatible with a future permanent Prussian Emperor as events were to show. But in the meantime the election of an Austrian was a sign of the low ebb to which the prestige of the Prussian state had sunk.

As the Vicar was an Austrian, it was all the more important to entrust key portfolios in the government to be appointed by the Archduke to Prussians of the first rank. But the attempt to secure Camphausen, who had just resigned as Prussian prime minister, failed. After his refusal, Camphausen was appointed Prussian plenipotentiary at Frankfurt. It proved impossible to find another Prussian of the same weight. A serving general, von Peucker, who did not belong to the National Assembly, was appointed Minister of War. Beckerath, one of the Rhenish liberals and *persona grata* with Frederick William IV, became Minister of Finance. The strongest personality in the new government was Schmerling, who took over the interior, a key function in the disturbed state of the country. The Hamburg lawyer Heckscher became Foreign Minister, another thorny post. Robert Mohl was appointed Minister of Justice and the Bremen merchant, Arnold Duckwitz,[1] who did not have a seat in the assembly, Minister of Trade. The first minister-president was Charles, Prince Leiningen, a half-brother of Queen Victoria. He had been advocating the assertion of the authority of the Reich government over the states.[2] Leiningen did not belong to the assembly. The under-secretaries included several prominent members of the parliament, among them Mathy and Bassermann from Baden, Max von Gagern from Nassau and the economist Fallati[3] from Wurtemberg. The parliamentarians were drawn exclusively from the Centre, rather more from the *Casino* (Right Centre) than from the *Würtemberger Hof* (Left Centre).

The government was only completed in August after the Vicar had returned to Frankfurt from a short visit to Austria to wind up his duties as deputy to the Emperor. In the meantime, the Minister of War, the Prussian general Peucker, on 16 July issued a decree to the ministers of war of the various states[4] which had a deep effect on the relations between the Central Power and the governments. Peucker had only accepted his new appointment on condition that he would not have to act against his king – his commander-in-chief – and that the

[1] *ADB* xlviii; Duckwitz, *Denkwürdigkeiten*; *BSTH.*
[2] Valentin, *Leiningen*; Eyck, *Prince Consort.*
[3] *ADB* vi; Klüpfel, 'Fallati'; *BSTH.*   [4] Huber, *Dokumente* i 278 f.

continued existence of the Prussian army was not in question. The letter did not go quite so far as to demand that the troops of the various states should swear an oath of loyalty to the Vicar, but it gave instructions that an attached declaration should be read to the military units and that they should give the Vicar a *vivat* as an expression of their homage (*Huldigung*). The letter also asked the ministers of war to communicate with General von Peucker about matters in the province of the Reich Minister of War and to instruct their troops to obey his direct orders in exceptional circumstances. The decree, which was virtually the first specific measure taken by the new Central Power in relation to the state governments, at once raised what was perhaps the most difficult problem pending between Frankfurt and the various capitals. Each ruler considered his army as within his personal prerogative and was likely to be supported in resistance to Frankfurt by his ministers whose continued existence in office and possibly even personal safety might depend on undiminished state control of the troops. It was the height of folly to issue this decree without taking steps to test the reaction of the state governments in less vital matters and to do so without the full co-operation of the Vicar.

It meant little that the smaller medium states and the small states carried out von Peucker's instructions. In Austria, only the troops in Vienna held a parade, but the Minister of War, von Latour, protested against Peucker's action to the Vicar, who dissociated himself from his minister. The Prussian king and government were determined to resist this interference to the uttermost. No parade was held either in Prussia or in Hanover. In Bavaria, the *vivat* to the Vicar of the Empire was combined with one for the King of Bavaria, thus leaving open the question who was commander-in-chief. Peucker could claim that he was only acting to apply a section of the law establishing the central power, which assumed for the new authority the supreme command of all the armed forces. But it was one thing for the Frankfurt Parliament to claim powers on paper and another to try and make them a reality.

Peucker's decree strained relations between Frankfurt and the major state governments right at the start. This tension was liable not only to limit the external effectiveness of the central power, but to weaken the prestige of the new authority abroad and thus to prejudice the chance of diplomatic recognition and of a say in such vital matters as the Schleswig-Holstein question.[1]

[1] See below, p. 288 ff.

6 Basic Rights

i. Constitutional Committee – Economic Committee

HOWEVER important the establishment of a provisional central power might have been, the prime task of the assembly was to draft a permanent constitution. On 24 May, a Constitutional Committee of thirty members had been elected by the sections to make recommendations to the plenum.[1] In view of the far-reaching effects of clauses of the constitution, the committee had to co-operate with other specialist committees, in particular with the Economic Committee, which was elected on the same day, also consisting of thirty members.[2]

Although both committees were elected by the sections, they differed in the balance of political opinion and personality. The Left was almost equally weak in both, counting five supporters in the Constitutional Committee and six in the Economic Committee. But the representation of the Left Centre on the Economic Committee was 8, double that on the Constitutional Committee. In the Constitutional Committee the orthodox Right Centre which met in the *Casino* had a majority, whereas on the Economic Committee it was merely the strongest group. The Right had 3 representatives on each.

The party political balance allowed the Right Centre to dominate the Constitutional Committee. Although on some of its sub-committees care was taken to have as many different views as possible represented, the three members who made the greatest impact on the work of the committee, Dahlmann, Georg Beseler and Droysen, all belonged to the *Casino*. Dahlmann's prominence can be easily understood. He was acknowledged as perhaps the greatest academic expert on constitutional theory in Germany and had played the leading part in drawing up the – admittedly abortive – proposals both of the Seventeen Men of Public Confidence and of the committee dealing with the central power.

---

[1] For their names see i 88. [2] For their names see i 88.

Like Dahlmann, Georg Beseler was qualified by his scholastic interests to give expert advice. Beseler was born in 1809 at Husum, in Schleswig, as a subject of the King of Denmark, studied law, but was not admitted as an advocate in Kiel because he refused to swear allegiance to the King. Political difficulties cut short his academic career in Kiel and he continued his studies at Göttingen, where Dahlmann – who had also in the meantime left Kiel after supporting the rights of the Duchies – was one of his teachers. After several other academic appointments, Beseler was called to a chair of law at the Prussian university of Greifswald in Pomerania. He was a leading authority on the history of law and in particular on the reception of Roman law in Germany. While he recognised the advantages of the spread of Roman law, he regretted that more had not been preserved of what he believed had constituted a Teutonic tradition of political freedom.[1] Like Dahlmann, he was an admirer of England. Whereas the older scholar, although he yielded to no one in his insistence on German rights, was mainly concerned to establish constitutional monarchy for which he had fought in Hanover, his disciple paid more attention to erecting the new state on typically German foundations.

Like Dahlmann and Georg Beseler, the third member of the trio on the Constitutional Committee, Droysen, was a North German Protestant, who also had strong connections with Schleswig-Holstein. Whereas the first two were the sons of officials, Johann Gustav Droysen was born in the vicarage, deeply imbued with religious belief. Unlike Dahlmann, who had been born as a Swedish subject, and Beseler, who was a Dane by birth, Droysen was a native Prussian. A year older than Georg Beseler, Droysen became an historian and specialised originally in the history of ancient Greece, interesting himself particularly in Alexander the Great. As was the case with other notable German scholars in this period, he was attracted to the study of antiquity by finding there many institutions which he missed in contemporary Germany, for instance a strong state organisation. Soon, however, he turned to more recent happenings and in 1846 published a history of the German wars of liberation from Napoleon.[2] In 1840 he was appointed to a chair of history in the university of Kiel. In the Elbe Duchies he took a prominent part in furthering the German cause. In 1848, the

---

[1] *ADB* xlvi; *NDB*; *BSTH*; G. Beseler, *Erlebtes*; H. v. Beseler, ' Aus Georg Beselers Briefen'.

[2] *Geschichte der Freiheitskriege*, 3 vols.

Provisional Government in Schleswig-Holstein sent him to Frankfurt to represent its interests with the Federal Assembly and he became one of the Seventeen Men of Public Confidence. He was elected to the National Assembly by a Schleswig-Holstein constituency.[1] While Dahlmann and Beseler appeared in the plenum as *rapporteurs*, Droysen never spoke in the assembly[2] and thus the gallery remained largely in ignorance of one of the most influential members of the Frankfurt Parliament. As secretary of the Constitutional Committee Droysen kept a record of the proceedings, the first part of which he published in 1849.[3] Droysen's political philosophy in 1848 is not easy to summarise, as it was an amalgam of many different forces. He was much more sceptical about the validity and relevance of historical rights than Dahlmann and Beseler, though he was not above having recourse to them in the question of the Elbe Duchies. There was a dynamism in his political outlook which was reminiscent of some of the Prussian leaders in the anti-Napoleonic struggle to whom he erected a monument in his works. A combination of religious faith and of a belief that he could project an almost inevitable future from an analysis of the past gave him a certain moral fervour which made him intolerant of those whom he regarded as being in error. He believed that Prussia was pre-destined to take over hegemony in Germany. While he expected resist-ance from the other powers he was surprised about the degree of resistance to these plans which came from Prussia itself. Droysen's career illustrates the difficulty of combining an active political life with the detachment of the historian. Curiously enough, Droysen's greatest miscalculations in 1848 – for instance in underestimating the deep-rooted particularism of the Prussian state – were due to a neglect of history. German historians at that time who felt so strongly as Droysen about the future of their country could hardly help subordinating their historical studies to some extent to their political plans.

Other representatives of the Right Centre (*Casino*) on the Consti-tutional Committee included Welcker, who was, however, absent for

---

[1] *ADB* xlviii; *NDB*; *BSTH*; Hübner, *Droysen, Briefwechsel*; 'Das Frankfurter Tagebuch Droysens', in Hübner, *Droysen*; Gilbert, *Droysen*; Hock, *Liberales Denken*.

[2] This may have been due to a certain detachment (see also Gilbert, *Droysen*, 91). Mevissen was another important member who never spoke in the plenum, partly because his voice could not cope with the poor acoustics of the Paulskirche (see Hansen, *Mevissen* I 554).

[3] Droysen, *Verhandlungen*, Erster Teil. The second part was published under the editorship of Rudolf Hübner and is cited as Hübner, *Droysen*.

some time on various missions; Bassermann, the chairman of the committee; Max von Gagern; the Protestant pastor from Brunswick, Jürgens,[1] who was one of the main organisers of the party; Soiron; and Lichnowsky, who was close to the Right.

The Right had its usual heterogeneous representation. On the one hand there was the philosopher Ernst von Lasaulx[2] whose uncompromising Catholicism had involved him in clashes with the Prussian and Bavarian governments. He sat side by side with the Hanoverian lawyer Detmold, the satirist of the assembly, who was a pronounced anti-Catholic. There was also the lawyer Eugen Megerle von Mühlfeld[3] from Vienna.

Two eminent jurists, Mittermaier (the chairman of the Pre-Parliament) and Robert Mohl, were among those on the committee who belonged to the Left Centre. Heinrich Simon, a radical opponent of the Prussian government before 1848, and Heinrich Ahrens,[4] who had held a chair of philosophy at Brussels after fleeing from Germany in 1831, represented *Westendhall*, the most moderate part of the Left. Robert Blum and Wigard, the editor of the short-hand reports of the assembly, incidentally both *Deutschkatholiken*, belonged to the *Deutscher Hof* (Main Left).[5]

Professionally, the emphasis in the Constitutional Committee was on scholarship and administrative experience. The most prominent group in the Economic Committee was that of the merchants. Among these was Eisenstuck[6] from Chemnitz in Saxony, who belonged to the Left, perhaps the dominant personality on the committee, at first its secretary, and later its chairman; Karl von Bruck,[7] of the Right, the director of the Austrian Lloyd in Trieste, soon to take up a ministerial appointment in Austria; Ernst Merck,[8] of the Right, from Hamburg; Karl Theodor Gevekoth[9] of the Right Centre, who pioneered the first direct steamer service from Germany to the United States of America, from

---

[1] *ADB* xiv; Karl Jürgens, *Zur Geschichte*; *BSTH*.

[2] Some of Lasaulx's works were later put on the papal index. See *ADB* xvii; Stölzle, *Lasaulx*; *BSTH*.

[3] Wurzbach xvii and xix; *BSTH*.   [4] *ADB* xlv; *NDB*; *BSTH*.

[5] A number of new members joined the Constitutional Committee on 7 September 1848 following the resignation of Bassermann, Mohl and others on their appointment to the Reich government.

[6] *ADB* v; H. Schneider, *Das Leben und Wirken J. B. Eisenstucks* (Leipzig dissertation, 1923).

[7] *ADB* iii; Charmatz, *v. Bruck*; *NDB*; *BSTH*.

[8] *ADB* xxi; *BSTH*.   [9] *ADB* ix; *NDB*.

Bremen; and Gustav Mevissen, of the Right Centre, one of the Rhenish liberals of the Prussian United Diet of 1847. Apart from Eisenstuck, all these men had been in charge of enterprises of some size. Others who made a mark in the committee included the chairman Friedrich Ludwig von Rönne,[1] of the Left Centre, who had served as Prussian minister in the United States of America, and as head of the newly created Prussian department of trade (*Handelsamt*); the Wurtemberg economist Fallati of the Left Centre; the Munich economist and official Friedrich von Hermann of the Left Centre; the Marburg economist Bruno Hildebrand[2] of the Moderate Left (*Westendhall*); Robert Mohl's left-wing brother Moritz,[3] a Wurtemberg economist and official; and Karl Mathy – to name only a few. In diversity of talent the Economic Committee was probably superior to the Constitutional Committee. Sub-committees investigated various subjects, such as labour questions and banking.

There was a certain amount of rivalry between the two committees, mainly due to a different approach and in the case of the Economic Committee possibly caused by resentment against a certain position of inferiority. No committee could touch the importance of the one which drafted the constitution. The Economic Committee had to be content with making comments on the proposals, with playing second fiddle. It had to follow suit. The Constitutional Committee proposed the order in which matters were to be handled. Thus at its second sitting on 26 May, the Constitutional Committee decided to compile a draft of the basic rights of every German, before discussing constitutional organisation. Previous constitutional proposals, such as those of the Seventeen Men of Confidence, had included sections of this kind. Droysen noted that the agitation of public opinion, which appeared to be concerned equally with freedom and unity, made this matter a very pressing one. Another advantage seemed to be that such a statement of rights appeared to be feasible almost outside the organic construction of the constitution.[4] A sub-committee consisting of Dahlmann, Robert Mohl and Megerle von Mühlfeld was entrusted with preparing a draft. At the fifth meeting of the Constitutional Committee on 1 June this draft was ready, but was rejected as being too abstract. The committee wanted to have a more concrete and popular formulation. As Droysen

[1] v. Rönne, *F. v. Rönne*; *ADB* xxix; *BSTH*.
[2] *ADB* xxii; *BSTH*; Bovensiepen, 'Bruno Hildebrand'.
[3] *ADB* lii; *BSTH*.   [4] Droysen, *Verhandlungen* i 2 f.

noted, with this arrangement the committee had made a fundamental alteration in the plans, though the matter of principle was little discussed. This decision of 1 June made the priority earlier given to basic rights even more fateful. The sub-committee could still hope at the end of May that their general statement would be passed quickly by the assembly, allowing it to concentrate on the substance of the constitution. After the committee meeting of 1 June it was inevitable that discussion of the basic rights would be prolonged, for the longer and the more detailed the draft, the longer and the more detailed debate in the assembly was bound to be. Compilation of the new draft took nearly three weeks and it was only on 3 July that the assembly was able to begin its debate on the draft.

Georg Beseler, as *rapporteur*, explained that the Constitutional Committee had been faced with the alternative of either beginning its deliberations by considering the superstructure – such as the head of state, the relationship between the centre and the state governments – or by starting with the lower levels of public life, i.e. those which affected everybody. In earlier times a document like the English *Magna Carta* contained very little but a catalogue of rights. The committee had decided to initiate its work with a compilation of basic rights (*Grundrechte*) for two major reasons. In view of the social agitation (*sociale Bewegung*) which had taken hold of the country, it was necessary for the assembly to declare itself, to state clearly where it stood in relation to popular demands. Also, members of the assembly did not yet know each other properly and it seemed inadvisable to tackle 'the highest political questions' while this was so. A 'neutral area' of discussion was therefore preferable where differences in opinion would not be so great.[1]

Beseler's first reason is more convincing than the second. After the experiences of the last thirty years, a widespread need was certainly felt for a precise delimitation of the frontier between the authority of the state and the rights of the citizen. This feeling was not confined to any particular class or political party. The extent to which government could interfere with the individual was a highly practical issue which affected and stirred members of parliament and the public at large more than the somewhat remote questions of whether the head of state should be elected or hereditary or even what the extent of the future Germany was to be. In a deeper psychological sense Germans first had

[1] I 700 f.

H

to bury the last thirty-three years, which many of them saw – somewhat one-sidedly – merely as a period of oppression, before they could think out their constitutional problems fully. Perhaps Beseler, when he stated his second reason, was too polite to say that the assembly – and the country – was not yet ready to face up to the key problems.

However understandable the priority given to Basic Rights may have been, it had some negative consequences. As American and French governments have found, 'rights of man' are easier to draft than to honour. Special situations may always arise which in the opinion of government require the setting aside of individual rights in the interest of the community. But rights which can be made inoperative in this way are hardly worth putting down solemnly in a constitution. In any case, the protection required for the individual will depend very much on the constitutional framework. Discussion of individual rights without having settled whether they would apply in a republic or a monarchy, in a state led by Austria or by Prussia, under a centralist or a federal system, was bound to be largely theoretical and to make it very difficult for the assembly to strike a balance between the various interests which would prove satisfactory in the long run. This situation played into the hands of the Left who argued that the people had certain inalienable rights. While fully convinced by their own reasoning, and being absolutely sincere, leaders of the Left did not pay enough attention to the very real difficulties in which governments might find themselves. The Left regarded the matter from the point of view of opposition, from outside. Even if members of the Left in the Frankfurt Parliament certainly did not all approve of the use of force against authority, for instance in the case of Hecker's rising, they shared a belief that to some extent the post-March governments only had themselves to blame for their troubles by relying too much on the old order and by not trusting 'the people' sufficiently. Strong individual safeguards might act as a brake on governments which were not fully 'democratic'. If the Left ever came into power, it was thought that any friction between state and individual would automatically disappear. Should these hopes fail to materialise, then the sovereignty of the people, vested in a government of the Left, would permit the temporary setting aside of individual rights. Neither Hecker nor the members of the Frankfurt Parliament who took revolutionary action in the summer of 1849 showed much tenderness for basic rights where these stood in their way.

As the state governments watched the progress of the assembly with

considerable attention, it was unfortunate that during the debate on
Basic Rights an impression of remoteness from the problems of
authority was often given, owing to the order followed by the Constitutional Committee. The Provisional Central Power was excluded from any
participation in the constitutional discussions by the law of 28 June
1848. No attempt was made to obtain the views of state governments
on the feasibility of the proposed Basic Rights, although state ministers
serving in the assembly could give their opinions as individuals.

The most serious consequence of the concentration on Basic Rights
was the delay to which practical issues, such as the relationship of
Austria and Prussia with the new state, were subjected. In the summer
of 1848 there was little premonition in the assembly that time was
running out on the Frankfurt Parliament. Those who worked to force
the pace, like the Left, did so more for tactical reasons than because
they believed that the tide was running against them. The historian
knows that time was, indeed, short. Members of the assembly could
not be expected to peer into the future, to be aware that by the end of
the year both the Habsburg and Hohenzollern monarchies would be
well on the way to recovery. Even then, most members of the assembly
misjudged the existing situation in two respects. They overrated the
power of the assembly and they underrated the vitality of the larger
states. The combination of these two factors led to a certain complacency. However, another factor also prevented the Frankfurt
Parliament from attacking the major part of its task at once. The
inability of the two major powers to take any far-reaching decisions
owing to their internal difficulties, which impeded their initiative in
June at the time of the establishment of the Provisional Central
Power, was not likely to be resolved quickly. The Pro-Prussians wanted
the Hohenzollern monarchy to recover first before raising the issue of
hegemony. Those who wished Austria to be kept in were hoping for
better days for the Habsburg monarchy. The leadership issue could
be raised too late – or too early – and the question was whether the
assembly would seize the ideal psychological moment for settling it. In
July, neither Prussia nor Austria was yet in a position to be fitted into
a scheme for unification and one of them at least was needed.

If priority for Basic Rights was perhaps unavoidable, these were
liable to remain unimplemented as long as the relationship between the
centre and the states was not settled. In view of the diversity of law
not only between one state and another, but also often within the same

state, a prolonged and complicated process of adapting state law to the requirements of the German constitution was needed in due course. A curious consequence of drafting the Basic Rights first was that it was left virtually to the Constitutional Committee – nominally subject to the approval of the assembly – to claim certain matters for the central authority before the general question of the relationship between centre and states was ever settled in principle.

Whereas the Constitutional Committee even under the revised draft was concerned mainly with establishing general principles, the Economic Committee adopted a more practical approach, always bearing in mind the problems which would have to be faced in applying the Basic Rights. Undoubtedly the draft benefited from suggestions made to the plenum by the Economic Committee. But the immediate consequence of the intervention of yet another committee was to add to the length and complexity of debate. Neither committee was united and there were sometimes two minority motions from each, so that it was not unusual to have six different motions before the assembly at the beginning, before any amendments from the floor were moved. All this was a long way from the original intention of Dahlmann and his colleagues to confine the declaration to the statement of a few general principles.

ii. National German citizenship – Freedom of movement

The draft of the Constitutional Committee consisted of 12 articles with altogether 48 clauses.[1] It covered freedom of movement, of speech, of publication, of meeting, of faith and conscience, and of learning. All citizens were to be equal before the law and to be entitled to public and oral trial. The judges were to be independent. Property was to be inviolable. Every part of the country was to be entitled to constitutional representation. Certain remaining feudal burdens were to be abolished. There was to be protection for national minorities in Germany and for Germans outside the country. In view of the importance of the subject, the Constitutional Committee suggested two readings.[2] This was agreed, against the wishes of the Left, who wanted to see the Basic Rights passed as quickly as possible.[3]

[1] i 681 ff.
[2] See Beseler, the *rapporteur* of the Constitutional Committee, Wigard i 702.
[3] i 709.

Article I dealt with the establishment of a general German nationality
(*das allgemeine deutsche Staatsbürgerrecht*). There had not been any
general German citizenship under the German Confederation. The
inhabitants were nationals of one of the 39 German states which made
up the Confederation. Whereas the other articles could have been
drafted for a single state, this first one dealt specifically with the
problem of how a national of any one of the German states could be
made a citizen of the whole of Germany. Article I was an attempt to
end what was called *das deutsche Ausländertum*, that a German could
be considered a foreigner (*Ausländer*) in another German state. Few
measures of political oppression had so discredited the pre-1848 régime
as the deportations of Germans from one state to another. There was
general agreement on the necessity of removing barriers which were
simply due to political discrimination. As the debate showed, it was
likely to be much more difficult to assimilate differences between the
various states where these were rooted in the variety of economic and
social conditions.

The complexity of the subject may be gathered from the difficulty
caused by the – apparently innocuous – first two words of the article.
Every German (*jeder Deutsche*) was to have the rights granted by the
constitution. It was pointed out at once[1] that this phrasing would cause
grave disquiet to the other nationalities in the German Confederation,
for instance to the Poles in the incorporated parts of Posen and to the
Slavs in the Habsburg territories. The debate on this point was part of
the attempt of the assembly to clarify its attitude to other nationalities.[2]
The *rapporteur* of the Constitutional Committee, Georg Beseler, explained that the Austro-Slavs would naturally have all the rights due
to Germans by virtue of the constitution.[3] He asked for the phraseology
'every German' to be retained, which was done.[4] Here was another
consequence of reversing the natural order of doing things. No further
definition could be given to the term 'every German' until it had
been decided what the extent and constitutional characteristics
of the proposed state were to be. Not even the name of the new state
had been settled. In effect, 'every German' was just a tentative
expression for citizens of the new state.

The draft of the Constitutional Committee began with the estab-

---

[1] By speakers from various political groups, beginning with an Austrian Fritsch who
belonged to the *Casino* (Right Centre), I 733.
[2] See below, p. 268 ff.   [3] I 738, 741 f.   [4] I 742.

lishment of a general German citizenship (*allgemeines deutsches Staats-bürgerrecht*). In order to avoid confusion with the citizenship of the various states, the term was changed to *Reichsbürgerrecht*.[1] In this form the first sentence which stated that every German had German citizenship was accepted unanimously on 20 July, with the votes of non-German members.[2] But unanimity ceased even with the second sentence of Article I, 1, however pale it might be, which only assured to every Reich citizen that he could exercise the rights due to him in this capacity in any German state. Those who did not vote for the sentence might have been just a few and the vast majority accepted it,[2] but the different voting behaviour was a straw in the wind, foreshadowing the clashes of opinion likely to occur over the key paragraph in the article, § 2, which spelled out the economic and social consequences of Reich citizenship.

In § 2, the Constitutional Committee bestowed on the citizen of the Reich the right to stay and reside, to acquire real estate, to trade and to obtain local community civic rights (*Gemeindebürgerrecht*) anywhere in any German state. At first this was to be under the same conditions as for the citizens of the state concerned, until a general Reich law removed the differences between the laws of the various states. On a superficial view, it was possible to write off any opposition to this version as obstructive particularism. But, on the Swiss parallel, one could be a good German without agreeing that the Reich should legislate in matters which deeply concerned the whole principle of self-government at local level. A case could even be made out for claiming that democracy had its roots in local government and that centralisation was destructive of representative institutions. Others, again, made a stand for the rights of the states, against the Reich, on the grounds that the views of duly elected representative bodies in the various parts had to be heard. § 2 asked the assembly to settle details which were consequent on not yet determined principles. Under this procedure, the principles largely emerged as a result of decisions on matters of detail.

With regard to state and community rights affecting the ordinary individual, the usual Left-Right division with intermediate shadings did not apply. Thus the Left Centre, which in principle was prepared to pay very little attention to the individual states when it came to settling the constitution, on the matter of economic rights stood out far more for state and community rights than the Right Centre. The

---

[1] II 971.   [2] II 1065.

Left on the whole was centralist in economic as in general constitutional questions, though not quite as united. The Right Centre wished the Reich to have a considerable say in economic matters, without riding roughshod over state rights and local community interests. The Right, in accordance with its usual policy, was sensitive about state rights.

The Constitutional Committee, with its *Casino* (Right Centre) majority, believed that a balance between the whole and the parts could be created by laying down certain broad principles for the whole country at once, without rushing into uniformity. The general approach of the Constitutional Committee was challenged by the Economic Committee, the majority of which doubted whether any assimilation of fundamentally different state laws was feasible.[1] Also the Economic Committee advocated a clear separation between the practical issues to be determined. In a much clearer version, the Reich citizen was given the right to stay, reside, trade and acquire property anywhere, in accordance with the conditions to be determined by a Reich law. On the whole, the right to acquire real estate was to be unrestricted. Whereas the Constitutional Committee was reasonably united on § 2, the Economic Committee reached its decision on this paragraph only by a narrow majority, on the proposal of Mathy of the Right Centre.[2] The Mathy compromise came under fire from both extremes, from the hyper-federalists as well as from the centralists of the Left. The Saxon industrialist Eisenstuck of the Main Left and the *rapporteur* of the committee, the Marburg economist Hildebrand of the *Westendhall* (Moderate Left), with a member of the *Casino* (Right Centre) put forward an amendment to the proposals of the Economic Committee which sought to allow Reich citizens to settle anywhere without necessarily being entitled to full community rights.[3] This amendment was eventually withdrawn.[4]

The more serious challenge came from 10 members of the Economic Committee who wanted to restrict intervention from the central power to an absolute minimum.[5] The signatories of this amendment to the proposals of the Economic Committee were opposed to a Reich law on trading and residence. They would go no further than to allow the

[1] I 689 ff.; see also the speech of the *rapporteur* of the Economic Committee, Hildebrand, I 756 f.
[2] Bundesarchiv, Minutes of the Economic Committee, which have been utilised for this chapter. The voting was 12 : 9.
[3] I 694.   [4] II 1066.   [5] I 694.

central government to see to it that the states revised their laws in accordance with the same principles, which was rather a vague formula. This minority of 10 even wished to allow states to restrict by legislation the right to acquire and to dispose of real estate on grounds of the public weal (*aus Gründen des öffentlichen Wohls*). 6 of the 10 signatories were drawn from the *Würtemberger Hof* (Left Centre), including the Munich civil servant and economist von Hermann and the professor of economics from Erlangen, Wilhelm Stahl, a brother of the more famous political theorist Julius. Scattered support for the amendment came from the Right and the Right Centre, but none from the Left.

The debate on Article I which began on 4 July[1] was of a very high standard. Members realised that they were discussing matters which were not only of considerable practical significance for their constituents but also of general portent for the principles of the constitution. The main problem was posed by von Hermann[2] right at the start: was there going to be absolute uniformity throughout the Reich in the matters under discussion or was variety to be permitted? Then, connected with that, would the whole of civil life throughout the country be regulated by the Reich or would it still be subject to state legislation? Hermann claimed for the state parliaments the right to settle these questions and expressed a justified doubt whether public opinion was really in favour of the Reich taking over. The opposite point of view was put by the spokesman for the other amendment from the Economic Committee. Eisenstuck[3] asserted that if Hermann had his way, there would be no need for them to continue with their deliberations at all. For everything would go on in the various states as before. He pleaded for free movement of people within Germany and dealt with the main objections which might be made to his proposals. Eisenstuck realised that the question of the right to reside anywhere was closely connected with the problem of poor relief. He admitted that local communities (*Gemeinden*) could not be forced to take on unlimited obligations of poor relief single-handed and therefore suggested supplementary state help where needed. There was strong applause when Eisenstuck referred to the wanderings of homeless people who had been sent from one parish to another and had nowhere found a home. Stahl[4] pleaded for trades giving themselves their own rules. He wanted as much *laisser-faire* as possible. The governments had been rightly criticized for interfering

[1] I 727 ff.   [2] I 757 ff.   [3] I 759 f.   [4] I 775 f.

too much, the assembly ought not to follow in their footsteps. The
senior Prussian judge and official Adolf Lette[1] asked the assembly to
support the proposals of the majority of the Economic Committee to
which he belonged. A member of the Centre, at first of its Left and later
of its Right wing (*Casino*), he was one of many, including representatives of the Left,[2] who paid tribute to the progressive Prussian legislation in the field of residence and trade. He did not think it was fair for
Prussia to be asked to open its doors to Hanoverians and Mecklen-
burgers without securing reciprocity. Lette regarded maximum
freedom of movement and trade as preferable to any declaration of a
right to work, a concept which was not new and advanced, as so often
claimed at the time, but had been well-known to the police state. The
main thing was to give everybody an opportunity to earn his livelihood.
He pleaded for the removal of restrictions, for instance on those
preventing Jews from acquiring real estate.[3] Other states should
follow the example of Prussia where these bars had been dropped in
1812. He ended by asking the assembly to create a fatherland not only
for the rich, but also for the poor German. The Catholic judge August
Reichensperger[4] of the *Casino* (Right Centre), from the Prussian
Rhineland, who was deputy chairman of the Catholic Association in
the assembly, claimed that there had been a reaction against freeing the
conduct of trades from regulation, though not in the sense that anybody wanted to restore the compulsion to belong to a guild. The
Bavarian Minister of Church and School Affairs (*Cultusminister*),
Beisler,[5] demanded that the freedom and rights of the Reich citizen
should not swallow up those of the state citizen and of the member of
the local community. France had suffered for two generations from
excessive centralisation. If there was too much interference with particularism, the local communities would rise up against the assembly
and they would be supported by the state governments. The senior
official Gustav von Salzwedell[6] from the province of Prussia, who belonged to the *Casino* (Right Centre), maintained that neither committee
had gone far enough in dealing with urgent social and economic

---

[1] i 777.
[2] For instance the prominent member of the *Deutscher Hof* (Main Left) Wilhelm Löwe
from Prussian Saxony (ii 861).
[3] For a detailed discussion of Jewish emancipation see below, p. 241 ff.
[4] ii 870.   [5] ii 871.
[6] *Deutscher Nekrolog* iv (1867), col. 19; Bundesarchiv; Deutsches Adelsarchiv. Speech, ii
871 ff.

H 2

problems, which were far more important in Europe at that time than the choice between monarchy and republic, or questions of nationality. What was at stake was the fate of the starving proletariat and this was bound up with the whole future of healthy independent local government. Poor relief should be left to the municipalities. Salzwedell did not quite face up to the restriction of freedom to take up residence that was implicit in his suggestions. This fundamental problem of reconciling the right to take up residence anywhere with the autonomy of the municipalities also affected § 3.

The Constitutional Committee had proposed as § 3 that state citizenship should not be refused to any German who was *unbescholten*, that is of good repute. Speakers in the debate pointed out that this term was vague and insufficiently defined in law. Beda Weber (independent), a Benedictine theologian from Tirol, and a prominent member of the Catholic association in the assembly, declared bluntly that in many Austrian provinces the clause would lead to civil war, that is if it meant anything at all.[1] If prior acceptance by a municipality was still required, then false hopes were being raised. In any case, the possession of state citizenship was useless unless arrangements were made for poor relief in case of need. In this context Weber referred to the tragic case of some Hanoverian Jews who wandered from community to community without knowing where they would be allowed to settle. Carl Nauwerck,[2] *Deutscher Hof* (Main Left), a Hegelian who had been dismissed from his teaching post at the university of Berlin for political reasons some years previously, pertinently remarked that it was petty (*eine grosse Kleinlichkeit*) to mention paltry monetary considerations on the first page of a declaration of rights.

The majority recommendations of the Economic Committee on § 2 were accepted on 21 July.[3] The Economic Committee was commissioned, by 244 votes to 242, to prepare drafts of laws on residence and regulation of trade before the second reading of the Basic Rights.[4] § 3 went through in the form proposed by a minority of the Constitutional Committee consisting of a mixed group ranging from the Right to the Left Centre. The only two permissible conditions which could be made in connection with the granting of citizenship in one of the states related to being of good repute and to the possession of sufficient means of

---

[1] *ADB* xli. See also Weber, *Charakterbilder*. Speech, ii 954 f.
[2] See Nerrlich, *Ruges Briefwechsel* i 387. Speech, ii 949 f.
[3] ii 1075.   [4] ii 1077 ff.

livelihood.[1] § 4 abolishing the punishment of civil death (*bürgerlicher Tod*), which deprived a (living) person of all legal rights as a consequence of certain heavy sentences, went through without difficulty.[2] During the debate the absurd consequences of this penalty imported from France, which could for instance void marriages, were pointed out.[3] In § 5, the assembly accepted the draft of the Constitutional Committee guaranteeing the right of emigration, but added that emigration was under the protection of the Reich.[4] According to the explanation of the *rapporteur* of the Economic Committee this somewhat menacing phrase merely referred to the help to be given to emigrants by the consular and diplomatic authorities of the Reich.[5]

Quite apart from the intrinsic importance of the matters under discussion, the outcome had given a clear indication of the assembly's attitude to certain basic constitutional issues. The majority had rejected a unitary structure without state governments as much as an unreformed particularism. There were many different ways of striking a balance between the whole and the parts which could be achieved under a federal system. Certainly sufficient support was lacking for a wilful dismantling of at least the larger state governments, though the plan for dividing up Prussia into Reich provinces had advocates even in the Right Centre. Fundamentally most members of the assembly were convinced that the Reich had to be given certain general powers of legislation to establish uniformity throughout the country in matters where excessive dissimilarities threatened to make a mockery of German unity. By taking the discussion away from the purely theoretical level and bringing it down to the hard facts of daily life, the debate had exposed the hollowness of the notion that particularism drew strength only from the princes. In this sense respect for state rights and local institutions was reinforced by consideration of article I of the Basic Rights. At the same time, while it was realised that the assembly could not simply ignore regional variations, any of these which conflicted with the essence of German unity were going to be subjected to critical examination.

---

[1] II 1087.   [2] II 1088.   [3] See the speech by the Munich jurist Ludwig Arndts, II 1039 ff.
[4] II 1089 f.   [5] Hildebrand, II 1062.

iii. Equality before the law – Position of the nobility – Freedom from arbitrary arrest – Abolition of the death penalty

During the following days, the assembly was preoccupied with other topics, mainly relating to foreign affairs[1] and the debate on article II of the Basic Rights was not begun until 1 August.[2] An attempt to speed up proceedings, mainly from the Left and the Left Centre, had failed to secure the approval of the assembly on 28 July.[3] The second article, though somewhat more straightforward than the first because it did not raise the relationship between Reich and states in such an acute form, was just as important. § 6 began with the statement that all Germans were equal before the law. The statement of principle was carried by a large majority, though some of its detailed application in the further clauses of the article was challenged.[4] The next sentence was much more controversial. The Constitutional Committee proposed the abolition of *Standesprivilegien*, i.e. privileges due to rank or estate. As explained in the commentary, this followed from the principle established in the first sentence which replaced the medieval state, with rights and liberties granted to individuals, by the more modern concept of equal rights and liberties for everybody. The term *Rechtsstaat* has often been translated as the state based on rights. But the commentary of the constitutional Committee makes it clear that it meant a state based on the principle of a law before which everybody was equal.[5] The estate concerned was the nobility and by a large majority the committee had rejected its complete abolition.[6] The clause proposed by the committee involved the ending of any privileges on the part of the nobility in public or private law, including the special representation of the landed aristocracy in the upper chambers of the states. On Beseler's suggestion the committee had, however, recommended that this clause should be subject to review where the assembly itself proposed to grant special representation.[7]

In the debate, critics of the nobility were more prominent than its defenders. The tone was set by the Wurtemberg representative Moritz Mohl,[8] the radical brother of the Reich Minister of Justice, who argued

---

[1] See below, p. 272 ff.   [2] II 1290.   [3] II 1260 ff.   [4] 2 August, II 1339.
[5] I 685: 'Zu Artikel II ... statt der Freiheiten die Freiheit, statt der Rechte das Recht...'
[6] By 20 votes to 3. See Droysen, *Verhandlungen* I 37 ff.   [7] I 685.   [8] II 1294 ff.

that the abolition of the nobility and of its titles followed from the principles established at the beginning of § 6. He called the existence of a superior caste an insult to the nation, for which he received due applause from the Left. No surprise is occasioned by the Left speaking against the nobility, but not even the *Casino* (Right Centre) was united in defending it. One of the most vehement attacks on the aristocracy came from a member of the *Casino*, Jacob Grimm,[1] the great scholar of the German language. His arguments at least had the stamp of originality. He said the bourgeoisie had been robbed by the ennoblement of Goethe and Schiller,[2] a remark greeted with applause not only from the Left but also from the Centre, at any rate according to the stenographer Wigard, not an impartial witness.[3] Grimm proposed that all legal differences between the nobility and other citizens should cease and that no more ennoblements should take place. Even members of the Right and those who were themselves involved were prepared to surrender important class privileges without firing a shot. The writer Arndt,[4] who had shed the radicalism of his younger days of the Napoleonic era and belonged to the Right in the Frankfurt Parliament, in an impressive speech found the abolition of the burdens which the nobility had imposed on the people quite natural. But he asked the assembly to leave the aristocracy its ancestors, coats of arms and emblems. Even Prince Lichnowsky,[5] who was never afraid to voice an unpopular opinion, made far-reaching concessions. He said that every decent nobleman would gladly give up privileges like exemption from taxation or the right to refuse to fight, that is not to share in the defence of his country. As to the rest, such as the proposed abolition of the nobility and even of its names and titles, he declared that any measures the assembly took would be fruitless. Nobility will remain nobility (*der Adel wird Adel bleiben*). The Left demanded a roll call for the vote on this issue and those who supported the abolition of the nobility were not confined to the Left, but were to be found even as far to the Right as the *Casino*. The Left Centre was split. The abolition of the nobility was defeated by 282 votes to 167, a clear majority against, but with a substantial minority.[6] The version of the Constitutional Committee

---

[1] *ADB* ix; *BSTH*. Speech, ii 1310 ff. [2] Grimm's phrase was '*Raub am Bürgertum*'.
[3] Wigard, with Blum, Heinrich Simon and another member of the Left belonged to the minority of the Constitutional Commitee which moved the abolition of the nobility.
[4] *ADB* i; *BSTH*; Brandis, 'Briefe von Arndt'. Speech, ii 1299 ff.
[5] ii 1307 ff. [6] ii 1340 ff.

removing caste privileges went through by a considerable majority.[1]
A clause was added that all titles not connected with a particular
function were to be abolished.[2] Jacob Grimm's motion was defeated,[3]
as was a move by the scientist Carl Vogt, one of the leaders of the Left,
allowing everybody to use the prefix *von*.[4] Whereas the Constitutional
Committee had merely proposed a general statement that compulsory
military service was to be the same for everybody, the Left succeeded
in adding a prohibition of arrangements to fulfil this obligation by
proxy. Also the right to bear arms (*Waffenrecht*) was to be the same for
everybody.[5]

§ 7 attempted to enact matters like rights of *habeas corpus* and the
famous English law was never far from members' minds. The Constitutional Committee proposed a short form establishing that except
when caught in the act, a person could only be arrested by virtue of a
judicial order, which had to be produced within twenty-four hours.
Nobody was to be withdrawn from his lawful judge, and extraordinary
courts (*Ausnahmsgerichte*) were not to be held. The principle on which
the clauses of the paragraph were based was that establishing a clear
separation between judicial and administrative processes. The sole
responsibility of the courts of law for the administration of the penal
law was unequivocally asserted. The days of administrative justice,
from which many members of the Frankfurt Parliament had themselves
suffered, were to be over. The powers of the police were to be severely
limited. The commentary by the Constitutional Committee emphasised
that the legal responsibility of the arresting authorities would become
operative if they could not obtain a judicial order for the arrest within
twenty-four hours. No longer would officials be protected from legal
action by sheltering behind superior orders.[6] Although § 7 even in this
form breached the whole former system of government at vital points,
it became apparent from the tabling of amendments and from the
opinions voiced in the debate that the assembly wanted to go much
further in spelling out the liberty of the subject from arbitrary arrest.
A wealth of knowledge and experience was brought to bear on the
question from this assembly of officials, judges and lawyers. Without
wishing to go so far as some members of the Left in writing every detail
into the Basic Rights, the assembly strengthened the paragraph by
plugging several gaps.[7] The independent authority of the police to

[1] II 1340. [2] II 1347. [3] II 1346 f.
[4] II 1346. [5] II 1347. [6] I 685. [7] II 1395 ff.

make arrests in certain circumstances was recognised, but was to be limited to about twenty-four hours. After this period had elapsed, the prisoner would either have to be freed or to be handed over to the judicial authority. Those responsible for unlawful arrest and, if necessary, the state were to give compensation and satisfaction to the prisoner. The assembly added a clause that accused persons were to be released on surety pending trial, unless there were urgent indications of a severe crime, although it was pointed out that the amendment would favour the rich. The most moving parts of the debate concerned the question of the death penalty and of corporal punishment.[1]

The majority of the Constitutional Committee had been opposed in general to including the prohibition of particular punishments in the Basic Rights, largely because of the belief that these matters had to be settled by the criminal law and that considerable confusion would be caused in the law of the various states by banning punishments prescribed for particular offences. This argument was countered by an eminent Prussian judge, Friedrich Ernst Scheller,[2] who belonged to the *Casino* (Right Centre). Scheller signed a minority motion in the Constitutional Committee with two members of the Left, Blum and Wigard, and the Wurtemberg minister Römer, demanding the abolition of the death penalty and of corporal punishment. He said that as these two punishments concerned life and honour, the Basic Rights were surely the right place for dealing with them. Whereas other speakers attacked the death penalty on general humanitarian or rationalist grounds, Scheller claimed that no human being had the right to deprive another of a single minute during which he could prepare for the after-life. Corporal punishment demoralised the convicted person and turned him into an enemy of the state. The punishment was unworthy of a free nation. These sentiments were echoed by the official of a Saxon court of law, Franz Heisterbergk,[3] who belonged to the *Deutscher Hof* (Main Left). Heisterbergk had been concerned with making arrangements for the various punishments. He described graphically how flogging, branding and putting in the pillory was carried out. In his opinion the consequences of flogging were disastrous. Any sense of honour still left in the offender was completely killed and many a woman had as a result become a whore. Corporal punishment was largely reserved for the poor, particularly for the vagabond. Social and economic problems which

---

[1] II 1369 ff.   [2] See *Umrisse*, 141; Simson, *E. v. Simson*, 336 ff. Speech, II 1369 ff.
[3] See *Umrisse* 25. Bundesarchiv. Speech, II 1382 f.

existed could not be solved by these crude means, they were only aggravated by them. This form of punishment also lowered the person who administered it. Heisterbergk's last point was developed by a judge from Westphalia, Carl Dham,[1] who belonged to the *Würtemberger Hof* (Left Centre). Dham had been sentenced for treason in 1833 owing to participating in the illegal *Burschenschaft* and had only been released from imprisonment in a fortress on the accession of Frederick William IV in 1840. He asserted that society had gradually over the centuries changed its whole attitude to the death penalty. Whereas at one time it was deemed an honour to execute a condemned person, the profession of executioner was now dishonoured. If the assembly decreed the maintenance of the death penalty, then every member would have to be prepared to execute it. Dham wanted capital punishment to be reserved for treason in time of war. The distinguished jurist Mittermaier[2] of the university of Heidelberg, who had presided over the Pre-Parliament, inferred from the ending of public executions in many places that states were now becoming ashamed of capital punishment.

The house was not, however, united. Notable speeches were made against the abolition of the death penalty from several sides. The Prussian judge Friedrich Leue[3] from Cologne of the *Würtemberger Hof* (Left Centre), a well-known law reformer, believed that capital punishment was necessary to keep discipline in the army in war-time. He could not support abolition even for political offences, quite apart from the difficulty of always being able to distinguish a political from an ordinary murder. The Bavarian Catholic priest Remigius Vogel[4] of the *Casino* (Right Centre) described how he had been obliged, in the course of his clerical duties, to accompany a condemned criminal to the scaffold and to give him spiritual aid. In spite of the terrible nature of the punishment which he had been obliged to witness, he still favoured its retention except for ordinary political crimes. The land-owner Philipp Wilhelm Wernher[5] (Centre) from the Hessian Grand-Duchy put forward the argument that in the absence of an official death penalty, some people might take the law into their own hands. It was absurd to ask for special treatment for political crimes. One could not put the traitor in the spinning-room, he belonged on the scaffold. He

---

[1] See Niebour, 'Die Westfälischen Abgeordneten' 37. Speech, II 1383 f.   [2] II 1379.

[3] See Hansen, *Mevissen*, I 433 f.; Hansen, *Rheinische Briefe* I 762, II 41; Pastor, *A. Reichensperger* I 203; Bundesarchiv. Speech, II 1369.

[4] Deuerlein, *Der katholische Klerus*. Speech, II 1373.

[5] See Wolfgang Klötzer in the appendix to Wentzcke, *Ideale* 305. Speech, II 1383.

even regarded the death penalty as a right of the criminal. There were crimes which could only be expiated by surrendering life itself. He called the death penalty a deep human necessity. It might be a paradox, but after all without crucifixion there would not be any Christianity. These final remarks were greeted with laughter. The *rapporteur*, Beseler, opposed abolition during his summing-up.[1]

The assembly decided by 265 votes to 175 to include the abolition of punishments in the Basic Rights.[2] In a division by name, the house voted to abolish the death penalty by 288 votes to 146.[3] The Left voted solidly in favour, supported by substantial parts of the Centre. The abolition of pillory, branding and corporal punishment went through by acclamation.[4]

The division on the death penalty took place on 4 August. Owing to various other preoccupations, mainly relating to foreign affairs, the debate on the Basic Rights was not resumed until 17 August. In the meantime, on 13 and 14 August, about half the membership of the assembly had attended a great national occasion, the Cologne Cathedral Festival (*Kölner Dombaufest*) at which the Vicar of the Empire and King Frederick William IV were the guests of honour. Although boycotted by the Left and in spite of some discordant notes, this represented in many ways the high-water mark of the assembly's prestige. There were great hopes for the future. Germany now possessed a ruler and a government, if only on a provisional basis. The presence of members of the Habsburg and Hohenzollern dynasties side by side with elected representatives from Germany and Austria could be the basis of a happy and prosperous future. Given strength and purpose, internal dissensions and external troubles might be overcome. One remark made by the King of Prussia to members of the Frankfurt Parliament during the festivities made many of them pensive. He asked the parliamentarians not to forget that there were princes in Germany and that he belonged to them. According to some accounts he added 'and I am one of the mightiest of them', but according to the Prussian official Wichmann (Right Centre), who stood close to the king, this was not so.[5]

The remaining paragraphs of Article II were settled much more expeditiously when the assembly returned to the subject of Basic Rights on 17 August.[6] The safeguards proposed by the Constitutional

---

[1] II 1388 ff. [2] II 1399 ff. [3] II 1405 ff. [4] II 1410.
[5] Wichmann, *Denkwürdigkeiten* 219. Cf. G. Beseler, *Erlebtes*, 66. [6] II 1575 ff.

Committee were considerably strengthened. The right to search homes was severely restricted.[1] Mail was to be confiscated only on the authority of a judge.[2] Even the debate on the freedom of the press took little time, because there was substantial agreement.[3] The press was to be free. Censorship of any kind was banned. All the thousand and one administrative measures which had been used to hamper the press – like postal prohibitions or advance payments required by the authorities – were specifically forbidden. Press offences were to be tried by juries according to a Reich law to be promulgated.[4] The comparative unity of the assembly was not, however, maintained, when the plenum began its debate on Article III of the Basic Rights, the relations of church and state, on 21 August.[5]

iv. Church and state

As was invariably the case in the Frankfurt Parliament, the raising of religious issues caused considerable passion. Few members felt entirely indifferent about religion, either positively or negatively. But even where a member had definite religious views, discussion of the future relations between church and state presented him with difficulties. If there was uncertainty about future developments in the sphere of politics, this was so at least as much as in that of religion. With many points of contact and certain similar problems, politics and religion affected each other. As both were in a state of flux, a debate on their relations presented an opportunity for new initiatives, but could not really finalise anything. The speaker's rostrum was in demand not only from those who wanted to maintain the influence of religion, but also from those who regarded the churches as impediments to any form of progress and wanted their power curbed.

The year 1848 marked the second centenary of the Treaty of Westphalia, which had regulated the position of the churches in Germany on the basis of *cujus regio, ejus religio*. A close relationship of the Protestants as well as Catholics with the temporal power often appeared a necessity in a country so uneasily balanced between two major and mutually hostile religions. Both churches accepted protection from the state against not only their external, but also their internal enemies. In

[1] III 1590 f.   [2] III 1608.   [3] III 1608 ff.   [4] III 1617 f.   [5] III 1631 f.

return for this assistance, the churches had to submit to far-reaching interference from the state. This was more obvious in the case of the Protestant Church, where the prince was *summus episcopus*, than with its rival. But the Catholic Church, too, had to accept state supervision in many internal matters which fell under the *ius circa sacra* (that is the rights of the state in religious matters), for instance in the communications of German bishops with the Papal Curia and in clerical appointments.[1] Among the Christians, however, the three recognised churches – Catholic, Lutheran and Reformed (Calvinist) – had a privileged position. They received financial help from the state – in many cases in partial compensation for what had been confiscated from them – and any secessionists from their ranks were kept at bay by being denied the advantages of official recognition. Victims of the old system were in particular all those who had broken away from the Catholic Church, like the *Deutschkatholiken*, or members of Protestant sects. The Jews were in an intermediate position. They were recognised, but were subject to discrimination. Several references were, however, made during the debate to the pressure on their flock exercised by Jewish rabbis in the same way as by the Christian clergy.[2]

The opposition of religious dissidents to the established churches and of anti-Christian circles to the existing relationship between church and state could be taken for granted. Less expected was the failure of spokesmen for the churches to put up an effective defence of the old order during the debate. Indeed, hardly any speaker had a good word to say for the system, not even a man like the Bavarian Catholic theologian Döllinger,[3] who a few years previously had not only defended but actively supported it. During the debate the Protestant and Catholic 'Christian state' was buried with almost indecent haste. This abandonment of concepts which had governed relations between the two spheres for at least a generation and in many respects much longer cannot merely be ascribed to disillusionment caused by severe crises like the Cologne church conflict or the Lola Montez affair. The causes go much deeper. In the debate, there was a tendency to blame the state and government interference for the troubles of the Christian

---

[1] See Huber, *Deutsche Verfassungsgeschichte* I 396 f. There were many complaints about the *ius circa sacra* from Catholic speakers during the debate, for instance from the East Prussian bishop Geritz (III 1680) and from the Munich historian Sepp (III 1691).
[2] By the unorthodox Catholic Sylvester Jordan (III 1647) and by the free-thinker Carl Nauwerck (III 1694).
[3] III 1673 ff.

Church, even for the often strained relations between the two con-fessions. Though this was not entirely good history, it was how leading Roman Catholics and Protestants saw the situation. The Catholics were certainly glad of the opportunity of freeing themselves not only from the fetters of the state but also from its support. For the Pro-testants the problem was much more complicated, but many of their faithful, too, longed at the very least for a greater say in the running of their affairs.

No doubt the political events of the spring of 1848 brought to a head many problems which had been troubling the churches for some time. Organisationally, neither church could ignore the repercussions which the granting of political representation was bound to have in the religious sphere. For many years the Catholic authorities had been faced with the demand for synods. In the Protestant Churches, there had been severe criticism of a state autocracy which had culminated in the forced founding of the United Church (*Unierte Kirche*) in Prussia. The changed political conditions of 1848 offered the churches the first real opportunity for many years to play a more active part. They felt revitalised by the quickened pace of events, by the greater urgency of their flocks and by the challenge the problems of the age – particularly the social ones – offered to them. The events of 1848 brought to fruition a religious revival which had been going on for some time. The churches, or at least the Catholics, now felt strong enough to stand on their own feet. There was a belief that the newly found freedom would more than compensate for the loss of state protection. In the absence of another political reversal, the state was unlikely to continue its partnership with the churches on the old basis. In a constitutional régime, the new ministers might not even officially be Christians. How could the churches agree to the far-reaching ecclesiastical powers of a Minister of Education and Religious Affairs (*Cultusminister*) being entrusted to a Jew or to an agnostic, perhaps even to a *Deutschkatholik*, or to a Protestant *Lichtfreund*?[1] The prospect which might have appeared bleak took on rosy colours when the opportunities of the future were surveyed.

On the face of it, greater democratisation of the churches in conse-quence of the changed political climate seemed likely. This was certainly the hope of many Protestants and Catholics. But a with-drawal of state direction might also have other consequences. In-

[1] A Protestant sect.

dependence for the churches (*Unabhängigkeit der Kirche vom Staat*) did not necessarily imply self-government in the political sense. In the general climate of opinion, the citizen who had been granted greater political rights might now expect the church to try and persuade rather than to command him. But there was also the argument leading to a tightened-up discipline. The leaders of the churches might assert that the withdrawal of state support did not permit a relaxation of the necessity of strict obedience. The churches were now almost like fortresses under siege, under attack from each other and from the enemies of religion. The latter feared that, freed from state tutelage, the churches might in fact prove so strong that they could threaten the liberty of the political order. Friendly and hostile observers agreed that any large church able to take advantage of independence from the state might become a very powerful force, in religion as well as in politics. Only the Catholic Church would be able to seize the opportunity at once. Many Protestants were reluctant to concede independence to the churches if only the Catholics could profit from their newly-won freedom.

The leaders of the Catholic Church in Germany came down firmly on the side of independence, rather than in favour of the separation of church and state. Each one of these formulas could not be more than a short-hand expression. Certainly the Catholics had a strong case for rejecting separation of church and state (*die Trennung von Kirche und Staat*) as a crude piece of surgery which did not make sense in the Germany of the period. There is also the more fundamental problem whether a Christian can agree to confine his influence to part of life. The next difficulty lay in the dividing line between the spheres of church and state. Both claimed a decisive say in school education, quite apart from questions like the conclusion of marriages. In any case, many political problems in Germany had a religious aspect, just as quite a few religious issues had a political side. Even if the principle of separation were established, this would not deter the major denominations from calculating which particular solution of the unification question would favour them. In view of these factors, the Catholics in Germany decided that their interests would best be served by demanding independence for the church.[1]

The advantages of independence for the Catholic Church were patent,

[1] See Schnabel, *Zusammenschluss*; Lill, *Bischofskonferenzen*; Bergsträsser, *Vorgeschichte der Zentrumspartei*.

but closer scrutiny revealed also serious disadvantages. Other churches would be entitled to a similar freedom or independence. One of the major benefits of the old system for the established churches, and especially for the Catholics, had been the help given by the state to keep down disobedient members. In future, the Catholics would have to fight their own dissentients entirely with spiritual weapons. In 1848, the German Catholics felt strong enough to do without the state, and there was certainly an element of separation here. But the Catholics did not want to be tied to separation all along the line. When this became clear, their enemies, already made suspicious by concessions so readily made, countered with a demand for the independence of the state from the church!

The Catholic association in the Frankfurt Parliament, which included a wide spectrum of theological attitudes[1] in this question, had the support of a leading Protestant minister in the assembly, the influential Jürgens of the *Casino* (Right Centre) from Brunswick. Jürgens had for many years fought state interference in religious affairs. On the whole, however, with a few exceptions, Protestants remained suspicious and kept aloof from the Catholic initiative. The outstretched hand was not so readily grasped. All those who had come into conflict with the Catholic Church either from inside or outside wanted to see evidence of a new spirit pervading the Roman Church before they were prepared to accept its assurances of a more liberal attitude to other ways of seeking salvation. All the established churches came in for severe condemnation during the debate. But there was nothing to equal the bitterness and hatred shown to the Catholic Church by priests in trouble with the ecclesiastical authorities and by laymen who had rebelled against what they regarded as spiritual authoritarianism. Leading Catholic speakers were deeply troubled by these attacks from speakers who were at least nominally within the fold. They were also disgusted with the indifference they encountered from many purely passive Catholics.

The only two other groups which had taken up firm positions were new churches, like that of the *Deutschkatholiken*, and those who wanted religious influence reduced to a minimum. Curiously, the two *Deutschkatholiken* Blum and Wigard in one respect found themselves asking for the same as the Catholics, namely for independence for the churches. But the rest of their programme showed a hostility to the established

[1] See Lempp, *Die Frage der Trennung.*

churches. No church was to receive a privileged position from the state and there was to be no state church.[1] The enemies of religion did not necessarily want to leave the churches free to run their own affairs. Many of them regarded the influence of the churches on society as evil. They wanted separation, but with a line of division quite unacceptable to the churches which would have been confined to a small corner of life.

The Constitutional Committee was not prepared to go all the way with any of the groups which had taken up fixed positions. Indeed the committee explained[2] that it refused to commit itself to any principle such as separation or independence, as it objected to linking denominational issues so closely with political ones. The restoration of Germany had already been prevented once by doing so, which was presumably a reference to the developments regularised by the Treaty of Westphalia in 1648. If independence were granted to the churches, it might be necessary to protect the state by special measures against encroachment. The committee also appreciated the difficulties in which the Protestant Church would find itself if any drastic changes in the relationship between church and state were contemplated. The committee's draft therefore contented itself with creating a large area of freedom in which the rights of the individual did not depend on professing a particular religion, while leaving the position of the established churches untouched in many respects. § 11 gave everybody full liberty of faith and conscience.[3] § 12 ensured the absence of any restrictions on common domestic or public worship. § 13 stated that the enjoyment of civic rights was not conditional on confessing a particular religion or limited by it. Civic duties must not suffer as a consequence of a religious faith. § 14 allowed new religious societies to be formed without any recognition on the part of the state. § 15 laid down that nobody was to be forced to take part in any religious act. §16 stated that the validity of a marriage in civil law was only dependent on civil registration; church solemnisation was not to take place until after the civil act. Article III in the existing form gave far more to the – admittedly very numerous – minority of non-Christians and members of break-away groups than to the vast majority who belonged to the major Christian churches.

[1] I 688.   [2] I 685.   [3] I 683.

v. Independence of the church from the state?

The first speaker in the debate on Article III which began on 21
August was the Protestant schoolteacher Wilhelm Weissenborn[1] from
the Grand-Duchy of Saxe-Weimar, who belonged to the *Würtemberger
Hof* (Left Centre). Weissenborn asked for the independence of the
churches from the state and he believed that it was essential for the
Protestants to face up to the new situation, whatever the difficulties.
The Protestant Church would have to go through a crisis before it
could recover its full health. He was not afraid for the future of Protestantism. Weissenborn regarded the mixing up of religious and political
rights during the last centuries as the true cause of many of the troubles
in which Germany found itself. These sentiments were echoed by the
Catholic speaker who followed, so that the debate opened on a note of
harmony between the two major churches. Georg Phillips[2] was born in
Königsberg in 1804 as the son of a wealthy merchant from Britain who
had settled there. He taught law at the university of Berlin and after
his conversion to Catholicism accepted a call to a chair in Munich in
1834, to be suspended as a follower of the clerical party during the
Lola Montez affair in 1847. Phillips, who tended to the Right, though
he did not belong to a parliamentary group in the assembly, expressed
agreement with many of the views put forward by Weissenborn. In his
opinion, the misfortunes of Germany were due not so much to the
religious divisions themselves, as to their exploitation for political
purposes. He similarly asked for the independence of the church from
the state, not only for the Catholics, but also for the Protestants. The
anticlerical unorthodox Protestant Karl Biedermann[3] of the *Würtemberger Hof* (Left Centre), a Leipzig university teacher of philosophy and
a prolific writer on political topics, expressed his surprise about the
apparently considerable measure of agreement between the various
interests and wondered whether the different parties meant the same
thing by terms like the independence of the churches from the state.
From his primarily secular point of view he preferred separation to
independence, but there was inadequate support for this solution. If
the churches were granted independence, there would have to be
reciprocity for the state. A similar note was struck by the school-

[1] *ADB* xli; Niebour, 'Vertreter Thüringens' 404. Speech, iii 1640 ff.
[2] *ADB* xxvi; Pöllnitz, 'G. Phillips'; *BSTH*. Speech, iii 1642.   [3] iii 1642 ff.

teacher Theodor Paur[1] from Silesia, a Catholic turned rationalist who
had been suspended from his teaching duties the year before at the
instigation of Bishop Diepenbrock of Breslau, now a fellow-deputy in
the Frankfurt Parliament. He was reinstated by Max, Count of
Schwerin-Putzar – now also a member of the assembly (on the Right) –
as Prussian Minister of Education and Religious Affairs (*Cultusminister*)
in the spring of 1848. Paur, who belonged to *Westendhall* (Moderate
Left), claimed a right for the state to safeguard its position where the
churches encroached on the political sphere. He was only the first of a
number of Catholics of greater or lesser unorthodoxy who gave no joy
to their stricter brethren. Where Paur had been comparatively mild,
Sylvester Jordan[2] from the Electorate of Hesse launched a severe
attack on the Catholic Church. It is significant that one of the most
effective speeches in the assembly of this political martyr was devoted
to a largely religious question. Jordan was born in a very humble home
in Tirol in 1792 and was only able to acquire a higher education with the
help of Catholic priests who took an interest in him. As his speech
showed, he had by 1848 moved a considerable way from a Catholic
position. He saw great dangers in granting the churches independence.
In the case of the Catholic Church, for instance, this would lead to an
excessive accumulation of power owing to the blind obedience of many
of the flock to the priests. He could bear witness to this from his own
long spiritual imprisonment.[3] The churches, as they had developed
historically, could not but hinder freedom of conscience. The only
solution was to abolish their authority. The Catholic priest Remigius
Vogel[4] from Bavaria (*Casino*, Right Centre) protested against the
description of the Catholic Church which had been given by Sylvester
Jordan. He was quite prepared to see any group granted the right in
civil law to form a religious society. There would be some awkward
consequences with an increasing number of sects. But truth could only
prevail through freedom.

A different line was taken by the next speaker, Franz Tafel (*Deutscher
Hof* – Main Left) from the Rhine Palatinate. Tafel had been ordained
a priest in the Catholic Church, but was forbidden in 1841 to officiate.[5]
He became a member of the Bavarian state parliament. In 1845 an
attempt was made to obtain for him a position as a minister of the

---

[1] *Umrisse*, 52; see also Paur, 'Briefe'. Speech, III 1644 ff. [2] 1646 ff.
[3] '*Aus einer langen geistigen Gefangenschaft*'.
[4] III 1651 ff. [5] Deuerlein, *Der katholische Klerus*.

Deutschkatholiken,[1] but apparently without success. Tafel expressed his surprise[2] about the position taken up by the official speakers for a church which had hitherto been very pleased to obtain the support of the state for its aims. He referred to the sufferings of the Hermesians, whose teachings were declared heretical by the Catholic Church, following which action was taken against them by the state.[3] Tafel opposed the establishment of independence for the church, for in the case of the Catholics this would only mean giving a *carte blanche* to the bishops to do what they liked. He supported the draft of the Constitutional Committee.

Another Catholic speaker, the Bavarian minister charged with church and educational affairs,[4] von Beisler[5] (Right), was certainly closer to that of Tafel than of Vogel. As the minister responsible for relations with the churches, von Beisler spoke with intimate knowledge of the workings of the existing system in a Catholic state. Beisler criticised the concept of freedom for the churches as too vague. The various groups which asked for it all meant something different. He regarded any separation of church and state as quite impracticable, because the two spheres were closely interwoven. For centuries Christianity had penetrated all aspects of life. The state in turn could not be indifferent to the Christian churches and treat them in the same way as a club.[6] The church had to reform itself. Otherwise there would be disharmony between the monarchical system of the church and the democratic institutions of the state. The church had to become democratic, like the state. Synods should be formed with the participation of laymen. Beisler called for the summoning of a Reich synod to regulate the affairs of the Christian Church in Germany and particularly its relationship with the state. In case of any denominational matters, these could be discussed by a section of the Reich synod consisting of members of the church concerned.

The tenor of the speech was anti-clerical. Beisler condemned the secularisation of the church, the way the clergy interfered in purely political matters, from the parish priest at election-time to the Pope

[1] Krautkrämer, *Kolb* 112 f., 178.
[2] III 1653.
[3] Thus the Hermesian Johann Wilhelm Joseph Braun, a professor of theology in the university of Bonn, who also sat in the assembly, was put on leave of absence by the state following his supension by the Catholic Church. He remained a practising Catholic.
[4] The post usually designated as *Cultusminister*.
[5] 1662 ff. [6] '*Wie eine Casinogesellschaft*'.

engaging in hostilities with another Catholic power. He would not accept that Pius IX had been forced to declare war on Austria in the spring of 1848. He admitted that the Pope had refused initially, but he had resisted like a bride.[1] These remarks were greeted with cheers and laughter. The chairman, Heinrich von Gagern, intervened to reprimand both the speaker and those who had laughed.

The following speaker, the Protestant minister of religion Karl Zittel[2] (Casino, Right Centre) from Baden, said he agreed with Beisler over the ends at which he aimed, but not in the means he suggested. The overthrow of ecclesiastical hierarchy must be achieved by the people on the basis of freedom, through the spirit of the age, and not by the Minister for Religious Affairs (Cultusminister). He wanted freedom for the churches, even if this was going to benefit the Catholics rather than the Protestants. Surely the Protestants would not wish to call in the protection of the state against their rivals. In the long run the Protestants would emerge from their trials with renewed strength.

One of the leaders of the Left, the zoologist Carl Vogt[3] from the university of Giessen in Hesse, forcefully put the case for the anti-religious section of the assembly. Vogt claimed that the Left was united on this issue. But though the majority of those hostile to religion sat on the Left, in fact many members were believing Christians, some of them Deutschkatholiken. Vogt called every church without exception a drag (Hemmschuh) on civilisation. He denied that there could be such a thing as a democratic church. He only supported a separation of church and state on condition that what was called a church was annihilated. A great struggle with religious fanaticism was imminent. But if complete freedom and democracy were granted to everybody, he and those who thought like him need not fear either a separation of church and state or those who stirred up trouble in the name of God and of religion. There had to be liberty not only for belief, but also for un-belief. This would provide the antidote (Gegengift) against the ultra-religious element. The great hope for the future lay in freeing school education completely from any influence of the church.

The Protestant minister of religion from Brunswick, Karl Jürgens[4] (Casino, Right Centre) who supported the Catholic minority in the Constitutional Committee on Article III, protested against the attempt of the committee to declare the indifference of the state to religion and

---

[1] 'Er hat sich aber gesträubt wie eine Braut.'
[2] ADB xlv; BSTH. Speech, iii 1665 ff.   [3] iii 1668 ff.   [4] iii 1670 ff.

to assign faith a place in the sphere of private affairs. He contrasted
the freedom given to new religious societies with the intolerable
obedience to the state (*Staats-Botmässigkeit*) which would still be
exacted from the official Catholic and Protestant churches. He opposed
any attempt to establish a complete separation of church and state,
because German political life had hitherto had a Christian basis and
would continue to do so. Neglect of religion might lead to a lowering of
moral standards. Church and state could help and benefit each other,
they could collaborate to solve, for instance, the social problem with
which they were faced. He referred to the argument of the majority of
the committee that the restoration of Germany had already once been
prevented by linking religious with political questions. What had caused
harm was not the independence of the church, but its dependence on
the state, which he had fought for the last twenty years.

Jürgens was followed by a distinguished Catholic speaker, Ignaz
Döllinger[1] (independent), who was suspended from his chair of ecclesiastical law in the university of Munich at the time of the Lola Montez
affair in 1847 as a prominent clerical politician. A leading personality
in the Catholic association of the assembly, Döllinger was one of its
main spokesmen during the debate. He inferred from the applause
given to speakers putting forward diametrically opposed views that the
house had not yet made up its mind. Indeed to some extent even he
could agree with Vogt. He admitted that religious freedom also implied
the right not to belong to any church. He could not go quite as far as
Vogt in accepting the liberty to profess atheism openly. Even in the
United States of America, which went furthest in granting religious
freedom, everybody who applied for citizenship had to declare his belief
in the existence of a Deity. He could not accept Vogt's reasoning that
freedom implied the liberty to destroy all religion. Next Döllinger
protested against the attack his temporal superior, the Bavarian
Minister for Religious Affairs, von Beisler, had made on the Pope. He
appealed to the sense of justice of members of the assembly, of Catholics
and Protestants alike, to recognise Beisler's account as a travesty of
the truth. The Pope had been powerless to prevent the declaration of
war against Austria, he had not been in a position to do more than to
protest and that he had done. He also contradicted Beisler's description
of the authoritarian structure of the Roman Church. The position of
the Pope in the church was far removed from despotic omnipotence.

[1] III 1673 ff.

Döllinger expressed agreement with the main tenor of Jürgens' speech and emphasised the considerable community of interests between the two major churches. Both had suffered from the old bureaucratic police state. Only when the churches had been granted independence would the two Christian denominations be able to live amicably side by side. Much of the friction between them had been caused by the state. Like Jürgens, he asked for equality of treatment for the old and the new religious communities.

The Prussian general von Radowitz[1] (*Steinernes Haus*, Right), who was chairman of the Catholic Association in the Frankfurt Parliament, tried to reassure Protestants about their position under a system of church independence proposed by his group. Independence did not imply a separation of church and state, merely that, as in other spheres, the state authorities would only be able to act strictly according to the law, without having vague police powers. It would still be open to the Protestant churches to give the various state governments a say in their affairs. But the authority of the state over the church would no longer be derived from the doctrine that the prince was *summus episcopus*, it would be a matter of voluntary, revocable treaties. He could not see how the Protestant churches would have disadvantages from a declaration of church independence. He hoped the day had not arrived where a step which was likely to benefit one church was therefore automatically condemned by the other. To put the fears of non-Catholics at rest, Radowitz said that he and his group – in this case the Catholic Association of the assembly – did not wish to take advantage of any independence granted to the Catholic Church to introduce the Jesuits into Germany. At the same time, any attempt to write a prohibition of the society into the law would be firmly resisted.

The general debate on Article III was followed by a detailed discussion of the various paragraphs, which began on 25 August.[2] The sentence proposed by the committee for § 11 about full freedom of faith and conscience went through almost unanimously, but an amendment moved by the judge Plathner (*Casino*, Right Centre) from Prussian Saxony, adding that nobody was obliged to reveal his religious convictions or to join any religious society, was also carried.[3] All other amendments were rejected.

Serious opposition to the ending of restrictions on freedom of

[1] iii 1695 ff.   [2] iii 1722 ff.
[3] *Umrisse*,133; Niebour, 'Die Abgeordneten der Provinz Sachsen' 56 f. Speech, iii 1767.

worship (§ 12) only came from a group of Tirolese Catholics of the clerical party. The ordained professor of theology Vincenz Gasser[1] (independent) asked that in applying the general principle of freedom of worship, with which he agreed, consideration should be given to the special situation in Tirol. In general it was necessary for the two major Christian denominations in Germany to make concessions to each other, but Tirol only had one religion in town and countryside, a remark received with unrest, as the report noted. Great excitement would be caused among the people if it were forced to receive all denominations in its midst. He asked that in due course a special agreement should be made between the Tirol estates and the Reich government to deal with the special religious conditions in the province.

Gasser's view was at once challenged from two quarters. The Protestant minister of religion from Austrian Silesia, Karl Kotschy[2] (*Deutscher Hof*, Main Left), denied that there were no Protestants left in Tirol. He said that he had been there and met Protestants, but discreetly in the evening by the light of a lamp.[3] He referred to the sufferings of the Protestants in the Zillerthal who had applied to the Tirolese estates for permission to found a congregation of their own, which was refused. They were given the alternative of either returning to the Catholic Church or of leaving Tirol, whereupon more than one hundred families emigrated.[4] The Italian priest and professor of theology, the Baron Giovanni a Prato[5] (*Deutscher Hof*, Main Left), claimed that the Italian-speaking parts of the province did not want any exemption from the operation of liberty of faith. The accuracy of this statement was questioned by the writer Johannes Schuler[6] (*Casino*, Right Centre) from Innsbruck, one of the secretaries of the assembly. Schuler, who expressed his regret about the expulsion of the Protestants, asserted that the Italian-speaking parts of the province were no more tolerant than the German ones. Jews were far better received in the German than in the Italian areas.

The draft of the committee for § 13 was accepted by the assembly,[7] whereupon 8 Catholic members from Tirol asked for a declaration to be entered in the record according to which they had given their assent to freedom of worship only on the assumption that in its application to Tirol consideration would be given to its peculiar (*eigentümlich*) con-

---

[1] Wurzbach v; *ÖBL*; *BSTH*; *NDB*. Speech, III 1736 f.
[2] Wurzbach XIII. Speech, III 1737 f.   [3] '*Beim Lampenschein*'.   [4] *Gegenwart* IV 87.
[5] III 1738.   [6] Wurzbach XXXII; *ADB* XXXII. Speech, III 1739.   [7] III 1769 f.

ditions.[1] Four of the eight signatories were members of the clergy.
Only one of them, Schuler, who belonged to the *Casino* (Right Centre),
had political party affiliations. Of the other 3 German representatives
from Tirol one was absent, and two who were present disagreed with
the protest.

vi. *The Jews – New religious societies – Civil marriage*

The main issue at stake in § 13, which abolished religious requirements for civic rights, was concerned with the position of the Jews.
Acceptance of the draft prepared by the Constitutional Committee
meant ending any special legal disabilities for those belonging to the
Jewish faith and making the Jews equal to Christians in law. When the
debate on § 13 was opened in the assembly on 28 August,[2] a strong lead
on the Jewish question was at once given by a Catholic priest from
Wurtemberg, Georg Kautzer, who was a member of the Catholic
Association. Not so long before Kautzer had been censured for refusing
to solemnise a marriage because insufficient guarantees were given for
the Catholic education of any children from it, and had been moved to
another parish.[3] Kautzer welcomed the paragraph,[4] which realised a
hope he had long and fervently nurtured. He expressed his conviction
that discrimination against the Jews in law – as against the Catholics
in Ireland before emancipation – had been harmful to the community
and unjust. He warned, however, that here and there popular prejudice
would be antipathetic to the opening of the ghetto, though only for a
time. It had often been said in the past that emancipation should wait
until the Jews had changed. He hoped rather that emancipation would
lead to change.

A different opinion was voiced by another speaker from Wurtemberg
soon afterwards. The official and economist Moritz Mohl,[5] an individualist of the Left and a Protestant, put forward an amendment to
§ 13. The German Jews were to have the vote and to be eligible for
election as members of parliament. But otherwise their 'peculiar
situation' (*eigentümliche Verhältnisse*) was to be a matter of special

---

[1] III 1770.   [2] III 1749 ff.

[3] Mainly *BSTH*; also Niebour in Schnurre, *Die Württembergischen Abgeordneten*;
Deuerlein, *Der katholische Klerus*.

[4] III 1750 f.   [5] Speech, III 1754 f.

legislation under the supervision of the Reich. Mohl claimed that with
their international ramifications the Jews could never completely
belong to the German people and that mixed marriages were an
impossibility.[1] The Jews were reluctant to engage in agriculture and
often sucked the poor peasant dry with their usurious practices. Once
the Jewish usurer (*Judenwucherer*) had his foot in the house of a peasant,
the latter was lost. These remarks were interrupted by hissing. Many
states, like his own, had salutary laws to divert the Jews into honest
trades and into agriculture. It was essential that the state should continue to have powers to deal with this problem. The whole life, tendency and occupation of the Jews in the lower classes was harmful to the
people (*volksverderblich*) and something had to be done to steer Jewish
youths into other careers. Mohl had a hostile reception from the
assembly. After one interruption he said: 'Gentlemen! I fulfil my duty
to the German people, knowing full well that this will make me unpopular.'

Mortiz Mohl at once received a reply from the leading Jewish spokesman in the assembly, Gabriel Riesser (*Würtemberger Hof*, Left Centre).
Riesser's own career illustrates the difficulties the Jews had to face in
Germany – and other countries – at that time. For many years he was
denied local citizenship (*Bürgerrecht*) and the permission to practise as
a lawyer by the city-republic of Hamburg, which was run by an oligarchy.
In 1840, his professional position was at last recognised. Thanks to his
writings, Riesser became well-known throughout Germany as an
advocate of Jewish emancipation. In May 1848, he was elected to the
Frankfurt Parliament by Lauenburg, an adjunct of the duchies of
Schleswig and Holstein close to Hamburg. He believed that he owed
his success to electors 'from the liberal, enlightened bourgeoisie
(*freisinniges, aufgeklärtes Bürgertum*)' against the opposition 'of the
higher officials, the nobility and the almost throughout pietistical
clergy.'[2]

Riesser claimed[3] the right to appear before the assembly in the name
of a class persecuted for thousands of years, to which he belonged by
birth and as a matter of honour; for he had scorned gaining by a
change of religion rights which had been basely denied to his people.
He protested against the way the Jews had been reviled. Moritz Mohl

---

[1] See above, p. 99 f.
[2] In a letter dated 13 May 1848 from Hamburg. See Isler, *G. Riessers Schriften* I
552. Further biographical information in *ADB* xxviii; Friedländer, *G. Riesser*; *BSTH.*
[3] III 1755 ff.

wished to have the Jews excluded by special legislation from equality before the law which was to apply to everybody else. The assembly had assured to the peoples on German soil who did not speak the German language the same rights as those who did.[1] Were the Jews going to be at a disadvantage because they spoke German? Riesser dealt with the specific arguments advanced by Moritz Mohl against the assimilation of the Jews. The difficulties over mixed marriages were caused by an intolerant civil legislation introduced by the Christian Church which played into the hands of prejudices on both sides. The removal of special conditions, such as those which insisted that all children from mixed marriages should be brought up as Christians, would lead to more frequent intermarriage and to an eventual end of the separation between the peoples (*Stammestrennung*). He rejected the account Mohl had given of the lower social classes among the Jews. If any acts were economically harmful to the community and were declared unlawful, they would have to be prohibited to Jews and Christians alike. Special economic laws against the Jews had been widely recognised to have furthered usury by Christians. He prophesied that under a just law the Jews would become increasingly enthusiastic and patriotic supporters of Germany, which had been impossible for them under the old régime. Special legislation against one section of the community would endanger the whole system of freedom. The speech was very well received and at the end obtained lively general applause.

Riesser was seconded by two leading Catholic speakers who followed. Heinrich Philipp Osterrath[2] (*Casino*, Right Centre) from Danzig said that as a Prussian judge he had resided in areas where Jews lived and some of them did many things which were not right. But he had also dwelled in districts where there were no Jews and had found that Christians behaved similarly. Osterrath asked for tolerance to other religious communities, including the Jews.

The Jewish question was treated even more fully by one of the most influential personalities of the pre-1848 era, the jurist Justin von Linde (independent), until the end of 1847 Chancellor of the university of Giessen in the Grand-Duchy of Hesse. Linde's advocacy of the Jewish cause is all the more remarkable in view of the vigour with which he had fought those holding other religious views, certainly in the case of the *Deutschkatholiken*. Like other prominent Catholics in this period, he is not an easy man to sum up in a few words. A strong defender of

---

[1] See below, p. 268 f.   [2] *ADB* xxiv; *BSTH*. Speech, iii 1757 f.

I

Catholic interests in the Grand-Duchy and deeply involved in the old system of relations between church and state, he yet preserved an independent religious attitude with his attachment to his old teacher Hermes, whose teachings had been condemned by the Roman church as heretical.[1] Linde argued[2] that as a religious denomination, the Jews were entitled to equality with other faiths. This followed from the vote on § 11 proclaiming liberty of faith which had removed any distinction between the rights of Christians and Jews made in the act setting up the German Confederation in 1815.[3] There was no justification for treating the Jews in Germany as a special nation. To qualify for that status it was necessary for a people not only to have a language, but also land and a country of its own. That was not the case with the Jews. Furthermore, if the Jews were a nation, then all barriers could not simply be removed, as they were, by joining another denomination. Because the Jews had been reduced to inferior status as a sect and not as a separate people, they regarded Christianity as the cause of the pressure on them. Naturally the Jews did everything in their power to escape the disadvantages of discrimination against them. On the Christian side, the oppression of the Jews had only led to arrogance.

The *rapporteur* of the Constitutional Committee, Beseler, firmly opposed[4] any special legislation affecting the Jews. He said this question had been decided in the public opinion of Germany. The legal position of the Jews could not be viewed from the angle of expediency. Whatever the practical consequences might be, the principle of freedom of religious faith and of equality before the law had to be applied without exception to all concerned. Beseler was – perhaps by accident – the first Protestant to speak up for the Jews during this debate in the plenum.[5]

Before the division was taken, the chairman went through all the motions and amendments to find out which of them had the necessary support of 20 members.[6] When Moritz Mohl's motion about the Jews was called, the necessary support was not found. Only a few members rose and the motion had to be dropped.[7] The house was thus almost united in wishing to see the German Jew recognised as a citizen with equal rights. Naturally this did not mean that all Germans would at

---

[1] *ADB* xviii; Treitschke, *Deutsche Geschichte* v 682; *BSTH*.   [2] iii 1758 f.
[3] Deutsche Bundesakte, article 16.   [4] iii 1762 ff.
[5] In the Constitutional Committee Römer (Protestant) and Beckerath (Mennonite) also supported Jewish emancipation. See Droysen, *Verhandlungen* i 8.
[6] iii 1764 ff.   [7] iii 1766.

once treat their Jewish co-citizens on terms of equality. The supporters of
Jewish emancipation realised that it would take many years for the more
subtle forms of discrimination against the Jews to disappear. But the
granting of equal legal rights was a substantial and concrete beginning.

Perhaps the best commentary on the attitude of the assembly to the
Jews was Riesser's election as second vice-president[1] five weeks after his
speech in defence of his co-religionists. He received 225 out of 368 votes,
an absolute majority and almost double that of his nearest opponent,
the Bavarian Protestant von Hermann. On the same day, 2 October,
Eduard Simson, whose father was the son of a Jewish merchant without
any school education and who himself had only been baptised at the age
of thirteen, was elected first vice-president on a similar vote, also
against von Hermann.[2] Simson succeeded Gagern in the presidency in
due course.

The debate on § 13 had only raised one matter of substance, the
treatment of the Jews. Though there had been a number of verbal
amendments, these were defeated and the committee draft went
through unchanged.[3]

The relationship between church and state came up in its most acute
form in § 14. Here the draft of the Constitutional Committee came
under fire from both the established and the new churches. The debate
on § 14 begun on 29 August[4] was soon overshadowed by the impact of
the Malmö armistice on the assembly. No time was found for a discussion of Basic Rights during the following sittings and the debate
on § 14 was only resumed on 9 September.[5] The vote was taken two
days later.[6] The joint Catholic–Protestant motion of a minority in the
Constitutional Committee, sponsored among others by Lasaulx and
Jürgens, asking for independence from the state for all churches, was
defeated by 357 votes to 99. This substantial defeat was due to the
refusal of the other minorities in the Constitutional Committee, such
as those led by the Mennonite Beckerath and by the *Deutschkatholiken*
Blum and Wigard, to make common cause with Lasaulx and Jürgens,
although their own motions were in substantial and even verbal agreement. The assembly did, however, carry a motion by Dominikus
Kuenzer,[7] the unorthodox Catholic priest from Constance, that while
every church should administer its own affairs independently, it should
remain subject to the laws of the state like any other society. The left-

---

[1] iv 2377.   [2] iv 2376.   [3] iii 1768.
[4] iii 1774.   [5] iii 1945 ff.   [6] iii 1990 ff.   [7] See above, p. 98.

wing minority in the Constitutional Committee led by Robert Blum and Wigard succeeded in obtaining the approval of the assembly for the principle that no religious society was entitled to any special privileges and that there was no state church. The passage proposed by the Constitutional Committee allowing the formation of new religious societies without approval by the state was also carried. But in view of the additions to § 14, the balance which the Constitutional Committee had in mind was changed. The influence of the state over the churches was restricted by the assembly and this potentially benefited the large established churches, which had suffered from the intervention of the secular authorities, rather than the smaller new ones. At the same time the abolition of special privileges for any church helped both the new societies and any large minority church in a particular state, whether Catholic or Protestant. The leading church in a state – of whatever denomination – was bound to lose some power, but as the debate had shown, there were grave doubts whether the work of a spiritual institution could be measured in such secular terms. While the new version did not state the principle of church independence in so many words, it went some way towards it. By defeating an attempt to enforce election of parish priests and church wardens by their congregations, the assembly showed that it wished to allow the religious societies to run their own affairs, from whichever quarter greater attempts at interference came.

Owing to the slow progress on the Basic Rights, the assembly decided to dispense with a debate on each clause unless demanded by 100 members[1] and to vote on § 15 without further discussion,[2] particularly in view of the careful prolonged general debate on Article III. The paragraph was passed in the form proposed by the Constitutional Committee.[3] The draft of the Constitutional Committee stipulating the priority of civil marriage was accepted, with the addition that religious differences did not constitute a bar to marriage and that the state authorities were in charge of registration.[4]

Another question of considerable interest to the churches came up in Article IV, that of school education. The debate in the assembly on this article opened on 18 September,[5] during the Frankfurt riots which transformed the entire situation in the assembly. As the disturbances formed part of a sequence of events which began with the news of the Malmö armistice, they are analysed in the following chapter.

[1] III 1984.   [2] III 2013.   [3] III 2014.   [4] § 16. III 2018.   [5] III 2167.

vii. Hecker's membership of the assembly – An amnesty? – Trouble with the gallery

The gulf between the Left and the remainder of the house became almost unbridgeable as a consequence of the September riots, but some fundamental differences of attitude had always existed. This was illustrated by the debates in August on the action to be taken about the election of the fugitive Friedrich Hecker to the Frankfurt Parliament by the Baden constituency of Thiengen on 7 June.[1] Hecker had fled to Switzerland following the collapse of his rising in Baden during April, had continued plotting from his exile and had refused to appear in the Grand-Duchy to answer the charges of treason against him. The Baden government considered him ineligible and was empowered by the constitution of the Grand-Duchy to call another election. In view of the grave and deliberate act of 77 out of 134 electors who participated in voting for a patent traitor, the Baden government was uncertain whether to hold a fresh election. The authorities in the Grand-Duchy were therefore considering either declaring the runner-up elected or leaving the constituency unrepresented for the time being. As all this was a matter of national importance, the Baden government was quite prepared to leave a decision to the Frankfurt Parliament and submitted all the relevant documents. In accordance with the usual procedure, the matter was considered by the credentials committee (*Central-Wahlausschuss*), but the committee found itself unable to deal with so grave a matter of principle.[2] The plenum decided on 1 July to refer the problem to a special committee, together with the question of what action the assembly should take about Hecker's fellow-conspirator Peter who actually sat in the house and for whose extradition the Baden government had applied. Though only procedural issues were involved, the debate quickly got heated.

The report of the special committee on Hecker's election was made on 3 August.[3] The committee had little difficulty in coming to a conclusion and made the unanimous recommendation that Hecker's election be declared invalid and that the government of Baden should be asked to hold fresh elections. Before the report could be debated,

---

[1] The following is based on the report of the committee in Supplement I to the proceedings of 2 August 1848 (following II 1376).

[2] I 658.   [3] Follows II 1376.

Hecker's fate came up in a more general way in connection with petitions, mainly from Baden, which asked for an amnesty for those who had been involved in his rising. The committee concerned[1] moved that no action be taken on this matter.[2]

At the other extreme, Ludwig Simon from Trier (*Donnersberg*, Extreme Left) asked the assembly to proclaim a complete amnesty for political offences, which was to be enforced by the Central Power.[3] In between these two extremes various compromises were suggested, including that of the Wurtemberg official Schoder (*Westendhall*, Moderate Left) moving 'next business' in the expectation that the state governments would use their power of mercy in the cases of the less guilty.[4]

Political amnesty was an awkward issue for the assembly, for both its advocates and its opponents.[5] Its supporters realised that the case of Hecker and of his followers was a weak one and only a few members of the Left were prepared to defend a rebellion against a constitutional government in public. As in the debate on Hecker's election which followed soon afterwards, the fight was carried on by a small band, mainly of close friends of Hecker, drawn almost entirely from the Extreme Left (*Donnersberg*): Ludwig Simon (*Donnersberg*), the writer Wiesner[6] (*Donnersberg*) from Vienna and two fellow members of the Baden state parliament, Adam von Itzstein (*Deutscher Hof*) and the lawyer Lorenz Brentano (*Donnersberg*). As the *rapporteur* of the committee, the lawyer Christian Wiedenmann[7] (*Würtemberger Hof*, Left Centre), pointed out, Itzstein and Brentano had voted by name in the Baden state parliament for the branding of Hecker's rising as a criminal enterprise.[8] Another member of the *Donnersberg*, the historian Carl Hagen[9] from the university of Heidelberg, was careful to express his condemnation of the rising when he spoke in support of a political amnesty.[10] The only consolation Hecker's friends had was that the broadening of the issue gave them more scope than the technical question of the representation of the constituency of Thiengen.

The opponents of amnesty did not wish to appear cruel or to be associated with such measures as the imprisonment of political opponents, which had become tainted during the previous period. As heirs

---

[1] *Ausschuss für Gesetzgebung.*   [2] II 1415 ff.   [3] II 1417.   [4] II 1435.
[5] II 1417 ff.   [6] Wurzbach LVI; Erasmus, *Die Juden.*
[7] Klötzer in Wentzcke, *Ideale* 305; Bundesarchiv.
[8] II 1455.   [9] *ADB* X; *BSTH.*   [10] II 1422 ff.

of revolution they were in an awkward position when it came to condemning revolutionaries. However, the *rapporteur*, Wiedenmann, was able to give figures of releases from arrest by the Baden government which showed that allegations of excessive harshness were quite unjustified. Only a comparatively small number was still in prison. In view of the political instability in Germany, there was obviously a danger in excessive leniency.[1]

In spite of a restless gallery, interest in the debate on the floor was beginning to flag after a few speeches on 7 August. A representative of the Right Centre (*Casino*) complained about empty benches.[2] But the situation changed rapidly when the next speaker, Brentano (*Donnersberg*), mounted the rostrum.[3] He was a member of that famous family of Catholic Frankfurt merchants which had immigrated from Italy and to which the pillar of the Romantic movement, Clemens Brentano, also belonged.[4] Brentano, a former collaborator of Hecker on the Extreme Left of the Baden state parliament, spoke of his friendship with the leader of the rebellion of which he was proud. When he was nearing the end of his speech, Brentano said: 'Do you want to treat those who took up arms in Baden worse than a Prince of Prussia?' This was a reference to the return home of the heir of the Prussian throne, the later King and Emperor William I, from his exile in England. William had fled from Berlin in March owing to his unpopularity as an advocate of tough measures to maintain order. A veritable tumult broke out in the chamber as soon as Brentano had spoken this sentence.[5] The Left of the assembly and some of the gallery broke into cheers. Right and Centre shouted 'away from the rostrum' and asked for the speaker to be called to order. The chairman, von Soiron, said he had not understood the sentence properly. He tried to restore order, but made no impression. A concourse of members formed near the rostrum and fighting nearly broke out.[6] According to some members of the Left, who recorded a protest the following day, several colleagues from the other side of the house tried to take the rostrum by force, insulted Brentano, challenged him to a duel and prevented him from finishing his speech.[7] As soon as von Soiron saw that he could not restore order, he closed the sitting.[8] When the debate on the amnesty question was resumed the following

---

[1] II 1455 f.   [2] Carl Edel, II 1434.   [3] II 1435 ff.
[4] For Lorenz Brentano see Weech, *Badische Biographien*, v; *BSTH*; *NDB*; Zucker, *Forty-Eighters*.
[5] II 1438.
[6] Droysen, Tagebuch, 7 August, in Hübner, *Droysen*, 823.   [7] II 1441.   [8] II 1438.

day, the atmosphere in the assembly was still at fever heat with mutual recriminations between the Left and the more moderate sections of the house. There were motions on the one hand asking that Brentano be called to order and on the other accusing his opponents of having outraged parliamentary decencies.[1] Without allowing any discussion, von Soiron called Brentano to order by virtue of his powers as chairman.[2] He was thereupon constantly interrupted by the Left, which was seconded by noise from the gallery, and threatened to suspend the sitting. His impartiality was challenged by several members of the Left. When he was defied by a member of the Left who refused to resume his seat and to be called to order, he once more suspended the sitting.[3] After the resumption, the situation was still so chaotic that Heinrich von Gagern, the president of the assembly, intervened.[4] He had not taken the chair as his brother had been killed in the Hecker rising which was the subject of the debate. Gagern asked the house to submit to the discipline of his deputy and to observe proper parliamentary procedure if dissatisfied with the way he chaired the meeting. Actually criticism of Soiron's handling of the vice-presidency was not confined to the Left, but extended right across the assembly.[5] Though re-elected once more, at the end of August,[6] he only came third with 18 votes on 2 October[7] when Eduard Simson succeeded to the vice-presidency.[8] In the meantime, Soiron found a niche as chairman of the Constitutional Committee, when Bassermann vacated the post on his appointment to the Reich government in August.

When von Soiron called on Brentano to resume his speech, another member of the Left asked to speak instead. The interruptions from the gallery during the dispute which followed were so loud that the chairman ordered those responsible to be removed. When this was of no avail, von Soiron ordered all visitors to leave.[9] This was easier said than done and it once more needed Heinrich von Gagern's intervention to have the galleries cleared. Gagern even personally went up to the gallery to persuade visitors to leave.[10] There followed an involved discussion[11] as to what the status of their sitting without visitors was. Did it constitute a secret session? Were the journalists to be re-

[1] II 1441 f.   [2] II 1442.   [3] II 1442.   [4] II 1443.
[5] Amongst others Droysen (*Casino*, Right Centre), see Tagebuch for 7 August previously quoted, p. 249, note 6; also Detmold (Right) in a letter of 9 August to Stüve, see Stüve, *Briefwechsel*, 83.
[6] 31 August (III 1806).   [7] IV 2376.
[8] See above, p. 245.   [9] II 1443.   [10] Paur, 'Briefe' 40.   [11] II 1444 f.

admitted? The latter was answered in the affirmative. The Left then
moved that the public was to be re-admitted, but in a vote by name this
was refused by 380 votes to 91.[1] An unrepentant and indeed offended
Brentano was then called to finish his speech of the previous day, but
mainly took the opportunity to defend his conduct and to protest about
his treatment.[2] When von Soiron wanted to press the debate to a conclusion, the Left unsuccessfully asked for a postponement.[3] Soon after,
Carl Vogt (Main Left, *Deutscher Hof*, but later in the more extreme
Donnersberg) interrupted to ask whether the presidium had given
orders to surround the Paulskirche building, in which the assembly met,
with troops. Soiron replied that he had given no such instructions and
added immediately afterwards that apparently the civic guard had
arrived. He said this was a security measure on the part of the town
which was not an appropriate subject for the house to debate. In any
case these arrangements were not directed against the assembly.[4] After
this there were constant references by speakers of the Left to outside
pressure and dictation. Itzstein stated that his friends would not
continue the discussion under bayonets, whereupon part of the Left
went out of the chamber.[5] When later the Left made a fresh effort
to obtain a postponement, although this had already been refused once,
Schoder of *Westendhall* (Moderate Left) protested against this attempt
of a small minority to terrorise the majority.[6] At last the chairman
was able to proceed to a division and the motion of the committee not
to take any action was carried by 317 votes to 90.[7] Some of the minority
favoured a compromise[8] and could not thus all be assumed to favour a
general political amnesty. There would have been more noes if it had
not been for the earlier departure of some of the Left as a protest.

The question of representation of the constituency of Thiengen
came up at the next sitting on 10 August.[9] This was a more precise
question than the vague issue of a political amnesty and unlike the
latter fell clearly within the competence of the house. This was so not
only because the assembly decided its own admissions, but also because
the Baden government had referred the problem to it. In a sense the
poet Wilhelm Jordan from Berlin, who was gradually abandoning the
Left for the Centre, was right in asking for a vote to be taken at once,
in view of the fact that a man who had just been refused an amnesty

---

[1] II 1445 ff.   [2] II 1450 ff.   [3] II 1452 ff.
[4] II 1453.   [5] II 1455.   [6] II 1456.
[7] II 1458 ff.   [8] Such as Schoder, who voted with the noes.   [9] II 1476 ff.

12

by the assembly could surely not become a member.[1] But his motion failed to get any support.[2] Only a few extremists like Itzstein[3] and Ludwig Simon[4] demanded Hecker's recognition as a member. Even Carl Vogt and others of the Left merely asked that no action be taken on the declaration of the Baden government, but moved that the assembly should indicate its readiness to consider motions from the authorities in the Grand-Duchy in connection with the continuation of the legal proceedings against Hecker.[5] This compromise motion begged the question, but – considering its sponsors – it is remarkable for its moderation. In the end the motion of the committee calling for fresh elections was passed by 350 votes to 116.[6] Not all those who voted with the minority were prepared to recognise Hecker as member.

Unfortunately the problem was not solved by the holding of a new election, as Hecker once more emerged at the top of the poll on 26 October. The Baden government decided to leave the constituency unrepresented for the time being.[7] The committee on Thiengen recommended accepting this situation[8] and the assembly agreed to this suggestion on 5 March 1849 against the opposition of Ludwig Simon and other members of the Left who wanted Hecker admitted as a member.[9]

The committee was also charged with investigating the related case of the Baden official Ignaz Peter whom Hecker had appointed as his governor in Constance during the rising.[10] Peter had been elected to the Frankfurt Parliament in that town. He was actually allowed to take his seat and joined the Extreme Left (*Donnersberg*). The Baden government asked the assembly to agree to Peter's arrest on charges of high treason. For a variety of reasons, parliamentary treatment of the whole affair was very dilatory. At first the committee refused to sanction the arrest, but later changed its mind in view of further evidence supplied by the Baden government. But the matter did not come up in the plenum until 17 April 1849, by which time many members with moderate political views were already resigning from the assembly. Parliament refused to agree to his arrest[11] so that Peter was able to continue sitting in the assembly right to the end.

The debates which centred round the Hecker rebellion had shown

---

[1] II 1480.   [2] II 1481.   [3] II 1483 ff.   [4] II 1481.   [5] II 1489 ff.
[6] II 1496 ff.   [7] v 3325.   [8] VIII 5585.   [9] VIII 5585.
[10] The following account is based on the reports of the Committee, VIII 6189 ff.
[11] VIII 6202.

clearly that arrangements for the admission of visitors were in need
of drastic overhaul, if the assembly was to function effectively in future.
According to the rules of the house[1] the president was charged with the
duty of maintaining order in the parliament building. With the support
of the other members of the management committee (*Gesamtvorstand*),
that is of the vice-presidents and the secretaries, Heinrich von Gagern
ordered a severe reduction in the number of visitors to be admitted to
the public gallery, which took effect on 10 August, when the question
of Hecker's election was debated. These measures were challenged by
a Saxon member of the Extreme Left (*Donnersberg*), Carl Theodor
Dietsch.[2] Gagern replied that so far arrangements within the building
had always been considered to fall within the discretion of the management committee (*Gesamtvorstand*). The large number of visitors had
not permitted the maintenance of order. Also some of the space was
needed for parliamentary office work and for committee rooms.[3] After
a short discussion, the matter was referred to the relevant committee,[4]
whose report was debated on 1 September.[5] The committee recommended that the rooms withdrawn from the gallery should be restored,
but that only a reduced number of visitors should be admitted so as to
allow order to be maintained. A minority of the committee asked that
the public gallery should be halved for visitors, which would still allow
the admission of about two thousand visitors, and that the other half
should be set aside for the use of members. After the debate, the
assembly decided by 278 votes to 134, mainly against the wishes of the
Left, to confirm the arrangements made by the management board
(*Gesamtvorstand*).[6]

On the purely domestic side, the division in the assembly had often
been other than on lines of purely political ideology during the first
four months. On many questions, such as the relationship between the
Reich, the states and the local communities, or of that between church
and state, the usual gradations from Left to Right did not apply.
Indeed, most of the issues raised in the Basic Rights did not fit into
this pattern. But the debates on Hecker and a political amnesty during
the early part of August widened rifts which had embittered the first
weeks of the assembly. It was not, however, a domestic, but a diplomatic
issue which brought tension between the Left and the moderates to a
climax.

[1] § 14.
[2] Bundesarchiv; Meinel, *Heubner* 46, 144. Speech, II 1509 f.
[3] II 1510.
[4] II 1510.
[5] III 1839 ff.
[6] III 1849 ff.

7 Germany's Frontiers: Posen and Schleswig-Holstein

i. Limburg – Luxemburg

ANY attempt to turn the German Confederation – a loose association of territories largely derived from the non-national Holy Roman Empire – into a single state based on German nationality was bound to raise in an acute form Germany's relations with foreign states and other nationalities which had lain dormant. German nationalism was only one expression of a general movement which went right through Europe and similarly affected other ethnic groups of deep concern to the Germans, like the Slavs, the Italians and the Danes. In some cases, accommodation might be reached between two national movements both claiming territories of mixed population, and indeed the assertion of national feeling could be regarded as a new emphasis on the inhabitant rather than on the prince and territorial state as heretofore. But viewed realistically it soon became clear that in the intricate political relationships in Europe national movements competed with each other, and thus the simultaneous national awakening of neighbours was liable to cause problems for German plans. The Frankfurt Parliament had to reckon with the opposition not only of other ethnic groups, but also of the European Great Powers loth to see the destruction of the German Confederation, which formed so important a part of the European system as they knew it. It might be asked why the Germans did not ally themselves with other national movements to achieve their aims. The answer to this is rather complex. Fundamentally most German nationalists at the time had not emancipated themselves from the cosmopolitan heritage of the Holy Roman Empire and were not content to found a purely German state shorn of all the territories mainly inhabited by other ethnic groups.[1]

There was an appeal both to self-determination and to historic rights or to either as the particular problem required, an approach

[1] See Meinecke, *Weltbürgertum* ([3]1915).

typical of national movements in general. Except for parts of the Left, there was little desire in the Frankfurt Parliament for an overthrow of the whole European system, merely for its adaptation where German concerns required. Quite apart from mutual antipathy – except in circles of the Left – the Poles, or the Slavs generally, were hardly considered suitable allies for the Germans in view of many apparently diverging interests. Thus it was difficult to draw a satisfactory border between the German and Polish areas of the Prussian province of Posen. The greatest impediment to alliances with foreign nationalities was, however, the close German relationship with the Habsburg Empire.

During the summer of 1848 the assembly was not prepared to face up to the possibility that the creation of a German national state might require the exclusion of Habsburg territories. This reluctance to part with Austria was not simply due to attachment to the frontiers of the German Confederation, though that played a part. Nineteenth-century nationalism was strongly motivated by historical memories seen through the flattering spectacles of the romantics. There was a longing to restore the former glory of Germany, represented in this view by German emperors ruling over a German Reich, the Holy Roman Empire. German emperors, the Habsburgs among them, made good German rule not only over Germans, over kith and kin – the Dutch, the Swiss, etc. – but also over the Latin (*die Wälschen*) and Slav races which were considered inferior. The Germans were seen as the cultural and even in some ways – at any rate before the Reformation – as the religious leaders of Europe, as more than simply one nationality, but as the representatives of civilisation.[1] On this interpretation the Habsburg Empire appeared as a continuation of Germany's mission over other races. Thus the exclusion of Austria from Germany (which was to become the programme of the *Kleindeutsche* who proposed the King of Prussia as hereditary German Emperor therefore also called *Erbkaiserliche*), was a betrayal of Germany's past. The reasons which prompted members of the Frankfurt Parliament to desire the retention of at least part of the Habsburg Empire were bound to prejudice the assembly against the claims of the non-Germans, at any rate in the territories which formed part of the German Confederation. This already became clear in May over the controversy about elections to the Frankfurt Parliament in constituencies inhabited entirely or mainly

---

[1] In this discussion the word *Kultur*, about which many learned treatises have been written, figures prominently.

by non-Germans, such as in Bohemia and in Styria, Carinthia and Carniola.[1] Indeed, not unnaturally some of the strongest supporters of the German connection in the Habsburg Empire were to be found in those provinces where German supremacy was threatened by the Slavs and the Italians. As long as the intention prevailed to keep Austria in, the assembly could hardly resist the pressure of Germans from border territories, such as Tirol and Bohemia, to support them against the non-Germans. This ruled out a German alliance with the Italians, the Czechs or the Slovenes. There was a brief flirtation with the Hungarians, who sent a delegation to the Frankfurt Parliament,[2] but nothing came of it. The failure of the Hungarians to support the radicals in Vienna effectively against a common enemy – the Austrian court and cabinet – in October 1848 shows how difficult it was to achieve co-operation between different national movements.

The Slavs, the Italians and the Danes left the Germans in no doubt about their national aspirations and therefore in a sense presented the Frankfurt Parliament with clear-cut issues. This clarity was lacking in one of the first problems of a partially international nature with which the assembly was confronted, that of Limburg and Luxemburg.

After the dissolution of the personal union between the United Kingdom and Hanover in 1837 on the accession of Queen Victoria in Great Britain, only two foreign monarchs still belonged to the German Confederation, the King of Denmark for Holstein and Lauenburg and the King of the Netherlands for Luxemburg. In 1839 the Netherlands formally ceded the Western half of the Grand-Duchy of Luxemburg to the newly-founded Kingdom of Belgium. In order to compensate the German Confederation – to which the whole of the Grand-Duchy of Luxemburg had belonged – for the loss of the 150,000 souls living in the parts ceded to Belgium, the King of the Netherlands, as Grand-Duke of Luxemburg, agreed to incorporate the Duchy of Limburg, with a population of similar size, over which he also ruled, in the Confederation. The King-Duke informed the German Confederation that the Duchy of Limburg would be under the same constitution and administration (*dieselbe Verfassung und Verwaltung*) as the Kingdom of the Netherlands, but gave assurances that this would not prevent the application of the constitution of the German Confederation (*deutsche Bundesverfassung*) to the duchy. The Federal Assembly agreed to these arrangements and accepted the assurances of the King-Duke about the applicability of

---

[1] See above, p. 71 ff.   [2] I 84 f., 677.

the constitution of the German Confederation in the expectation that the wisdom of his majesty would prevent any inconveniences (*Unzukömmlichkeiten*) from arising in connection with the dual status of Limburg. The population of Limburg, which had in effect been united with the Kingdom of Belgium since 1830, would on the whole have preferred the continuation of that arrangement and there was some hostility to its allocation to the Northern kingdom.[1]

Elections for the Frankfurt Parliament had been duly held in Limburg and the two members to which the duchy was entitled were returned. On 25 May 1848, the land-owner Stedmann from Rhenish Prussia, who was then close to the Left Centre, informed the assembly that Baron von Scherpenzeel from Limburg had scruples about taking his seat in the assembly until the position of the duchy had been clarified by the Frankfurt Parliament. While the duchy had been asked to send members to Frankfurt, representatives had also gone to The Hague to take part in the deliberations of the States-General there. Stedmann asserted that though the inhabitants were loyal to their prince, they wished to see the relationship with the Netherlands confined to a personal union. He claimed that the population of Limburg was purely German and asked for investigation by a committee.[2] Wigard (*Deutscher Hof*, Main Left) regretted that Scherpenzeel had refused to follow the usual procedure of presenting his credentials and seeking admission to the assembly. If he had done so, any matter of principle arising would have been duly investigated.[3] In the end it was decided to refer Stedmann's motion to the central committee for admissions (*Centralausschuss für Legitimationen*).[4]

The reasons for von Scherpenzeel's scruples became clearer with the report of the committee on 5 June.[5] Scherpenzeel asked the assembly to declare Limburg German federal territory separate from the Kingdom of the Netherlands and to save it from any participation in the Netherlands debt. The committee refused to get involved in these issues and simply declared that von Scherpenzeel was to be admitted at once as a member of the assembly, but that the other questions should be investigated by the appropriate committee. The report came under attack from several members of the Left Centre for failing to protest

---

[1] This summary of the exceedingly complicated position of the Duchy of Limburg is based mainly on the report of the International Committee (called briefly *Internationaler Ausschuss*) of the Frankfurt Parliament, II 1011 ff.

[2] I 80. [3] I 81. [4] I 83. [5] I 218 f.

against the exploitation of Limburg by the Netherlands and against its treatment as a Dutch province. The *rapporteur* of the committee, the former Saxon minister von Lindenau, who also belonged to the Left Centre, asserted against these views that the dual relationship of Limburg, with both the Netherlands and the German Confederation, could not be denied. He reiterated that it was essential to have the intricate legal issues examined by the appropriate committee.[1] The assembly decided to refer the question of the legal relationship of the Duchy of Limburg with the Kingdom of the Netherlands to the newly formed committee for international affairs (*Internationaler Ausschuss*). A further motion to ask the committee to investigate complaints about maltreatment of Germans in the duchy was rejected.[2]

The committee for international affairs was elected at the end of May[3] and had a distinguished membership. The writer Arndt (Right), the Göttingen jurist Heinrich Zachariä[4] (*Casino*, Right Centre), the Berlin historian Friedrich von Raumer[5] (*Casino*, Right Centre) and the Weimar minister Oskar von Wydenbrugk (*Würtemberger Hof*, Left Centre) were among those who sat on the committee. The Left and the Habsburg Empire were only represented by the writer Franz Schuselka (*Deutscher Hof*), a *Deutschkatholik* from Bohemia who wanted to preserve the Austrian connection with Germany.[6] The Left Centre was almost as strong on the committee as the Right Centre. The Catholics did not have their due share.

Considering the complexity of the whole question, the committee did very well in having an exhaustive report ready by 14 July[7] and the debate took place on 19 July.[8] The report began by describing the Duchy of Limburg, as it now formed part of the German Confederation, as one of the most disastrous creations of recent diplomacy and as a mongrel (*Zwittergestalt*) creation of constitutional and international law which could not go on as before. There was now an opportunity to restore to Germany the Maas district, which had – at least partly – belonged to it before, under the rule of such states as Prussia and the Palatinate. The almost entirely nominal relationship which the weakness of the German Federal Assembly had permitted had to be converted into a real union. The committee affirmed the competence of

<hr>

[1] I 222 f.   [2] I 223.   [3] I 183.   [4] *ADB* XLIV.

[5] *ADB* XXVII; Raumer, *Briefe* and *Lebenserinnerungen*; *BSTH*.

[6] *ADB* XXXIV; Wurzbach XXXII; *BSTH*; Schuselka, *Österreichische Vor- und Rückschritte*; Schuselka, *Deutsche Fahrten*; see also Namier, *1848: Revolution* 25.

[7] II 912.   [8] II 1011 ff.

the National Assembly to make changes in the status of Limburg without the agreement of its duke, the King of the Netherlands. The report argued that the relationship between Limburg and the German Confederation was a purely internal German matter, because Limburg had been incorporated in the Confederation as a result of the obligations of one of its members, the King of the Netherlands as Grand-Duke of Luxemburg. The King-Grand-Duke was merely honouring the federal compact by compensating the Confederation for losses it had incurred in Luxemburg. In essence the relationship between Limburg and the German Confederation was therefore based on the legislation of the Confederation and not on international treaties. The German National Assembly, as the heir – in some respects – of the German Federal Assembly, was therefore entirely within its rights in turning Limburg into part of a German federal state. This was impossible as long as Limburg was administered as an integral part of the Kingdom of the Netherlands. The report rejected the Dutch claim that it was the Netherlands itself which had been compensated by Belgium through the cession of Limburg. On its interpretation of the relevant treaties and declarations the committee argued that Limburg should have been under a separate régime, as Luxemburg had been. On the general question of the constitutional position of Limburg the committee made two motions. Firstly, the union of Limburg with the Kingdom of the Netherlands under one constitution and administration was to be declared incompatible with the German federal constitution (*deutsche Bundesverfassung*). Secondly, the decision of the National Assembly of 27 May about the subordination of state constitutions to the general German constitution[1] was to apply to Limburg.

The report also dealt with Scherpenzeel's other point, that Limburg should be exempt from a share in the Dutch national debt. The committee realised that the population of Limburg was drawn more to Belgium than to the Netherlands, and that reluctance to share in the large Dutch national debt aggravated the distaste for the Northern state. On this question the committee moved that the German Provisional Central Power should try to find a solution safeguarding the rights of the duchy, subject to the approval of the National Assembly.

With two exceptions, the speeches in the debate from all sides of the house which followed went at least as far as the committee in asserting German rights in Limburg. The famous poet and writer Ernst Moritz

[1] See above, p. 130 ff.

Arndt (Right), a member of the committee, claimed[1] that Belgium and Holland were German lands (*germanische, deutsche Lande*). He spoke of the longing of Germans to regain in the future their great Western rivers, with which world domination over the seas was connected. Holland would be forced by necessity – owing to the increasing power of the Anglo-Saxon fleets and to the eventual loss of its overseas possessions – to become Germanic (*germanisch*). It would not do so voluntarily. The Bohemian German Schuselka (*Deutscher Hof*, Main Left), also a member of the committee, similarly spoke[2] of Holland as German soil and described Dutch as a German dialect. He denied the right of the Netherlands government to make Limburg share in the national debt and moved that any contribution on the part of the population of the duchy should be freely negotiated under the supervision of the German Provisional Central Power, subject to the ratification of the German National Assembly. The tone of Schuselka's speech was often vehement, particularly when he protested against what he described as the arrogant tone of the Dutch government and against any attempt of the Great Powers to interfere in what to him were purely German concerns. The Hamburg schoolteacher and journalist Christian Friedrich Wurm[3] (Left Centre), who came from Wurtemberg, drew attention[4] to the failure of the German Confederation to fulfil its contractual obligation of coming to the aid of the Grand-Duke of Luxemburg during the Belgian troubles. He believed that the attraction of the larger – German – state when founded would be such that the Dutch would not be ashamed of remembering their German blood and origin. He looked forward to a great future full of deeds for Germany in union with the free peoples of Germanic origin. A discordant voice was that of the distinguished historian Andreas Michelsen[5] (*Casino*, Right Centre), who gave up his chair in Kiel after difficulties with the Danish government arising from his support for the rights of the Germans in Schleswig-Holstein. In the spring Michelsen, who had in the meantime been called to a professorship in Jena, was sent to Berlin on a special mission by the Provisional Government in the Duchies. In spite of his involvement in the German national movement, Michelsen was fair-minded enough to subject the arguments of the committee to a critical examination.[6] He contested the conclusion reached in the report on the key issue of the legal basis for the

[1] II 1020 f.   [2] II 1021 ff.   [3] *ADB* XLIV; Wohlwill, 'C. F. Wurm'.
[4] II 1023 ff.   [5] *ADB* XXI; *BSTH*.   [6] II 1026 f.

relationship between Limburg and the German Confederation. On Michelsen's interpretation of the evidence, Limburg's membership of the Confederation arose primarily from international treaties and not in the first instance from a legislative act of the Federal Assembly which only followed the treaties. Therefore Germany was bound by a contractual obligation which could not be disavowed unilaterally. The Duchy of Limburg remained politically part of the Kingdom of the Netherlands, it merely accepted certain duties towards the German Confederation. There was no difficulty about belonging to two state systems, as long as one of them was a confederation. Once Germany constituted itself as *one* state, the subordination of any part to another power was impossible. But all this was matter of negotiation with the Duke of Limburg and King of the Netherlands, not something that could simply be decided by Germany, as the committee stated. The only speaker in the debate who supported Michelsen's legal interpretation was von Linde (independent).[1] But Linde believed[2] that the decision of the assembly of 27 May about the overriding nature of the German constitution was binding on Limburg. The writer Jacob Venedey[3] (*Westendhall*, Moderate Left) from Cologne made the remarkable suggestion[4] that Germany should present a counter-claim to the Netherlands for charging a fraction of their debt to Limburg, a part of Germany. The debts had arisen in connection with the colonies, the fleet, arsenals and fortresses. Germany should be prepared to settle the Limburg part of the Netherlands debt in return for a proportionate share of these assets, such as the fleet. Otherwise, not a penny should be paid. The argument neatly combined an attack on military expenditure and standing armies – an article of faith for the Left – with support for national aims. Another member of the Moderate Left (*Westendhall*), the Prussian official Friedrich Wilhelm von Reden,[5] who had earlier been in the service of the Hanoverian state, wanted[6] the German Provisional Central Power to make an attempt by negotiation to put the fortresses in Limburg under some German control. He predicted that the sympathy of the population of Limburg for Germany would decline unless the Germans succeeded in at least reducing the share of the Netherlands debt to be borne by Limburg.

The *rapporteur* of the committee, Zachariä, when commenting[7] on

---

[1] See above, p. 243 f.   [2] II 1029.   [3] *ADB* xxxix.   [4] II 1028.
[5] *ADB* xxvii; *BSTH*; see also Stüve, *Briefwechsel*, 38 (Detmold to Stüve, 20 May 1848).
[6] II 1028 f.   [7] II 1031 f.

the debate, drew attention to the internal repercussions of any decision of the assembly on this matter. The right claimed by the King of the Netherlands that he had only joined a confederation and not a federal state could be asserted by every German prince.

Several members of the Left put forward amendments to the report asking for stronger action. The Berlin historian Carl Nauwerck (*Deutscher Hof*, Main Left) wanted[1] a declaration that the union of Limburg with the Netherlands was to be dissolved, which went further than the statement of incompatibility for which the committee had asked. Schuselka and the journalist and owner of a printing business from the Rhine Palatinate, Georg Friedrich Kolb, both members of the *Deutscher Hof* (Main Left), in separate motions[2] denied the right of the Netherlands government to charge part of its debt to Limburg. In the division at the end of the debate, the recommendations of the committee were accepted by a large majority. A small addition expressing the urgency of the matter was also carried.[3]

These resolutions were not the end of the matter for the assembly. Members had the right to address questions to ministers of the Reich government and to parliamentary committees in the form of *Interpellationen* which had to be answered as soon as possible and could lead to a debate if the assembly so wished. On 1 September, as the assembly was waiting for detailed information about the Malmö armistice,[4] the Minister for Foreign Affairs, Johann Gustav Heckscher (*Casino*, Right Centre), answered an interpellation by the Rhenish land-owner Philipp Wilhelm Wernher (Left Centre) which asked for news about the steps the government had taken since the resolution of the assembly on 19 July. Heckscher, a Hamburg lawyer, gave a short summary[5] of the legal background of the question which was on the whole rather favourable to the Netherlands point of view. He could not report any progress in the debt question. Most of Heckscher's statement dealt with complaints from inhabitants that the German flag had been forcibly hauled down by Dutch troops which had been heavily and excessively reinforced. The Netherlands government had given assurances that the additional troops had been sent merely in order to maintain law and order. The house was critical of what was regarded as the inactivity of the Central Power and there were demands for stronger action and for a vote of no confidence in the government. One of the leaders of the Left, Carl Vogt, said[6] that German troops should

[1] II 1032.   [2] II 1033.   [3] II 1033.   [4] See below, p. 288 f.   [5] III 1822 ff.   [6] III 1826 f.

have entered Limburg in reply to the contemptuous treatment meted
out to the German government by the Netherlands. He accused the
Reich government of dilatoriness over the despatch of a minister to the
Netherlands to ask for explanations. All this was not the way to found
German unity and to instil foreign countries with a respect for Germany.
Venedey (*Westendhall*, Moderate Left) believed[1] that the Reich govern-
ment had been so weak because the Great Powers were against
Germany. But was this submissiveness really necessary? At present
Germany, with its 45 million inhabitants and the driving power of its
people, was the strongest power of the world. Nobody wanted war, the
Germans included. All that was needed for Germany was to show
courage and energy to foreign countries. The demand for strong action
against the Netherlands was echoed by Ludwig Simon,[2] a prominent
personality of the *Donnersberg* (Extreme Left). Another important
member of the *Donnersberg*, Wesendonck from Düsseldorf, however,
moved 'next business'.[3] The more moderate sections of the assembly
recognised that if the censure was pressed too far, the government
might be forced to resign, just as decisions were required on the Malmö
armistice. The government promised the publication of documents and
in the end the assembly resolved on next business.[4]

As negotiations with the Netherlands government made little
progress and as the Netherlands States-General at The Hague had
drawn up a constitution for the whole of the kingdom including
Limburg, Gustav Höfken[5] (*Würtemberger Hof*, Left Centre) raised the
matter again on 10 November.[6] The International Committee came to
the conclusion[7] that the introduction of the new Dutch constitution in
the Duchy of Limburg violated the resolution of the German National
Assembly of 19 July and asked the Provisional German Central Power
to oppose the execution of the Dutch constitutional measures in
Limburg in every way possible. The committee did not exclude negotiations with the Netherlands government. The debate on the report on
24 November 1848 began with a request by von Scherpenzeel[8] asking
to be allowed to have a statement by him read out to the assembly by
one of the secretaries, as he only knew German slightly. The wish was
granted. Scherpenzeel proposed[9] that the Netherlands should be given
an ultimatum demanding the separation of the administration of

[1] iii 1834 f.　　[2] iii 1835 f.　　[3] iii 1836.
[4] iii 1838. The documents are to be found in Hassler ii 214 ff.　[5] *ADB* l; *ÖBL*; *BSTH*.
[6] Follows v 3250.　[7] v 3549 ff.　[8] v 3552.　[9] v 3552 ff.

Limburg from that of the Netherlands. After a brief discussion the report of the committee was carried, apparently unanimously.[1]

The postscript to the assembly's treatment of the Limburg question came in May 1849, when the Frankfurt Parliament was disintegrating. The reading out of lists of resignations became a ritual at the opening of sittings. Among those whose names figured on 14 May[2] were those of the two members for Limburg, von Scherpenzeel and Schönmäckers. Scherpenzeel did not, however, simply resign from the assembly, but protested against the further union of Limburg with Germany.

The Luxemburg members took their seats in the assembly without demur, but also raised a problem for the Frankfurt Parliament. When the house passed a motion about the subordination of state law to the future Reich constitution on 27 May,[3] the three members for Luxemburg protested. They declared that their mandate was a limited one and that they had been delegated to object to any decision of the assembly threatening the independence of the Grand-Duchy. They informed the president of their inability to take any further part in the deliberations of the parliament for the time being. Their case was referred to the Constitutional Committee on 29 May.[4] The committee curtly denied the right of any part of the country to limit the mandate of its representatives or to issue instructions to them in any way. The Luxemburg members were asked to resume their seats in the assembly.[5] On 14 June, Heinrich von Gagern was able to report that the Luxemburg representatives were no longer so adamant in their refusal to take part in the work of the assembly and their absence proved short.

The Limburg dispute is useful for assessing the attitude of the Frankfurt Parliament to other states and nationalities. Unlike the Slav question, the Limburg problem was not aggravated by any hostility between the nationalities involved. The issue was in the first instance forced on the assembly and not sought by it. As the matter was raised in connection with the admission of new members, it was within the competence of the parliament. There was a wide choice open to the assembly. The house could have followed the same line as over Luxemburg and simply asked the members to take their seats, refusing to be drawn over the other issues until they had done so. There was no dispute about Limburg's participation in the German Confederation. Members for the Frankfurt Parliament had been elected quite legally

[1] v 3558.   [2] ix 6543.   [3] See above, p. 133.
Hassler, *Verhandlungen* i 14–15; Wigard i 160 f.   [5] i 251.

and it would not have been right for the two successful candidates to have left Limburg unrepresented in the assembly. Parliament was certainly very much concerned to ensure attendance, and in the case of Luxemburg something like a definite order to participate in the work of parliament went out. The assembly accepted some of the demands of the Limburg members because in this case yielding seemed a profitable business for the Germans, whereas giving in to the representatives from Luxemburg had only disadvantages. Unlike the Luxemburg members, the Limburg representatives held out a bait which the assembly could not resist. The assembly as a whole was tempted to draw the frontiers of Germany as wide as possible. This conduct is in accordance with the practice of other large national groups in the nineteenth century. In the case of the Germans, the tendency was strengthened by the key place occupied by the Holy Roman Empire in what they regarded as their national heritage. The blinkers of a historical romanticism and the enthusiasm of the new national era prevented the assembly from examining critically its identification of an obsolete conglomeration of territories, led to some extent by what might be regarded as Germans, with a modern national state. A mixture of cosmopolitanism (*Weltbürgertum*) and nationalism deluded the assembly into assuming that German hegemony, such as was to be found in the Empire, could be preserved in the new era of nationalities. The Romantic and cosmopolitan heritage certainly made the evolution of a modern German theory of nationality more difficult.

The German part of the assembly at least was united over Limburg and in the defence of national interests the Left was not backward. The Left Centre was the most active part of the assembly in this field. The Right Centre was more conciliatory and, certainly from the time of the formation of the Reich government onwards, made cautious by the realisation of responsibility. The Right was hardly engaged in the question, with the exception of Arndt, who spoke for himself rather than for his group.

For the Left and in some ways for the Left Centre, the attitude to nationalities and states was to some extent influenced by domestic constitutional considerations. In the case of Limburg, the opportunity to assert the power of the assembly against organs of a state and indirectly against its ruler, who had been a protégé of the Eastern Powers, was eagerly taken.

The International Committee based its rejection of Netherlands claims mainly on historical and legal reasons, and only marginally on ethnic considerations. Any committee of investigation was bound to start with a review of the legal situation, particularly one which was concerned with the law of nations as its full title (*Ausschuss für völker-rechtliche und internationale Angelegenheiten*) made clear. The committee interpreted the relevant treaties and official declarations very much in its way. The view that the title of the German Confederation to Limburg rested primarily on a legislative – and therefore internal – act of the Confederation was quite untenable, because the territorial arrangements formed part of the wider Belgian settlement in which many parties – including the Great Powers – were involved. The committee was fair enough to condemn the refusal of the German Confederation to answer the call of the Grand-Duke of Luxemburg for assistance. But it did not draw the obvious conclusion that it was adding insult to injury to ask the Grand-Duke to compensate the Confederation for territory the Germans should have defended. Legal considerations apart, it was better for European peace that the German Confederation did not get involved in what was primarily a civil war in the Low Countries. The King of the Netherlands left the Federal Assembly in no doubt that Limburg would be administered along with the other parts of his kingdom except for any special duties it owed to the German Confederation. There were no difficulties about this, as long as there was a loose association of states on the German side, any more than there were problems about the Habsburg terri-tories belonging to the Confederation. The committee was blind to any flaws in its argument that the Duke of Limburg had to submit to whatever the German constitutional organs decided at Frankfurt. All objections were simply ignored, because it was feared that any weak-ness shown by the assembly in enforcing the May resolution about the over-riding nature of the Reich constitution might threaten the very existence of the assembly. As will be examined later,[1] it can be ques-tioned whether the May resolution was realistic even for purely German states. The constitutional doctrine proclaimed by the assembly certainly did not fit the position of a foreign monarch who had joined the Confederation under certain conditions embodied in a treaty and had compensated this body for loss of territory. The King of the Netherlands could not be expected to submit without demur to a complete alteration of the whole situation. From a practical point of view, unless the King-Duke regarded yielding to the German demands

---

[1] See next chapter.

as a dictate of prudence, war might ensue, which could easily spread to the neighbouring Great Powers. Moreover, the legal position was certainly not so simple as the committee claimed. The Federal Act (*Bundesakte*) laid down than any organic changes could only be made unanimously. The Netherlands on behalf of Luxemburg and Limburg accepted the handing-over of the power of the Federal Assembly to the Vicar of the Empire. But the German Confederation had not thereby ceased to exist, indeed any such development would have undermined German claims. The King of the Netherlands had joined the German Confederation on certain terms and these could not be changed without his consent in view of the unanimity rule. Any new constitutional arrangement could only come about as a result of negotiation. The committee did not wish to deprive the King of the Netherlands of his rule over Limburg, but simply to obtain such administrative arrangements on the Dutch side as would permit Limburg to become a full part of the German state. Any such change would have frustrated the overdue efforts of the Netherlands authorities to modernise the political organisation of the kingdom. Not unnaturally, attempts to overhaul the machinery of government were no more confined to Germany than the emergence of national consciousness. The committee was really trying to reverse the emphasis in the dual relationship of Limburg by weakening its bonds with the Netherlands and strengthening the hitherto tenuous ties with Germany. In recommending this drastic alteration in the position of Limburg, the committee merely followed its own legal reasoning. The committee could hardly help being influenced by some of Scherpenzeel's statements about feelings in the Duchy, but it was careful – unlike some speakers in the debate – not to commit itself too closely to them. The report debated on 19 July indicated the realisation of the committee that for the Limburgers drawing nearer to Germany was merely a second-best, if they could not have union with Belgium.[1] Wurm had a flash of understanding when he remarked that the continuation of pro-German feeling in the Duchy depended on the success of German efforts in the question of the Limburg share of the Netherlands debt. The assembly was gullible about alleged pro-German tendencies, fell for Scherpenzeel's arguments and was taken for a ride by him. When Scherpenzeel realised that the Frankfurt Parliament and the Provisional Central Power could not help him in the question of the debt, he no longer wanted to have anything to do

[1] II 1015.

with Germany. Linguistic differences – for instance Scherpenzeel's open admission in the plenum that he could not speak German – failed to raise any doubts in the minds of members about the feasibility of incorporating the Duchy in a German national state. Quite apart from any practical difficulties about running a multi-lingual state, language played so vital a part in providing the common cultural heritage round which each national movement centred, that the failure to ventilate the question whether the Limburgers would be able to share in this is rather odd. Much was made of a common history, but this rested largely on the Holy Roman Empire, on the dynastic ties of the Netherlands dynasty with the German line of Nassau and on German princes having at various times ruled over parts of Limburg.

On Limburg, the assembly was largely united, whereas it was divided on most other nationality issues. Thus the Limburg question brings out most clearly the general attitude of the assembly to foreign nationalities and other states. This unanimity ceased when it came to discussion of relations between German and Slav.

ii. Germans and Slavs – Posen

The Slav question could be viewed from many different angles and had more complex international implications than the Limburg problem. The whole matter of relations between the Germans and the Slavs was bound to come up in the assembly, as their destinies were closely bound up with each other, particularly in the case of the Poles. The Germans found themselves in competition with another strong national move-ment and as has been seen[1] the assembly was nervous about the effects of the Slav congress in Prague early in June.

On 27 May, just before the congress commenced, Titus Mareck[2] (Left), a young lawyer from Styria, who described himself in the membership register as a 'citizen from Gratz', proposed a motion to reassure the Slavs about the intentions of the Frankfurt Parliament. He felt that this would counteract any hostile pan-Slav propaganda at the congress.[3] The assembly referred the motion to the Constitutional Committee as a matter of urgency.[4] The committee recommended acceptance of the motion drafted in a slightly different form which the

[1] See above, p. 73.   [2] Niebour, 'Die Abgeordneten Steiermarks'.
[3] I 118 f.   [4] I 121.

assembly passed by acclamation. In the resolution the non-German races (*Volksstämme*) living on German territory were assured of the right to their own culture, language, education, religion and interior administration. The Slavs, the Danish-speaking North Slesvigers and the Italian-speaking inhabitants of Southern Germany were specifically mentioned.[1] These considerable concessions were meant in the first place for regions with large foreign populations, rather than for small scattered minorities.

The most acute Slav problem for the assembly was the Posen question. In this Eastern province of the Kingdom of Prussia, something like civil war between the ruling German minority and the Polish majority was in progress, after an initial period of fraternisation in March 1848. The pattern of relations between the two peoples during the spring and summer of 1848 was in some ways similar to that of the Czechs and the Germans in Bohemia. Before 1848, the Grand-Duchy of Posen did not form part of the German Confederation. In March 1848, the Poles in the province asked for what was called a national reorganisation of the territory, by which they meant that as much of it as possible should be governed by Poles, though – certainly in the first instance – within the framework of the Prussian monarchy. Under the influence of his Foreign Minister Heinrich von Arnim-Suckow, who had plans for the renewal of Polish independence, Frederick William IV agreed on 24 March to a mixed German-Polish commission in the province of Posen to make proposals for a national reorganisation.[2] The King asked for the maintenance of law and order to allow reforms to proceed, but his hope was not fulfilled. The German population of Posen felt threatened and asked for the incorporation of the parts inhabited by Germans in the German Confederation. This in turn antagonised the Poles who regarded the whole of the province historically as theirs. The Prussian government obtained the incorporation of parts of the province in the Confederation and the quota of representatives for the Frankfurt Parliament was fixed at 12. The Poles felt seriously aggrieved by this development, particularly as the estates of the province – mainly Poles – had certainly not agreed to these changes and as many of them had made their opposition clear.[3] The division of the province

---

[1] I 183 f.   [2] Huber, *Deutsche Verfassungsgeschichte* II 640.

[3] I 1126. The rejection of the incorporation in the Confederation by 26 votes to 17 by the estates is not conclusive, as they were asked whether they wanted the whole of the province to join. In fact, only part of the province was transferred.

for certain purposes which was thus effected violated existing rights, as any attempt at a solution was bound to do. Details apart, it is remarkable as the one case in connection with the proposed unification of Germany where a division along ethnic lines was tried and where the Germans were prepared to leave some German-held territory out of their intended national state. Admittedly, the province of Posen did not form part of the German Confederation before 1848 and had first been annexed to Prussia during the Polish partitions at the end of the eighteenth century. In the case of Posen, the Prussian government did not stand pat on its own legal rights, but was prepared to surrender some of these. But the position of many Poles in the province was also changed, against their will, by annexing them to the German Confederation.

A period of intermittent strife, punctuated by military oppression, was not a happy time to try and disentangle the two nationalities by partition, for unhappily for this solution the two peoples were far from being neatly separated in two distinct areas. There was some dispute about the exact strengths of the two national groups. The main criterion was language, but religion also played a considerable part and it was sometimes argued on the Polish side that the Catholics generally did not want to join the German Confederation.[1] The International Committee[2] estimated that in a population of just under 1,300,000 in 1843, nearly 800,000 were Poles, 420,000 Germans and almost 80,000, Jews. The Polish memorandum to which reference has been made did not give a definite figure for the Polish population, but asserted that it was considerably more than 800,000 in a population of about 1,200,000. Disregarding Prussian officials and their families only temporarily resident in the province, the Germans were only credited with a strength of hardly 250,000. The rest were Jews. The encyclopaedia *Die Gegenwart*, the general tone of which was moderately radical, reduced the gap between Polish and German strength by including all the Jews in the latter. According to *Die Gegenwart*, there were 750,000 Poles as against 530,000 Germans.[3] These statistics were too flattering to the Germans. With some small adjustments, the figures given by the committee are likely to come near the truth. The Poles were found more in the Eastern and the Germans more in the Western

---

[1] I 1128 f. In the memorandum written by the Polish members of the Prussian National Assembly for the province of Posen which was read out to the Frankfurt Parliament.

[2] See its report debated on 24 July, II 1124 ff.   [3] I 70.

parts. But there was no neat division between the two nationalities and most districts were mixed, often with strong minorities of either side. Matters were further complicated by the fact that the fortress of Posen, which had been established by the Prussian authorities at considerable cost, lay in the part of the province mainly inhabited by Poles, though it was claimed by the committee that Germans and Jews in the town itself together outnumbered the Poles. The Prussian government had hesitated for ethnic reasons about incorporating the area round the town of Posen in the German Confederation and had only done so after some pressure from the German population. Strategic considerations thus frustrated a solution along ethnic lines, which was difficult enough in itself, and the demarcation line was so drawn as to confine the Polish majority to a corner of the province.

The Posen issue was raised in the Frankfurt Parliament as soon as it assembled. On 19 May, the Left Centre member Leue, the law reformer, moved that the King of Prussia should be asked for a public assurance that the Grand-Duchy of Posen would never be returned voluntarily to Poland, but would remain attached to Germany under a separate administration.[1] The motion was referred to the sections (*Abteilungen*),[2] as committees were not yet functioning. On 22 May, some members of a Polish national committee, an unofficial body in the absence of a Polish state, protested against the admission of any Posen representatives to the Frankfurt Parliament.[3] On the same day, the Cologne writer Venedey of the Left moved the exclusion of the representative of the town of Posen from the assembly.[4] The central committee for admissions (*Centralausschuss für Wahllegitimationen*) was bound to make a special report about the Posen representatives in view of the Polish protest and of the motion by Venedey. The committee reported on 3 June that there were no formal objections to the seating of the Posen representatives, but as the question of the validity of the elections in the province had been raised, the Posen members should only be provisionally admitted, pending an examination of the question of principle which was beyond the brief of the central committee.[5] Even this limited recommendation and the primarily technical issue of whether the question should be referred to a committee led to a clash of opinion in the plenum on 5 June. The Mainz lawyer Zitz (Left) objected[6] to the admission of the Posen deputies as long as there was any doubt about their status. He held that even their proposed temporary mem-

[1] I 31.   [2] I 32.   [3] I 196.   [4] Hassler, *Verhandlungen* v 6.   [5] I 196 f.   [6] I 225 f.

bership prejudiced the final issue. On the other side, one of the affected representatives, the Protestant minister Ernst Louis Nerreter[1] (*Casino, Right Centre*), made an impassioned appeal to members of the assembly not to abandon their German brethren. He asked for the unconditional admission of the Posen members.[2] A motion by the Trier lawyer Ludwig Simon (Extreme Left) demanded the complete exclusion of all the Posen members.[3] During this preliminary skirmish the Left thus staked a clear claim to act as the main defenders of the long-oppressed Poles. Heinrich von Gagern ruled that in accordance with standing orders the Posen members were entitled to sit while their membership was under consideration.[4] He maintained his point of view in the teeth of opposition from the Left. When he put the question to a vote, the assembled decided by a majority to refer the matter of principle to the International Committee.[5] All sides realised that the big battle was yet to come.

The report of the International Committee on Posen[6] came up in the plenum on 24 July and led to one of the great debates of the Frankfurt Parliament. For most of three successive sittings the house was occupied with a discussion of the question and on the fourth the division was taken. The report gave a careful historical survey from the German point of view, emphasising the economic contribution of the German colonist in the formerly Polish territories. The committee was sufficiently candid to realise that all the good the Prussian officials had done could not compensate the Polish people for the loss of their national independence. There was an admission that the Prussian authorities had not succeeded in making friends of the conquered. In the spring of 1848, there at last appeared to be a chance of reconciliation. The Germans sincerely offered their fraternal hand to atone for the crimes of their princes. But at the very moment that the Poles accepted the proffered hand, the paths of the two nations diverged once more. According to the committee, the aim of the Poles was to restore their state at the very least within the limits it possessed before the beginning of the partitions in 1772. The effect of the establishment of the pre-1772 frontiers of Poland would have been the loss of most of the Eastern possessions of Prussia, not only of the Grand-Duchy of Posen, but also of West Prussia. East Prussia would have been isolated from the main part of the Prussian state. The Germans wanted to help

---

[1] *Umrisse*, 131; Niebour, 'Die Vertreter der Provinz Posen'.
[2] I 224 f.   [3] I 224.   [4] I 228.   [5] I 229.   [6] Text, II 1124 ff.

the Poles to regain their own national state, but they did not themselves wish to be ruled by Poles. In their view the soil was neutral, the land in the Grand-Duchy was neither German nor Polish, it was the inhabitants who gave it the character of their nationality. The committee recorded the unhappy course of events since March, when disorder in the province had been endemic. Concessions to one side aroused disquiet in the other. Thus the contingent promise of national reorganisation to the Poles led to German pressure for the incorporation of a considerable part of the Grand-Duchy in the German Confederation. This in turn embittered the Poles. The committee concluded that owing to the intermixture of nationalities a complete geographical separation of the two peoples and full justice for both was an impossibility. The committee on the whole favoured an allocation of districts (*Kreise*)[1] to either side on the basis of the local majority nationality, apart from the mainly Polish hinterland of the fortress of Posen which should remain in German hands for strategic reasons. The report admitted that these suggestions would result in the Polish majority finding itself confined to the smaller part of the Grand-Duchy. But as against that the Polish part was the more fertile and it would be easier for Poles to live under German rule than *vice versa*. Even so many Germans would find themselves in the Polish regions.

The committee recommended the definite admission of the 12 Posen representatives to the assembly, and the provisional acceptance of the tentative demarcation line fixed by the Prussian commissioner, General Pfuel, but to reserve for the assembly approval for the definite arrangements. The Prussian government was to be asked to give guarantees for the preservation of their nationality to the Germans in the Polish parts even in the contingency that they ceased to be under Prussian rule. The non-German inhabitants of West Prussia were – in answer to several petitions – to be assured of the right to their own culture in accordance with Mareck's resolution of 31 May.[2] Though the last two recommendations were not unimportant, the debate was bound to centre round the admission of the Posen members and the demarcation line.

---

[1] Often rendered as 'circles'.   [2] See above, p. 268 f.

iii. Attitude of Left and Catholics to Posen question – Wilhelm Jordan –
'German intoxication with the Poles'

Floor motions and amendments came almost entirely from the Left
and from the Catholics. Blum (*Deutscher Hof*, Main Left) asked for a
commission of enquiry.[1] The Berlin radical writer Nauwerck (also
Deutscher Hof) endorsed the incorporation in the Confederation of
those parts of the province which had a preponderantly German
population. Pending the fixing of permanent frontiers, the Posen
representatives should remain members of the assembly on a provisional
basis. The three Eastern Powers were to be asked to free those of their
territories inhabited by Poles and to unite them in an independent
state which was to be assured of the protection and assistance of the
German nation against all enemies.[2] The lawyer Theodor Reh[3] from
Hesse-Darmstadt (*Westendhall*, Moderate Left), moved that the
Prussian and Austrian governments be asked to call a Polish National
Assembly for the purpose of the national reorganisation of Galicia and
Cracow (which belonged to Austria) and of Posen.[4] The omission of
West Prussia from this list is of some interest. The Extreme Left
(*Donnersberg*) proposed that for the time being no part of the Grand-
Duchy was to be incorporated in the German Confederation and that
the Posen members were not to be definitely admitted. An international
congress was to be summoned to restore a free and independent Poland.[5]
Another motion from the *Donnersberg*, partly with the same signatories,
desired a declaration from the assembly that the partitions of Poland had
been a shameful injustice and that it was the sacred duty of the German
people to collaborate in the restoration of an independent Poland.[6]

Apart from the Left, some Catholic groups showed an interest in the
Poles. Eight members, all of whom were Catholics, except for one about
to be converted,[7] with Ignaz Döllinger and von Ketteler at the head,
moved the revocation of the incorporation of parts of the Grand-Duchy
in the German Confederation and asked for the summoning of an
assembly representing the whole population of the province for the
purpose of establishing a permanent union (*Realunion*) of the Grand-

---

[1] II 1129.   [2] II 1130.
[3] *Umrisse*, 57; Wentzcke and Klötzer, *Deutscher Liberalismus*, 453; Bundesarchiv.
[4] II 1131.   [5] II 1131.
[6] II 1131.   [7] The Freiburg historian August Friedrich Gfrörer. *ADB* IX; *BSTH*.

Duchy with Germany. Both nationalities were to be guaranteed equal rights. The fortress of Posen was to remain a Prussian and German fortress and to keep a German garrison.[1] While this motion did not go so far in meeting Polish demands as some of those emanating from the Left, it tried to remedy some measures, like the forced incorporations in the German Confederation, which the Poles deeply resented. This group of German Catholics tried to combine allegiance to their German nationality with an endeavour to help their suffering co-religionists.

After the *rapporteur*'s speech, the debate from the floor was opened by two German members from Posen. One of these, the lawyer Emil Senff,[2] who also sat as a member of the Left in the Prussian National Assembly, criticised the house for the way it had proceeded. The question of principle, as to whether parts of Posen had been rightly incorporated in the German Confederation, should have been decided before admitting the Posen representatives. Senff accused the Poles of inconsistency when they, who had always appealed to the rights of nationality, now denied the German parts of the Grand-Duchy the right to opt for Germany. The Poles had become territorialists who objected to the incorporation of any part of the Grand-Duchy in the German Confederation because they claimed the whole of it for themselves. In view of the situation which had arisen between the two peoples, separation was the only practicable policy. Constitutionally the King of Prussia was quite entitled to have parts of the Grand-Duchy incorporated even if the estates did not agree.[3] Senff, though a member of the Left (at least in the Prussian National Assembly), was thus prepared to concede near-absolute rights to the King when it suited his nationalism.

Robert Blum, the leader of the Main Left (*Deutscher Hof*), who had helped the Poles in the years before 1848 at considerable risk to himself, criticised the committee for giving insufficient demographic and topographical information. He asked the assembly to be consistent in its treatment of other nationalities and not to alternate between territorial and ethnic conceptions as appeared most appropriate in the particular case. If ethnic considerations were to be decisive in the Polish question, how could the assembly lay claim to the Danish districts of Schleswig or to the Italian parts of Tirol? Only either the one or the other principle could be right. Adherence to a firm principle was essential as the basis of anything which could fairly be called a policy. Blum rejected war as a solution of the Polish problem. There

---

[1] II 1130.   [2] See Niebour, 'Die Vertreter der Provinz Posen'.   [3] II 1138 ff.

K

was a general concern for the strengthening of what had developed (*dass das Gewordene sich befestige*) and for the maintenance of treaties. Changes in the frontiers had to be made in consultation with the other interested powers. It was best to wait for the detailed investigations which the Prussian government was carrying out and for the recommendations which were going to be made as a result. The whole question was far too complicated to decide without much more factual information and that was why he asked for a commission of enquiry.[1]

Blum's speech was very thoughtful and moderate, somewhat resigned. It was a statesmanlike contribution to the debate. He castigated the tendency of the assembly to rush into decisions without proper knowledge of the facts. He also exposed the inconsistencies the house showed in its attitude to other nationalities. The tone of the speech was unusual for Blum, who had often appealed to passion and tried to obtain a quick vote without proper investigation.

Blum was followed by another member of the Left, who took a completely different line, Wilhelm Jordan.[2] Whatever view may be taken of the opinions expressed by Jordan, his speech was one of the most stirring and skilful ever made in the Frankfurt Parliament and, incidentally, one of the longest.[3] Jordan said that those who proposed to hand over half a million Germans in Posen to the Poles were at least unconscious traitors to the German people (*unbewusste Volksverräter*). The demarcation line had to take account of strategic necessities and he whole-heartedly supported the decision of the Prussian government to retain the district around the fortress of Posen, even if the ethnic principle was thus violated to the disadvantage of the Poles. Anyway the German intoxication with the Poles (*der Polenrausch*)[4] was declining. The Poles were more popular in the West than in the East. Apparently the liking for them increased the further one got away from them. Thus it appeared that any attraction to them was due not to real merits of the Polish character, but to a certain cosmopolitan idealism among the German people which refused to face facts where political articles of faith were involved. He admired the patriotism (*Vaterlandsliebe*) of the Polish people and wished that these feelings were equally strong in Germany. He was moved by the Polish tragedy, but it was quite a

---

[1] II 1141 ff.   [2] See above, p. 182.

[3] II 1143–1151. One page is taken up with the reading of a document. A speech of average length runs to about two pages.

[4] The term by which the debate is often called (*Polenrauschdebatte*).

different matter to try and undo the tragedy, to turn back the wheel of history. It was feeble-minded sentimentality to desire the restoration of Poland merely because its destruction filled us with just grief. This remark was greeted with cheers from the Right (presumably mainly from the Right Centre) and with hissing from the Left. Jordan remarked that it was a change for him to be hissed by the Left on which he sat. He spoke as he did, not although but because he was a democrat. What evidence was there that the Poles, who had been the mortal enemies (*Todfeinde*) of the German people, would forget the past and become a reliable bulwark against the Russians to whom they were related (*stammesverwandt*)? He believed that instead the Poles – once independent – would join forces with the Russians against the Germans. Also the new Polish state would not be content to remain confined to inland territory but would try to obtain access to the sea. This would threaten German rule over the Baltic coast. The Poles might not be able to maintain their independence against Russia. The friends of the Poles expected the Germans to go to war with Russia, if necessary, to make good the freedom of Poland. Those who preached hatred of Russia did not know what they were doing. Hatred between nations was a barbarism incompatible with the culture of the nineteenth century. There was nothing wrong with the Russian people, only with its system of government. He referred to threats that if the Germans did not release their Polish territories, the French would force Germany to do so by occupying parts of the Rhineland. He for one, who had recently been to Paris, discounted any warlike tendencies on the part of the French. In any case, fear of foreign countries should not deflect the assembly from the course it considered right. It was time to wake up at last from that dreaming forgetfulness of oneself in which they raved about all sorts of nationalities while being trampled under foot by all the world. What was now needed was a healthy egotism on the part of the German people which put the welfare and the honour of the fatherland first in all questions. The right of the Germans in Posen was that of the stronger, the right of conquest, not only by the sword, but also by the plough. In the West the Germans had been conquered, but in the East theirs had been the terrible misfortune of having themselves been the conquerors, thus giving to whole swarms of German poets the opportunity for touching jeremiads about the diverse nationalities which succumbed to the Germans. (Laughter on the Right, hissing on the Left.) The predominance of the German over the Slav races, perhaps with the sole exception of the Russians, was a fact, against which decrees of cosmopolitan justice could do nothing. The partition of Poland was only the proclamation of a death which had already taken place. He, Jordan, had the courage to challenge what had been a commonplace of German liberalism for almost a generation and to defend an action of cabinet policy (violent hissing in the Centre and on the Left). The spirit of world history in this case spoke to the nations in the language of exalted, tragic irony. In the partitions of Poland the princes, who were so soon to conspire together against revolution, carried out in the sense of the as yet unborn revolution its sentence against a nationality which in itself did not have the strength to break the feudal system. Jordan blamed the Catholic clergy for much of the friction between the Poles and the Germans. During the recent fighting the Polish people was motivated by religious fanaticism more than by national enthusiasm. In the present state of affairs, restoring Poland meant handing the peasants, who had been freed from their serfdom by the Prussians, back to the lash of the Polish aristocracy. It was a duty of the German people to further truly national development among the Poles and in this way to expiate some odious aspects of the manner in which the partitions had been carried out. He closed with the motto: 'Freedom for all, but the strength and welfare of the fatherland above all!' There was continuing tempestuous applause.

Jordan's speech illustrates the difficulties faced by an assembly consisting largely of members who had until a few months previously found themselves in opposition not only to the government, but to the whole political order. Jordan seriously attempted to free himself from the lack of realism which had been one of the unhappy consequences of the dichotomy prevailing before 1848. The tone of his speech may have been even shriller than necessary because he was in some ways thinking out his position aloud. While he mainly criticised the political attitude of the Left, his message affected all parties. In effect he called for an abandonment of the ideological approach to European diplomacy and instead for consideration of the *real* interests of the German people. The Left was – on this view – only repeating in a different way the mistake of the Eastern Powers in subordinating the interests of their states to their general ideological aims. Jordan thus foreshadowed the concept of *Realpolitik*, a few years before the term was coined.[1] In

---

[1] Probably first by A. L. v. Rochau in his *Grundsätze der Realpolitik* (1853).

itself there was nothing dangerous for the peace of Europe in calling on Germans to look first to their own interests. This was after all something which many other European nations had been doing for some time. The rejection of cosmopolitanism in itself did not make the Germans more warlike. Indeed some of the most explosive nationalist mixture may well have consisted of a combination of nationalism with the idea of a general German cultural mission in Europe. In detail, Jordan was at times unpleasantly chauvinist, for instance in his contempt for the Poles. There were elements of the master-race concept and of the doctrine that might is right. For Jordan personally the speech meant the beginning of a break with the Left.[1]

iv. Approval of Posen incorporations – Bohemia

On the second day of the debate, 25 July, von Radowitz, the leader of the Right (*Steinernes Haus*) and the chairman of the Catholic Association in the assembly, regretted the introduction of religious controversy into a national and legal matter. He regarded the proposals of the committee, which he supported, as the only way of avoiding either a complete incorporation of the whole province or its exclusion from the Confederation, both of which he rejected. Posen outside the Confederation might prove the nucleus of a Polish state. He wondered whether the restoration of Poland would be in the German interest.[2]

The Bohemian-born writer Franz Schuselka (*Deutscher Hof*, Main Left) from Austria, a *Deutschkatholik*, belonged to the International Committee, but dissociated himself from all its recommendations. He argued in his speech in the plenum that a partition of Posen conflicted with the policy of the assembly in other matters. On territorial grounds, South Tirol, Czech Bohemia and Danish North Schleswig were regarded as German. This was quite right, for a great people needs space in order to fulfil its world calling (*Weltberuf*). He would rather die than admit that Trieste should be ceded, although Italians lived there. But similarly – on this territorial argument – the Poles had a right to say that Posen was theirs; the Germans had only immigrated there. Nobody could tell how the Russians would react to the division of Posen and great dangers for Germany might follow. Schuselka rejected division as

---

[1] See below, p. 296.   [2] II 1155 ff.

impracticable and moved that the province be governed as a single unit for the time being.[1]

The only Polish member for Posen, the director of the Catholic clerical seminary in the town of Posen and a participant in the Slav Congress, Jan Chryzostom Janiszewski (independent), defended the Poles with great dignity and moderation. No court of law had yet judged who was to blame for the outbreak of violence in the province of Posen. As to German industriousness having conquered parts of Posen, he was quite prepared to recognise German application. He would, however, point out that there were badly run German and Polish villages, as there were some Polish estates which were as well run as any German ones. He denied the right of the Prussian government to incorporate the province in the German Confederation and to hold elections for the Frankfurt Parliament there. He himself had only accepted his seat in the assembly after long deliberation. The Poles in the Prussian monarchy demanded that they should cease to be second-class citizens and that attempts at Germanisation should be stopped. Charities which had been pressed upon the Poles (*aufgedrungene Wohltaten*), and of which they had been reminded *ad nauseam*, were no substitute for these human rights. Janiszewski received a prolonged applause at the end of his lengthy speech.[2]

Janiszewski was followed by a German member from the province, the headmaster Samuel Gottfried Kerst (then *Casino*, Right Centre), a Protestant from East Prussia who had earlier served in the Brazilian army, where he had distinguished himself as a cartographer.[3] Kerst said the German people could not be made responsible for making good all historic injustice, for conditions had changed. The right of peoples to a separate existence on the basis of nationality had nowhere been officially recognised. The claim was new. Kerst warned against any declaration of the right by the assembly, for they might find themselves obliged to surrender half of Germany. Any attempt to apply the principles of self-determination strictly in a central Europe where the nationalities were intermixed was an absolute impossibility. Kerst asked the assembly to support the incorporations in the German Confederation which had taken place.[4]

---

[1] II 1157 ff.   [2] II 1163–9.

[3] Niebour, 'Die Vertreter der Provinz Posen'; Kerst, 'Briefe'; Becker, 'Kerst'; Bundesarchiv.

[4] II 1169 ff.

The Catholic lecturer (*Privatdozent*) at Bonn, Jakob Clemens[1] (*Würtemberger Hof*, Left Centre), rejected the attacks which had been made on Catholics and objected to the discrimination against his co-religionists in the Kingdom of Prussia. He condemned the way the Polish majority had only been allocated a corner of the province. He moved that the whole Grand-Duchy be incorporated in the German Confederation, but only temporarily, until a possible restoration of Poland.[2] Clemens wanted to help the Poles, but it was doubtful whether his proposal was in any way acceptable to them, except that the division of the province would be avoided.

The Bavarian Catholic priest Friedrich Thinnes[3] (*Casino*, Right Centre) spoke to the Catholic motion by Döllinger, which was not an easy task. The Left and the Catholics both had considerable sympathy with the Poles and wanted to do something for them, but the Left was much more prepared to come out into the open. At the beginning Thinnes defended his co-religionists against the charge of opposing the recommendations of the committee because they shared the Polish prejudice that the incorporation of part of Catholic Posen in the German Confederation was treason against the Catholic religion. Indeed, he and his group were advocating the incorporation of the whole of the Grand-Duchy. They had no fear for the Catholic religion. They were against a demarcation line because it led to a new partition.[4]

The Poles certainly had the strongest objections to the division of the Grand-Duchy and any solution which avoided a split was preferable to them. But the price Thinnes was prepared to pay on their behalf – incorporation in the German Confederation – was rather high, though if seen to be necessary, the Poles might accept it in return for a withdrawal of partition. Altogether, however, the support the Poles received from the Catholic group was disappointing.

One of the toughest speeches against the Poles came from another Catholic, but of the anti-clerical party. Karl Giskra (*Würtemberger Hof*, Left Centre), who was to be Austrian Minister of the Interior from 1867 to 1870, was born in Moravia in 1820 and according to one source[5] was of Slav origin. He rose from humble circumstances to become a teacher of law at the University of Vienna, and was one of the radical leaders in the March revolution in Vienna.[6] Giskra said that even Polish

---

[1] *ADB* LV; *BSTH*; *NDB*.   [2] II 1172 ff.   [3] *Umrisse* 71   [4] II 1201 ff.   [5] Wurzbach v.
[6] Friedrich Schütz, *Werden und Wirken des Bürgerministeriums* (1909) 48 ff; *ÖBL* I; *BSTH*.

fanaticism in Galicia and in Posen had not been able to destroy his sympathy for the Polish people. In principle, he was in favour of the restoration of an independent constitutional Polish state, but he doubted whether the time was ripe for it. Polish claims had to be carefully scrutinised. In general the Poles viewed matters from a territorial point of view, not from that of the nationality of the population occupying the soil. Polish hopes were directed towards the restoration of the old empire of the Jagiellon dynasty stretching from the Baltic to the Black Sea. The Germans had to consider their own interests and like every other nation they had the duty of self-preservation. For that Posen was necessary. He believed it was essential to adhere to the principle of demarcation in Posen. Any sign of hesitation would weaken the whole German position towards the Slavs, in Bohemia, Moravia, Styria and Illyria. He rejected any French interference in the Posen question, which was purely a German affair. 'Should you suffer the shame of allowing yourselves to give up our good right owing to the protest of a neighbouring people (tempestuous cheers), then I would despair of your future, my German people, then you, gentlemen, would have murdered yourselves. (Long continuing applause . . .)'[1]

The debate from the floor was closed on 26 July, after three sittings. The division was taken on the following day. The Posen members had been allowed to take part in the debate, but not to vote in a matter which concerned their status.[2] The motion by Robert Blum to send a commission of investigation to Posen to obtain the necessary facts for a decision was rejected by 333 votes to 139, whereupon Blum declared that his political friends would have to absent themselves from further voting, as they were insufficiently informed.[3] The first recommendation of the committee, to recognise the incorporation of parts of the Grand-Duchy of Posen in the German Confederation and to admit definitely the representatives for the region, was carried by 342 votes to 31.[4] Owing to the abstention of many members from all sides of the house who believed that the matter had not been sufficiently aired for a decision, not only on the Left, but also among the Catholics,[5] the total vote was nearly one hundred down. The absentees were mainly opponents of the recommendations of the committee. The second recommendation of the committee, about the demarcation line, was carried with an amendment by Giskra stipulating that the Provisional German Central Power

[1] II 1203 ff.   [2] II 1134 f.
[3] II 1233.   [4] II 1238.   [5] II 1238: declaration by Döllinger and several others.

should carry out further investigations before the line was finally accepted.[1] The third recommendation of the committee was rejected. Instead an amendment by Prince Lichnowsky was carried according to which the assembly expressed its firm expectation that the Prussian government would assure to the Germans living in the Polish part of the Grand-Duchy the protection of their nationality in all circumstances.[2] The fourth recommendation of the committee about the position of the non-Germans in West Prussia was also rejected. An amendment moving next business in view of the resolution of the assembly of 31 May with regard to other nationalities was carried.[3] The Extreme Left motion condemning the partitions of Poland and declaring it a duty of the German people to help to restore Poland was defeated by 331 votes to 101, with 26 abstentions. In this division Blum and his collaborators voted again. A great many declarations were made by members explaining why they had felt unable to vote for the motion, for instance because they did not regard it as the duty of the assembly to make judgments on past history.[4] It certainly cannot be inferred that all those who refused to vote for the motion regarded the Polish partitions as justified or that they were opposed to a restoration of Poland.

The further debates in the assembly on the Posen question were never on the same scale as those from 24 to 27 July which have been called *Polenrauschdebatten* after the term used in Jordan's speech. The threefold division of the Frankfurt Parliament established in July regarding this question continued to apply whenever the matter was raised again. The majority which supported the incorporation of the larger part of the Grand-Duchy in the German Confederation was opposed by the Left which wanted to see the Polish part considerably increased. A small Catholic group led by Döllinger condemned the annexation of the larger part of the province to Germany, regarded partition as impractical and wished to maintain the integrity of Posen in close association with Prussia and Germany. Döllinger's solution bristled with difficulties and its defeat in the Frankfurt Parliament was a foregone conclusion. But the plan was in fact revived, in a somewhat different form, by an unexpected ally, the Prussian National Assembly, which was following a much more radical course than the Frankfurt Parliament. On 26 October 1848, the Prussian National Assembly in Berlin by a narrow majority passed article I of the Prussian constitution. According to this article, all parts of the Prussian monarchy were

---

[1] II 1239.   [2] II 1240.   [3] II 1240.   [4] II 1247.

K2

to belong to the Prussian state. The inhabitants of the Grand-Duchy of Posen were guaranteed the rights which they were given on being incorporated in Prussia. The Berlin assembly took these decisions in spite of a warning by the Prussian Minister of the Interior, von Eichmann, that it was risking a collision with the German National Assembly in Frankfurt.[1] But the Prussian assembly was only too glad to show its strength to the German National Assembly and to the Provisional Central Power in Frankfurt. From this time onwards, the Posen question became engulfed in the conflict between Berlin and Frankfurt, complicated by the ideological struggle which had been going on all the time. In answer to several interpellations, the Reich Minister of the Interior, von Schmerling, declared in the Frankfurt Parliament on 6 November that the resolutions of the Prussian National Assembly were void as they contradicted decisions of the Frankfurt Parliament. He added his surprise that the Left, which had earlier defended the omnipotence of the Frankfurt Parliament, was now encouraging particularist interests.[2] There had, indeed, been a reversal of positions. At the end of the period reserved for interpellations of ministers, Wilhelm Jordan, by now a pillar of one of the Right Centre groups (the *Landsberg*),[3] attempted to follow up Schmerling's attack on the inconsistencies of the Left by moving that the assembly should reaffirm its resolution of 27 May over Raveaux's motion.[4] Jordan's move was bound to place the Left in a tactical dilemma. On the matter of substance, the future of the Grand-Duchy of Posen, the Left at Frankfurt was quite pleased with the work of the Berlin assembly. Article I of the Prussian constitution offered a way out of the defeat the Left at Frankfurt had suffered over Posen on 27 July. On the other hand, the Frankfurt Left had tied its hands to some extent by supporting the moves in the assembly at the end of May aimed at subordinating the constitutions of the states to that worked out for the whole of Germany by the Frankfurt Parliament. Vogt's way out of the dilemma was to claim that there was no contradiction between the decisions of the two assemblies.[5] Jordan took the opportunity to make another long speech full of brilliant rhetoric.[6] In the end, the assembly accepted a motion proposed by Kerst from Posen (like Jordan a member

---

[1] *Verhandlungen der Versammlung zur Vereinbarung der Preussischen Staats-Verfassung* (1848), 23 October, 1733 ff.; 26 October, 1803 ff.

[2] iv 3078 f.   [3] See below, p. 296.

[4] See above, p. 133.   [5] iv 3128 ff.   [6] iv 3119 ff.

of the Right Centre *Landsberg*), to pass on to 'next business' after reaffirming its previous decisions.[1]

The last phase of the Posen controversy in the Frankfurt Parliament came in February 1849, when the house was in the throes of the hegemony issue.[2] On 6 February the assembly debated a report by the International Committee on the demarcation line in the Grand-Duchy of Posen. The boundary was finally fixed by a commissioner appointed by the German Provisional Central Power, in collaboration with the Prussian Government. The line proposed by the Reich commissioner was even less favourable to the Poles than the provisional boundary fixed earlier by the Prussian Government. The International Committee of the Frankfurt Parliament recommended acceptance.[3] The most effective criticism of the demarcation line came from the spokesman of the Catholic group, Döllinger (independent).[4] He drew attention to the fact, which was common ground, that only about 350,000 Poles – out of about more than 800,000 – would find themselves in the Polish part, which would contain considerably less than one-third of the population of the Grand-Duchy. Another leading Catholic, von Radowitz (Right), argued that the proposed demarcation line was essential for strategic reasons.[5] Several speakers of the Left defended Polish interests. In the end, the demarcation line was approved by 280 votes to 124. The minority consisted mainly of the Left, with some support from Catholics (including Döllinger) and other elements.[6]

Whereas in the case of Limburg the argument centred around treaties and historical memories, with Posen the interests of the population, both German and Polish, were very much in the centre of the debate. While the Limburgers used the Germans to fight out their differences with the Dutch, the Germans themselves were involved over Posen as inhabitants. But as comparative late-comers and as recent conquerors, the Germans realised that with Posen treaties and history were not sufficient allies, as they believed these were in the case of Limburg. In law, there was no doubt about the title of the King of Prussia to the Grand-Duchy of Posen. Indeed, what was at stake during the debates was not Prussian rule over Posen, but how exactly the Grand-Duchy or parts of it would fit into the German state. Not unnaturally, the majority of the Frankfurt Parliament – apart from the Left and a Catholic group – supported the partition carried out by the

[1] IV 3138. [2] See below, Ch. 8. [3] VII 5045 ff.
[4] VII 5066 ff. [5] VII 5072 ff. [6] VII 5089.

Prussian government. It was not easy for a parliament charged with the task of founding a national state to give up territory to another. The dictates of nationalism and strategic necessities prevented the assembly from rising to the level of higher statesmanship. The minority failed to convince because it fought with its hands tied. The Left was the slave of its own dogma, of a crude and insufficiently developed doctrine of democratic rights. It was tied down by the centralism of the Raveaux motion which boomeranged over the 'particularism' of the Prussian parliament in the case of Posen and it was prevented by its dream-world of international brotherhood from facing up to the diplomatic consequences of its German nationalism. The Catholics were half-hearted and the solution they proposed hardly remedied the ills of which they – rightly – complained. In spite of a certain harshness, most of the assembly did, however, bear in mind the injustice the Poles had suffered in the partitions of the eighteenth century. The Poles received a certain consideration, subject to the safeguarding of German interests, which was largely denied to the other Slavs with which the Frankfurt Parliament was concerned.

The assembly, including the Left, showed little understanding for the refusal of the Czechs to elect representatives for the Frankfurt Parliament. Some members of the Left were forward in asking for German military measures in Bohemia to protect the Germans against the Czechs.[1] There was general agreement in the assembly, in spite of the far-reaching changes made in Germany by the establishment of national institutions, that Bohemia should be represented at Frankfurt even for its Czech districts and there was no support for any division along ethnic lines, such as was envisaged in Posen. There was no guilty conscience, as in the case of Poles, and Bohemia was largely considered as German.[2] The moderate majority of the committee of investigation (*Ausschuss für die Begutachtung der österreichisch-slavischen Frage*) and of the assembly managed to ward off any extreme action in Bohemia when the matter was debated on 1 July.[3] On the question of represen-

[1] I 418. Motion of 20 June by Johann Nepomuk Berger (Extreme Left), who was later a Minister of the Austrian crown, and by the medical practitioner Ernst Schilling (*Deutscher Hof*, Moderate Left; see above, p. 70) that Bavarian and Saxon troops should be sent to Bohemia. See also Hassler I 45.

[2] See for instance I 212, the motion of 5 June by the distinguished writer Gustav Höfken (*Würtemberger Hof*, Left Centre) asking for energetic measures to ensure elections in Bohemia, 'an originally German territory, inseparably connected with Germany through nature, history, education, law and justice'.

[3] I 660 ff.

tation of Czech districts, the assembly remained adamant, however, though this was bound to remain a dead letter. Little could be achieved by any show of sternness and an inexpensive generosity might have created a better climate between the Czechs and the Germans.

v. South Tirol – The French Republic – Defence

The assembly also viewed the desire of the Italians in South Tirol to be released from their association with Germany with little sympathy. As in the case of Posen, the German representatives of Tirol were active in opposing any concessions. On 12 August 1848, the assembly on the recommendation of the International Committee refused to release the districts of Tirol inhabited by Italians from Germany.[1] So far, in all these questions – from Limburg to Posen – the assembly had been dealing with matters which were to a greater or lesser extent within its competence. Like the Polish problem, Italian concerns took the Frankfurt Parliament right into the sphere of high diplomacy. A debate about the war between Austria and Italy held on 12 August[2] was largely inconclusive, because Germany was only indirectly involved and relations with other states were a matter for the Provisional Central Power, which was asked to consider the report of the International Committee and the motions which had been put, in the expectation that German interests would be maintained.[3]

For similar reasons, a general foreign policy debate on 22 July[4] ended with a reference to the Provisional Central Power. The assembly unanimously accepted a number of generalities about living in peace with other states and expressed itself in favour of recognising the French Republic. The most important practical issue, the raising of the strength of German troops in the East in view of reported Russian military reinforcements on the other side of the border, was referred to the Central Power.[5]

The assembly realised that an active foreign policy required an increase in armaments and the two committees concerned with the armed forces were quite active. After two debates, the assembly agreed on 15 July by 303 votes to 149 – mainly of the Left – to a recommendation of the military committee (*Ausschuss für Wehrangelegenheiten*)

[1] II 1547 ff.   [2] II 1560 ff.   [3] II 1568.   [4] II 1097 ff.   [5] II 1117 ff.

that the army should be brought up to the strength of two per cent of the actual population.[1]

There were many reservations in the assembly, even outside the Left, to standing armies. There was much more general agreement on the need to create a navy. On 14 June, the recommendations of the naval committee (*Ausschuss für eine deutsche Marine*) – one of the most active committees of the assembly – to raise six million thaler[2] was accepted almost unanimously.[3] The need for a navy was felt so strongly at that time particularly because of the Schleswig-Holstein war, which became a vital question for the assembly. Indeed, in many ways support for Schleswig-Holstein and for a navy were the two articles of faith of the German national movement.

vi. Malmö armistice

On 26 August, Prussia and Denmark concluded an armistice at Malmö. Hostilities on land and on sea were to be suspended for seven months, prisoners to be exchanged, the Danish blockade to be lifted and all German ships to be restored to their owners. In general, all Danish and German troops were to be withdrawn from Schleswig and Holstein, each of which was to be garrisoned by local troops under separate command. For the time being the Duchies were put under a common administration, to be nominated jointly by Denmark and Prussia, which was to govern in the name of the King of Denmark as Duke. In principle, all laws made by the German Provisional Government of the Duchy were to be regarded as annulled, but they could in certain cases be re-enacted. The stipulations of the armistice were not to prejudice the conditions of peace for which negotiations were to be opened at once.

Prussia signed the treaty not only on her own behalf, but also on that of the German Confederation. There was no mention of the German Provisional Central Power. Denmark could not be officially informed of the constitutional changes which had taken place within Germany while the two countries were at war. Prussia had been authorised by the Provisional Central Power to conclude an armistice, on certain conditions, which had not been met in full.

---

[1] II 940.   [2] I 305.   [3] I 319.

The terms of the armistice came as a shock to German public opinion. The aims for which the Duchies had risen had certainly not been realised in full. The main demand of a permanent joint administration for the Duchies separate from that of the rest of the Danish monarchy had not been granted. Some of the armistice arrangements made a distinction between Holstein, which continued to come under the German Confederation, and Schleswig, which was outside it, though there was to be a joint government. The treaty was a compromise, for the Danish authorities were not restored to the full power they had possessed before the March uprising. Indeed, criticism of the treaty was not confined to the Germans, but was also vocal among the Danes.

For the Germans, the moment was one of rude awakening. The public debate, including that conducted on the floor of the Frankfurt Parliament, had so far been very much in terms of securing German rights. The assumption was that Germany had been victorious. There had, indeed, been some German military successes on land, as well as some defeats. But the war could not be won on land alone. German achievements on land had been balanced by Danish mastery of the seas and the blockade of the German North Sea and Baltic ports. The damage done not only to the ports themselves, but to an ever-increasing hinterland, was well realised in Germany and helped to strengthen the agitation for a German fleet so that a situation of this kind would not be allowed to recur. While the Danes could not easily defeat Germany decisively simply by a blockade, they could certainly keep victory out of Germany's grasp. The Germans found it difficult to accept that a small state, like that of Denmark, could resist the larger Germany in the long run, particularly as so considerable a part of the Danish dominions had been overrun by German troops or was threatened by them. This incredulity encouraged the belief that the German military effort, which had apparently come so near complete success, had been sabotaged by those who did not have the interests of Germany truly at heart, in particular by the Prussian court and government. Those who thought thus omitted from their calculations not only the impossibility of snatching Danish mastery of the sea from the Danes in the near future, but also the realities of the diplomatic situation. The two leading Great Powers, Britain and Russia, were not prepared to see Denmark humiliated, and France was at best neutral and potentially hostile. Also it was often forgotten in Germany that the war in the Duchies was to the Danes a matter of survival. The Danes had little alternative but to resist demands which would have reduced their state from a second-rate to a third-rate power and prevented them from proceeding with the integration of Schleswig in the Danish monarchy. They could not accept the complete abandonment of the duchy of Schleswig, including its Northern part mainly inhabited by Danes. The Danes felt that the Germans had pushed their claims far beyond any point where they could be supported by legal rights. Thus the Danes had no incentive to end the war, for in the summer of 1848 they were not even offered an ethnic frontier – with the partitioning of the Duchy of Schleswig – as the eternal indivisibility of the Duchies had become sacrosanct in Germany. There was no basis for discussion or compromise from the Danish point of view.

The Danes drew strength from being on the defensive and from regarding themselves as the injured party. They were united. This could not be said of the Germans, even outside the Habsburg Empire. However much enthusiasm there was on the German side, neither the German governments nor the German people were as much at one in this as the Danes. Many voices were raised in Germany questioning whether the sacrifices demanded in this war were necessary, particularly in the North which was mainly affected by the blockade. While there was great bravery on the battle-field, the will to adopt economic counter-measures against Denmark was lacking even in the Duchies themselves. In Frankfurt, few members of the National Assembly were indifferent to the fate of the German areas in the Duchies. But there was a substantial body of opinion, including the Reich government, which had come to the conclusion that a halt had to be called to a war which could not be won quickly and which was bound to cause increasing misery to wide parts of the country the longer it went on.

For the Reich government under Prince Leiningen, with Heckscher as Foreign Minister and Schmerling responsible for the Interior, the armistice negotiations were a testing time. The Reich government had responsibility – to Germany and to its representative, the National Assembly – without power. The Danish war was a legacy left by the German Federal Assembly, from which the Vicar of the Empire and his government had taken over in July. The government was only completed in the first half of August, at the end of which month the armistice at Malmö was signed. Owing to the war the formal steps which were necessary to inform the Danish government of the political reorganisation in Germany had not been taken. Indeed, the new order had not been recognised by the European Great Powers, except for Prussia and Austria, and even by them only to a limited extent in practice. The ministers themselves did their best in difficult circumstances, handicapped by the lack of nearly everything from proper control over a state apparatus to proper assistance. They were heartily sick and tired of being blamed for their failure to solve complex problems,[1] such as that of Limburg,[2] in which there was not the slightest reason on any sober consideration to anticipate concessions from the other side. Ministers now found themselves criticised for allowing the Prussians to conclude and ratify the Malmö armistice with Denmark without securing the German objectives. Once more the assembly was confronted with all the complications of the relationship between the state governments and the Provisional Central Power. Thus diplomatic and constitutional issues were closely linked in this whole question. To the critics of the government in the Frankfurt Parliament it appeared that better terms could have been obtained if the Reich government had kept a closer hold over the negotiations which Prussia was conducting. Unfortunately the mission of Max von Gagern to the Duchies during the final stages of the negotiations proved an utter failure, though it was probably a hopeless task.

Whatever the Frankfurt Parliament might in fact be able to do, the interest of the assembly in the Malmö armistice was patent and the competence of the house to vote on the question was common ground between the parties. Before the setting up of the Central Power it was tenable to argue that the assembly should confine itself entirely to the drafting of a constitution. But once a Reich government, however shadowy, had come into existence, the assembly was bound to scrutinise the policy of this government which had to be answerable to the house. On these general grounds there could thus be little doubt about the right and indeed the duty of the assembly to hold the Reich government to account for its role in the armistice negotiations. The responsibility or even culpability of the Reich government in allowing the armistice to be concluded on the terms of Malmö would depend on the view taken by the critic of the relative strengths of power both within Germany itself, and between Germany and other countries. The constitutional and diplomatic issues were inextricably enmeshed in

---

[1] For instance the Reich Minister of Trade, the Bremen businessman Arnold Duckwitz. See his *Denkwürdigkeiten* 82 ff.

[2] See above, p. 256 ff.

each other. The different attitudes adopted towards the Malmö armistice revealed a fundamental cleavage on leading questions of home and foreign policy. The solid rejection of the armistice by the Left is probably the most striking feature of the Malmö debates in September.

The Left accepted the legal reasoning based on historical rights in the case of the Elbe Duchies as much as over Limburg. Unlike the case of Posen, no interest was expressed by the radicals in seeing any documentary evidence about the national allegiance or language of the inhabitants of, say, the Duchy of Schleswig. No attempt was made by the Left in the Malmö debates to secure the right of self-determination for the Northern districts of the Duchies, although this question was being ventilated at the time, for instance in diplomatic circles.[1] The arguments of the German party in the Duchies were thus swallowed in full by the Left in the Frankfurt Parliament, and quite uncritically. Over Schleswig-Holstein, the Left occupied a leading position in German nationalism in the Frankfurt Parliament, much more radical than most of the Right Centre which was prepared to accept a compromise. The extremism of the Left in external policy matched the uncompromising line it took in internal affairs. The moderates were prepared to work within much of the existing governmental framework, because they believed that it represented historical traditions based at least to some extent on popular wishes. The Left postulated a division between government and people which their constitutional concepts had not bridged and perhaps could not bridge until they had themselves become ministers. Seemingly condemned to the role of a permanent opposition, the Left in the Frankfurt Parliament saw its hope for the realisation of its plans outside rather than inside the chamber. The Left increasingly regarded the assembly itself as unrepresentative of opinion in the country, drawing evidence from the greater radicalism of some of the state parliaments, for instance in Prussia. This shift in the balance of power led to some revision of the belief of the Left in unitary government for Germany. In many ways, there was even a lack of faith in political institutions generally, not only in governments, but also in parliaments of the type which had been created in Germany. In their desperation, many members of the Left saw another revolution and the establishment of a Convention and of an Executive Committee (*Vollziehungsausschuss*) modelled on France after 1789 as the only way

---

[1] The British government showed some interest in this plan.

out. Altogether, in the heady atmosphere of 1848, many extremists believed they were on the brink of a new era in which governments and state boundaries would have little meaning and in which the normal laws of economics would not operate. In their idealism, these extremists were in fact quite remote from the political, diplomatic and economic conditions in which they were operating. 'The people' did not conform to the image in the minds of the extremists. Attachment to the traditions of a state, however small and insignificant, did not cease because it appeared irrational to the radicals. With more intense national feeling, which the radicals supported, the differences between peoples were in fact accentuated and frontiers became more and not less important. Finally, the indifference of so many radicals in theory to the realities of the economic situation – although some, like the philosopher Ruge, were in fact quite shrewd businessmen on their own account – made them blind to the necessities of the situation. There was in general a refusal to follow through theory to its logical conclusions. Few of the extremists had the nerve to carry out in cold blood the brutalities which were constantly in their mouths.

The Left believed, or at least professed to believe, that all the National Assembly had to do was to say the word to bring recalcitrant state governments into line and to make them obey the will of the people, in this particular case to continue the war until Denmark had been forced to her knees. Diplomatic complexities, problems of strategy and economic necessities were simply ignored. The Left did not explain how a people which was so divided, partly as the result of the action of the radicals themselves, could muster the unity necessary to fight a European war. As the heirs of the French Revolution, the German radicals were certainly far from being adherents of non-violence or pacifists. They showed frighteningly little fear of unleashing a war involving all Europe.

While the radicals were quite sincere in condemning the Malmö armistice, they were too experienced as parliamentarians to ignore certain tactical advantages accruing to them as a result of their attitude. Here was an opportunity to inflict punishment on a Reich government consisting entirely of moderates which was deeply involved in the conclusion of an unpopular armistice. With help from other quarters, the government might be overthrown and there was even a chance of eventually reorganising the whole central power more in accordance with the wishes of the Left. Also the agitation against the

Prussian monarchy could be revived, though care would have to be taken not to beat the anti-Prussian drum so hard as to frighten off any of the temporary allies of the Left in this question. If wisely used, the Malmö treaty could help the Left to break out of its isolation. The Left Centre in the *Würtemberger Hof*, which had always been in the lead in defending German national interests, was likely to join forces with the Left – at least in large part – over this issue, in spite of being represented in the government. There was also bitter opposition to the armistice among some members of the Right Centre in the *Casino* representing Schleswig-Holstein interests. For once, Dahlmann (*Casino*) and the Left found themselves on the same side.

On 4 September, after a statement by the Reich Foreign Minister, Heckscher (*Casino*, Right Centre), giving details of the armistice,[1] Dahlmann at once began a bitter attack on the treaty. He interpellated the Foreign Minister about the attitude of the Reich government to the armistice. He concluded a series of questions with the statement that on 9 June the assembly had resolved to preserve the honour of Germany over Schleswig-Holstein.[2] This remark was greated by tempestuous applause and at one stroke Dahlmann, hitherto a pillar of the main government party, had become leader of the opposition. In spite of considerable pressure from the Left, supported by parts of the Left Centre, to reject the armistice at once, the calmer parts of the assembly managed to obtain reference of the question to a committee. A joint body consisting of the committees for international affairs and for those of the central power (*Ausschuss für Centralgewalt*) was instructed to report with all possible speed.[3] The exclusion of the Foreign Minister, a member of the International Committee, from the deliberations of the body, moved by a representative of the Left Centre,[4] was defeated, but Heckscher promised to abstain voluntarily from voting on the armistice.[5]

vii. Vote to inhibit armistice measures

The report on the Malmö armistice was quickly produced and the assembly debated the matter on the following day. The committee, which was attended by 20 members, was unable to agree and Dahlmann

---

[1] III 1857 ff.   [2] III 1861 f.   [3] III 1868.
[4] The lawyer Compes from Cologne (*Würtemberger Hof*).   [5] III 1869 f.

acted as *rapporteur* for the bare majority of 11, which recommended the arrest (*Sistierung*) of the measures for executing the armistice. The committee published the successive projects for an armistice, from which the treaty of Malmö eventually emerged,[1] but did not have time to agree on a written report which could be laid before the assembly. The committee found itself handicapped by the lack of papers, but was helped by the oral evidence of the Foreign Minister, Heckscher, who sat on the committee. In his commentary, Dahlmann criticised the Prussian negotiators for accepting Danish proposals to conclude the armistice for seven months, instead of the three months originally contemplated, on the basis of which the German Central Power had authorised the signing of the treaty. The Germans would thus be deprived of the opportunity of resuming operations in winter when circumstances favoured them. Dahlmann could not resign himself to the dissolution of the German Provisional Government in the Duchies, and claimed that the representation of Schleswig-Holstein in the Frankfurt Parliament was dependent on the continued existence of that body. He condemned Prussian approval of the appointment of Count Carl Moltke, who was hated by the Germans in the Duchies, as head of the interim authority.[2] The separation of the Schleswig from the Holstein troops could not be tolerated. He believed that any attempt to apply the armistice would lead to anarchy in the Duchies. Dahlmann concluded by expressing his conviction that the Germans would never again be able to hold their heads high if they meekly subjected themselves to the foreign powers at the first moment of danger. At the end of the speech, the shorthand reports recorded lively, continuing applause from the Centres, the Left and the galleries.[3]

The statistician and historian Friedrich Wilhelm Schubert[4] from Königsberg, like Dahlmann a member of the *Casino* in the Right Centre, spoke for the 8 members of the joint committee, out of the 20 who attended, opposing the majority recommendations. They had the support of Heckscher, who, however, abstained as Foreign Minister. The minority moved that a vote on arresting the execution of the armistice should be deferred until a resolution had been taken on the treaty itself, which could only be done when all the papers had been carefully examined. The armistice had been ratified in Lübeck on 2 September. Any refusal

---

[1] III 1876 ff.
[2] The resignation of Count Moltke from his office took place very quickly (III 2027).
[3] III 1880 ff.   [4] *ADB* LIV.

to execute the stipulations of the armistice amounted to a breach of the treaty itself and was liable to lead to war with Prussia. The Prussian government had been under considerable pressure from the population of Pomerania and of the Province of Prussia to bring hostilities with Denmark to an end. Untold misery would be caused in these parts by any attempt to prolong the fighting. The South and West of Germany hardly understood the extent of the economic crisis.[1]

The Reich Minister of the Interior, von Schmerling (*Casino*, Right Centre), agreed with Schubert that any attempt to prevent the execution of the armistice amounted to a unilateral abrogation. He read a statement from the Reich government that, after prolonged and careful considerations, the ministers had come to the conclusion from undeniable necessity not to recommend a rejection of the armistice. At the same time, they were dissatisfied with the attitude to the Provisional Central Power revealed by the negotiations. In view of these circumstances, the Reich government was asking the states to recognise explicitly the law relating to the Provisional Central Power passed by the Frankfurt Parliament on 28 June.[2] Schmerling urged the assembly to accept the recommendations of the minority of the joint committee.[3]

It was realised on all sides during the debate that the vote at the end would depend very much on the quality of the speeches from the floor on either side. Constant fluctuations in membership rendered even a calculation of the strengths of the various groups a somewhat intricate task. The early days of September saw the formation of a new club, that of the *Landsberg*, consisting of about 45 members. Most of them had seceded from the *Casino* (Right Centre) ostensibly because they had failed to obtain the acceptance of a statement of principles. Theoretically, the *Landsberg* had views somewhat to the Left of the *Casino*. The main reason for the secession was their resentment of what they regarded as the domination of the *Casino* by the university professors. Those who left the *Casino* did not like being lectured constantly by men like Dahlmann and Georg Beseler.[4] As there was little practical difference in their views, *Casino* and *Landsberg* co-operated on many questions. A very important recruit was the poet Wilhelm Jordan, who had formerly belonged to the *Deutscher Hof* (Main Left) and became one of the leading personalities of the new group.

[1] III 1882 f.
[2] See above, p. 195 ff.   [3] III 1884.   [4] Cf. Wichmann, *Denkwürdigkeiten* 124 ff.

After the formation of the *Landsberg* at the beginning of September, the strengths of the various parties were approximately:

Right (mainly in *Steinernes Haus*)	41
Right Centre (*Casino*)	126
Right Centre (*Landsberg*)	48
Left Centre (*Würtemberger Hof*)	71
Moderate Left (*Westendhall*)	50
Main Left (*Deutscher Hof*)	50
Extreme Left (*Donnersberg*)	48
Independent	129
	563

Discounting the independents, the Right and the Right Centre were a few votes short of a majority. On the assumption that the independents split equally,[1] the Left Centre could turn the scales against the moderates by throwing in the whole of its weight with the Left. The moderates were at an additional disadvantage owing to the high number of their absentees.

As the example of Dahlmann showed, party discipline in the Right Centre was undermined by a question which aroused the strongest patriotic emotions and thus weakened allegiance to the parliamentary group in case of a clash of loyalties. As the Left adopted the nationalist point of view, there was no problem for the party organisers there. For the *Casino* the Malmö armistice was certainly a severe test because of the group's leading role in trying to bring about the unification of Germany and because it naturally had strong links with Schleswig-Holstein. Many of its most prominent personalities besides Dahlmann, like Droysen, Georg Beseler and Waitz, had been born or lived there, in some cases representing Schleswig-Holstein constituencies. The attitude of Dahlmann and the other Schleswig-Holsteiners was only symptomatic of these deeper stresses.

Right at the beginning of the debate, the *Landsberg*, the secessionist Right Centre, came out against a suspension of the armistice. There was thus an expectation of a reasonably united support for the Reich government from the whole of the Right and the Right Centre, apart from an unpredictable number of conscientious objectors, mainly from

---

[1] Actually rather more favoured the armistice than voted against it. See below, p. 301.

the Duchies. The first speaker from the floor, Heinrich Simon (*West-endhall*, Moderate Left) from Breslau, backed the attack of the Left on the armistice whole-heartedly.[1] But the attitude of the *Würtemberger Hof* (Left Centre) was still in doubt. Both because of its strong nationalism and because of its insistence on the supremacy of the national assembly, the Left Centre was likely to give some support to suspension of the armistice. One of its representatives in the Reich government, the Minister of Justice Robert Mohl, indeed at first opposed endorsement of the armistice by the Central Power, but in the end agreed with the majority in the council of ministers.[2] Another native of Wurtemberg and member of the Left Centre, the Hamburg schoolteacher and journalist Christian Friedrich Wurm, was one of the most active opponents of the armistice on the joint committee.

In his speech, Heinrich Simon claimed that the armistice agreement only became a valid treaty after approval by the Frankfurt Parliament and subsequent ratification by the German Central Power. It was up to the assembly to approve or to reject the treaty. He moved that measures be taken at once to arrest the execution of the armistice. 'May Russia, may France, may England dare to interfere with us in our just cause! we will reply to them with one and a half million armed men . . . they will not dare . . . because they know that . . . this would lead to a German national rising such as world history may perhaps not yet have seen, . . . which might, incidentally, easily also like an avalanche make the thirty-four German thrones and much else reel before it.' Similar arguments were repeated by other speakers of the Left. The Stuttgart schoolteacher Wilhelm Zimmermann (*Donnersberg*, Extreme Left) asserted that if the armistice were accepted, the Central Power and the assembly would be finished,[3] a feeling which was echoed by the Düsseldorf lawyer Wesendonck of the same group.[4] The leader of the Main Left (*Deutscher Hof*), Robert Blum, in a powerful speech insisted on Prussia honouring the law about the German Provisional Central Power. It was better for the Germans to be annihilated with honour than to be guilty of a shameful surrender.[5] The Trier lawyer Ludwig Simon (*Donnersberg*, Extreme Left) claimed that if the Tsar sent troops to the Rhine, he would have to fear for his throne.[6]

For the Left Centre (*Würtemberger Hof*), the Hamburg school-

[1] III 1884.   [2] Arneth, *Schmerling* 187.
[3] III 1886 ff.   [4] III 1890 ff.   [5] III 1896 ff.   [6] III 1900 ff.

teacher Christian Friedrich Wurm, who had voted with the majority on the joint committee, deemed the approval of the Frankfurt Parliament as necessary for the armistice treaty to become fully effective. He regarded the ignoring of the Central Power and of the assembly as shameful. Wurm did not believe that a European war would follow the rejection of the armistice, but even if it did, fighting foreign countries was better than being despised by them.[1]

Many speakers from the *Casino* (Right Centre) pleaded with the assembly to avert the calamity of a European war and of a conflict with Prussia. One of the most effective speeches was made at the beginning of the debate by the publisher Friedrich Daniel Bassermann from Mannheim, who served in the Reich government as Under-Secretary in the Ministry of the Interior. He reminded the assembly that the armistice was a compromise and that there were severe critics in Denmark, too. Some of the stipulations to which exception was taken on the German side, for instance the appointment of Count Carl Moltke as head of the new authority in the Duchies, were in the process of being modified. He denied Dahlmann's assertion that the members of the Frankfurt Parliament who represented Schleswig would have to resign from the assembly.[2]

The official Wilhelm Wichmann[3] from Prussian Saxony, who belonged to the newly formed *Landsberg* in the Right Centre, ably seconded Bassermann. He did not regard the measures proposed by the majority of the joint committee as just. So far as foreign powers like Denmark were concerned, ratification by the German Provisional Central Power or by the assembly did not arise. From a military point of view it was unwise to hinder the armistice, which had many advantages for Germany, for the Danes could act more quickly. He referred to the patriotic songs which spoke of Germany comprising Schleswig-Holstein *meerumschlungen* (surrounded by the sea), 'but the power of the enemy is not sung down with songs.' He spoke bitterly of the difficulties with which the German troops in Schleswig had to contend from the local population who betrayed them to the Danes. The assertions of representatives from Schleswig who claimed that the Duchy was solidly German were quite incorrect.[4]

[1] III 1906 f.
[2] III 1888 ff. Dahlmann was certainly wrong about the representatives of Holstein, which had always been in the German Confederation. See above, p. 46.
[3] Niebour, 'Die Abgeordneten der Provinz Sachsen' 60; Wichmann, *Denkwürdigkeiten*.
[4] III 1892 f.

The leader of the *Steinernes Haus* (Right), von Radowitz, regarded an armistice as a necessity, not only for the Baltic regions of Prussia and Mecklenburg, but also for the Duchies themselves. The armistice did not prejudge a permanent settlement. In a closely reasoned exposition he was frank enough to point out that some of the German measures in the Duchies could not be justified by positive law and that certain foreign countries had concluded that these actions were part of a German policy of conquest. From a diplomatic and a military point of view any attempt to continue the war was highly dangerous.[1]

When the voting started, there was a preliminary though highly significant skirmish when the division on the minority report was taken. This asked that any resolution about inhibiting the armistice should wait until the decision on the treaty itself was taken. The recommendation was rejected[2] by 244 votes to 230, and though the majority was narrow, the vote showed that a substantial body of opinion in the assembly was determined to take some action against the armistice without further delay. Victory for the majority recommendations was now likely, but still not certain. When the roll call began once more for the division on the inhibition of the armistice, tension was high. 15 members left the chamber as they could not make up their minds and at half-past six in the evening Heinrich von Gagern was at last able to announce the result. The inhibition of the measures to carry out the armistice was carried by 238 votes to 221.[3] The reading of the result of the division was received with continuing applause on the Left and on the gallery. Both the victorious and the defeated realised that the evening was a turning-point for the assembly. The Left hoped to quicken the radicalisation of political life. The moderates saw their attempt to establish constitutional government by adapting the existing framework threatened. The day closed with high hopes and great fears. The division is analysed by political parties on the left side of table 5A (p. 301) and by states and regions on the left side of table 5B (p. 302).

As the section on the left side of table 5A shows, with some notable exceptions the division was along party lines. The Left voted solidly for inhibition of the armistice and were supported by the overwhelming majority of the *Würtemberger Hof* (Left Centre), whereas the whole of the Right and nearly 90 per cent of the Right Centre (*Casino* and *Landsberg*) opposed the motion. In this case the decisive dividing line

[1] III 1895 f.   [2] III 1912.   [3] III 1917.

TABLE 5A

	Vote on motion to inhibit the execution of the Malmö armistice (5 September 1848)				Vote on motion to reject the Malmö armistice (16 September 1848)			
	Yes	*No*	*Absent*	*Total**	*Yes*	*No*	*Absent*	*Total**
Right (*Steinernes Haus* etc.)	—	30	11	41	—	33	8	41
Right Centre (*Casino*)	12	89	25	126	9	103	15‡	127
Right Centre (*Landsberg*)	5	34	9	48	4	39	5	48
Left Centre (*Würtemberger Hof*)	52	7	12	71	54	11	7	72
Moderate Left (*Westendhall*)	45	2	3	50	47	3	1	51
Main Left (*Deutscher Hof*)	44	—	6	50	46	1	4	51
Extreme Left (*Donnersberg*)	40	—	8	48	42	—	6	48
Independent	40	59	30†	129	35	68	28§	131
	238	221	104	563	237	258	74	569

* There are slight fluctuations in party strengths between the two divisions owing to members entering or leaving the assembly in this period.

† This includes Heinrich v. Gagern who abstained as chairman.

‡ This includes v. Soiron who abstained as chairman.

§ This includes one abstention.

certainly ran between the Left Centre and the Right Centre, between the *Würtemberger Hof* and the *Landsberg*. On balance the alliance of the Left Centre with the Left on this occasion was probably due even more to nationalist than to ideological considerations. The independents split in a proportion of nearly three to two against inhibition of the armistice. This is not surprising as for instance some Catholics did not join a political group, although they were known to favour moderation. The Right Centre was both absolutely and relatively handicapped more than the Left by the high number of absentees.

The regional distribution of the vote is shown in the section on the left side of table 5B. The backbone of the vote against stopping the execution of the armistice certainly came from Prussia. This is not surprising in view of the strength of moderate opinion among the representatives of Prussian constituencies. Most Prussian members failed to see any advantage for their state – or even for Germany, in which the Hohenzollern monarchy played so important a part – in bearing the burden of a war which could not be won. They thus supported the policy of their government in concluding an armistice. The claims of the Left in the Frankfurt Parliament that there was grave dissatisfaction with the treaty in Prussia were not borne out by the

TABLE 5B

	Vote on motion to inhibit the execution of the Malmö armistice (5 September 1848)				Vote on motion to reject the Malmö armistice (16 September 1848)			
	Yes	No	Absent	Total	Yes	No	Absent	Total
A. Prussia (Kingdom)	47	113	33	193	40	132	25	197
B. Northern Germany (except Prussia)								
Schleswig-Holstein, Lauenburg	10	—	1	11	6	5	—	11
Hamburg, Bremen, Lübeck	—	3	2	5	—	5	—	5
Mecklenburg (Schwerin & Strelitz)	5	2	1	8	6	2	—	8
Hanover, Oldenburg, Lippe, Anhalt, Brunswick	11	23	4	38	11	25	3	39
Luxemburg, Limburg	1	2	2	5	1	3	1	5
Hesse region (Cassel, Nassau, Homburg, Waldeck, Frankfurt)	12	2	6	20	14	5	1	20
Thuringian territories (Saxon Duchies, Schwarzburg, Reuss)	7	4	2	13	6	5	2	13
Saxony (Kingdom)	18	1	3	22	19	1	3	23
sub-total	64	37	21	122	63	51	10	124
C. Southern Germany								
Hesse (Grand-Duchy)*	8	—	2†	10	9	2	—	11
Baden, Lichtenstein	14	1	4	19	17	—	2‡	19
Wurtemberg, Hohenzollern	24	3	3	30	23	3	3	29
Bavaria (Kingdom)	31	30	9	70	34	27	9	70
sub-total	77	34	18	129	83	32	14	129
D. Habsburg Empire	50	37	32	119	51	43	25§	119
grand total	238	221	104	563	237	258	74	569

* Mainly south of the line of the River Main.
† This includes Heinrich v. Gagern who abstained as chairman.
‡ This includes v. Soiron who abstained as chairman.
§ This includes one abstention.

behaviour of the National Assembly in Berlin, in spite of its radical majority. The Prussian Parliament was at this time far too busy with purely domestic issues to have any time to spare for a full-scale debate on the Malmö armistice.

The only other major state with a majority against the inhibition of the armistice in the Frankfurt Parliament was Hanover. Most of the

North German region (apart from Prussia) was for arresting the execution of the treaty. Southern Germany showed an even higher proportionate support for Dahlmann's policy. The Habsburg Empire, so far removed from the scene of battle, had a majority for the committee, if not a substantial one. Could it be said that feeling against the armistice increased the further removed members were from the problems caused by the war? This was largely, if not universally, true. As one would expect, members for the Elbe Duchies voted solidly against the armistice. In spite of the damage Mecklenburg suffered from the Danish blockade, most of its representatives voted for stopping the execution of the armistice, possibly mainly on ideological grounds.

There was only a limited feeling of solidarity against excessive German national aspirations among the members of the assembly belonging to other nationalities. Three of the Italians from South Tirol[1] voted for inhibition of the armistice. They do not seem to have had much sympathy with the Danes, or else they wished to humour the German majority for their own purposes.

viii. Resignation of Leiningen government – Reversal of vote

Although the division was only completed at half-past six, the council of ministers resigned the same evening. In accordance with the constitutional practice of responsible government they had observed in Britain and elsewhere, the ministers found they had no option. They agreed to carry on with any business unconnected with any political responsibility, but refused to accept formal notification of the resolution of the assembly about the Malmö armistice.[2] An attempt by the Left to make the retiring ministers execute the resolution of the assembly failed.[3] The Archduke John as Vicar of the Empire at once entrusted Dahlmann with the formation of the new government,[4] acting with perfect constitutional propriety, as it was undoubtedly the merit or demerit of the famous historian to have turned the feeling about the Malmö armistice in the assembly decisively against Heckscher and Schmerling. The Archduke was too much a man of the world to rate Dahlmann's chances very highly and there were many members of the

[1] Esterle, Marsilli and a Prato.   [2] III 1919.   [3] III 1920 ff.   [4] III 1919.

assembly who, after having had to suffer their colleague's authoritative manner about all sorts of constitutional matters in theory, were quite glad that the professor was having to pass a test of practical statesmanship. Dahlmann certainly tried to form a new government. He approached several of the former ministers, but not the Left. On 9 September Dahlmann had to admit defeat.[1] He emerged from this interlude sobered, after learning in a somewhat painful manner that an eminent scholar did not necessarily make a good politician. Dahlmann was not prepared to make that sacrifice so essential for the politician, the abandonment of his own professional career if circumstances required. The authority of the university professors in the assembly could no longer be the same after Dahlmann's fiasco. More generally, Dahlmann's initiative in the debate coupled with his failure to form a government was part of the gradual awakening of the assembly to sober reality, from the dreamland of classical perfection and of the romanticised period of German glory in the Middle Ages.

The next member of the assembly to be entrusted with the task of forming the government, von Hermann,[2] fared no better than Dahlmann. Friedrich von Hermann was the second vice-president of the assembly and a member of the *Würtemberger Hof* (Left Centre), who like most of his party had voted for the arrest of the execution of the armistice treaty on 5 September. He was a distinguished economist who had become a senior Bavarian government official. He had failed by 14 September, when the debate to decide whether the armistice should be approved or rejected had started. Technically, the vote of 5 September only dealt with a preliminary question which left the fate of the armistice itself untouched, though in practice the resolution of the assembly amounted to an abrogation of the treaty. The joint committee had in the meantime prepared a fuller report,[3] based on a study of further relevant documents, but had once more been unable to agree. A narrow majority – of 12 to 10 with one member adopting an intermediate position – recommended rejection of the armistice and the reopening of hostilities, unless Denmark was prepared to negotiate with the Central Power. The committee did not divide entirely along party lines, even apart from Dahlmann. The minority which desired approval for the treaty consisted almost entirely of members of the *Casino* (Right Centre) and of the Right. Another member of the *Casino* besides Dahlmann, the official Karl Wippermann[4] from Hesse-Cassel,

---

[1] III 1967.   [2] III 1967 ff.   [3] III 2020 ff.   [4] *ADB* XLIII.

recommended rejection, with Arndt, a member of the Right. Arndt, however, voted on the opposite side in the division. Three members of the Left, von Trützschler (*Donnersberg*, Extreme Left), Blum (*Deutscher Hof*, Main Left) and the lawyer Hans Reimer Claussen[1] (*Westendhall*, Moderate Left) from Kiel were active on the committee for rejection of the treaty. They were supported by some members of the *Würtemberger Hof* (Left Centre) like the official Hans von Raumer[2] from Franconia, an old enthusiast for the cause of the Elbe Duchies, by the Hamburg schoolteacher Wurm, and by the writer Gustav Höfken, a strong defender of German rights against other nationalities.[3]

The debate from the floor began on Thursday, 14 September in the morning and went on for three days, ending on Saturday, 16 September at a quarter past eight in the evening. A clarification of the parliamentary situation was overdue, as the failure of Dahlmann and von Hermann to form a government showed. The former Foreign Minister, Heckscher, gave a careful survey of the negotiations which had taken place, emphasising the determination of most of the Great Powers not to see Denmark overawed by Germany.[4] Heckscher certainly knew – as a lawyer – how to marshal his facts, but he offended by a biting sarcasm, for instance when he accused critics of the treaty of wishing to throw down a challenge to everybody in the manner of Don Quixote. He is not likely to have won many votes, and only added to his already considerable unpopularity. The failure of this able man as a politician puzzled the Right Centre perhaps more than that of Dahlmann.

Naturally this second debate on Malmö covered some of the same ground as the first. But neither side spared any trouble, as there were many waverers. Great efforts were made by the party groups to call up absentees and it was vital to make sure that any prodigal sons who returned to the fold would hear the right arguments.

The speech by a distinguished member from the Elbe Duchies, the former senior Danish official Karl Philipp Francke,[5] who belonged to the Centre, was a straw in the wind. Francke had voted for inhibition of the armistice, but he now recommended acceptance of the treaty, coupled with an attempt to negotiate modifications with Denmark.[6] Francke was a confidant of the dukes of Augustenburg, the German

---

[1] Hubner, *Droysen, Briefwechsel* I 256 for 1843; Zucker, *Forty-Eighters*; Carr, *Schleswig-Holstein* 133, 287.

[2] *Umrisse*, 56; *ADB* xxvii; Raab, *H. v. Raumer.*

[3] Also over Limburg, see above, p. 263.

[4] III 2034 ff.   [5] *ADB* vii; *NDB.*   [6] III 2052 ff.

claimants of the Duchies in the event of the extinction of the male line
of the Danish dynasty. The speech created a considerable stir as it
indicated a weakening of the determination to fight among the leaders
of the German movement in the Duchies. Similar sentiments were
voiced in a carefully reasoned speech by the Göttingen historian
Waitz[1] (*Casino*, Right Centre)[2] who represented a Holstein constituency
and had, like Francke, voted for inhibition of the armistice.

The Left did not weaken in its hostility to the treaty. The Wurtemberg official Schoder (*Westendhall*, Moderate Left) put the matter in a
nutshell when he asserted that the vote on the armistice would decide
whether the March revolution was going to lead to the unification of
Germany.[3] The Austrian jurist Giskra (*Würtemberger Hof*, Left Centre)
applied to the Malmö armistice Blücher's famous dictum about the pens
of the diplomats spoiling what the sword had achieved.[4] The leader of
the *Deutscher Hof* (Main Left), Robert Blum, argued that the Reich
government showed the same ineptitude over its handling of the
Schleswig-Holstein question as it had done in the case of Limburg.
He ridiculed the ministers for their inactivity.[5] The Trier lawyer
Ludwig Simon (*Donnersberg*, Extreme Left) interestingly enough
appealed to the memory of the Great Elector and of Frederick II of
Prussia in his speech advocating rejection of the armistice.[6] On the
other side, able speeches advocating acceptance of the Malmö treaty
included those by von Vincke (Right),[7] the merchant Merck (Right)
from Hamburg,[8] Prince Lichnowsky (*Casino*, Right Centre)[9] and Max
von Gagern (also *Casino*),[10] who reported with great dignity on his
diplomatic mission. Wilhelm Jordan (*Landsberg*, Right Centre)[11] once
more appealed for realism. He claimed that the German aims had been
achieved by the armistice, thus reconciling acceptance with his former
belligerent attitude over Schleswig-Holstein[12] as a member of the Left.
He was given a hot reception by his erstwhile allies. At the end of the
debate Heckscher spoke[13] with so much passion that Heinrich von
Gagern, who was in the chair, had to ask him to moderate himself.[14]
The debate concluded with summings-up by representatives of the
majority and minority of the joint committee.[15] Certainly members were
now much better informed about the advantages and disadvantages of

[1] *ADB* xl; E. Waitz, *G. Waitz*; Hagenah, 'G. Waitz'; *BSTH*.   [2] iii 2066 ff.
[3] iii 2076 ff.   [4] iii 2083 ff.   [5] iii 2114 ff.   [6] iii 2122 ff.
[7] iii 2099 ff.   [8] iii 2110 f.   [9] iii 2119 ff.   [10] iii 2128 ff.
[11] iii 2086 ff.   [12] i 276 ff.   [13] iii 2131 ff.   [14] iii 2132.   [15] iii 2137 ff.

the armistice than on 5 September. All aspects of the question, as they affected not only the Duchies themselves, but also the North German states hit by the Danish blockade and, indeed, the future of Germany – constitutional and diplomatic – had been fully aired. On the whole, defenders of the armistice had – apart from Heckscher and Wilhelm Jordan – appealed mainly to calmness and common sense, whereas the critics of the treaty had tried to raise the temperature by arousing a righteous indignation. Once more, a roll call was taken for voting. Both sides could have reasonable hopes of success.

Thanks to the efforts of the parliamentary groups, 30 absentees in the division on 5 September were brought in to vote on 16 September. In the interval, the assembly had made a net gain of 6 members. Uncertainty was not only confined to the absentees and new-comers. Many members who had divided on either side on 5 September were wavering – by no means only those who had voted to inhibit the execution of the armistice – and were now beginning to be afraid of their own courage.

In the event, the assembly in effect reversed its previous position by defeating the majority recommendation to reject the armistice by 258 votes to 237.[1] Many members voted differently from the previous time, changing in either direction. Opponents of the treaty only suffered the net loss of one vote. As a detailed analysis of the considerable number of individual transfers from one of the three categories of ayes, noes and absentees to another between the two divisions shows, the victory of the moderates was gained more by a net accession of absentees than by gains made from members who had voted for inhibition on 5 September.

A comparison of the sections for the two divisions in tables 5A and 5B[2] indicates the net gains and losses for both sides in the various parliamentary groups and regions. The Left fractionally increased its support for rejection of the armistice, whereas the balance between the ayes and noes in the *Würtemberger Hof* (Left Centre) remained largely unchanged. The biggest gains for the moderates were in the Right Centre, both in the *Casino* and the *Landsberg*.

Regionally, the greatest help naturally came from Prussia. A significant change was the breach in the solidarity of the representatives for Schleswig, Holstein and Lauenburg in opposing the treaty. Nearly half of these members – among them Droysen, Francke and Waitz – now voted for the armistice. In Northern Germany generally (even

[1] III 2149.   [2] See above, pp. 301–2.

L

apart from Prussia), support for Malmö increased substantially, whereas it decreased slightly in Southern Germany. The vote from the Habsburg monarchy was on balance somewhat higher for the treaty.

In the following division the recommendations of the minority of the committee, not to hinder the execution of the treaty – in as far as it could be put into practice – was accepted by 257 to 236 votes.[1] The discontent of the defeated was now vented on procedural matters in general and on the chairman, von Soiron, in particular. Soiron presided as Heinrich von Gagern wanted to vote for the armistice. The following division was boycotted by the Left,[2] though the relevant motion, asking the committee of the assembly on the Central Power (*Ausschuss für Centralgewalt*) to report on the conduct of the Prussian government towards the Reich government during the negotiations for an armistice, suited the Left. Owing to these mass abstentions, the motion was defeated by 205 votes to 165,[3] although it could easily have been carried with the aid of the Left.

Swallowing the Malmö armistice was a bitter pill for the German National Assembly, considering the central place held by the cause of the Elbe Duchies in the whole national movement. In view of the stalemate in the fighting and of the damage inflicted on German trade by the Danish blockade, an armistice was inevitable and was bound to be a compromise. The Germans received solid advantages from the treaty in the lifting of the blockade and the return of captured shipping. The Danes were not allowed to restore their actual control over the Duchies in full. The armistice did not permanently prejudice German claims. At the same time the Danes preserved their long-term rights, whatever they were. In a sense the moderates were right in claiming that the treaty did not destroy the future German position. For the ending of the armistice by the Danes in the spring of 1849 gave the Germans another opportunity of restoring their rule over the Duchies for a time. If Schleswig-Holstein was put back under Danish rule once more in 1851, this cannot be blamed on the Malmö armistice.

What could be achieved by inhibiting the execution of the treaty? If a stop meant anything at all it applied to both sides. The German troops would have remained in their positions, instead of withdrawing in accordance with the terms of the treaty. On the Danish side, the blockade would have been resumed and any return of confiscated ships would have been suspended. In fairness to the Left, it must be empha-

[1] iii 2154.   [2] iii 2155.   [3] iii 2159.

sised that it regarded inhibition as preliminary to an abrogation of the armistice and to a resumption of fighting, unless the Danes conceded the German demands. Further substantial Danish concessions after the withdrawal of the nomination of Count Carl Moltke were not likely. The Danes could not be expected to accept the German view about the indivisibility of the Duchies which they had so long contested and any admission of which undermined their whole position. The problem can thus be narrowed down to the question whether the Germans could have renewed war with the Danes to any advantage. The only military power capable of helping the Germans to victory was Prussia, which was not going to resume hostilities at the dictation of the Frankfurt Parliament. No substantial group in Prussia, the Left included, wanted to continue the war. Denmark could not be defeated by sending irregulars (*Freischaren*) to the Duchies. Indeed, whatever military successes the Germans might have, the Great Powers would see to it that Denmark did not suffer unduly.

The more extreme parts of the Left in the Frankfurt Parliament saw the Schleswig-Holstein issue as part of a wider theme, that of the creation of a more radical order in Germany and in Europe. Many of the leading personalities, particularly in the *Deutscher Hof* (Main Left) and the *Donnersberg* (Extreme Left), but even in *Westendhall* (Moderate Left), envisaged revolution and war with a light heart. The historian cannot condemn means which were common in that age, but he may perhaps ask whether those members of the Left who were prepared to risk major conflicts were fully aware of the dangers involved. The radicals and extremists in the Frankfurt Parliament were not the stuff from which Jacobin dictators are made and it is very doubtful whether they could have seen through a policy of revolution and war, assuming that it had any chance of success. The charge must be laid at the door of the leaders of the Left in the Frankfurt Parliament that they were prepared to throw Germany and Europe into the most terrible turmoil without any reasonable expectation of the means of mastering it. The diplomatic conventions and the historical traditions which many of the members of the Left despised played a part in the real world which their idealism would not let them see.

The Left wanted all or nothing. There was no hesitation in risking those achievements which came about directly or indirectly through the March revolutions, if the institutions concerned – like the Frankfurt Parliament or the Central Power – were not sufficiently radical for them. Whatever the effect of the actions of the Frankfurt Parliament on the affairs of the nation, the debates and divisions of the last fortnight were bound to affect deeply the future of the assembly. The repercussions came more quickly than most members on either side of the house in the Malmö question imagined.

ix. The September riots in Frankfurt – Schmerling as Minister-President

The Left in the Frankfurt Parliament leant heavily on the support of radical public opinion outside the assembly, if only to obtain added weight in view of its inferior numerical position in the house. The radicals outside, in turn, were encouraged and often further excited by the vehement attacks on the moderates made by the Left both in the assembly and in the press organ *Die Reichstagszeitung* edited by Robert Blum (*Deutscher Hof*, Main Left) and his brother-in-law Georg Günther (*Donnersberg*, Extreme Left). In the *Reichstagzeitung* Blum and his collaborators were in fact able to go much further in their attacks on the Reich government than they were allowed to do in the assembly. The *Reichstagszeitung* did not for a moment admit that there were two sides to the Schleswig-Holstein question, but instead treated all defenders of the Malmö armistice as traitors to the German people and accused them of corruption.[1] While for instance the journal of the *Casino* (Right Centre), *Die Flugblätter aus der Deutschen National-Versammlung*,[2] also adopted a strong polemical tone, the *Reichstagszeitung* was much more virulent and also paid less attention to truth. Many members of the Left in the assembly were quite reckless in the verbal attacks they made on those who disagreed with them. They ought to have realised that this campaign of representing ministers and their followers as enemies of the people was liable to expose the moderates to physical assault from the crowd and to threaten the independence of parliament. While Blum and his political friends did not approve of everything which the radical organisations in and around Frankfurt did, they cannot be absolved from some blame for the tragedy about to begin.

After all they had been told about the obstructive tactics of the

[1] III 2198 f.   [2] See Jürgens, *Zur Geschichte* I 165 ff.

Right Centre and the Right in the Frankfurt Parliament, the radicals who had listened to the speeches of Blum and Vogt from the gallery of the assembly could not be expected to honour the decision of the house about Malmö in a strict constitutional manner. Already on the evening of 16 September a series of meetings began at which some kind of action was demanded. It may well be true that the Left in the assembly tried to dissuade the activists outside from action against parliament,[1] but this advice hardly carried conviction in view of the speeches the parliamentarians of the Left had made for many months. In any case, the agitation had assumed such proportions that the movement could hardly be controlled any longer. An open-air meeting just outside the town[2] was arranged for the following afternoon, a Sunday. This meeting, which was attended by several thousand people, passed a resolution addressed to the Frankfurt Parliament declaring those who had voted for the 'shameful armistice' to be traitors against the German people.[3] In view of the threat to law and order, and in particular to the safety of the National Assembly and of the Central Power, the acting Minister of the Interior (pending the formation of a new government), von Schmerling, took energetic action. As the town of Frankfurt could no longer guarantee the security of the assembly, Schmerling called on the federal fortress of Mainz for military reinforcements during the night from Sunday to Monday, 18 September, and some units were sent at once. The troops had orders to protect above all the assembly and the government. In the meantime, barricades began to go up in the usual fashion of 1848. As on previous occasions, the arrival of more soldiers – however necessary in the interest of law and order – at first raised the temperature. The assembly sat from 9 o'clock in the morning, mainly concerned with the section in the Basic Rights dealing with school education. At the beginning of the sitting an announcement was made that Schmerling and several other ministers had acceded to a wish of the Vicar of the Empire to conduct official business with full responsibility until a new government had been formed.[4] An attempt to storm the assembly made by a part of the crowd which had eluded the vigilance of the military failed thanks to the presence of mind and the courage of the president of the assembly, Heinrich von Gagern. The schoolteacher Theodor Paur (*Westendhall*, Moderate Left) from Silesia, who spoke in the debate, described the scene in a letter written on the

[1] As Eisenmann claimed, III 2189.
[2] In the *Pfingstweide.*   [3] III 2184.   [4] III 2164.

following day.[1] According to Paur, the crowd was already forcing its way into the building by demolishing one of the doors when Gagern with a thundering voice called out to them: 'I declare every transgressor against this holy place a traitor to the fatherland!' Paur added: 'Curiously enough, they withdrew at once.' The writer, a free-thinker and a rationalist, was surprised by the effect which this appeal to sentiment, partly semi-religious or pseudo-religious and partly patriotic, had on the crowd. The incident reveals in a flash the strength and weakness of the German national movement at the time. In some ways leaders and people spoke the same language, but the idiom was vague and could only be understood with the help of the right atmosphere. All this was useful and a good beginning, but had to be translated into practical terms and to correspond to real interests.

Even if the situation in the assembly remained under control, the work of parliament was now being threatened by the hunt of the crowd for unpopular members of the assembly. The former Foreign Minister, Heckscher, whose portfolio was now being administered by Schmerling,[2] had left Frankfurt, but he was recognised at nearby Höchst and beaten up, though he escaped with his life. Two colleagues from the assembly were not so fortunate. Prince Lichnowsky (*Casino*, Right Centre) decided to reconnoitre on horseback outside the town boundaries and asked the Prussian General Hans von Auerswald (also of the *Casino*) to join him. Both men were recognised by the crowd and brutally murdered. In the meantime, fighting in the town was demanding casualties on both sides. Schmerling now became the dominant personality in the – officially still caretaker – Reich government and was shortly afterwards made head of the government in succession to Leiningen, who did not take office again. He showed great determination. Several members of the Left in the assembly tried to mediate between the authorities and the men on the barricades, but Schmerling insisted on unconditional surrender. While this refusal to parley may have been demanded by the exigencies of the situation, it might also reflect a certain rigidity in Schmerling's outlook. When order was not fully restored by the evening of Monday, 18 September, a state of siege (*Belagerungszustand*) was declared.[3] The Left in the assembly strained every nerve to have the state of siege lifted as quickly as possible, claiming that the work of parliament was adversely affected.[4] No

---

[1] Paur, 'Briefe' 57.   [2] iii 2162.   [3] iii 2266.
[4] See for instance the motion by Schaffrath (*Donnersberg*, Extreme Left) iii 2217.

sooner had the Frankfurt rising been put down, than Struve opened
another – abortive – revolt in Baden on 21 September.

The effect of the first three weeks of September on the fortunes of
the assembly can hardly be exaggerated. The votes on Malmö and the
Frankfurt disturbances dealt a blow to the prestige of the assembly
from which it took many months to recover. The illusions of the summer
may have been shattered, but hope and confidence in the future were
weakened as well. Above all, the assembly was for the next period
divided more rigidly into moderates and radicals than before, thus
removing any fundamental basis of unity which was so essential for
nationhood. The Left in the assembly certainly suffered a severe
reverse on 18 September. It was damned by its association – however
indirect in many cases – with the odium of murder and of the lynch-
law. A successful coup might have been useful and even glorious. An
unsuccessful *Putsch* was neither. A pamphlet about the rising by Carl
Vogt, who was to succeed Blum as the main leader of the Left, commissioned by the *Deutscher Hof* (Main Left) and the *Donnersberg*
(Extreme Left), published soon after, shows the Left very much on the
defensive.[1] Under the pressure of these events, the Left Centre in the
Würtemberger Hof, which had already shed *Westendhall*, split once
more in the second half of September. This time about 40 members,
among them several ministers,[2] moved closer to the *Casino* by forming
the *Augsburger Hof*. The *Würtemberger Hof*, which had earlier played
a key part, was now reduced to relative insignificance and numbered
only rather more than 40 representatives.

The Reich government was strengthened by the formation of the
Augsburger Hof, which became, with the *Casino* and the *Landsberg*,
one of the parliamentary groups of the Right Centre. The three clubs
co-ordinated their tactics. The Right also streamlined its organisation
by forming at the end of September a comprehensive club in the *Milani*,
more clearly distinguished in meeting place and leader from the
Catholic Association in the *Steinernes Haus* than previously. Vincke
took over the leadership from Radowitz and at once displayed his
accustomed energy.

Right Centre and Right between them now controlled a majority in
the assembly. Under their influence the assembly was certainly determined to support the upholders of law and order. This was the –

---

[1] Vogt, *Der Achtzehnte September*.
[2] The Reich Minister of Justice, Robert Mohl, as well as some secretaries of state.

necessary – negative side of a programme on which the moderates were agreed. But certain positive decisions also had to be taken about the position of Prussia and of the Habsburg monarchy in Germany. As deliberations on the constitution, which was after all the primary task of the assembly, were reaching the stage where the question of the headship of state had to be faced, the assembly, which was only slowly recovering from its tribulations of September, was once more thrown into turmoil.

8 Austrian or Prussian Hegemony?

i. October rising in Vienna – Two Frankfurt missions to Austria

THE September disturbances in Frankfurt proved to be the first of a series of monthly uprisings which affected Vienna in October and Berlin in November. In many ways, the work of the Frankfurt Parliament was as much affected by happenings in the two major capitals as by those on its doorstep in Frankfurt. In view of that, the Left in the German National Assembly strained every nerve to throw in the weight of the Frankfurt Parliament against the Austrian and Prussian governments. Similarly, the moderates at Frankfurt were determined not to allow the assembly to give any succour to forces which they had fought, in and out of parliament, since March. The crisis in Vienna and Berlin was also that of the German national movement.

By the beginning of October, an armed clash between the Austrian government and the Hungarian national movement had become inevitable. After months of temporising, the Austrian court and minister had thrown down a challenge to Kossuth and his allies by decreeing the dissolution of the Hungarian Reichstag, by declaring its last resolutions void, by putting the country under a state of siege and, above all, by appointing the mortal enemy of the Magyars, the Croat Jelačič, as deputy of the King-Emperor. The Austrian Minister of War, Count Latour, was determined to send every available soldier to the Hungarian front, even at the risk of baring Vienna of troops which might be needed to maintain law and order. He realised that the fate of the Habsburg Empire was being settled in Hungary and acted accordingly. The radicals in Vienna shared Latour's view about the importance of what was happening in Hungary, but for a number of reasons they did not, from an opposite viewpoint, draw all the necessary conclusions for their plan of operations. This was not only due to the odds against which they were struggling. The failure of the Vienna revolution in October was caused just as much by various inconsis-

tencies in the position of the insurgents. For several months, the
German radicals in the Austrian Reichstag had made matters very
difficult for the government, but they certainly did not want to break
up the Habsburg Empire, an institution from which both Vienna and
the Germans in the Monarchy benefited considerably. When they
crossed the thin line between legitimate defiance and open rebellion,
they shrank from asking the secessionist Hungarians for help which –
if successful – would have brought the Danube Monarchy to an end.
In October the German radicals in Vienna came nowhere near leading
a united opposition of the peoples of the Habsburg Monarchy against
a government suspected of reactionary tendencies. They did not win
over all Germans or even all radicals of other nationalities. The radicals
in the Habsburg Empire were no more agreed than the Germans there
on their political aims in 1848. Furthermore, the complex relationship
between national and ideological factors defied the oversimplifications
of the extremists. The October revolution in Vienna, with its national,
ideological and social aspects, baffled contemporary observers, including
members of the Frankfurt Parliament.

If the German radicals in Vienna were not prepared to go so far as to
ask the Hungarian insurgents for help against the government in
Vienna, they were certainly determined to do everything in their power
to prevent the authorities from crushing Magyar resistance. They
realised that their turn would come once Hungary had been brought
under control. It was therefore no coincidence that the Vienna rising –
the fourth in 1848 – began on 6 October, the day that a German
battalion was due to leave the capital to reinforce the Hungarian front.
The radical leaders resolved to prevent the departure of the troops, in
which they succeeded. In the disturbances which ensued, the com-
manding general was killed. Many of the soldiers joined the insurgents.
The Minister of War, Count Latour, was slaughtered by the mob.
Bach, an opposition leader who had accepted a post in the government,
only escaped from Vienna with difficulty. Soon the city was in the
hands of the revolutionaries.

From 12 October, the Frankfurt Parliament was concerned almost
daily, sometimes on several occasions, with the happenings in Vienna
and in Hungary. On 12 October, the Viennese lawyer Johann Nepomuk
Berger[1] (*Donnersberg*, Extreme Left), the later Austrian minister, put
down an urgent motion expressing the thanks of the assembly to the

[1] *ADB* ii; *BSTH*; *NDB*; G. Franz, *Liberalismus* 29 ff.

German city of Vienna for mounting the barricades in the cause of German and Hungarian freedom. He was supported by many members from his own group and from the *Deutscher Hof* (Main Left). The assembly refused to allow an immediate debate. Berger thereupon withdrew the motion,[1] because he and his friends regarded the matter as far too urgent to await consideration by a committee. As Berger hinted when he withdrew his motion, the Left was, in fact, prepared to act on its own. The same evening a deputation from both clubs was elected to go to Vienna with fraternal greetings to the Reichstag and to the people in Vienna. The two representatives of the *Donnersberg* were the writer and university teacher Julius Fröbel[2] and the poet Moritz Hartmann. The Main Left (*Deutscher Hof*) decided to send a Viennese lawyer, Albert Trampusch,[3] and another delegate. The club felt that one of its leading personalities, either Vogt or Blum, should also go. In the end Blum asked that he should be sent, and this was agreed.[4] The high hopes Blum had entertained for the radical party and for himself in March had not been fulfilled. The September riots in Frankfurt had reduced the Left in the German National Assembly to the position of an impotent minority. Blum – like Ruge, who formally resigned his seat in the Frankfurt Parliament in November, after a prolonged absence – had become very sceptical about the usefulness of the German National Assembly from the point of view of the Left. Blum went to Vienna after abandoning any expectation of being able to realise the aims of the radicals on the floor of the Frankfurt Parliament. His decision to take on the mission proved more fateful than he imagined at the time. The delegation left at once for the Austrian capital, arriving there on 17 October.

The decision to send envoys to Austria was also taken in another quarter on 12 October. The German Provisional Central Power did not want to stand idly by while a fight to the finish was in progress between the Austrian authorities and the insurgents in Vienna. The Reich government regarded happenings in the parts of the Habsburg Empire which had belonged to the German Confederation as matters coming within their province. Two Reich commissioners, the member of the Frankfurt Parliament and plenipotentiary of Baden in Frankfurt,

---

[1] IV 2557. [2] *ADB* XLIX; Fröbel, *Lebenslauf*; Feuz, *J. Fröbel*; *BSTH*.

[3] See Hartmann, 'Bruchstücke' 40; Wittner, *M. Hartmann* I 266; *Deutscher Nekrolog* V.

[4] H. Blum, *R. Blum* 466 f.

Welcker, and a senior army officer from Oldenburg, Mosle, were therefore dispatched to Austria with instructions to help in bringing the
civil war to an end and restoring law and order. In accordance with the
law about the Central Power of 28 June, the Austrian authorities were
ordered to obey the instructions of the commissioners. It was the Reich
Minister of the Interior, von Schmerling – lately Austrian plenipotentiary in Frankfurt – who announced these moves to the Frankfurt
Parliament in reply to an interpellation.[1] Schmerling was certainly as
determined as any other member of the Reich government, while he
belonged to it, to emphasise the authority of the Central Power, even
towards his native Austria. The Minister of the Interior must have
realised that his insistence on the rights of the Central Power was not
likely to dispose the Austrian court and government in his favour. The
Archduke John was much more careful and refused to discuss the
situation in Austria with Welcker when the Reich commissioner had a
private audience just before his departure.[2] The sympathies of the Reich
government were certainly as little with the radicals in Vienna as they
had been with the extremists in Frankfurt in September. But the
Austrian government was bound to resent what it regarded as an
attempt by the Central Power to interfere in the internal affairs of the
Habsburg Empire. The Austrian court and government had certainly
never agreed to the conversion of the German confederation into a
federal state, in which the Western half of the Monarchy became
subject to the orders emanating from Frankfurt. After the various
rebuffs at the hands of the two major states in Germany – Prussia and
Austria – the Central Power regarded the moment as propitious for
making good its claims. Superficially, the weakness of the Habsburg
Empire might have appeared a good time for that, but actually the
crisis was so grave that the responsible commanders and ministers
were not inclined to take advice from anybody. No doubt the decision
to despatch the commissioners was taken partly with an eye to the
feeling in the Frankfurt Parliament. Even Malmö had failed to convince
large sections of the assembly that the Central Power had to rely on
persuasion rather than on commands.

While the official and unofficial delegations made their way from
Frankfurt to Austria, the situation in Vienna became increasingly
critical. The Austrian authorities withdrew almost entirely from the

[1] iv 2620 f.
[2] Wild, *K. T. Welcker* 268.

capital and surrounded it, the court fled to Olmütz in Moravia and members of the Reichstag who did not belong to the German radicals also left Vienna. On 23 October the Frankfurt Parliament debated the report on the situation in the Habsburg Empire made by the committee on Austrian affairs (*Ausschuss für die österreichischen Angelegenheiten*) which had been elected on 17 October. The committee split in a proportion of 2 : 1 between moderates and radicals. The majority merely moved that any action should await the report of the commissioners, whereas the radical minority called on the Central Power to ensure that troops in the 'German-Austrian territories' would only obey the constitutional and legally responsible organs. This wording was a compromise, in order to obtain support from the Left Centre on the committee. The Left wanted the assembly to declare that the Viennese Reichstag – a rump – and the committee of public safety in the capital were in fact the government of German Austria and that the Emperor and most of the ministers had abdicated their functions by their flight.[1] The radicals in the Frankfurt Parliament looked on a break-up of the Habsburg Empire with equanimity. Without having considered the situation in all its implications, there was a vague feeling among them that the Viennese democrats might be useful allies for breaking the stranglehold of the moderates in Germany. This may well have been a factor in Blum's decision to take on the Austrian mission.

The historian Carl Nauwerck (*Deutscher Hof*, Main Left) from Berlin had gone so far as to move on 17 October that the penetration of German Confederation territory in Austria by the Croat army under Jelačič amounted to a *casus belli* against Germany, although the Ban was under the orders of the Austrian Emperor. But Nauwerck – with the Left in general – regarded the Emperor as at least temporarily suspended from power. He asked for a Reich army to come to the assistance of the Viennese.[2] The lawyer Johann Nepomuk Berger (*Donnersberg*, Extreme Left) from Vienna moved an amendment to the recommendations of the committee, urging the Central Power to summon back the Austrian Emperor at once to the capital, whose siege should be lifted. Any Reich troops required for the ending of hostilities should be put under the command of the Austrian Reichstag.[3] The debate was opened by a member of the committee, the official of the Austrian National Bank in Prague, Heinrich Reitter (*Westendhall*, Moderate Left), who represented a Bohemian constituency. Reitter

[1] iv 2809 f.   [2] iv 2678.   [3] iv 2810.

had earlier belonged to the *Würtemberger Hof* (Left Centre).[1] The speaker argued that the defenders of Vienna were fighting the battle of the Germans against the Slavs rather than that of the extremists against the forces of law and order. Though he condemned the murder of Latour, he charged the Minister of War with having behaved in a non-German (*undeutsch*) manner and with having by his actions supported an enterprise against the German nation. Reitter claimed that the guns which had been sent against Vienna from Prague had been decorated with flowers by Czech students![2] Reitter was seconded in his general thesis by another member of the committee and of his group *Westendhall*, the writer Venedey from Cologne. The issue at stake in Vienna was whether Austria would be German. '. . . should the Slavs win, then Austria will become Slav and we shall have to reconquer it, whatever the cost . . .'[3] The opposite point of view was voiced by the Austrian official Franz Philipp von Somaruga. He doubted whether the Reichstag in Vienna was the supreme legal body in Austria. Ever since the radicals had taken over in Vienna, German interests had suffered in the Monarchy. The extremists had misused the German colours for their own purposes. He strongly advised the Frankfurt Parliament against committing itself to supporting the Vienna Reichstag and the Magyar national movement. The Magyars under Kossuth were not, as was often imagined in Germany, either politically progressive or tolerant to other nationalities. The Germans in Hungary had suffered from bad treatment at their hands, like the Croats. Jelačič, the Ban of Croatia, was only standing up for the interests of his people and did not deserve the opprobrium which had been heaped on him in the Frankfurt Parliament.[4] Somaruga's anti-Magyar theme was taken up by Friedrich Daniel Bassermann (*Casino*, Right Centre), who was an Under-Secretary in the Reich government.[5] In the division, the cautious recommendations of the majority of the committee were carried by 250 votes to 166. The minority consisted not only of the Left, but also of members of the Left Centre.

---

[1] Biedermann, *Erinnerungen* 226, 358; minutes of *Westendhall* in Bundesarchiv.
[2] iv 2811 ff.   [3] iv 2827 ff.
[4] iv 2817 ff.   [5] iv 2829 ff.

ii. The Reich, § 2 and § 3 – Gagern's plan

The debate about the Viennese revolution was interpolated into the discussion by the plenum of clauses of the constitution which very much concerned the position of Austria in the proposed German state. The first reading of the Basic Rights had been completed on 12 October.[1] After 18 September, the intense interest in the Basic Rights had worn off somewhat, with the exception of article IV on education which was being debated at the height of the disturbances. Partly owing to the efforts of the committee on schools (*Ausschuss für Unterrichts- und Volkserziehungswesen*), in which several anti-clerical members played a leading part,[2] the Catholic party in the assembly suffered a severe defeat. In spite of exertions by the Catholic Association and by some Protestant members of the house, the schools were withdrawn from the care of the clergy by 316 votes to 74,[3] and put under the general supervision (*Oberaufsicht*) of the state.[4] Once this issue had been settled, many of the leading Catholics lost interest in the Frankfurt Parliament. Wilhelm von Ketteler, who had forcefully put the Catholic case on school education in the plenum on the fatal 18 September[5] and preached a stirring sermon at the funeral of the victims of the disturbances[6], formally resigned his seat in January 1849. Many of the most distinguished members of the Catholic clergy left the assembly before the end of 1848.[7]

After submitting the first draft of the Basic Rights to the plenum, the Constitutional Committee had turned in July and August to defining the relationship between the central power and the states in the section entitled *Die Reichsgewalt* (the authority of the Reich). The proposals on this section of the constitution had been finalised by the committee at its last meeting before the disturbances of 18 September. The Constitutional Committee had so far left out of account the question of the extent of the Reich and in particular the whole position of the Habsburg Monarchy. At a meeting on 19 September, the com-

---

[1] IV 2581. [2] For instance the Silesian schoolteacher Theodor Paur, see above, p. 235.
[3] III 2298 ff.
[4] III 2296. See also Radowitz, *Gesammelte Schriften* III 428 ff. [5] III 2182 ff.
[6] See also Lenhart, *Bischof Ketteler*.
[7] Diepenbrock, Bishop of Breslau, and Johann Georg Müller, Bishop of Münster, resigned their seats in August. Joseph Ambrosius Geritz, the bishop in charge of the diocese of Ermland, withdrew from the assembly in September.

mittee decided that the Austrian question had to be resolved before any further progress could be made with the constitution. The section *Das Reich* was therefore called a question to Austria (*eine Frage an Öster-reich*).[1] The sections *Das Reich* and *Die Reichsgewalt* came before the plenum on 19 October.[2]

The majority of the Constitutional Committee submitted a draft aiming at a federal state, with a strong central power, although a minority consisting of radicals wanted to go even further in creating unitary institutions. A minority of members of the Right objected to many clauses restricting state rights more than necessary.[3] Section I *Das Reich* was debated first. § 1, about the extent of the Reich, was accepted in the form proposed by the committee, which stipulated that the new state would consist of the territories of the German Confederation. The status of Schleswig and the fixing of the frontier in Posen was to be left for later decision.[4] Although the passing of § 1 committed the assembly to the intention of including in the new state not only German-speaking Austria, but also Bohemia, Moravia and parts of the Adriatic area, the Austrian question was only faced in the following two paragraphs, which led to a lengthy debate.

The majority of the Constitutional Committee proposed as § 2: 'No part of the German Reich may be united in one state with non-German territories.'[5] A minority consisting of 4 members of the *Milani* (Right)[6] asked for special consideration to be given to Austria in view of its peculiar position and urged that the closest possible union between Austria and Germany should be achieved by diplomatic (*völkerrechtlich*) negotiations between the Provisional Central Power and the Austrian government. Closely linked with § 2 were the recommendations of the Constitutional Committee contained in § 3 which laid down that wherever German and non-German territories had the same head of state, they were to be governed on the basis of a pure personal union of the two crowns.[7]

---

[1] Droysen, *Verhandlungen* I 312.   [2] IV 2717 ff.   [3] IV 2739 ff.   [4] IV 2767.

[5] For details of the discussions in the Constitutional Committee, see Droysen, *Verhandlungen* I 318 ff.

[6] The Viennese lawyer Eugen Megerle v. Mühlfeld, the Catholic philosopher Ernst v. Lasaulx (who had been suspended from his chair in Munich as a member of the clerical party by King Louis I), the Hanoverian particularist Johann Hermann Detmold and a Protestant Franconian land-owner, Hermann v. Rotenhan.

[7] IV 2770 f.

The debate, in which most of the speeches were made by Austrian members, was opened by the government official Johann Nepomuk Fritsch[1] (*Casino*, Right Centre) from Tirol, who was born in the German speaking part of Bohemia. Fritsch asserted that the strict application of § 2 and § 3 would make it impossible for Austria to remain a part of Germany. A personal union was unsuitable for the Habsburg Empire and, in any case, presented particular difficulties under a constitutional system. If the will of the majority of the Constitutional Committee prevailed, the consequence would be the separation of the German from the non-German territories of Austria. This would not be in the interests of either side. While he did not wish to challenge the sovereignty of the Frankfurt Parliament, the resolutions of the house would only have any force if they were in accordance with the will of the people; otherwise the assembly would be building castles in the air. The common life of nationalities in the Habsburg Monarchy was not only rooted in treaties, but in the will of the people. The German and non-German provinces did not want to be separated from each other. Such a separation could only be enforced by civil war. There was a grave danger that Germany would, by following the recommendations of the committee, lose its influence over the non-German parts of the Habsburg Empire and that its trade with these territories and their adjacent areas would be harmed. Generally the Slavs and the Magyars would benefit at the expense of the Germans. Any German minorities would be totally at the mercy of the other dominant races. Germany's task of bringing culture, scholarship and freedom to the Danube region, its influence over Italy and its world position would be endangered. He implored the assembly not to make any rash decisions while the Habsburg Empire was in a state of ferment, but to wait until the situation had become stabilised. Fritsch had a hostile reception from many quarters of the house, but managed to deal with interruptions, though he required some support from the chair.[2]

Many other speakers from Austria, including the historian Alfred Arneth (*Augsburger Hof*, Right Centre),[3] the Reich Secretary of State von Würth (*Casino*, Right Centre),[4] the university teacher Carl Beidtel (independent) from Moravia,[5] the Viennese lawyers Ignaz Kaiser (*Augsburger Hof*, Right Centre)[6] and von Mühlfeld (*Milani*, Right),[7] the Benedictine theologian Beda Weber (independent) from

---

[1] *Umrisse* 104; Bundesarchiv. [2] IV 2772 ff. [3] IV 2779 ff.
[4] IV 2789 ff. [5] IV 2846 ff. [6] IV 2853 ff. [7] IV 2854 ff.

Tirol,[1] the landowner Friedrich von Deym (*Casino*, Right Centre) from Prague[2] like Fritsch emphasised the difficulties posed for Austria by the recommendations of the committee and expressed their belief that German interests would not be advanced by it. But the representatives from Austria were not united on this issue. All the Austrian critics of § 2 and § 3 came from the more moderate side of the house, from the Right Centre or the Right if they belonged to a club. On the whole the Austrians of the Left and even of the Left Centre took quite a different line. An official of the Austrian National Bank in Prague, Heinrich Reitter (*Westendhall*, Moderate Left) saw the integration of German Austria in Germany as the only way to avert the Slav threat to the Germans in the Habsburg Monarchy. He therefore backed the proposals of the Constitutional Committee for a separate administration of the German and the non-German parts on the basis of personal union. He mistrusted the Habsburg dynasty which he suspected of having decided to back the Slavs against the Germans. Reitter was quite prepared to see greater national rights granted to some of the non-Germans outside the German Confederation, in particular to the Magyars. But he was opposed to any concessions to the Czechs in Bohemia and he played down the strength of the Czech national movement, which he believed was confined to scholars in Prague and had not spread to the peasants in the countryside. The Germans had to have Bohemia, even if not a single inhabitant of their people lived there; for Germany needed a firm base in the East for a war against Russia which was bound to come sooner or later.[3]

Similar arguments were put forward by a law lecturer from the University of Vienna, Karl Giskra (*Würtemberger Hof*, Left Centre), who represented a Moravian constituency. He, too, regarded amalgamation with Germany as the only way of preserving German hegemony in the Western half of the Monarchy. Personal union offered a way of separating hostile parts, though he did not apparently extend this principle to the non-Germans in the German Confederation territories. Giskra vehemently rejected any suggestion that negotiations should take place with the Austrian government about the position of the German parts. The Frankfurt Parliament was solely constituent (*allein constituierend*). Nobody was to interfere, not the Emperor, or the King,

---

[1] iv 2877 ff. Weber wanted the whole of the Habsburg Empire to enter the German Reich.

[2] iv 2881 ff.   [3] iv 2781 ff.

or the government or the provincial assembly (*Provinziallandtag*). A united Germany had to be created, even if all the thrones tumbled. His remarks were received with tumultuous applause.[1] Giskra combined strict insistence on German rights with a political ideology which was both democratic and anti-democratic. He claimed absolute sovereignty for the Frankfurt Parliament and denied any say to other representative organs.

The Viennese writer Adolf Wiesner (*Donnersberg*, Extreme Left) was one of the few opponents of § 2 and § 3 on the Left. The foundation of republics might make personal union superfluous. Wiesner was also against any negotiations with the Austrian government, which he suspected of conspiring with the Prussian cabinet to exclude Austria from Germany altogether.[2] The speech was passionate and sincere, but not always quite clear in its arguments.

The Styrian lawyer Titus Mareck (*Donnersberg*, Extreme Left) also took an independent line and this was of some interest for the future. He thought it unlikely that the Danube Empire could be preserved. But if events proved him wrong and a united Austria could be maintained, there would no longer be any question of an *Anschluss* with Germany. That would be against Austrian interests and he, too, would in those circumstances be opposed to tying down the Austrian eagle. In this respect, he was also *schwarzgelb*.[3] These remarks were greeted with laughter in the Right half of the house.[4]

The speeches of many Austrian members certainly reflected grave disquiet about the recommendations of the committee. Indeed, differences of opinion about the relationship with Austria threatened the very co-operation of Austrians and non-Austrians in two parliamentary groups of the Right Centre, the *Casino* and the *Augsburger Hof*. The *Landsberg* did not contain any Austrians. The few speeches by non-Austrian members which were made during the debate were mainly in favour of the recommendations of the committee. Only a minority was critical. But the division was not clearly along ideological lines, as among the Austrian members. Prominent personalities of the Right Centre among the German members were found on opposite sides. The main speech in support of § 2 and § 3 was made by a member of the majority of the Constitutional Committee, the Göttingen historian Waitz (*Casino*, Right Centre). Waitz began by pointing out that the

---

[1] iv 2791 ff.   [2] iv 2784 ff.
[3] Black-yellow, the colours of the Austrian coat of arms.   [4] iv 2892 ff.

two paragraphs under discussion applied not only to Austria, but also to Limburg, Luxemburg, Schleswig-Holstein and Posen. Any weakening in order to take account of the special position of Austria would carry grave risks elsewhere. Waitz regarded a separation of German Austria from the rest of the Monarchy as a natural outcome of the development of the national principle which had taken place. Indeed, he did not think that the Habsburg Empire would survive in the long run. There were only two possibilities for German Austria, either to join Germany completely or to remain entirely and exclusively with the Habsburg Monarchy. The decision for the Germans in Austria was not an easy one. It would be difficult for the Germans in Austria to give up the idea of ruling over millions of non-Germans. There were rights on both sides. From the German point of view, there was the right to hold fast to whatever was German of Austrian territory, not only to what belonged to the German Confederation, but to what had always formed part of the body of the German Reich (*deutscher Reichskörper*), i.e. to the Holy Roman Empire, which Waitz regarded as such. Bohemia and Moravia had been German before they became Austrian and they could be reclaimed from Austria. It would be easier to build Germany without Austria, but the difficulties must not be shirked. May German Austria stay with Germany! But if this could not be, then the edifice would have to be completed without Austria. There was then always the hope that the Austrians would join eventually. Waitz ended by exclaiming: Germany wants to be united, must be united and will be united. There was strong applause in the Centre and the Left.[1] Other speeches in support of § 2 and § 3 were made from the benches of the Right Centre by Biedermann (*Augsburger Hof*) from the Kingdom of Saxony[2] and by Wichmann (*Landsberg*) from Prussian Saxony,[3] as well as by several speakers close to the Left, by Vogt (*Deutscher Hof*)[4] and by the poet Uhland from Wurtemberg.[5]

There were three German speakers from the floor against the recommendations of the committee. The leader of the Right (*Milani*), the Prussian von Vincke, wanted a Confederation with the whole of Austria and a German federal state without the Habsburg Empire. He believed that was the only proper solution. If he had been advancing purely Prussian interests, he would have supported the two paragraphs, for he believed that they would – if applied – lead to the withdrawal of Austria, which would leave the way clear for Prussian hegemony in Germany.[6]

[1] IV 2786 ff.   [2] IV 2866 ff.   [3] IV 2883 ff.   [4] IV 2888 ff.   [5] IV 2875 ff.   [6] IV 2857 ff.

The German opponents of § 2 and § 3 were certainly not agreed amongst themselves about their aims in relation to Austria. While Vincke wanted to see a German federal state formed without Austria, two Catholic speakers from the Prussian Rhineland spoke against the recommendations as they were opposed to the exclusion of Austria which they believed – like Vincke – would result from a strict application of the two paragraphs. The philosophy lecturer Jakob Clemens (*Augsburger Hof*, Right Centre) criticised the recommendations because he was not prepared to accept the separation of Austria from Germany in any circumstances.[1] The judge August Reichensperger (*Casino*, Right Centre) regarded the two paragraphs as a crude solution to a problem which required considerable subtlety. He warned against their acceptance.[2]

As in the debates on the establishment of the Central Power, Heinrich von Gagern descended from the presidential chair to make the last speech from the speaker's rostrum. For some time before the opening of the debate in the plenum on 19 October, von Gagern had been trying to find a way out of the Austrian dilemma posed by the Constitutional Committee. He had received little encouragement from members of the Centre and of the Right he had assembled informally at his house,[3] but he still persevered. In his speech in the Frankfurt Parliament on 26 October, Gagern argued that the two paragraphs would, if applied, lead to a break-up of the Habsburg Empire, a development not in the interest of Germany or of Europe. Great disruption would be caused, peace would be disturbed and a fresh crop of revolutions would ensue. The Germans in Austria wanted to remain in the Habsburg Empire and they also wished to have their ties with Germany preserved. Surely there were intermediate phases between a federal state and a confederation. At present Austria did not wish to join the closer federal state (*engere Bundesstaat*) which the remainder of Germany wanted. He therefore moved an amendment to be inserted before § 2: 'Austria remains, in view of its connection with non-German territories, in a permanent and indissoluble federation (*Bund*) with the remainder of Germany . . .'[4]

Gagern's programme, which was further developed during the following months, was an imaginative attempt to get away from the doctrinaire attitude of some of the leading members of the Con-

---

[1] iv 2863 ff.
[2] iv 2868 ff.   [3] Laube, *Das erste Parlament* iii 47 ff.   [4] iv 2896 ff.

stitutional Committee, like Dahlmann, Georg Beseler, Waitz and Droysen, and to try and find a solution of the Austrian question which did justice to Germany and to the Habsburg Empire. The speech constituted one of the great acts of statesmanship witnessed by the assembly, but its echo at the time was very small. The spokesman of the Constitutional Committee, Riesser, on 27 October adhered to the paragraphs as they stood.[1] Thereupon Gagern withdrew his amendment until the second reading.[2] § 2 was carried by 340 votes to 76[3] and § 3 by 316 votes to 90.[4] All the amendments and additions were rejected.

iii. Capture of Vienna by Windischgrätz – Execution of Blum – Strong conservative governments in Austria and Prussia – Move of Prussian Parliament from Berlin

The ease with which the two paragraphs were passed by the assembly is surprising in view of the doubts of so many Austrians of moderate views. But owing to a combination of circumstances the critical speeches had little effect. On 27 October a belief still prevailed in the assembly that the Austrian Empire would not continue in its old form. Most of the non-Austrian Right and nearly all the Left were prepared to ride rough-shod over the wishes of other parties, including the constitutional organs of the Habsburg Monarchy. The reasons for the attitude of the Left – which was hoping for a greater radicalism – are easier to understand than those of the main supporters of § 2 and § 3 in the Right Centre. It hardly suited the political theory of the moderate liberals to deny the right of a say to other representative assemblies affected by its recommendations about the relationship between Germany and Austria. The unilateral decreeing of the new order by the Frankfurt Parliament irrespective of the wishes of other parties involved, simply on the basis of the sovereignty of the assembly, accorded more with the doctrine of the radicals than of the moderate liberals. The radicals believed in fitting the existing situation into the theoretical concept which they regarded as right whatever the consequences. The moderate section of the Frankfurt Parliament was much more sensitive to what had grown up in the past and not sufficiently ruthless to sweep aside all resistance. There must be serious doubt as to whether men like

---

[1] IV 2909 ff.   [2] IV 2916.   [3] IV 2918 ff.   [4] IV 2933 ff.

Georg Beseler and Droysen who defended the two paragraphs in the Constitutional Committee[1] fully realised all the implications of the recommendations. It was certainly illogical to call the unilateral regulation of the relationship with Austria by the committee a question put to Austria. Any stipulations in the constitution should have been preceded by negotiations with the Austrian government, for they were likely to remain a dead letter unless they received the assent of whatever authorities were in charge in the Habsburg Empire. However, the peak of the battle for Vienna was hardly a propitious occasion for negotiations with the Austrian government. One of the dilemmas of 1848 was that neither disturbed nor really stable situations were always suitable for making weighty changes affecting the long-term future. On the one hand, at times of tension the calm consideration of future policy by all the parties concerned was often an impossibility. On the other hand, the chance for change had frequently passed once the situation had settled down. Action at the right moment between these two extremes was not easy, particularly for a representative assembly, and in any case the favourable time was often very short, if it occurred at all. The Frankfurt Parliament – or even the Central Power – did not always have accurate and up-to-date information about events in other parts of the German Confederation, such as a well-trained and well-functioning diplomatic service could have provided.[2] The mission of the Reich Commissioners, Welcker and Mosle, to Austria was not primarily designed to keep the Central Power quickly informed about what was happening in the Habsburg Monarchy and for various reasons certainly failed to do so.[3] As matters turned out, the decision to persevere with the debate on § 2 and § 3, although – or perhaps because – the situation in Austria was quite unsettled, proved mistaken. Events already in train at the time of the debate rendered the resolutions of the Frankfurt Parliament academic, and fully justified the doubts voiced by Austrian members and by von Gagern about the recommendations of the Constitutional Committee.

On 26 October, Prince Windischgrätz began his systematic attack on Vienna, but the city only capitulated on 31 October, when there could no longer be any hope of the scales being turned by a Hungarian relief

---

[1] Droysen, *Verhandlungen* i 331 ff.

[2] The emissaries sent to various capitals by the Provisional Central Power were no substitute.

[3] For the correspondence between the Central Power and the Commissioners see v 3660 ff.

army, following its defeat by Jelačić on the previous day. Though Hungary still remained in a state of rebellion, the Western part of the Monarchy had now been reduced to order. Within a few days of the grand debate in the Frankfurt Parliament on the constitutional relationship with Austria, any assumption of a break-up of the Western part of the Monarchy had thus proved completely unjustified.

Windischgrätz took severe measures on reoccupying the city. There were numerous executions, including that of Robert Blum. Blum and Fröbel had taken part in the fighting in Vienna and found themselves cut off when the city was taken. Hartmann and Trampusch, who had also been in the delegation from the Left of the Frankfurt Parliament to the rump Reichstag in Vienna, had been able to make good their escape. When Blum and Fröbel asked the Austrian military authorities for passports to leave the city, they were both arrested on 4 November, and their claim to special status as members of the German National Assembly was rejected. On the following day, they tried to send a communication to the Frankfurt Parliament telling of their predicament. On 8 November they solemnly protested to the Austrian military authorities against their arrest. A few hours later, Blum was summarily tried, condemned to death and executed early on the following day. Fröbel's court martial took place on 10 and 11 November. According to the account which he gave to the Frankfurt Parliament on 18 November, he admitted participating in the fighting after Windischgrätz had declared the city in a state of siege. He was, however, invited by the judges to state anything in his favour. Fröbel believed that he owed his release after the trial to his mention of a pamphlet he had published some months earlier in which he had rejected any solution of the German-Austrian question by a division of Austria, but had pleaded for some association of the whole of the Habsburg Monarchy with Germany. On 11 November Fröbel was formally condemned to death, but at once reprieved and ordered to be released and deported. Fröbel's statement to the Frankfurt Parliament,[1] which was made with a minimum of emotion, created a deep impression in the assembly.

Blum, whose political fortunes had declined in life, in death became a political martyr. Whatever the formal justification, his execution was a political blunder of the worst order and quite an unnecessary brutality. The Left could only benefit from the excessive severity of its opponents. For some time various questions in connection with the

[1] v 3419.

execution were to engage the attention of the Frankfurt Parliament.[1]
Moves were now on foot to strengthen the Habsburg Empire at the
centre. On 21 November an energetic conservative Austrian government was appointed under Felix von Schwarzenberg, the brother-in-
law of Windischgrätz, with the erstwhile liberal Alexander Bach
retaining the portfolio of justice and with Karl Bruck as Minister of
Commerce. Bruck resigned from the Frankfurt Parliament, in which
he had sat on the Right. He had also for a few weeks been Austrian
plenipotentiary to the German Central Power. The Austrian Reichstag
was moved to Kremsier, near the temporary Moravian residence of the
court at Olmütz. On 27 November, Schwarzenberg formulated his
famous programme of Kremsier to the Austrian Reichstag there. The
bonds uniting the different parts of the Habsburg Empire were to be
strengthened and any dismemberment was to be resisted. The relationship between Austria and Germany was to be regulated when they had
found their new form. In the meantime, Austria would faithfully carry
out its duties as a member of the German Confederation.[2] This was the
Austrian answer to the demand of the Frankfurt Parliament that the
Habsburg Monarchy should establish a personal union between its
German and non-German territories. After the crushing of the Vienna
revolt there could be no doubt about the ability of the Austrian government to make its voice heard, which could only be ignored at grave
peril. The internal strengthening of the Habsburg Monarchy was
completed with the abdication of the imbecile Emperor Ferdinand and
the accession of his great-nephew Francis Joseph.

Almost parallel with the recovery of the Habsburg Empire, the
Prussian monarchy went through a remarkable consolidation, after a
period of severe crisis. In many ways the pattern in Berlin was similar
to that in Vienna. In October, the Vienna rising was certainly an
encouragement to the radicals in the Prussian National Assembly to
push matters to extremes. Frederick William IV came to the conclusion
by the end of October that the Prussian National Assembly in Berlin,
which was in the hands of extremists and subject to the pressure of the
mob, could not be allowed to continue its activities. On 1 November,
Count Brandenburg, a son of King Frederick William II by a morganatic
marriage, informed the Prussian parliament that he had been asked to

---

[1] There were three attempts, naturally unsuccessful, to bring to book the 'murderers'
of Blum. v 3321, 3323 ff.

[2] '*Seine Bundespflichten*'. Extract in Huber, *Dokumente* i 291.

form a government. On the following day, the assembly passed a vote of no confidence in a government which had not yet been formed, warned the King against the appointment of Count Brandenburg and asked for the establishment of a more popular cabinet. This resolution was an interference with the constitutional prerogatives of the head of state. On 3 November the King declined to abandon the formation of a government under Count Brandenburg. Six days later, the Prussian National Assembly was adjourned and moved from Berlin to the town of Brandenburg. A substantial number of representatives, however, continued their sittings in Berlin in spite of these measures by the executive. The assembly was closed by troops, but some members decided to go on meeting. On 12 November, the government proclaimed a state of siege in Berlin and General Wrangel occupied the city. On 15 November, a number of members of the Prussian National Assembly, sufficient for a quorum, met in a Berlin café and declared that the government under Count Brandenburg was not entitled to levy taxes as long as the National Assembly was not allowed to meet in Berlin. The meeting was dissolved by soldiers.

iv. Bassermann's mission to Berlin

After a month in which the happenings in Vienna came up almost daily in the Frankfurt Parliament, attention now shifted mainly to Berlin. As with Austria, the Left in the Frankfurt Parliament attempted to secure the help of the assembly for their political friends in Berlin, while the moderate section of the house was not prepared to tolerate any assistance to those planning or perpetrating a second revolution. Whereas there had been little doubt about the revolutionary nature of the actions of the Austrian Reichstag in Vienna, the constitutional position in Berlin was confused. The Prussian National Assembly had been called to agree a constitution with the crown. Co-operation between the assembly and the king had broken down. Both sides now took the law into their own hands. From a strictly legal and constitutional point of view, the crown was more in the right than the assembly. But the whole matter was one of individual judgment, depending on the political outlook of the observer. Fundamentally, a trial of strength had started between the crown, supported not only by conservatives, but also by many moderate liberals, and the forces of movement.

On events in Prussia, the Frankfurt Parliament was split along party lines. The Left wanted the assembly to throw in its whole weight and that of the Central Power to stop the move of the Prussian parliament to Brandenburg and to force the resignation of the new government. The Right believed that the matter was entirely one for Prussia and had nothing to do with the Frankfurt Parliament or the Central Power. The Left Centre on the whole supported the Left, though in softer tones. The Right Centre certainly had no sympathy with the party of movement, from which it had suffered in September. But many of its members were unhappy about the appointment of the Brandenburg ministry and wanted to see an attempt made to obtain the appointment of a government of a less conservative character. Those in the Right Centre who desired the establishment of a German federal state without Austria under Prussian leadership were uncertain about the attitude of the new Prussian government to such plans. They were worried about the image of the new Prussian régime in Germany.

For the Frankfurt Parliament and the Central Power, the struggle in Berlin was significant not only as a phase in the battle between order and movement. The effect of the outcome of the constitutional conflict in Prussia on prospects for the unification of Germany also had to be considered. The Prussian state was – apart from Austria – the largest morsel that a united Germany would have to swallow. In the Frankfurt Parliament no parliamentary group was solidly for state rights, except for the Right. Even in the Right Centre, there were many who supported large-scale mediatisation of small states and the break-up of the Hohenzollern Monarchy into provinces. The Left in theory tended to see the states as the artificial creations of monarchs and to identify particularism with the vested interests of the princes. States were regarded in general (except by the Right) as a nuisance which made the task of unification more difficult. Many members of the Right Centre – and not only those who advocated a form of unitary government for Germany – were worried about the new lease of life the states received from the constitutional reforms of 1848. State parliaments and constitutions made the particularism of the states even more formidable. This possible conflict between the constitutional Germany and the constitutional states was believed to be particularly acute in the case of Prussia. From the beginning, the Frankfurt Parliament had been jealous of the other national assembly in Berlin. There had recently

been a difference of opinion over Posen.[1] As the Left in the Frankfurt
Parliament was in this case given a chance of making good its defeat,
the usual emphasis on the superior power of the German National
Assembly was omitted. Altogether, since September, the Left at
Frankfurt was having second thoughts about the relative merits of the
central government and the states. In Vienna in October and in Berlin
in November, the radicals seemed to have a chance of restoring their
fortunes after the defeat they had suffered in Frankfurt in September.
Support for the revolution in Vienna could be fitted more easily into
the general concept of the Left than its backing for the Prussian
National Assembly. The Austrian Reichstag in Vienna could certainly
be viewed as a friend of German unification. This was not so clear in
the case of the Prussian National Assembly. Indeed, the Prussian
Parliament had hardly been any more compliant with the Frankfurt
law of 28 June setting up the Central Power than the Prussian government, sometimes actually less so, as over Posen. It was in order to
further its vision of freedom that the Left exerted itself in favour of the
Prussian Parliament. The effect that the establishment of a strong,
politically radical Prussia would have on plans for unity was hardly
considered. The Left in the Frankfurt Parliament, which now became
the champion of the strongest – if democratic – particularist interests,
had moved a long way since its unequivocal support for centralism in
June. For once, the radicals had a measure of success, because for
different reasons the Right Centre was prepared to go some way with
them.

The parliamentary groups of the Right Centre – *Casino, Landsberg,
Augsburger Hof* – certainly did not wish for the victory of the democrats in Berlin. But they were quite glad to use the Prussian constitutional crisis to tighten the hold of the Central Power on the Prussian
government in the interests of German unification. Whatever happened
about Austria, Prussia had to be fitted into the proposed German state.
Ever since the conclusion of the Malmö armistice, there had been widespread dissatisfaction in many quarters, not only on the Left, with the
attitude of the Prussian government to the Central Power, irrespective
of the merits of bringing hostilities with Denmark to an end. For once,
the continual agitation of the Left of the Frankfurt Parliament might
come in useful to increase the pressure of the Central Power on the
Prussian government. In its weakness – so the argument ran – the

---

[1] See above, p. 283 ff.

Prussian government might be quite glad of the support of the moderate liberals in the Frankfurt Parliament, represented by the Central Power. The more evenly the two sides in Berlin were balanced, the better was the chance that the Central Power would at last be taken seriously by the Prussian authorities. There might even be an opportunity for mediation in the conflict this time, after the disappointment of this hope in Austria. The Central Power might be able to work for a solution in Berlin which would favour neither reaction nor revolution, and which would at the same time create conditions in the Hohenzollern Monarchy propitious for unification. With these aims in mind, the Central Power decided on 6 November to send the Under-Secretary in the Ministry of the Interior, Friedrich Daniel Bassermann (*Casino*, Right Centre), to Berlin as a Reich Commissioner.[1]

Bassermann was one of the ablest members of the Reich Government and of the *Casino*, one of the best speakers in the assembly and a man of great determination. In those days when order was severely disturbed particularly in Prussia, it required considerable courage for a man of Bassermann's known opposition to the radical movement to undertake this mission. Quite apart from the danger of assassination, the voyage from Frankfurt to Berlin in winter was not a holiday, as there was no railway all the way through and as the journey had to be undertaken partly in draughty horse-drawn coaches. It took Bassermann 48 hours to reach Berlin. On the return journey, the combined strain of a harassed political life and of uncomfortable travelling conditions led to his being laid up at the house of a relative. This is only one example among many of leading members of the Frankfurt Parliament reaching a point of complete exhaustion.

In Berlin, where he stayed from 9 to 14 November, Bassermann quickly took sides against the Prussian National Assembly as an extremist body unwilling to come to any understanding with the crown. He had only contempt for those members of moderate views who according to their own explanation remained in Berlin in order to curb the more radical elements in the parliament. Bassermann accepted at their face value assurances he received from the new Prime Minister, Count Brandenburg, and from the Minister of the Interior, Otto von Manteuffel, that they did not intend to take advantage of their victory over the Berlin assembly in order to follow a 'reactionary' policy.[2]

---

[1] v 3252, 3266; Bassermann, *Denkwürdigkeiten* 246 ff.

[2] Bassermann, *Denkwürdigkeiten* 253 f.

Later Bassermann felt bitter about being duped by Manteuffel. However, it does not necessarily follow that Manteuffel had already made up his mind in November 1848 to turn not only against the radicals, but also against the moderate liberals. The latter cannot be absolved from some responsibility for missing valuable opportunities and thus for their own eventual plight. Fundamentally Bassermann agreed with the assessment of the new government that the Prussian National Assembly could not do any useful work in the politically unhealthy climate of Berlin at that time. In the report he gave to the Frankfurt Parliament on his mission, he mentioned that he saw near the parliament building in Berlin figures (*Gestalten*) whom he did not wish to describe any further.[1] These became famous throughout Germany as 'Bassermannsche Gestalten'. In his memoirs he spoke of them as hired executioner's assistants who made their appearance anywhere in Germany in times of disorder.[2] The immediate threat of left-wing extremism was more real to Bassermann than the potential menace of a right-wing reaction.

Bassermann was well received at court and had several audiences with King Frederick William IV. He explained to the King the main official purpose of his mission, the clarification of the relationship between the Central Power and Prussia. Here he was only successful in one respect, in obtaining support for the resolutions of the Frankfurt Parliament on Posen which had been opposed by the Prussian National Assembly. At the height of the Prussian constitutional conflict, this was hardly a great concession on the part of the King. Bassermann made no headway with his other requests, such as that Prussia should allow herself to be represented abroad by the Central Power and that the Prussian government should agree in advance to accept the Reich constitution as drafted by the Frankfurt Parliament. The emissary also used his audiences with the King to promote the idea of the bestowal of the imperial hereditary crown of Germany on Frederick William IV, for which his instructions gave him no authority. Bassermann believed that the moment was propitious for a general deal between the Central Power and Prussia. The Central Power could help Prussia – at least morally – in the restoration of law and order. A conflict between the interests of the Central Power and the Prussian authorities could best be reconciled by their joining forces, by something along the lines of Frederick William IV's own programme of the

---

[1] v 3407 ff.　　　[2] Bassermann, *Denkwürdigkeiten* 256.

merger of Prussia in Germany (*Preussen geht fortan in Deutschland auf*) proclaimed on 21 March. Bassermann was sufficiently discerning to see that the demands of submission to the Central Power he was commissioned to present to the Prussian government had no attraction unless accompanied by the bait of the imperial crown. He had seen for himself that the Prussian government was sufficiently strong to be able to quell the attempt at a further revolution. While the ministers and the Prince and Princess of Prussia expressed some interest in the imperial crown, the King discouraged any such idea. Frederick William emphasised in the first audience, on 11 November, that Prussia, with its glorious past, must not be allowed to be submerged in Germany. There was also the whole position of Austria, the previous holder of the imperial dignity, to be considered. In any case, he could not take the imperial crown without the consent of the other princes. In the second audience, on 14 November, just before Bassermann's departure, the difference of opinion and attitude became crystallised in a clash over the King's plan of a house of princes (*Fürstenkollegium*) which was to be added to the Frankfurt Parliament as an upper house. Bassermann expressed his view that an institution of this kind was not feasible as matters stood. Once more Bassermann was asking the King to throw himself and the Prussian state on the mercy of the Frankfurt Parliament, with its unstable and potentially unpredictable majorities. Like so many leading personalities in the Right Centre, Bassermann overrated the 'moral' power of the assembly and of the government to which he belonged, and underrated the strength and stabilising influence of the large states, particularly of Prussia. In his speech of 26 October to the Frankfurt Parliament on the Austrian question, Heinrich von Gagern had recognised fully the duty of self-preservation of every constitutional (*verfassungsmässig*) state. He was speaking about Austria, but the principle similarly applied to Prussia. Bassermann was expecting Frederick William IV to leave the solution of the complex question of the relationship between Prussia and a Germany under a Hohenzollern Emperor entirely to the Frankfurt Parliament, thus deeply interfering with the rights of the various Prussian constitutional organs, from crown and government to parliament. The King would have acted quite recklessly if he had agreed to Bassermann's suggestions as they stood, for no responsible Prussian would have followed him on this course. The result would have been at least a crisis of the throne and at worst the break-up of the Prussian state, the very body which had sent soldiers to Schleswig-Holstein for the German cause and which had dispatched a contingent of troops to protect the Frankfurt Parliament against the forces of subversion in September. Bassermann himself would at the time of the next rising have been the first to regret the destruction of the main pillar of law and order in Germany. When the King made a practical suggestion as to how the interests of the parts and of the whole could be harmonised, by a body representing the rulers, Bassermann at once rejected the idea. Even this comparatively realistic Baden politician had breathed the air of the Frankfurt Parliament and of the Central Power for too long to shake himself free from the dream-world doctrine of the duty of the states to do what Frankfurt commanded. Prussia did not need Frankfurt to re-establish law and order in Berlin, as Bassermann himself saw during his stay. He still deluded himself that the Central Power and the Frankfurt Parliament had so much to offer to the Prussian crown over the unification of Germany that Berlin would be glad to accept on almost any terms. Frederick William IV was quite right to point out all the difficulties which would arise from his acceptance of the imperial crown, even if offered by the Frankfurt Parliament. Though Bassermann quite rightly noted in his memoirs that the King only had a dim idea of what was involved for Prussia in a restoration of the imperial crown to the Habsburg dynasty, Frederick William faced reality in drawing attention to the necessity of considering Austria. He also had a greater appreciation of the importance of rulers and states than Bassermann. There is some irony in the fact that the first major approach to Prussia by the Right Centre in the Frankfurt Parliament was made in the first half of November, when Prussia had just, for the first time since March, received a Conservative government. The ministries in which leading liberals like Camphausen and Hansemann had participated had not shown any particular enthusiasm for subordinating Prussian interests to the German cause. It was thus impossible to speak of any definite agreement among moderate liberals in Germany generally on unification plans on the basis of what was proposed at Frankfurt. In Hanover, too, the conservative liberal Stüve, the former opposition politician, was a strong supporter of state rights and had come under severe censure in the Frankfurt Parliament in July.[1] Count Brandenburg's government was at least as approachable to suggestions on Prussia's part in German unification as its predecessors. Bassermann does not seem to have

[1] II 879 ff.

fully grasped the illogicality of his position in his negotiations with the King of Prussia. Here the emissary of the Central Power, which had always claimed the right to issue orders to the state governments, was conspiring with Frederick William IV behind the backs of the Habsburg Vicar of the Empire and of his colleagues – including the Minister-President von Schmerling, also an Austrian – to get the King to accept the imperial crown at the hands of the Frankfurt Parliament, which had not yet even considered such a plan. There was also the technical consideration that the Central Power was excluded by law from taking part in the drawing up of the Reich constitution, although this was soon to become completely a dead letter. Still, Bassermann himself had been forced to resign his chairmanship of the Constitutional Committee of the Frankfurt Parliament for this very reason on being appointed to the Reich government.

Bassermann brought his mission to an end after his final visit to the court at Potsdam on the evening of 14 November. On his return journey he saw from newspapers that on this very day the Frankfurt Parliament had debated the situation in Berlin and passed a motion without waiting for his arrival. The resolution was based on a view of the situation in Berlin totally different from the one he had adopted, and as he was not prepared to carry out any instructions from the Central Power based on the decision of the assembly, he determined to return to Frankfurt rather than go back to Berlin. His position in Berlin had become untenable.[1]

v. Simson's and Gagern's negotiations with Frederick William IV

Already two days before the debate in the Frankfurt Parliament on 14 November, the Central Power had sent fresh instructions to Bassermann which were diametrically opposed to the policy he had been following in Berlin and to the assessment he had made of the situation. The note said that as the Prussian National Assembly had expressed a vote of no confidence in the Brandenburg government, in accordance with the principles of constitutional monarchy a new ministry ought to be

---

[1] The account of Bassermann's mission is based on an interpretation of evidence scattered over several sources. These include Wigard v, particularly 3252, 3266 ff.; Bassermann, *Denkwürdigkeiten* 246 ff.; Gerlach, *Denkwürdigkeiten* I 232 ff.

M

formed which would have the trust of king and country. In general the instructions were aimed at effecting a compromise between the authorities and the assembly. The latter was to be urged to accept its move to Brandenburg for the time being. Government and assembly were to continue striving together for a constitution. The authorities were supported in their efforts to restore law and order.[1] Bassermann had learned from the newspapers during his return journey that fresh instructions were on their way to him, but as he did not go back to Berlin he escaped the dilemma of a conflict between his official duties and his conscience. The assumption behind the instructions, that the Prussian National Assembly was a body whose judgment could be trusted and that a compromise between parliament and crown was feasible, was not shared by Bassermann. On 14 November, the Frankfurt Parliament by a large majority accepted a resolution very much along the lines of the instructions to Bassermann.[2] The Central Power, on 18 November, immediately after Bassermann's return, sent two further Reich Commissioners to Berlin in order to carry out the resolution of the assembly, including the demand for a new Prussian government. This time a vice-president of the assembly, Eduard Simson, and the Minister-President of Nassau, Hergenhahn, both members of the *Casino* (Right Centre), were chosen.[3] Theirs was the impossible task of negotiating with a government for whose resignation they were supposed to be asking. Their position was slightly eased by the Frankfurt Parliament on 20 November declaring the suspension of taxes by the rump of the Prussian National Assembly in Berlin null and void.[4] But the following day the Vicar, with the endorsement of several ministers, issued a proclamation to the Prussian people couched in arrogant and condescending terms.[5] The commissioners reached Berlin on 20 November. They were well received by both sides in the constitutional conflict, but – as was to be expected – did not make any headway in its settlement. Simson soon came to the conclusion that affairs in Berlin were reaching so decisive a stage as to require the presence of the president of the Frankfurt Parliament, Heinrich von Gagern. One of the matters which worried Simson was his belief that Frederick William IV was about to grant a Prussian constitution without agreement with his parliament. This development was on two grounds objectionable to the moderate liberals in Frankfurt who hoped

---

[1] Text in Bassermann, *Denkwürdigkeiten* 279 n. 1.   [2] v 3316 ff.
[3] v 3405.   [4] v 3470 ff. By 275 votes to 150.   [5] v 3510.

for a Hohenzollern emperor. In general, the principles of constitutional monarchy required negotiations between crown and parliament in constitution making. Also, those in Frankfurt who advocated bestowing the imperial crown on Frederick William thought in terms of Prussia merging in Germany. As long as the Prussian assembly and government were deadlocked over the constitution, the Frankfurt Parliament had a good chance of finishing its task before that of its rival. The existence of a Prussian constitution and the strengthening of the Prussian state would make the fitting of the Hohenzollern monarchy into the unified Germany along the lines envisaged by Heinrich von Gagern's circle even more difficult.

Simson returned to Frankfurt on 22 November. On the following day he reported to the council of ministers and on 24 November once more undertook the journey to Berlin, this time in the company of Heinrich von Gagern. The latter had obtained the approval of the Frankfurt Parliament for a week's leave of absence for the purpose of personally investigating the situation in Berlin.[1] He went with the approval of the Central Power, but not as its emissary.

Gagern's two main aims on his mission seem to have been to try and prevent the King from single-handed constitution-making and to get him to agree to accept the imperial crown. The first objective was official and undertaken with the approval of the Central Power, but the second – as in Bassermann's case – entirely unofficial. Gagern could pursue the imperial plan more legitimately than Bassermann, because he was not a member of the Reich government or its official emissary.

It is worthy of note that the main drive for an offer of the imperial crown to Frederick William at the beginning of the campaign which culminated in the vote of the Frankfurt Parliament at the end of March came from two politicians of the South-West of Germany, both subjects of Grand-Duchies below the status of kingdoms. Familiar above all with conditions in their home states, which were of comparatively recent origin even as third-rate powers, they lacked an understanding for the history and traditions of the Prussian kingdom. Gagern had never been to Berlin before November 1848. Admittedly even some representatives from Prussia shared Gagern's belief that the Hohenzollern monarchy could merge in Germany under an emperor of the Prussian dynasty. But this conviction was to be found more among

[1] v 3537.

politicians from the Rhineland and Westphalia, like Beckerath and Mevissen, than among influential personages from the heartlands of the Prussian monarchy in the main continuous area, in Brandenburg, Silesia and East Prussia.

Gagern and Simson arrived in Berlin on the evening of 25 November. On the two following days, Gagern had conversations with Frederick William. Besides pressing the official objectives, he used all the persuasiveness at his disposal to obtain the agreement of the King to the plan of a Hohenzollern emperor. He failed to have his way. As may be inferred from some references in his speech to the Frankfurt Parliament of 26 October on the Austrian question[1] he regarded some modification of the Prussian state as necessary in the interests of German unity at that time. He was thus bound to encounter the same point-blank refusal which Bassermann had already experienced. Both Gagern and the King got rather heated and Gagern returned to his hotel from one audience completely shaken, even ill. He could not understand how a wonderful offer could be turned down in this way. Like many other leading members of the Frankfurt Parliament, Gagern was an enthusiast who was perplexed by conversation partners who did not share their premises or reached other conclusions. After a farewell audience with the King, Gagern left Berlin on 2 December and on 4 December once more presided over the Frankfurt Parliament[2] where he felt more at home. The King afterwards told Simson that he liked Gagern, but added: 'It is only a pity that I do not understand him, for he constantly talks with enthusiasm, of which I have enough anyway. I do not understand him and he does not understand what I say to him.'[3] This is a shrewd comment on one side of Gagern's personality, on the whole his strength in the Paulskirche and his weakness in complex negotiations, certainly when he was emotionally involved.

In spite of the King's negative attitude, Gagern did not write off his plan of a Hohenzollern emperor, because he believed that he had received some encouragement from other members of the royal family and from the government. Even Prince Charles, a younger brother of

---

[1] See above, p. 327. In the sentence in question (IV 2900, col. 1, lines 39–42) he spoke about the headship of state which he had in mind excluding the concept of a Prussian hegemony. Gagern was a speaker of deep convictions, but not always fluent, and even some close friends had difficulty in following him on this occasion. He explained later that he visualised the gradual disappearance of the states and their replacement by provinces all equally under an emperor. See Bergsträsser, *R. C. T. Eigenbrodt* 233.

[2] v 3797.   [3] Simson, *E. v. Simson* 151 f.

the King and an ultra-conservative, was against letting the imperial crown slip through the fingers of the Hohenzollern dynasty. He could thus reasonably feel that there was still some hope and that Frederick William IV would not be an obstacle as long as the royal family and the government supported acceptance of the crown. A formula had to be found which would satisfy both Frankfurt and Berlin. Unfortunately Gagern in his righteous zeal failed to narrow down the differences to the key points, such as the attitude of Austria and the kingdoms, and the future of the Prussian state. It cannot have been easy for his Prussian opposite numbers to get him to see the problem from their point of view and to obtain concessions from him. A favourable opportunity at a time when matters were still comparatively fluid was thus missed. Although Gagern later did patient work in eliciting the views of the state governments on the Reich constitution, valuable time was lost.[1]

Simson's suspicion that the King would proclaim a constitution unilaterally without reference to parliament proved justified. The constitution (*oktroyierte Verfassung*) was announced on 5 December, while Simson was still in Berlin. Gagern and Simson believed that the constitution would make their unification plans more difficult to realise. Gagern saw danger in some of the more radical provisions of the constitution, which had been inserted to take the wind out of the sails of the opposition.[2] The internal situation in Prussia certainly now became more stable. By the middle of the month the Frankfurt Parliament was preoccupied with another problem, the crisis which led to the resignation of von Schmerling from the Reich government and to his replacement by Heinrich von Gagern.[3]

vi. Schmerling's replacement by Gagern as Minister-President

Schmerling was a man of great determination and the upholder of the principle of the subordination of the state governments to the Central

---

[1] For the Simson and Gagern missions, see Simson, *E. v. Simson* 129 ff.; Meinecke, *Weltbürgertum* 380 ff.; Gerlach, *Denkwürdigkeiten* 1 253 ff.; Sachsen-Coburg-Gotha, *Aus meinem Leben* 1 322 ff.

[2] See Gagern's letter to Hergenhahn and Simson, Frankfurt, 14 December 1848, in Simson, *E. v. Simson* 146 ff.

[3] For this period, see Ernst Bammel, 'Gagerns Plan'.

Power even in the case of Austria.[1] He was a man of integrity and charges that he used unfair methods are only indicative of the pollution of the atmosphere and of the inability of dedicated men to regard opposition to their views as anything else but obstruction. Schmerling had many enemies, not only because of his policies, for instance in repressing with the utmost vigour the September uprising in Frankfurt, but also because of his often abrupt manner. He was one of those rather ruthless high-level administrators thrown up by the revolution of 1848 who had, if anything, less tenderness for the feelings of individuals than Metternich and his colleagues. The Left loathed Schmerling. He was not really at home in his own party, the *Casino* (Right Centre). The predominant Prussian element there on the whole did not understand him and therefore mistrusted him. As a man of action, he was bound to be impatient with the theoreticians of the *Casino*, like Georg Beseler. Schmerling was unlucky in having to expiate all the sins of the Central Power, as seen from various quarters. The Left identified the behaviour of the Reich government in the Frankfurt disorders mainly with Schmerling personally, to a large extent fairly. The minister also seems – rather belatedly – to have aroused the ire of the Schleswig-Holstein pressure group, particularly of Georg Beseler (*Casino*), of his brother Wilhelm (*Augsburger Hof*, Right Centre) – formerly a member of the Provisional Government in the Duchies and from November to March a Vice-President of the Frankfurt Parliament – as well as of Dahlmann, Droysen and Waitz. If this was a revenge for Schmerling's firm opposition to a rejection of the Malmö armistice in September, it was a belated move, with particular irony at this juncture. By his attitude then, Schmerling and his colleagues in the Reich government had prevented a complete breach of the Frankfurt Parliament and of the Central Power with Prussia which would have followed from the policy advocated by the pro-Prussian Dahlmann.[2] In any case, the Reich government decided its attitude to the Malmö armistice corporately and to have singled out one minister in particular would have been unfair.

These personal animosities helped to explain the campaign mounted

---

[1] This is quite clear from the correspondence submitted to the Frankfurt Parliament by the Central Power, for instance on the mission of the Reich Commissioners Welcker and Mosle to Austria in October 1848. See iv 2620 ff., v 3660 ff. and especially Schmerling's instructions of 24 and 29 October and 1 November.

[2] See Laube, *Das erste Parlament* ii 209.

against Schmerling in the Right Centre, for any differences in policy could have been bridged. Schmerling realised after the formation of the Schwarzenberg government and the proclamation of the programme of Kremsier[1] that the changed situation in the Habsburg Monarchy necessitated negotiations between the Central Power and Austria. He sensed that the tough theoretical line about the superiority of the Central Power could not be maintained towards the invigorated Austria. Like other Austrian members of the Frankfurt Parliament he began to have doubts about the value of § 2 and § 3 on the relationship between German and non-German territories belonging to the same state. Almost all the Austrian members now wanted to find a solution which would allow German Austria to maintain its links with Germany, while preserving the coherence of the Habsburg Monarchy.

Heinrich von Gagern, the president of the Frankfurt Parliament, who was close to the Right Centre, had full understanding for the difficulties in which the German Austrians found themselves and his programme of 26 October had been designed to resolve the dilemma. At that time he had regarded his plan as an alternative to § 2 and § 3 which in his opinion were a crude way of dealing with a complex problem deeply rooted in history. In October, the very group which now wanted to overthrow Schmerling – the core of the Constitutional Committee and of the Right Centre, Georg Beseler, Dahlmann, Droysen, Waitz – had stood firm on § 2 and § 3 and had forced Gagern to withdraw his motion. They now worked for the substitution of Gagern for Schmerling, although Gagern had not renounced his ideas and had indeed been proved right by events in his insistence on negotiations with Austria. Gagern and Schmerling were ready to come to terms on a programme and to sit together in the Reich government.[2] Quite rightly Gagern wanted to have his programme accepted by the assembly before entering the government. But the palace revolution against Schmerling in the clubs of the Right Centre foiled this plan. On 15 December the resignation of the two Austrian members of the Reich government, the Minister-President von Schmerling (*Casino*) and the Under-Secretary von Würth (*Casino*), which had taken place the previous day, was announced to the Frankfurt Parliament. Immediately afterwards, Heinrich von Gagern rose to announce his own appoint-

---

[1] See above, p. 331.
[2] For the text of the motion Gagern and Schmerling intended to introduce in the Frankfurt Parliament, see Haym, *Die Deutsche Nationalversammlung* II 127 f.

ment as Minister-President and his resignation as President of the assembly. He made a brief statement on the developments which had led to the changes in the government couched in conciliatory terms. He had been reluctant to enter the government before the assembly had accepted his programme, but in the new circumstances he had no option.[1]

Schmerling's withdrawal from the government marked the end of a chapter in the history of the Frankfurt Parliament and of its groupings. So far, the Reich government had represented, to a greater or lesser extent, all the various regions of Germany, even if there were certain notable gaps.[2] The dropping of all the Austrian members from the Central Power, leaving the Vicar without any of his countrymen, was a serious matter, bound to undermine any unity of the assembly which has still been preserved in many essentials among the moderates. The days of the alignment of the assembly based on political ideology were over. The moderates now split along regional and religious lines, between those who wanted to keep Austria in the new German state and those who had come to the conclusion that it was better to go ahead without Austria. As the leadership issue was closely connected with the position of Austria, and as the Habsburg and the Hohenzollern monarchies represented the two great Christian Churches of Central Europe, the struggle between the two parties which involved so much became extremely bitter. Naturally, Schmerling's fall was connected with these deeper causes and reflected the divisions which had been created. But many of the more far-sighted members of the Right Centre – among them the Baden politicians Bassermann and Mathy of the *Casino* – had grave misgivings about dropping Schmerling from the government. Many observers afterwards regarded Schmerling's exclusion as a mistake. The question was whether the Central Power could have followed a clear and promising policy with Schmerling continuing as a member, stepping down as Minister-President, as he was quite prepared to do.

On the matter officially at issue, the relationship with Austria, there were no outstanding differences between Schmerling and Gagern. Both wanted to negotiate with Austria and both wished in principle to keep in the German parts of the Habsburg Monarchy. Unlike Georg

---

[1] VI 4223.

[2] While South-Western Germany was strongly represented, there was, after Leiningen's resignation, nobody from Bavaria.

Beseler or Dahlmann, Heinrich von Gagern was not doctrinaire about the precise constitutional form which the new state ought to take and would have been prepared to go as far as was at all practicable in finding such an arrangement as would allow all the German Confederation territories to be included. If Austria could not enter the more intimate circle, he advocated a wider federation between a German federal state and the German territories of Austria. The difference between Schmerling and Gagern at that time was mainly one of emphasis. If it came to a final choice, the Austrian statesman might have been prepared to have sacrificed a slightly greater degree of coherence for Germany than Gagern in order to avoid the exclusion of his homeland from the new Reich. But Schmerling had shown throughout his tenure of office as a member of the Central Power that he was averse to making concessions to the states, even to Austria. In his insistence on the superior authority of the Central Power he hardly yielded pride of place to the unitarians of the Right Centre or of the Left. As Minister-President Schmerling had quite deliberately done very little to cultivate relations between the Central Power and the state governments, in order to avoid countenancing any claims on the part of the latter. It was only Gagern who on taking over as Minister-President arranged regular meetings between his government and the plenipotentiaries of the states.[1]

There was thus a wide measure of agreement between Gagern and Schmerling on the overt issue of the relationship with Austria. The same could not be said of the disposal of the imperial crown and its possible bestowal on the King of Prussia which had not yet reached an acute stage in the National Assembly. Rightly or wrongly, the presence of Schmerling in the Reich government had not prevented his under-secretary, Bassermann, while on a mission as Reich Commissioner, from trying to persuade Frederick William to agree in advance to accept the imperial crown, although the Frankfurt Parliament had not considered the matter and in spite of the fact that the Central Power was by law prevented from intervening over the constitution. Gagern himself certainly took the view that Schmerling's membership of the government would not prevent him from pursuing his plans, including that of offering the crown to Frederick William. Presumably he wished to tackle the Austrian problem before he got on to the leadership question, and saw no reason why Schmerling should not remain a

[1] See Bergsträsser, *R. C. T. Eigenbrodt.*

M 2

member of the government as long as Austria had not been definitely excluded from the closer union. Indeed, for the negotiations with Austria, the advice of the former Austrian presidial delegate to the Confederation might be useful to the cabinet.

Gagern's caution and moderation was frustrated by the impetuosity of the Schleswig-Holstein hotheads. So far, though left-wing criticism had increased after the September disturbances,[1] Heinrich von Gagern had remained a national figure, to some extent above party. Now that he became, against his intention, the leader of a government not containing any Austrians, the base of his influence was narrowed. This Germany could ill afford, for he occupied at that time a singular position. What happened to the symbol of German unity was only a reflection of the general decline in the fortune of the national cause. Schmerling's fall precipitated an internecine political warfare between various regions of Germany, above all between the two great religious confessions, which made all protestations of national solidarity appear hollow. This, coming on top of the old division between moderates and radicals, split the German National Assembly in three. There was an obvious conflict between moderates and radicals which could be simply and clearly presented. Though the relationship with Austria affected vital and to some extent conflicting interests, and was therefore bound to become a topic of political controversy, the terms in which the public debate were conducted befogged rather than clarified the issues by reducing them to an apparently straightforward alternative. The opening of the battle forced all participants to array themselves on either side and prevented compromise. The pace was set by the extremists in both camps and the more moderate elements were relegated to the background. Either side made it appear that the option it advocated was still open. In fact, by the end of 1848 the possibilities available to the Frankfurt Parliament had become strictly limited by the restoration of strong government in Austria and Prussia. Gagern had wished to explore the practical possibilities step by step, ignoring – inevitably – the absurd exclusion of the Central Power from the establishment of the constitution. Contrary to his intentions, the public discussion of the future relationship with Austria and related issues now began before the practical possibilities had been established by negotiation. Thus an air of unreality and a failure to come to grips with the arguments of the opponents hung over the whole debate. On

[1] See Paur, 'Briefe' 75.

the whole members of the Frankfurt Parliament made up their minds as to what they wanted and then claimed that their aims could be realised. Gagern was in a rather exceptional position because he looked first at what he believed could be achieved and then cut his cloth accordingly. He certainly would have liked to have maintained as close an association as possible with Austria. He only reluctantly became the leader of the party whose programme in fact involved the exclusion of Austria. He was certainly not an anti-Austrian. If these points are borne in mind, his political career as a whole assumes much more consistency than is sometimes admitted. Although Gagern adopted a considerably more practical approach to the Austrian problem than most of the other protagonists – on both sides – in the Frankfurt Parliament, it might well be that the moment for realising the key point of his programme, the opening of negotiations with the Austrian government, had passed owing to the changed position in the Habsburg Monarchy. In the end, the Austrian stake in Germany was not negotiable and Prince Schwarzenberg was able to veto any exclusion of Austria from the proposed state. In spite of these reservations, the debate on the Gagern programme of the relationship with Austria was an important stage in the clarification of ideas in Germany on this complex problem.[1]

vii. Simson's election as President of the Frankfurt Parliament – Debate on Gagern's Austrian programme

On 18 December, Heinrich von Gagern put forward his government programme to the Frankfurt Parliament. In substance, this was not radically different from the draft to which Schmerling would have been ready to agree. Gagern insisted on the necessity of the Central Power being permitted to assist in smoothing the path for the constitution, whatever was said in the law establishing the Reich government. He claimed that with the declaration of Kremsier the Austrian government had answered the question posed by § 2 and § 3, by affirming its unwillingness to join the German federal state. This attitude had

---

[1] Most of the authorities contain material on the replacement of Schmerling by Gagern, including Jürgens, *Zur Geschichte* ı, particularly 387 ff.; Wichmann, *Denkwürdigkeiten* 301 ff.; Biedermann, *Erinnerungen* 53 ff.; Haym, *Die Deutsche Nationalversammlung* ıı 116 ff.; Laube, *Das erste Parlament* ııı 177 ff.; Schweickhardt, *W. Beseler* 142 ff.

apparently found the approval of the vast majority of the population of German Austria, which remained in a permanent federation (*in einem unauflöslichen Bunde*) with Germany. He asked the assembly to authorise the Central Power to conduct diplomatic negotiations with the Austrian government to establish the future relationship between Austria and the proposed German federal state. The constitution of the German federal state could not, however, form a subject of negotiation with the Austrian government.[1] After some debate and a number of divisions, the assembly resolved to elect a special committee to report on the recommendations of the government. The nominations of the 15 sections (*Abteilungen*) for the committee were eagerly awaited as an indication of the attitude of the assembly to the new government and to Gagern's Austrian programme. What had happened over the election of Gagern's successor in the presidency of the assembly on 18 December was hardly likely to give much comfort to the new government. Although Eduard Simson (*Casino*, Right Centre) had already as vice-president won the almost universal respect of the Frankfurt Parliament for his able and impartial handling of the chairmanship, three ballots were necessary before he could muster the necessary absolute majority of all the votes cast. Even then he only received 2 more votes than the required minimum. In the second and third ballot, Carl Kirchgessner (*Würtemberger Hof*, Left Centre),[2] a Bavarian lawyer, ran Simson very close. With the dropping of Schmerling and the raising of the Austrian issue in an acute form, the Reich government lost the clear lead it had possessed in the assembly since the September riots. Kirchgessner had the support of the Left and of the Left Centre, as well as that of those moderates who could not accept Gagern's Austrian programme.[3] It took little more for a coalition of these two groups to beat the Gagern party.

In fact, on the committee to consider his programme, Gagern did even worse. The committee was dominated by the Left and the Left Centre. Only about a third of the committee backed Gagern.[4]

The report of the committee came up in the plenum on 11 January 1849. The majority of the committee reiterated the sole right of the Frankfurt Parliament to draft the constitution and emphatically

[1] vi 4233 f.

[2] *BSTH*; Bassermann, *Denkwürdigkeiten* 314; W. Klötzer, 'Abgeordnete', in Wentzcke, *Ideale* 291.

[3] vi 4229 ff.   [4] vi 4281; Rümelin, *Aus der Paulskirche* 143.

rejected any participation of the state governments in constitution making. As the assembly had been given the task of establishing a common constitution for the territories of the former German Confederation, the exclusion of German Austria was outside its brief. Germany must not give up the Germans in Austria, for they would then be at the mercy of the Slavs and non-Germans there. Germany had already suffered too much loss of territory, of Alsace, Lorraine, Switzerland, Belgium, Holland and the Baltic provinces. A North German Empire (*Kaisertum*) without Austria, Bohemia, Tirol and Bavaria would be lost at the next onslaught of the Slavs against Germany, for the German fortress (*Zwingburg*) of Bohemia would irrevocably deliver up Germany to any enemy from the East. Any negotiations conducted with the Austrian government by the Central Power should only be to regulate the relationship of the new German state with those parts of Austria which had been outside the German Confederation. A minority of the committee, consisting of 4 members of the Right Centre and of one independent member, recommended that the government should be given the authority for which it had asked in the statement of 18 December, but that this should be interpreted in the light of the declaration made to the committee by the Minister-President on 5 January.[1] This second statement was made in response to an intervention by the Austrian government.

Following his resignation from the Central Power, Schmerling decided to pay a visit to Austria. While on his journey home, despatches reached him from the Austrian government asking him to enter its service once more. As will be recalled, it was Schmerling as Austrian presidial delegate at the German Confederation who had handed over the authority of the Federal Assembly (*Bundesversammlung*) to the Vicar of the Empire in July.[2] Prince Schwarzenberg offered him the appointment of Austrian plenipotentiary in Frankfurt and he was seconded in his persuasion by two other ministers, Stadion and Bruck. The latter had served for a time as a member of the Frankfurt Parliament. One of Schmerling's main duties was to be to stiffen the resolve of the Archduke John as an upholder of Austrian interests. Schmerling accepted and on 27 December took part in an Austrian council of ministers at which the relationship between Austria and Germany was discussed. On his return to Frankfurt he handed to Heinrich von Gagern a rescript of the Austrian government of 28 December. The

new Austrian note rejected Gagern's interpretation of the programme
of Kremsier and his assumption that Austria had decided not to join
the German federal state. Austria remained a German federal power
(*deutsche Bundesmacht*). Any new arrangements could only be made in
agreement with the German governments, among which that of Austria
took the first place. In view of these circumstances, Gagern was
requested not to pursue his intention of establishing diplomatic
relations, as these were inappropriate between German governments.[1]
Heinrich von Gagern submitted the Austrian note to the parliamentary
committee with his own comments. He rejected the Austrian thesis
that the constitution had to be agreed with the state governments. The
German National Assembly, which alone had to lay down the future
constitution, had already shown during the first reading of the constitution its determination to establish one – federal – German state, instead of a confederation. In the opinion of the Central Power, the insistence of the Austrian government on the continuance of the unity of the
Habsburg Empire clearly prevented the inclusion of German Austria
in the proposed German federal state. As to the rejection of diplomatic
negotiations by Prince Schwarzenberg, Heinrich von Gagern stated
that he did not attach particular importance to the form in which these
contacts were conducted. He had, indeed, favoured diplomatic channels
in order to avoid hurting the susceptibilities of the Austrian government by the despatch of Reich commissioners.[2]

The Austrian note was a severe blow to Gagern's programme. Prince
Schwarzenberg declined to negotiate about Austria's position in
Germany. He reserved all Austrian rights in Germany for the future.
For the first time a leading state government quite openly and directly
challenged the claim of the Frankfurt Parliament to carry out constitution-making single-handed. Schwarzenberg did not merely insist that
the views of the Austrian government on the constitution should be
heard, he also denied the right of the Frankfurt Parliament to go
ahead with constitutional planning in any meaningful sense until the
Austrian government gave the signal. As the Habsburg Monarchy
was still involved in major internal struggles at the beginning of 1849
and was therefore unable to finalise its own internal reorganisation, this
effectively meant an Austrian veto against constitutional developments
in Germany for some time ahead. Unfortunately the debate largely
ignored the practical issue of Austrian power to stop constitution-

[1] VI 4554.   [2] VI 4553 f.

making in Frankfurt and revolved mainly on the ability or inability of Austria to take part in the kind of German state which the assembly favoured. Those who challenged Gagern's view were driven to the assertion that German Austria could in fact at one and the same time join a German federal state and continue as an integral part of the Habsburg Empire. But this in turn was bound to depend on arrangements within the Monarchy which had not yet been fixed. The dual status was in fact only feasible if the links of German Austria with the rest of the Habsburg Monarchy were weakened. This would have been an exact reversal of the position before 1848 and would have hardly commended itself to the inhabitants.

The *rapporteur* of the committee, Jacob Venedey (*Westendhall*, Moderate Left), accused his opponents of wishing to create a Prussian Empire. He described that as the real issue in the debate. He rejected the exclusion of Austria, because he believed that it would lead to war between a Prussian-led Germany and the Habsburg Empire.[1] Venedey was followed by Gagern.

The Minister-President made it quite clear that he realised the difficulties the larger states had in accepting subordination to the authority of a federal government. The problems were particularly acute in the case of Austria. He would be only too delighted if Austria could after all enter the German federal state with her German provinces. In any case he regarded the ties between German Austria and Germany which had been formed in 1815 as the very minimum for the future. He advocated negotiations with the Habsburg Empire because he wished to see these ties strengthened. It was the Habsburg Monarchy which in 1815 had quite deliberately refrained from resuming its full influence in Germany and with it the imperial crown. Once these claims had been given up, they could not so easily be revived again. He quite appreciated that Austria would have to be asked how it wished its relationship with Germany to be regulated in the future. It never occurred to him to assume that Austria could be forced into a particular position in this respect against its will. Some members might feel that negotiations with Austria would limit the sovereignty of the assembly and thus conflict with previous declarations of its sole right to determine the constitution. But the sovereignty of the assembly did not imply that ruthless decisions could be taken by the Frankfurt Parliament. Only those decisions would become effective which had the

[1] vi 4561.

support of public opinion. Gagern defended Prussia against accusations of wishing to obtain hegemony over Germany. Indeed, the representatives of what was called specific Prussianism (*spezifisches Preussentum*) objected to a merging of their state in Germany. He himself did not advocate the leadership of any one of the German peoples over the others, but a powerful, beneficent government over the whole country in those matters which were of vital national concern. This was his personal view, but he was speaking from the government bench of the assembly as the representative of the whole Reich ministry and the question of the headship of the state was outside the sphere of competence of the Central Power. Gagern concluded by asking the assembly to give the government power to negotiate with Austria for which he had asked and not to limit the authorisation as the majority of the committee proposed. In view of the declaration of the Austrian government of 28 December, the unwillingness of Austria to take part in the German federal state could no longer be assumed.[1]

The historian and official Alfred Arneth (*Augsburger Hof*, Right Centre), one of the most generally popular members of the assembly, followed Gagern with a speech putting the point of view of the German Austrian. He complained bitterly about § 2 and § 3 by which the German provinces of Austria were veritably being pushed out of Germany. The assembly had neither the right nor the power to enforce these articles. The vast majority of the Germans in Austria protested against these paragraphs and supported the stand of the Austrian government against them. He appealed to the assembly to drop the offending clauses from the constitution. It would be far better if the ties of the new state were somewhat looser so that Austria could be included. The second reading provided an opportunity for reconsideration of these aspects. He asked for the whole question of the relationship with Austria to be deferred to the time when the assembly had finally settled the constitution. If it then proved impossible even by concessions to Austria to retain her German provinces in the proposed state, then there would still be enough time to conduct negotiations. The speech was not only directed against Prussia but also against the Left. He rejected the use of force as a means of settling differences between Germany and Austria and castigated the Left for suggesting repeatedly the use of Reich troops to unify the country.[2]

Another Austrian member, Camillo Wagner[3] (*Westendhall*, Moderate

---

[1] VI 4562 ff.   [2] VI 4566 ff.   [3] *Umrisse* 73; *ADB* XLII.

Left), denied the right of the assembly to exclude any part of Germany. Unlike Arneth, Wagner supported § 2 and § 3. He asserted that Austria could accept the principle of personal union without harm. Wagner believed that the agitation against the two paragraphs in Austria had been organised by the state and church authorities. He opposed any special treatment for Austria, maintaining the orthodox position about the sole right of the assembly to lay down the constitution.[1]

The first day of the debate ended with a speech by von Schmerling, now Austrian plenipotentiary to the Central Power. Schmerling defended the right of the Austrian government to reserve its right over the German constitution. § 2 and § 3 indirectly affected the non-German parts of Austria and could therefore not be settled solely by an assembly in which the non-German territories were not represented. The Austrian government could not formulate its views on the relationship with Germany until the main decisions on its own future organisation had been taken. He did not think it right to exclude Austria from Germany simply because the Austrian attitude to Germany was not yet properly determined. In any case, it behoved the assembly to arrange matters in such a way that Austria could stay with Germany.[2] Schmerling had to tread very warily in his speech as he could count on but a small following and was viewed with suspicion not only by many erstwhile political collaborators, but also by some Austrian members, particularly those of the Left. He had to build up a new following slowly and carefully. The abrupt change from Minister-President to plenipotentiary of a leading state to the Central Power laid him open to a charge of inconsistency. The sternest advocate of the superior authority of the Reich government in the ministry now became the foremost defender of state rights.

On the second day of the debate, 12 January, the Trier lawyer Ludwig Simon (*Donnersberg*, Extreme Left) made a sustained attack on Schmerling both for his methods in quelling the September riots, and for the part he was now playing as a servant of the Schwarzenberg régime. He reminded the assembly of the fate of Robert Blum at the hands of this very government. The Left wanted neither Austrian nor Prussian hegemony. Whatever the assembly did, the reaction might prove victorious, and if that happened he would not like to choose a solution which involved the division of the fatherland. He rejected the exclusion of Austria.[3]

[1] vi 4571 ff.   [2] vi 4581 ff.   [3] vi 4586.

In a very thoughtful speech, Oskar von Wydenbrugk (*Würtemberger Hof*, Left Centre), the chief minister of the Grand-Duchy of Saxe-Weimar, rejected the Gagern programme and advocated a presidency alternating between Austria and Prussia. He was not prepared to give the Reich ministry in advance the right to exclude Austria from the German state. He wanted the assembly to be asked to approve every step as it was about to be taken. He believed that Austria would join the German state. But if that should not happen, then the assembly would not be able to force Austria to do so. In that case, German rights should be reserved by drafting an additional clause in the constitution leaving a place in Germany open for Austria whenever it decided to join. Wydenbrugk rejected as Utopian any plan of including the whole of the Habsburg Monarchy in the new German state. He asked for the insistence on the formation of a personal union between the German and the non-German territories of the Habsburg Monarchy to be dropped from § 3. The assembly merely had a right to insist on those territories belonging to Germany not being hindered from obeying the German constitution. Even that deeply affected the other states concerned, such as the Habsburg Monarchy.[1] Wydenbrugk dissociated himself from the extreme form in which the Left put forward its demands for the sovereignty of the assembly and for the abandonment of monarchical institutions, while going some way with the radicals. By adopting this intermediate position so characteristic of the Left Centre both in ideology and in the Austro-Prussian issue, he became a key figure in the assembly during the phase which was about to open.

Like the Thuringian statesman, the Bavarian Catholic church historian Johann Nepomuk Sepp,[2] who had moved into the Right Centre after initially belonging to a club of the Right, wished to avoid hegemony falling into the hands of either of the two German Great Powers. He supported Wydenbrugk's appeal for a revision of § 2 and § 3 during the second reading.[3]

The schoolteacher and journalist Christian Friedrich Wurm (*Augsburger Hof*, Right Centre) from Hamburg, a native of Wurtemberg, openly professed his support for bestowing the German imperial crown on Frederick William IV. He did so on the assumption that Austria could not participate in the German federal state. He would be delighted if he was proved wrong in this supposition. Should Austria, after all, be able to enter the German federal state, then the Habsburg

---

[1] vi 4597 ff.   [2] *Umrisse* 65; Sepp, *Bild seines Lebens*.   [3] vi 4604 ff.

Emperor would be the natural leader. But he could not see any move towards Germany in the policy of Prince Schwarzenberg. He suspected the Austrian government of wishing to return to the old unhealthy system of dualism in Germany.[1]

On the third and final day of the debate, 13 January, the leader of the *Milani* (Right), Georg von Vincke, argued that the Germans in Austria did not want to be separated from the non-German parts of the Habsburg Monarchy and that they could not possibly belong both to a German federal state and to the Danube Empire. He rejected any forced division of the Habsburg Empire, such as the Left desired, as contrary to German interests. The Slavs in the Austrian territories which belonged to the German Confederation could never be expected to submit to incorporation in a German state. He supported the programme of the Minister-President. Vincke was a signatory of a formal amendment to the minority recommendations of the committee which asked the assembly to approve von Gagern's programme as explained at the beginning of the debate.[2]

viii. Narrow victory for Gagern

The division of 13 January on a major issue of policy revealed for the first time the new balance of strength in the assembly. The vote was taken on the minority recommendations as amended by Vincke and his political friends. The Gagern programme was approved by 261 votes to 224. There were 3 abstentions, giving a voting strength of 488. As many as 70 members were absent, many of them more or less permanently. Gagern still had a majority, if not a large one. But he could not necessarily count on keeping his following together when the more controversial implications of his policy became apparent. The authorisation for which he had asked was comparatively harmless, indeed quite innocuous as it could, in the event, never be used. Gagern realised that the losses the moderate majority had suffered might only herald worse things to come when the crucial issue of the headship of the state became acute. During the early winter, the moderates had usually been able to keep the Left in check without difficulty. But from now on, the alignment of parties could no longer be simply along ideological lines.

[1] vi 4616 ff.   [2] Vincke's speech, vi 4635 ff.; amendment, vi 4593.

Regional and confessional loyalties came increasingly to the fore. These were bound to split the Right Centre and the Right, as will be seen from the following tables.

TABLE 6A

Motion to approve Heinrich von Gagern's programme concerning the relationship with Austria (13 January 1849)

		Yes	No	Abstentions	Absent	Total
Right		24	5	—	9	38
Casino	Right	97	9	1	10	117
Landsberg	Centre	36	1	—	4	41
Augsburger Hof		30	7	2	8	47
Würtemberger Hof (Left Centre)		23	19	—	7	49
Westendhall		14	38	—	1	53
Deutscher Hof	Left	1	39	—	9	49
Donnersberg		—	40	—	9	49
Independent		36	66	—	13	115
Total:		261	224	3	70	558

As table 6A shows, the Left was only vulnerable on its right wing (*Westendhall*) to the raising of the Austrian issue and the related one of the headship of the state. The official party line of not abandoning any part of the German Confederation territories kept the South Germans and Austrians contented, and the North German radicals were not on the whole likely to sponsor a Prussian emperor. Republicanism remained the official dogma, but its realisation had little chance in the short term. The Left could achieve technical advantages by throwing in its weight with the Austrian or with the Prussian party. But on the whole, any attempt to remain pure in the pursuit of radical objectives condemned the Left to sterility in the assembly. The battle was mainly fought out by the other two groups. The only part of the Left affected to any extent by the questions now under discussion was thus *Westendhall* (Moderate Left), an offshoot of the Left Centre, which faced an increasingly serious crisis in the following weeks. The three groups of the Left (*Westendhall, Deutscher Hof, Donnersberg*) collaborated very much in the same way as the clubs of the Right Centre. In addition, the parliamentary groups of the Left were linked with the national radical organisation, the *Zentralmärzverein*, which was founded in Frankfurt at the end of November. This was the central body which brought together the radical associations all over the country, many of which took their name from the March revolution. Even some members of the Left Centre in the Frankfurt Parliament, notably Wydenbrugk and Giskra, belonged to the *Zentralmärzverein*. The Left Centre in the Frankfurt Parliament thus had one foot in the Left, but as table 6A shows, it was even more seriously affected by the problems now before the assembly than the Moderate Left (*Westendhall*).

As the voting demonstrates, the three groups of the Right Centre were only marginally affected in the division on 13 January, least of them the *Landsberg* (an offshoot of the *Casino*) which was almost entirely North German and did not contain a single Austrian. Of the three groups, the *Augsburger Hof*, an offshoot of the Left Centre, was most seriously threatened, as it contained a majority of Austrians and South Germans, and few Prussians. (See p. 360.)

As table 6B shows, not a single Austrian representative voted for the Gagern programme. Even disregarding Austria, only 36 per cent of the representatives from Southern Germany supported Gagern. At the opposite end, 5 out of 6 members from Prussia backed the ministerial plan. In the other states of Northern Germany, 66 per cent were in favour of the policy of the government and 34 per cent against, roughly the converse of the situation in Southern Germany. Regionally, the basis of Gagern's support therefore came from Prussia and the other North German states. The Minister-President could not carry with him the South-West of Germany, the cradle of the liberal and national movement from which he himself came. Bavaria was divided, rather against than for him. The Rhine Palatinate was opposed to his programme, as it was represented entirely by the Left. With the rest of Bavaria, the predominant factor was denominational. The desire to keep Austria in was particularly strong amongst the Catholics, whereas the Protestants on the whole favoured more a compact German state under Prussian leadership. In this division, however, Gagern still managed to carry with him a number of Bavarian Catholics, though he was to lose their support during the coming months.

Table 6c shows that overall, religion was the most powerful and the clearest motive in the division of parties on the question of hegemony. About 70 per cent of the Protestant membership was quite ready to see Austria go, whereas 75 per cent of the Catholics were opposed to the exclusion of the Habsburg monarchy. (See p. 361.)

TABLE 6B

Motion to approve Heinrich von Gagern's programme concerning the
relationship with Austria (13 January 1849)

	Yes	No	Absent	Total
A. Prussia (kingdom)	150	30	17	197
B. *Northern Germany* (except Prussia) Schleswig-Holstein, Lauenburg	8	2	1	11
Hamburg, Bremen, Lübeck	4	—	1	5
Mecklenburg (Schwerin & Strelitz)	6	1	1	8
Hanover, Oldenburg, Lippe, Anhalt, Brunswick	29	8	3	40
Luxemburg, Limburg	2	—	3	5
Hesse (Cassel, Nassau, Homburg, Waldeck, Frankfurt)	10	9	1	20
Thuringian territories (Saxon Duchies, Schwarzenburg, Reuss)	8	4	1	13
Saxony (kingdom)	5	13	3	21
sub-total	72	37	14	123
C. *Southern Germany* Hesse (Grand-Duchy*)	5	6	1	12
Baden, Lichtenstein	4	12	4	20
Wurtemberg, Hohenzollern	7	20	2	29
Bavaria (kingdom)	23	31	12	66
sub-total	39	69	19	127
D. *Habsburg Empire*	—	88	23†	111
Total:	261	224	73†	558

* Mainly south of the line of the River Main.   † Includes 3 abstentions.

The assembly had been divided before, but up to the middle of
December 1848 it had at least had a common purpose, that of drawing
up a constitution for the whole of the German Confederation. Even in
October, when § 2 and § 3 of the constitution received their first
reading, owing to the confused state of affairs in the Habsburg

TABLE 6c

Motion to approve Heinrich von Gagern's programme concerning the relationship with Austria (13 January 1849)

	Yes	No	Abstentions	Absent	Total
Protestant	167	69	—	25	261
Roman Catholic	42	120	3	36	201
Deutschkatholisch	1	5	—	—	6
Mennonite	2	—	—	—	2
Jewish	2	—	—	1	3
No Religion	1	2	—	—	3
Not known	46	28	—	8	82
Total:	261	224	3	70	558

Monarchy there remained some hope of keeping German Austria in the new state. All members, including those representing Austrian constituencies, could with sincerity speak and vote on the assumption that they would or at least might be affected by what was being decided. On the two most important – and connected – issues, that of the ideological basis of the constitution and of state rights, there was a wide spectrum of views, facilitating compromise without any suspicion of horse-trading. There was often great bitterness. But the matters under discussion could at least be related to clearly stated and well-known principles represented by the various groups. Even when the assembly was faced with more than two recommendations, suggestion could usually be fitted into some pattern of progression, normally from Right to Left.

All this was now changed, as Frankfurt was once more being overshadowed as a centre by the capitals of the two Great Powers, at this stage certainly by Vienna. One of the few members of the Frankfurt Parliament to recognise the changed position of the assembly was Heinrich von Gagern, who did everything to cultivate contacts with the state governments, mainly through their plenipotentiaries to the Central Power, and had some measure of success in his efforts, though he failed entirely with Austria. The air of unreality which hung over the debate on Heinrich von Gagern's plan between 11 and 12 January has already been noted.[1] Any constituent assembly is in some danger of living in a world of theory and of being insufficiently attuned to practical conditions. The greatest brake on irresponsibility in a parliament,

[1] See above, p. 352 f.

that victory in the assembly might result in having to put the ideas advocated in debate into practice in government, is missing in the case of a constituent body. The majority of the Frankfurt Parliament aggravated its remoteness from actual conditions by under-rating the resilience of the states, including that of the Habsburg Monarchy. With the recovery of governmental authority in Austria, the real difficulties in applying the constitution to the Danube Empire became apparent. There now had to be at least a strong doubt in the minds of Austrian members as to whether the constitution they were drawing up would in fact be applied to the territories they represented. None of the three main groups had a majority. For any of the three which did not have any chance of getting their way there was bound to be a temptation of voting against their best convictions simply to block a solution they were determined to prevent. This was all the easier in the case of the Austrian members when they realised that the territories they represented were unlikely to be affected by the constitution they helped in drawing up. Thus, even Austrian members of moderate political views and their allies in other parts of the assembly were liable for purely tactical reasons to join with the Left in making the constitution more democratic, so as to make the acceptance of the imperial crown by Frederick William IV less likely. All these factors did great harm to the Frankfurt Parliament and reduced the importance of the plenum, whose robustness was in many ways a good indication of the general health of the assembly. The strength of the plenum had lain in the patent conviction with which members had spoken, in the straight clash of principles. Discussion in smaller groups, in the official committees and in the unofficial clubs, had only served to facilitate the public debate in the plenum. The deals which now took place between groups were of a different order from what had gone before and they were bound to undermine the authority of parliament. They increased mutual distrust and suspicion. All this did not augur well for the next stage, the constitutional clauses about the headship of the Reich, which came up in the assembly on 15 January.[1]

---

[1] vi 4675 ff.

ix. Erbkaiserliche – Grossdeutsche – *Left*

The consequences of the threefold division of the assembly could be seen in the inability of the Constitutional Committee to obtain a majority for any concrete proposal about the headship of the state, except that one of the ruling princes was to become Emperor of the Germans (*Kaiser der Deutschen*). All the more detailed stipulations were therefore simply opinions of various groups in the Constitutional Committee – four altogether – which all remained in the minority.[1] The strongest section of the committee, consisting of 9 members mainly drawn from the *Casino* (Right Centre) and including Dahlmann, Georg Beseler and Droysen, proposed a hereditary emperor.[2] Taken in conjunction with the remainder of the section, and particularly with the clause that the head of state had to reside at the seat of the Reich government, only the King of Prussia could become hereditary emperor. The alternative choice, the Emperor of Austria, could not be expected to reside outside Austria,[3] and Vienna was not seriously considered as a Reich capital. The group which advocated the election of the King of Prussia as hereditary emperor was called simply *Erbkaiserpartei* (hereditary emperor party). This term is more satisfactory than that of *Kleindeutsch*, which puts the exclusion of Austria from the proposed German state in the foreground of this movement. The exclusion of Austria was not primarily a consequence of Prussian leadership, but of the general difficulty of reconciling the membership of German Austria in the Habsburg Empire with its participation in the new German state. The antithesis of *Kleindeutsch* (Lesser German) and *Grossdeutsch* (Greater German) is not sufficiently subtle to describe the real difference between the parties. In any case, the party opposed to Prussian leadership consisted of heterogeneous elements, some of which would not have been unhappy to have seen the establishment of a large South German state including Austria and excluding Prussia. As the programme of the Prussian hereditary imperialists is much more definite than that of its opponents, the division into *Erbkaiserliche* and their opponents, under various guises, such as *Grossdeutsche* and

[1] vi 4675 ff.

[2] '*Diese Würde [des Reichsoberhauptes] ist erblich im Hause des Fürsten, dem sie übertragen worden; sie vererbt im Mannesstamme nach dem Rechte der Erstgeburt.*'

[3] The Munich professor Ernst v. Lasaulx was among the few who advocated the bestowal of the German imperial crown on the Austrian Emperor. vi 4776 (on 18 January 1849).

particularists, is preferred. The use of the term *Kleindeutsch* was a clever move on the part of the *Grossdeutsche* and their allies, to put the onus of the exclusion of Austria on the party supporting the Prussian hereditary emperor.[1] The first months of 1849 saw an intensification of the use of the press by the political parties, with the help of the *Parteikorrespondenzen* issued by the various parliamentary groups in the Frankfurt Parliament.[2]

There were three other proposals about the headship of state. A small mixed group of the Left Centre and the Right Centre[3] suggested the election of an emperor for life. One of the pillars of the *Casino* (Right Centre) in the Constitutional Committee, the historian Georg Waitz from Göttingen joined with the lawyer Friedrich Zell[4] (*Würtemberger Hof*, Left Centre) from Trier in proposing the election of the head of state from among the leading princes – the Emperor of Austria and the Kings – for a period of twelve years. A group consisting mainly of the Left, but including Welcker from the *Casino* (Right Centre), recommended the election of the head of state for six years. The amendment left open the form of government. Some of the sponsors of this motion on the Left[5] elsewhere opposed any restriction of the headship of state to ruling princes, while Welcker was committed to a monarchical summit. The compromise was quite proper, but would not have provided the basis for a solution of the question. This illustrates the difficulty the Left and the anti-*Erbkaiserliche* of moderate political views had in finding common ground.

There was not even agreement in the committee on having a single person as head of state. A minority consisting of two Austrians[6] proposed a directory (*Reichsdirectorium*) of five members appointed by the princes, with the chairmanship alternating every two years between Austria and Prussia.

The debate which followed the presentation of the proposals of the Constitutional Committee did nothing to reconcile differences and, if

---

[1] See Möller, *Grossdeutsch und Kleindeutsch*.

[2] Bundesarchiv; see Ludwig Bergsträsser, 'Partei-Korrespondenzen'.

[3] The Baden jurist Mittermaier (*Würtemberger Hof*, Left Centre) and the lawyer Gülich (*Landsberg*, Right Centre) from Schleswig.

[4] *ADB* lv; *BSTH*.

[5] Including the former judge Heinrich Simon (*Westendhall*, Moderate Left) from Breslau and the teacher of short-hand Franz Wigard (*Deutscher Hof*, Main Left) from Dresden.

[6] The official Franz Philipp v. Somaruga (*Casino*, Right Centre) from Vienna, and the statistician Gustav Franz Schreiner (*Würtemberger Hof*, Left Centre).

anything, only served to exacerbate and embitter feelings. It seemed as if nothing could bridge the gulf between the *Erbkaiserliche*, the *Grossdeutsche* and the Left. A few members of the Right Centre who had so far not been able to make up their minds joined the opposition to the plan of a Prussian hereditary emperor. The divisions at the end of the debate revealed the strengths of the various groups. On 19 January 122 members of the Left voted for the amendment making any German eligible for the headship of the state which was lost by a large majority. However, not the whole of *Westendhall* (Moderate Left) backed the amendment, so that the full voting strength of the united Left (*vereinigte Linke*), the backbone of parliamentary support for the national organisation (*Zentralmärzverein*), was about 150. 339 representatives voted against the amendment.[1] The recommendation of the majority of the committee bestowing the imperial dignity on a reigning prince was carried by 258 to 211 votes immediately afterwards. Once more, a minority of the Left voted in favour of monarchy.[2] A comparison of the two divisions would suggest that there were about 90 moderates who had seceded from the traditional clubs of the Right Centre and the Right, and aligned themselves with the group of *Grossdeutsche* and defenders of state rights who had their headquarters in the *Pariser Hof*, though not all of them were firm supporters during this period of party confusion and instability. The break between those who seceded from the traditional clubs of the Right Centre and of the Right on the one hand, and those who remained behind on the other, was not complete, as the rejection of the republican amendment by the joining together of the two moderate groups, mustering 339 votes, shows. On 23 January, the proposal of the *Casino* (Right Centre) representatives on the Constitutional Committee for a hereditary emperor was lost by 263 votes to 211.[3] For this division all groups made a great effort to rouse their followers and bring in absentees. In rough figures, the effective voting strength of the parties at that time was:

For a Prussian hereditary emperor	210
(moderates only)	
Left	150
Grossdeutsche, particularists	120
Total:	480

[1] vii 4800 ff.   [2] vii 4802 ff.   [3] vii 4851 ff.

A coalition of the Left with the *Grossdeutsche* and particularists in the *Pariser Hof* could thus block the plan of a Prussian hereditary emperor but there was little to unite the two groups except for their aversion to the Hohenzollern dynasty and to the Prussian state. What divided them was their totally different conception of how a German state should be organised. The Left was mainly republican and centralist, whereas the *Grossdeutsche* were in favour of monarchical institutions and the preservation of state rights. Schmerling, the plenipotentiary of the Schwarzenberg régime which had executed Blum, now found himself in the same lobby with the radical Austrians who had supported the cause of the Vienna rising. Indeed, even the *Grossdeutsch* party itself consisted of disparate elements. Its backbone were the Austrians who had their own national organisation in the Hotel Schröder under the chairmanship of Schmerling, as well as some Bavarians. Nearly all the Austrians and Bavarians were Catholics, many of them strong defenders of Catholic rights in their states. These two peoples were opposed to the Prussian emperor because of their loyalty both to their states and to their religion. The Baden politician Welcker, the Brunswick minister of religion Jürgens, the Hanoverian advocate Detmold and the Hamburg lawyer Heckscher shared the dislike of their Bavarian and Austrian colleagues for a Prussian empire. But they were Protestants. Jürgens believed in the necessity for cooperation between the two confessions, but Detmold was – like his friend Stüve at Hanover – suspicious of Catholic influence in politics. Unlike Schmerling with his centralist tendencies (at least formerly), Detmold wished to see the powers of any national government, to which he looked forward with limited enthusiasm, confined to an absolute minimum.

It took the *Erbkaiserliche* somewhat longer to organise their forces. At last, on 17 February, they founded their own organisation in the *Weidenbusch*. The three groups of the Right Centre (*Casino, Augsburger Hof, Landsberg*) formed the kernel of the party supporting the Prussian hereditary emperor, in spite of some losses by the first two to the *Grossdeutsch* party. The Right (*Milani*) was divided and was represented on both sides. The Left Centre (*Würtemberger Hof*) and the Moderate Left (*Westendhall*) lost any coherence with the opening of the Austrian and imperial issues. The Left Centre was the worst sufferer, as always whenever any conflict of principle came to a head, as it was also affected by the ideological issue. A minority in the *Würtemberger*

Hof aligned itself with the Left by joining the *Zentralmärzverein*. A considerable part of the Left Centre in the end supported the Prussian emperor. The smaller part of the Moderate Left formed a splinter group *Neuwestendhall* supporting the Prussian emperor, under the leadership of a lawyer from Darmstadt in the Grand-Duchy of Hesse, Theodor Reh. The *Weidenbusch* club supporting the programme of the Prussian emperor comprised nearly half the assembly. It was touch and go whether it would secure a majority.

The key to the position was held by the Left. The leader of the Left, Carl Vogt, was quite candid in offering a deal to either of the two main contenders. He was prepared to throw in the support of the Left to whichever of them was ready to make concessions for a strengthening of popular liberties.[1] In view of the parliamentary situation, both parties had to humour the Left but there does not seem to have been any kind of coalition of the *Grossdeutsche* with Vogt as has sometimes been alleged by writers of the *Erbkaiserliche*.[2] The *Grossdeutsche* were constantly haunted by reports that a deal between the Left and the Prussian party was imminent. There was certainly a common interest – though not necessarily a concerted action – to prevent the second reading of the constitution at the earliest possible moment after the middle of February as intended by the *Erbkaiserliche*. The *Grossdeutsche* needed more time to prepare their position for the second reading. The Left wanted to have the electoral law for the Reichstag settled first. When Vogt moved on 13 February that the electoral law should be taken next, he and other speakers of the Left put forward quite respectable reasons for settling the detailed regulations for Reichstag elections before the second reading of the constitution. He succeeded with the help of the *Grossdeutsche* and in the teeth of the opposition of the *Erbkaiserliche*.[3] It has often been asserted that the *Grossdeutsche* deliberately made the constitution as democratic as possible, in order to prevent Frederick William IV's acceptance of the imperial crown, for instance by helping to carry manhood suffrage. In fact, in the division of 20 February, about one hundred *Erbkaiserliche* supported the granting of the vote to every German above the age of 25 who was of good repute (*unbescholten*), as well as a smaller number of

---

[1] vii 5257. Vogt's formula in negotiations with the *Erbkaiserliche* outside the assembly was: '*Für jeden Paragraph vermehrter Volksfreiheiten einen Zoll Oberhaupt!*'

[2] Biedermann, *Erinnerungen* 86. See also Schneider, *Grossdeutsch oder Kleindeutsch* 159 ff.

[3] vii 5199 ff.

Grossdeutsche.[1] An assembly elected at least in considerable part by manhood suffrage was uneasy about the exclusion of large sections of the labouring classes, such as factory workers, domestic servants and casual labourers, from the franchise, as proposed by the Constitutional Committee.[2] Public voting was similarly rejected and the secret ballot substituted.[3] Voting was to be direct. Accusations made by the followers of the Prussian hereditary emperor that the amendments to the proposals of the Constitutional Committee on the franchise were a plot hatched between the Left and the *Grossdeutsche* are quite unfounded and only reveal the suspicions which rent the assembly. On other occasions, the *Grossdeutsche* voted with the *Erbkaiserliche*.

Both with the strengthening of the power of the state governments and with the approaching end of the main task of the constituent assembly, members of the Frankfurt Parliament could not close their eyes to developments in the German capitals, particularly in Vienna and Berlin, however much they believed in the sole right of the assembly to draw up a constitution. The *Erbkaiserliche* could not hope for the realisation of their plans unless the King of Prussia agreed to become German Emperor. The *Grossdeutsche* were dependent on the Austrian government at least not crossing their plans. All through the three months from the middle of December to that of March, negotiations were being conducted at various levels, between the state governments, by groups in the assembly with the plenipotentiaries in Frankfurt and sometimes directly with the state governments, and, above all, by the Central Power with the plenipotentiaries accredited to them. The decision which King Frederick William IV and the Prussian government had to make in relation to the plans of the *Erbkaiserliche* was much more difficult than has sometimes been allowed. Negotiations between Prussia and Austria established quite clearly that Austria would not voluntarily abandon the leading position in Germany she had held in the German Confederation. If Frederick William accepted the imperial crown proffered by the Frankfurt Parliament, he risked war with Austria. His constant reiteration of his preparedness to submit to the Austrian emperor, even if clothed in romantic terms, only expressed his correct appreciation that any provocation of the Habsburg Empire might be fraught with dire consequences for Prussia. But not only Prussian interests were affected. Frederick William regarded the harmony of the two German Great Powers as a European necessity,

[1] vii 5337 ff.   [2] Draft of electoral law, vii 5218 ff.   [3] vii 5529 ff.

for the preservation of peace and of monarchical institutions. In this he was quite right, both in the short and in the long term. If Frederick William also insisted on the approval of his fellow princes in general before he accepted more responsibility in Germany, this was not merely due to the arrogance of a monarch. The king had a far better understanding for the strength of particularist loyalties and the place of the rulers in them than the constitutional experts of the Frankfurt Parliament, like Dahlmann and Georg Beseler. In respecting the wishes of the princes, who certainly in many instances – such as in Bavaria – represented old and deeply rooted traditions, Frederick William was in fact being more 'democratic' than those who wanted to settle the future of Germany by two readings of a constitution passed by a single chamber, in which the smaller states could be over-ruled by the two larger ones, or the Catholics by the Protestants. The lack of proper representation for the state governments in the Frankfurt Parliament, with all the consequences that flowed from it, was Frederick William's greatest objection to the proceedings of the National Assembly, and a valid one. Compared with that, any particular decisions of the assembly – for instance on a democratic franchise – were comparatively unimportant. The absence of a proper federal organ during the process of drafting a constitution, which in fact provided a limited representation for the state governments, did not make sense. Surely if the necessity of having the state governments represented in the future parliament was granted, it was absurd to deny them a place in the constituent assembly. In this connection it was perhaps unfortunate that the constitutional development of the two countries which probably influenced a greater range of members of the Frankfurt Parliament than any other, France and Britain, did not have any bearing on the kind of federal problem faced by Germany.

x. Hereditary emperorship narrowly passed – Election of the King of Prussia as Emperor

Heinrich von Gagern as Minister-President tried to find a way of reconciling the need to hear the views of the state governments with the right of the Frankfurt Parliament to have the last word. On 28 January, Gagern asked the plenipotentiaries of the state governments accredited to the Central Power to communicate their views on the first reading of the constitution by the Frankfurt Parliament.[1] Gagern's step was in spirit, if not in letter, a breach of the law setting up the Provisional Central Power voted by the Frankfurt Parliament on 28 June 1848. With his new approach, the Minister-President achieved a certain positive clarification of the situation which was helped by a fresh initiative on the part of the Prussian government. A few days before, on 23 January, after some opposition by Frederick William, the Prussian government was able to issue a note which expressed support for plans designed to promote the closer union of some territories, while preserving the Austro-German link in a German Confederation. Prussia would only put herself at the head of a German federal state with the consent of the German governments. In the view of the Prussian authorities, the establishment of a new imperial dignity was not necessary for the completion of these plans.[2] The Prussian note was largely in harmony with Gagern's plan for a closer and looser union. In accordance with the new policy of the Brandenburg government, the Prussian representative in Frankfurt, Camphausen, succeeded in obtaining the consent of nearly 30 governments for a common approach to the Central Power, accepting the basic concept of the Reich constitution, while making detailed criticisms.[3] Austria and the four other kingdoms, however, expressed their opposition to the constitution as passed in the first reading by the Frankfurt Parliament.

Matters came to a head with developments in Austria. On 7 March, the Emperor Francis Joseph dissolved the Reichstag at Kremsier and unilaterally imposed a constitution as Frederick William had done. The new constitution proclaimed the unity of the whole of the Habsburg Monarchy and thus made any entry of the German provinces of Austria into a German federal state quite impossible. These and various other Austrian moves led to the break-up of the *Pariser Hof* and to the disintegration of the *Grossdeutsche* in the Frankfurt Parliament. As soon as news of the Austrian constitution reached Frankfurt, the leader of the *Grossdeutsche*, Welcker, rose in the assembly to move an urgent motion proposing the speeding up of the passing of the constitution and the bestowal of the hereditary imperial German dignity on the King

---

[1] Roth and Merck, *Quellensammlung* II 282 ff.; see also Huber, *Dokumente* I 297.

[2] Roth and Merck, *Quellensammlung* II 253 ff.; see also Huber, *Dokumente* I 294 ff.

[3] Collective declarations of 23 February and 1 March. See Roth and Merck, *Quellensammlung* II 299 ff.

of Prussia. When Welcker reached the latter point, there was a great sensation in the house.[1] In a moving speech, Welcker said that the aim of his previous policy had merely been to try and preserve the whole fatherland. He had opposed the plans for a Prussian emperor only for that reason and not because he was in any way anti-Prussian. But now the Babylonian constitution of Austria made any participation of the German provinces of the Habsburg Monarchy in the German federal state quite impossible. Welcker urged that the assembly should accept en bloc the draft of the Constitutional Committee for the second reading which took account of the views of the state governments. Any changes could be made by later parliaments.

This was certainly a sweeping suggestion, perhaps unnecessarily so. Still, the majority of the Constitutional Committee accepted the general principle, with only small modifications. An insertion was to be made into § 1 of the constitution on the territory of the new state, that a place was to be kept open for the Austrian federal territories (*österreichische Bundeslande*), that is for those parts of the Habsburg Empire which belonged to the German Confederation. In the meantime, there were to be attempts to arrive at a close association with them. The first Reichstag was to be allowed to make changes in the constitution by ordinary legislation in co-operation with the Reich government. After the end of the first Reichstag, a two-thirds majority of parliament was to be required. The Constitutional Committee revived its proposal, rejected in the first reading, that the voting for parliamentary representatives should be public. In its draft, the majority of the committee once more proposed the establishment of a hereditary empire, although this had been rejected earlier by the plenum. The committee now asked for the hereditary imperial dignity to be bestowed on the King of Prussia.[2] The majority view was contested in various respects by the Left and by the *Grossdeutsche* and particularists. The Left objected to a restoration of voting in public. The minority of the Left and *Grossdeutsche* on the committee moved next business.[3] Although the plenum rejected this minority motion after a lengthy debate from 17 to 21 March, the majority recommendations were also defeated, by 283 votes to 252.[4] Welcker's impetuosity was rather unfortunate and he might have done better if he had made slightly less radical procedural proposals. As Heinrich von Gagern in a powerful speech had committed himself to the view of the majority of the Constitutional

[1] VIII 5666. '*Grosse Sensation.*'   [2] VIII 5793 ff.   [3] VIII 5795.   [4] VIII 5915 ff.

N

Committee, he had no option but to tender the resignation of the Reich government on 22 March, though he carried on provisionally.[1] The same day, however, the Saxon industrialist Eisenstuck, who belonged to a moderate section of the Main Left,[2] carried more reasonable proposals for a speeding up of the constitution-making in the plenum by 282 votes to 246. There was to be no discussion of individual clauses. Amendments could only be moved if supported by at least 50 members. The section of the constitution dealing with the headship of the state was to be taken last. From now on, the house was to be concerned with a speedy completion of the constitution.[3] Under the new procedure, the second reading was indeed finished on 27 March.

The most controversial section of the constitution remained that dealing with the headship of the state, which was to be taken last. There was particularly the second paragraph, dealing with the hereditary emperorship. The discomfiture of the *Grossdeutsch* group in the assembly increased the chance of success, but did not make it certain. Not only Welcker, but also Schmerling had to come to an important decision on 12 March. The position of the Austrian plenipotentiary accredited to the Central Power had become untenable owing to recent developments in the Habsburg Empire, and Schmerling therefore tendered his resignation from the post while remaining a member of the Frankfurt Parliament. Schmerling had striven for the retention of the German Confederation in the proposed German federal state. The proclamation of the new Austrian constitution rendered this mission quite impossible. If he still remained a member of the assembly, it was to try and at least prevent the creation of a German federal state – in which he believed in principle – as long as Austria could not join. It may well be that, even before the granting of the Austrian constitution, the task he had set himself was an impossible one. After the disavowal of his objectives by the Austrian government his position in Frankfurt became still more hopeless and was certainly unenviable. He carried on as acting Austrian plenipotentiary until the end of April, when he also resigned from the National Assembly.[4]

In March, the Left in the Frankfurt Parliament was still very much in demand from both major contestants. Parallel negotiations were

---

[1] VIII 5938.
[2] Eisenstuck was during the winter a member of a small and fairly moderate offshoot of the *Deutscher Hof, Nürnberger Hof I*.
[3] VIII 5931 ff.   [4] Arneth, *Schmerling* 310 ff.

carried on with the Left almost all the time by the *Grossdeutsche* as well as by the *Erbkaiserliche*. One, but only one, of the many interesting transactions going on in the second half of March was the conclusion of a pact between a large number of protagonists of the Prussian hereditary emperorship with a small group of about 15 members led by the former Prussian judge Heinrich Simon, a prominent personality on the Moderate Left who had belonged to *Westendhall* and had now formed his own club at *Braunfels*. After long drawn out and difficult negotiations, large numbers of *Erbkaiserliche* signed two bonds on 26 March. In one, 114 members pledged themselves to support the suspensive – as opposed to the absolute – veto of the head of state, as well as the electoral law, in the form passed in the first reading. In the other, 86 members of the party abjured any participation in attempts to change the constitution materially in the future after it had gone through the second reading. Leading figures among the *Erbkaiserliche*, including the acting Minister-President Heinrich von Gagern and the Minister of Justice, Robert Mohl, signed both declarations. In return Heinrich Simon and his group promised to vote for the hereditary emperorship.[1] Heinrich Simon's action, though perhaps misguided from his own point of view, can certainly not be dismissed as a shady political manoeuvre. He and his friends basically wanted to vote for the Prussian hereditary emperorship because they believed that this solution offered the only chance of achieving their aim of German unity. They sought a golden bridge for their republican consciences by obtaining concessions for the democratic cause in return for their vote for the hereditary emperor. In fact, the bargain might well have been unnecessary to make sure of the attainment of democratic safeguards. The first reading had shown that a substantial number of members of the Right Centre – that is to say of those who now formed the bulk of the *Erbkaiserliche* – disliked the absolute veto. On 14 December 1848, the assembly rejected by 267 votes to 207 the proposal of the majority of the Constitutional Committee to invest the head of state with the right of an absolute veto, for instance on legislation passed by parliament. The *rapporteur* of the committee, Dahlmann, who quoted extensively from English history, admitted that the matter was more of theoretical than practical importance. Eventually the

---

[1] Jacoby, *H. Simon*, which contains on 271 ff. Simon's public declaration of 31 March published in the press in which he explained the reasons for his conduct; Biedermann, *Erinnerungen*, particularly 106 ff.; Bammel, 'Pakt Simon-Gagern'.

suspensive veto was passed by 274 votes to 187.[1] In addition, many *Grossdeutsche* were ready to vote against the absolute veto in March, in order to increase the difficulties in the way of the acceptance of the imperial dignity by Frederick William, Schmerling among them.[2] On 26 March, the suspensive veto was carried by 385 votes to 127,[3] so that the signing of the bond by 114 *Erbkaiserliche* hardly proved necessary. On the following day the electoral law was finally passed, in a moment, as it stood, even without voting by name,[4] although these roll calls had become rather a habit, even in comparatively unimportant matters.

Simon might thus have done without the support of the *Erbkaiserliche* in the matter of the veto and – probably – of the electoral law. In both questions, the decision already reached by the assembly during the first passage was only endorsed in the second and final reading. But the party favouring the Prussian hereditary emperorship could not have done without Simon. On 27 March, the clause establishing a hereditary emperorship was passed by 267 votes to 263, with 8 abstentions.[5] The majority was so narrow that even the handful of votes from Heinrich Simon's group could not have been missed.

TABLE 7

Motion to establish hereditary emperorship (27 March 1849)

	Yes	No	Abstentions	Absent	Total
Protestant	176	66	3	13	258
Roman Catholic	29	158	3	13	203
Deutschkatholisch	1	5	—	—	6
Mennonite	2	—	—	—	2
Jewish	3	1	—	—	4
No religion	1	1	1	—	3
Not known	55	32	1	3	91
Total :	267	263	8	29	567

As Table 7 shows, only 29 Catholics (about 15 per cent) out of the 190 who were present when the division was taken supported the hereditary emperorship. Opposition to Prussian leadership had thus increased considerably among the Catholics since the division on 13 January on Gagern's programme.[6]

This vote and the completion of the constitution by the assembly on

[1] vi 4096 ff.   [2] Bammel, 'Pakt Simon-Gagern' 79.
[3] viii 6030 ff.   [4] viii 6070.   [5] viii 6061 ff.   [6] See above, p. 361.

the same day left the way open for the holding of the election of the emperor on 28 March. There was only one candidate and those who were not prepared to record their vote for Frederick William IV of Prussia when called upon in effect abstained, instead of voting for a counter-candidate. The King of Prussia received 290 votes, 248 members abstained and 29 were absent from the chamber when the vote was taken.[1] After what had gone before, the election of the King of Prussia was a foregone conclusion, but the exact size of the vote for him could not be predicted with any certainty. The *Erbkaiserlich* party had some hope that there would be some rallying to Frederick William even on the Left, but except for a substantial measure of support from the former *Westendhall* (Moderate Left), including the Heinrich Simon group, the Left abstained almost entirely.

TABLE 8A

Election of the Emperor (28 March 1849)

	For Frederick William IV	Abstentions	Absent	Total
Protestant	193	55	13	261
Roman Catholic	32	156	13	201
Deutschkatholisch	2	4	—	6
Mennonite	2	—	—	2
Jewish	3	—	—	3
No religion	2	1	—	3
Not known	56	32	3	91
Total :	290	248	29	567

Thus Catholic support increased only very slightly compared with the previous day.

Regionally, the broad picture did not change as compared with the position in January. Support for the Hohenzollern dynasty on the German imperial throne increased in Prussia and in the rest of Northern Germany, but diminished in Southern Germany. The question was whether the Frankfurt Parliament could assure Frederick William of sufficiently wide national support for his imperial throne. When the president of the Frankfurt Parliament, Eduard Simson, announced in moving words the election of the King of Prussia as hereditary German emperor, the house and the nation were deeply stirred. But could the

[1] VIII 6084 ff.

TABLE 8B

Election of the Emperor (28 March 1849)

	For Frederick William IV	Abstentions	Absent	Total
A. Prussia (Kingdom)	167	24	10	201
B. *Northern Germany* (except Prussia)				
Schleswig-Holstein, Lauenburg	10	—	1	11
Hamburg, Bremen, Lübeck	4	1	—	5
Mecklenburg (Schwerin and Strelitz)	6	1	—	7
Hanover, Oldenburg, Lippe, Anhalt, Brunswick	29	10	—	39
Luxemburg, Limburg	4	—	1	5
Hesse region (Cassel, Nassau, Homburg, Waldeck, Frankfurt)	17	3	—	20
Thuringian territories (Saxon Duchies, Schwarzburg, Reuss)	10	3	3	16
Saxony (Kingdom)	4	12	1	17
sub-total	84	30	6	120
C. *Southern Germany* Hesse (Grand Duchy)*	5	6	—	11
Baden, Lichtenstein	6	10	5	21
Wurtemberg, Hohenzollern	12	18	—	30
Bavaria (Kingdom)	16	49	—	65
sub-total	39	83	5	127
D. Habsburg Empire	—	111	7	118
Total:	290	248	29	567

* Mainly south of the line of the River Main.

scheme of the Frankfurt Parliament be implemented? The next week or so was to give the answer.

xi. The Reich constitution

The hereditary emperorship was in many ways the most important feature of the constitution, for the whole edifice stood or fell with it. But quite apart from the provisions for the headship of the state, the constitution[1] drawn up by the Frankfurt Parliament was no mean achievement.

As defined in section I, the German Reich was to consist of the territories of the former German Confederation. The status of the Duchy of Schleswig was reserved for future settlement.[2] The harsh and controversial § 2 and § 3[3] were softened in the second reading on 23 March[4] by the omission of the requirement of a personal union. Though the words were less unconciliatory, there was still the insistence on German territories having a constitution, government and administration separate from that of the other lands under the rule of the same prince. The Reich constitution and all legislation was to have the same binding force in these mixed dominions as in purely German ones.[5] Any prince ruling over mixed territories was to reside in the German part or to appoint a regency for it, to which only Germans could be appointed.[6] The German states were to keep their independence, in so far as it was not limited by the Reich constitution.[7]

Section II, Die Reichsgewalt, regulated the relationship between the Reich and the states. The international representation of Germany was to be entirely in the hands of the Reich authorities.[8] War and peace was a matter for the Reich.[9] The whole armed forces of all the German states were to be at the disposal of the Reich.[10] But subject to that, the state governments retained considerable powers over their own armies.[11] The first part of the oath to be taken by all soldiers was to be to the Emperor and to the Reich constitution.[12] The navy was to be a matter exclusively for the Reich.[13] The German Reich was to form one customs and trade area, surrounded by a common customs frontier, without

---

[1] Text in Huber, Dokumente I 304 ff. [2] § 1. [3] See above, p. 321 ff.
[4] VIII 5953 ff. [5] § 2. [6] § 3. [7] § 5. [8] § 6–9.
[9] § 10. [10] § 11. [11] § 13, § 17. [12] § 14. [13] § 19.

any internal frontier dues. The exclusion of individual territories from the customs area was a matter for the Reich.[1] In the first reading, the wording 'surrounded by a common customs frontier' proposed by the Economic Committee, as an amendment to the draft of the Constitutional Committee, was only very narrowly carried, by 194 votes to 185.[2] The Left was protectionist almost to a man and the Left Centre was preponderantly so, whereas the Free Traders drew their strength mainly from the Right Centre and the Right. In regional terms, the North of Germany was more inclined to Free Trade and the South and Austria more to protection. The clause about special arrangements in § 33 was inserted for the benefit of an international port like Hamburg.

The Reich was entitled to part of the revenue from customs and excise,[3] and if necessary to contributions from the states (*Matrikular-beiträge*).[4] In extraordinary cases, the Reich was permitted to levy a Reich tax and to contract debts.[5]

In certain circumstances, the Reich authorities had the right to intervene in the affairs of the states in order to preserve law and order.[6] In general, the Reich government had the task of ensuring that the constitution and the laws made centrally were observed in the states.[7] The Reich could legislate about any matter necessary for carrying out its constitutional duties, even to the extent of creating further common institutions and introducing fresh measures of co-ordination.[8] It was left to the Reich authorities, subject to the approval of the legislature, to determine the limits of Reich authority in relation to the states. Thus the Reich had what the Germans call *Kompetenz-Kompetenz*. The Reich took what authority it needed and the rest was left to the states. Reich law normally took precedence over state law.[9] The Reich was charged with the task of introducing a national law code.[10]

Section III laid down that the ruling prince who was to be hereditary 'Emperor of the Germans' (*Kaiser der Deutschen*) was to have his permanent residence at the seat of the Reich government. The location of the capital was to be settled by Reich legislation.[11] The Emperor appointed Reich ministers, who were to countersign his acts of government and to have constitutional responsibility for them.[12] He represented Germany internationally, appointed diplomatic envoys and consuls, declared war and concluded peace and other treaties with foreign powers.[13] The Emperor summoned and closed the Reichstag and had

[1] § 33.   [2] v 3486 f.   [3] § 35.   [4] § 50.   [5] § 51.   [6] § 54–6.   [7] § 53, § 57–9.
[8] § 62–3.   [9] § 66, § 194.   [10] § 64.   [11] § 68–71.   [12] § 73–4.   [13] § 75–7.

the right to dissolve the popular chamber.[1] He had the right of making proposals for legislation; he proclaimed Reich laws and had to issue the decrees necessary for their implementation.[2] He disposed over the armed forces.[3] The Emperor had all the necessary authority to exercise the powers assigned to the Reich in so far as these were not specifically granted to the Reichstag.[4]

The Reichstag[5] was to consist of a house of states (*Staatenhaus*) and a house of the people (*Volkshaus*).[6] In the *Staatenhaus*, each state, however small, was represented by at least one member. Prussia was to have 40 members, Bavaria 20[7] and the other states varying numbers depending on their size.[8] Half the members were to be elected by the state government and half by the state parliament.[9] Members were to serve for 6 years. Half the seats were to come up for re-election every 3 years.[10] The *Volkshaus* was to be normally elected every 3 years.[11] Members of neither house were to be committed by any instructions issued to them by their constituents.[12] The agreement of both houses was necessary for are solution of the Reichstag.[13] A resolution by the Reichstag needed the consent of the Reich government to become law. But if passed three times in successive sessions (lasting at least four weeks) it became law even without the consent of the Reich government.[14] This was the suspensive veto.[15] The consent of the Reichstag was required over a wide field, including legislation, the budget, loans, cessions and acquisition of territory.[16] There were to be annual budgets. The Reichstag was to have strict control over the raising and spending of money.[17] Both houses were normally to sit in public.[18] There were various clauses to secure members from arrest.[19] Reich ministers had the right to be present at meetings of both houses and to be heard[20]. They could not be members of the *Staatenhaus*.[21] A member of the *Volkshaus* who was appointed to Reich office or promoted had to submit himself to a fresh election, but retained his seat in the house until the by-election had taken place.[22]

---

[1] § 79. [2] § 80. [3] § 83. [4] § 84. [5] Section IV. [6] § 85.
[7] As long as Austria did not belong to the Reich. Otherwise Bavaria was to have 18 members.
[8] § 87.
[9] § 88. There were special provisions for states with an odd number of members.
[10] § 92. [11] § 94. A special law regulated the procedure for elections. See below, p. 382.
[12] § 96. [13] § 100. [14] § 101. [15] See above, p. 373 f. [16] § 102. [17] § 103.
[18] § 111. [19] § 117–20. [20] § 121. [21] § 123.
[22] § 124. This was a variation of the current English practice which inspired it.

N2

380 THE FRANKFURT PARLIAMENT

A Reich court of law (*Reichsgericht*)[1] was to settle legal disputes between the states and the Reich, and between various Reich or state organs, and to secure redress of grievances for the citizen.[2] Section VI consisted of the Basic Rights[3] which thus became binding on all the German states.

The final section, VII, *Die Gewähr der Verfassung*, dealt with the safeguarding of the constitution. It prescribed the form of the oath to be taken by the Emperor and by Reich officials.[4] A change in the form of government of one of the states could take place only with the approval of the Reich.[5] A two-thirds majority in both houses was required for any changes in the constitution.[6]

The *Reichsrat* was eliminated on 27 March during the second reading by 269 votes to 245, mainly by a combination of votes from the *Grossdeutsche* and from the Left.[7] This body was to have consisted of 12 members, one each to be appointed by the governments of the 7 largest states and the remainder by groups of the others. But the *Reichsrat* would only have had advisory functions.[8]

In some ways the constitution drawn up by the Frankfurt Parliament was a skilful attempt to secure the essentials of unity while preserving separate states. Attempts at forced mediatisation of the small states were abandoned. But there was inadequate representation for the interests of the states at the centre. The uni-cameral Frankfurt Parliament, which was forever asserting its claim to be the sole arbiter of the constitution, had little sympathy for the problems of the states. The two most influential groups in the assembly, the *Casino* (Right Centre) and the Left, wanted to keep their power down to an absolute minimum. There was no representation of the state governments at the centre, and even the defeated *Reichsrat* would have been quite an inadequate substitute. Not only the rulers, but many of the governments and parliaments of the states were not likely to view with favour the considerable surrender of their sovereignty demanded of them by the Frankfurt Parliament after a minimum of consultation with them. The states lost their separate existence in the international community. They were no longer entitled to their own diplomatic representation. For Prussia this would have been an impossible condition without the imperial crown. But even for Bavaria, which had for long played a notable part in European diplomacy, the abandonment of her

---

[1] Section V.   [2] § 126.   [3] See above, p. 214 ff.   [4] § 190–1.
[5] § 195.   [6] § 196.   [7] VIII 6067 ff.   [8] VIII 5766 ff.

sovereignty in this respect was a bitter pill. A fear of separatism ran through parts of the constitution, understandable in view of the historical past, with living memories of the Holy Roman Empire and of the Confederation of the Rhine in many cases. Separatism could not be prevented by a denial of diplomatic representation. If the Bavarians benefited from German unification, they were not likely to make any difficulties. In that case, it would probably have been better to have left them the semblance of sovereignty. The denial of a separate foreign policy was resented by the states, particularly the larger ones. Also the states had no redress against a gradual extension of the power of the central government at their expense. The Basic Rights, which were obligatory all over Germany, interfered deeply in everyday affairs, not only at the level of the state, but also at that of the local community. The South of Germany had yet to be convinced that its material interests would be safeguarded in a unified Germany without Austria, instead of being sacrificed to those of Prussia and of the North. Many South Germans were worried about the introduction of general regulations, without taking account of their needs, as had already become apparent during the debates on the Basic Rights.[1] Some of their representatives feared that the abandonment of protection, which suited Prussia and Hamburg, would expose their nascent industries to deadly competition.[2] Would the numerically and economically weaker South receive a fair deal from Prussia?

As Droysen, the secretary of the Constitutional Committee, often complained,[3] the constitution was not based on a basic concept, but emerged from the piece-meal drafting and amendment of individual clauses, many of which owed their final form to a compromise. The constitution was never tried, but its main failing might well have been that it did too little to enlist the voluntary co-operation of the states, while not putting enough force – for instance in the shape of an army under the sole control of the Reich – into the hands of the central government to bring them into line if recalcitrant. The unitarians of the Right Centre and of the Left thus achieved their aim in theory, without being able to give the Reich government the practical means for living up to their pretensions. The central and the state governments could frustrate each other. A trial of strength, perhaps a critical one, was almost inevitable. The constitution lacked the federal chamber

---

[1] See above, p. 218 ff.   [2] See also Rümelin, *Aus der Paulskirche* 151.
[3] For instance on 11 August 1848. Droysen, *Verhandlungen* I 180.

which might have helped to resolve these differences at the centre. Particularly in view of the suspensive veto, emperor, Reich government and Reichstag kept each other in check. There was no establishment of parliamentary government in the British sense, but the possibility of strong parliamentary control of government under a system containing elements of a separation of powers.

The electoral law was passed as voted in the first reading. The popular chamber (*Volkshaus*) was to be elected directly by secret ballot by male Germans of good repute (*unbescholten*) at least 25 years of age.[1] All attempts by the *Casino* group in the Constitutional Committee to introduce property or other qualification, or public voting, failed. A parliament elected by something like manhood suffrage could hardly be 'Whig', especially at a time when Prussia was governed by a constitution imposed by her king which did without any restrictions on the franchise. Gradualism was difficult to practise at a time of revolution and rapid change.

xii. Refusal of the imperial crown by Frederick William IV – Break-up of the Frankfurt Parliament – Rump Parliament – Gotha meeting

The leaders of the *Erbkaiserliche* certainly wanted a restricted franchise partly in order to make acceptance of the imperial crown easier for the Hohenzollern dynasty. After the election of the King of Prussia as Emperor of the Germans, the assembly resolved to send a deputation to Frederick William IV. Care was taken by the office of the assembly, to whom the choice of the deputation was left, to make the delegation as widely representative as possible ideologically and regionally.[2] As the envoys of the first German parliament travelled to Berlin on their memorable mission, the spirit which had characterised the entry of the assembly into the Paulskirche in May 1848 was once more recaptured. On 3 April, the solemn audience at which the imperial crown was offered to Frederick William IV took place at the royal castle in Berlin. The president of the Frankfurt Parliament, Eduard Simson, who was accompanied by the 32 fellow-members of the deputation, read to the king the formal address which informed him that the constitution passed by the Frankfurt Parliament had been proclaimed as law and

[1] Text in Huber, *Dokumente* i 324 ff.   [2] viii 6095 f.; 6098.

that the hereditary imperial dignity established in the constitution had been bestowed on him. Simson asked the king to accept the crown on the basis of the constitution. The address was couched in respectful and at times in stirring terms, which appealed to Frederick William's romanticism. The king replied in a conciliatory tone, which did not, however, mask his disinclination to undertake the office assigned to him. He said that he was deeply moved by the resolution conveyed to him which he recognised as the voice of the people. He adhered to his previous determination that he would not agree to act unless asked to do so by the princes and the free towns of Germany. The next stage ought to be an examination of the constitution by the governments to see whether it suited the parts as well as the whole. In an official communication to the Prussian government the following day, the deputation interpreted the king's reply as a refusal of the offer. In the unanimous opinion of the deputation, this was so once Frederick William had expressed his view that the constitution passed by the Frankfurt Parliament had not yet acquired legal validity, but was subject to the approval of the German governments. As long as the constitution was not recognised as being valid, it could not provide the basis for the lawful authority of an emperor.[1]

The refusal of the imperial crown by Frederick William IV has often been interpreted too much in purely personal terms and has been misunderstood owing to being isolated from the history of the Frankfurt Parliament as a whole. A wide gulf separated the attitude of Frederick William IV from that of the majority of the Frankfurt Parliament. The difference in outlook was deeply rooted in the events of the preceding year and can only be understood against the background of the origins and development of the Frankfurt Parliament.[2]

What followed the refusal of the imperial crown by the King of Prussia was the gradual disintegration of the Frankfurt Parliament, a slow and painful death.[3] So far the assembly had been able to avoid violent clashes with the governments. There had been many differences of opinion and at various times those in authority in Austria, in Prussia

---

[1] VIII 6125 ff. Report by Simson to the Frankfurt Parliament on 11 April. See also Simson, *E. v. Simson* 173 ff. Declarations in Huber, *Dokumente* I 328 ff.

[2] See p. 336 ff above and the Epilogue, p. 393 below.

[3] A law regulating the use of bills of exchange (*Wechselordnung*) throughout Germany which the assembly passed on 24 November 1848 (v 3558 ff.) came into force in 1849 and was not affected by the failure of the constitution. See also Wichmann, *Denkwürdigkeiten* 335.

and in Hanover were severely critical of certain acts of the Frankfurt Parliament which they regarded as unwarranted interference in their internal affairs. But basically it suited most of the governments to humour the Frankfurt Parliament, partly because it was a buffer against greater radicalisation and also because it might prove to be the source of rewards, as well as of reprimands. The passing of the constitution and the election of the emperor were the first really decisive acts of the assembly and any attempt to enforce the constitution could hardly be ignored by the state governments. The assembly itself was now faced with the alternative of abandoning the constitution it had composed or of trying to apply it. Neither course was easy. On the one hand the assembly could hardly now draw back, or try an entirely new approach to the governments, giving up the claim to sole constituent powers which it had professed almost since the beginning. On the other hand any attempt to impose the constitution was liable to require the use of force. And thus once more, as in September, the assembly was back to the fundamental question of moderation versus radicalism and, therefore, to its ideological division, which had to some extent become submerged in the issue of the Prussian hereditary emperor. Once more members drifted uneasily from one side to the other. Thus Karl Biedermann, who had started in the Left Centre (*Würtemberger Hof*) and then helped to sponsor the secession to the *Augsburger Hof* in the Right Centre, now became one of the leading advocates of attempts to enforce the constitution, but in the end found that he could not go all the way with the Left.

For a time Heinrich von Gagern attempted as acting Reich Minister-President to steer a middle course, to secure approval of the Reich constitution by peaceful means and to prevent the use of force. On 11 April he and his group voted for the establishment of the committee of 30 (commonly called *Dreissigerausschuss*) which was charged with the task of executing the constitution (*Durchführung der Verfassung*).[1] This committee now became the leading organ of the National Assembly. Although it had a majority of moderates[2] the very definition of its duties and the logic of events drove it further along on the road of intervention in the affairs of the states. The question of acceptance of the Reich constitution became an apple of discord in the states, leading to conflicts between the popular chamber and the government in Prussia, Wurtemberg, Saxony and elsewhere. Finally, the two civil

[1] viii 6142 ff.   [2] viii 6149.

wars which arose out of the dispute over the Reich constitution in the Kingdom of Saxony and in the Rhine Palatinate (part of the Kingdom of Bavaria) revealed the dangers of a policy which tried to combine striving for the Reich constitution with some consideration for particularist interests. In spite of Gagern's opposition, the Reich commissioner Eisenstuck (Main Left), who had been sent to the Rhine Palatinate, backed the revolutionary movement there.[1] Several members of the Frankfurt Parliament served on the revolutionary bodies set up in Saxony and the Rhine Palatinate, as well as in Baden, which was once more the scene of an uprising. When Prussian troops came to the aid of the King of Saxony, the Frankfurt Parliament on 10 May passed a motion by 188 votes to 147 condemning this action as a breach of the Reich peace.[2] On 14 May, the Prussian government recalled the Prussian representatives from the Frankfurt Parliament. On 16 May, a motion to ignore the Prussian order was carried in the assembly by 287 votes to 2, with 10 abstentions.[3] The Austrian government had already recalled its representatives on 5 April,[4] although not all of them had obeyed the instructions.

The positive side of the balance-sheet, the acceptance of the constitution by nearly 30 governments, but mainly the smaller ones, could not make up for the increasing hostility of Austria, Prussia and some of the other kingdoms. On 10 May, Heinrich von Gagern resigned after the Vicar had refused to continue giving him his support.[5] In an assembly in which the radicals were getting stronger every day, Heinrich von Gagern could hardly maintain himself. But the Vicar did not accept Gagern's resignation in order to appoint somebody more in tune with the feeling of the assembly. On 16 May he announced the nomination of Wilhelm Grävell,[6] a Prussian individualist of the Right, who did not have any following. The Hanoverian lawyer Detmold, also of the Right, was another minister.[7] The following day, a vote of no confidence in the new government was carried by 191 votes to 12, with 44 abstentions.[8] On 19 May, the assembly resolved by 126 votes to 116 to elect a *Reichstatthalter*.[9] On 21 May, a large group of moderates, led by Dahlmann and Heinrich von Gagern, decided to resign.[10]

The constant blood-letting, with mass resignations, partly as the result of recall of representatives by several states, could have been

[1] IX 6580 ff.   [2] IX 6503 ff.   [3] IX 6600.
[4] Laube, *das erste Parlament* III 419.   [5] IX 6496.
[6] *ADB* IX.   [7] IX 6611 ff., 6617 f.   [8] IX 6629 ff.   [9] IX 6690 ff.   [10] IX 6697 f.

expected to lead to the end of the assembly. Standing orders prescribed 200 members as a quorum. On 30 April, however, the number was reduced to 150[1] and on 24 May to 100.[2] Great efforts were made to call up substitutes for the members who had resigned and these were normally radicals, as there was hardly any longer a place for moderates in the assembly. By 24 May attendance had dropped to 155 members[3] and on 30 May to 130 members.[4] On the latter day, a motion was carried by 71 votes to 64 to transfer the assembly to Stuttgart. The Frankfurt Parliament had ceased to exist.

Whatever view may be taken of the reduction of the quorum to 100 in a house whose voting total had normally been well above 400, the assembly had become unrepresentative of Germany well before the end of May. The Rump Parliament (*Rumpfparlament*), which met in Stuttgart several times between 6 June and 18 June and just managed to scrape together the necessary 100 members with the help of recently elected substitutes, was a travesty of the German National Assembly of the Paulskirche. The increasing radicalism of the assembly after the move from Frankfurt to Stuttgart was inevitable. The position of any member that was not an extremist was daily becoming more difficult. Although a few comparatively moderate members, like the poet Uhland and the aesthete Vischer, belonged to the Rump Parliament, the vast majority were far more radical. The assembly could only become a Convention and on 6 June decided to elect a Reich Regency of five which included four former members of the Frankfurt Parliament, Raveaux, Vogt, Heinrich Simon and the writer Friedrich Schüler from the Bavarian Rhine Palatinate.[5] The Wurtemberg Prime Minister Friedrich Römer had at first not been unsympathetic to the Rump Parliament. In the Frankfurt Parliament he had inclined to the Left Centre and he stayed on in the Rump Parliament. But by 13 June, when he resigned from the assembly,[6] he had concluded rather belatedly that he could not be on the side both of order and of revolution. On 17 June, Römer and his fellow-ministers in the Wurtemberg government decided that the activities of the Rump Parliament and of the Reich Regency could no longer be tolerated. When the assembly still persisted in meeting on 18 June, it was prevented from entering its usual meeting place by troops.[7] Although the assembly met once more – in a hotel – on 18 June, and resolved to stay together, the days of the Rump Parlia-

[1] VIII 6356.   [2] IX 6725.   [3] IX 6720.
[4] IX 6780.   [5] IX 6821 f.   [6] IX 6841.   [7] IX 6875 ff.

ment were numbered. Some of the bitterest hatred of the extremists fell on Römer.

While the Rump Parliament does not form part of the story of the Frankfurt Parliament, the assembly at Stuttgart revealed the difficulties under which all those laboured who, like Uhland and Vischer, wanted to combine radical political ideas with respect for law and order. At the same time, the leaders of the Moderate Left (*Westendhall*) in the Frankfurt Parliament, Raveaux and Heinrich Simon, at Stuttgart became as extreme as any former members of more radical clubs of the Left in Frankfurt. Simon, who had helped to achieve the election of Frederick William IV as Emperor at the end of March, had become a Reich Regent by June.

The dispersal of the Rump Parliament by soldiers was an ignominious end for the remnants of an assembly which had made history. The Rump Parliament was not simply a sequel. For many of its members, it was the beginning of bitter days in exile. It was the tragedy of many radical representatives at this testing time that they felt committed to political principles which could not then be realised.

On 26 June 1849 about 130 former members of the Frankfurt Parliament who had supported the Prussian hereditary emperor began a short meeting at Gotha to rally the moderates who had been opposed to the Rump Parliament. Once more, the Gagern brothers sat side-by-side not only with Dahlmann and Georg Beseler, but also with Biedermann and others more to the Left.[1] Barely fifteen months lay between the Pre-Parliament and the two rival assemblies which met in June 1849. The transformation of the political scene during that period was closely interwoven with the work of the Frankfurt Parliament and is a measure of its importance.

[1] See Laube, *Das erste Parlament* III 441 ff. Gotha declaration also in Huber, *Dokumente* I 430 ff.

9 Epilogue

THERE have been few periods in history which offered such great
opportunities for solving the problems of an age as the months following
the revolutions of March 1848. The achievements of the various bodies,
including the Frankfurt Parliament, which had their chance then were
almost bound to disappoint. For the scope for change could not possibly
be as great as it seemed. The conservative forces had been only caught
temporarily off their balance. While there was widespread popular
demand for change, there was little agreement as to the areas in which
it was to take place and how it should be carried out. As in other
epochs, there was a tendency on the part of many to expect all the
concessions from others. Difficulties were often brushed aside in a
general atmosphere of over-simplification. Whatever political unselfish-
ness was to be found in Germany at that time only too easily became an
unworldly enthusiasm which refused to face up to the real problems,
particularly among the political extremists and among some romantic
supporters of German unification, as in Schleswig-Holstein.

On the whole historians have been more sympathetic to the advocates
of change than to their opponents. Too little understanding has been
shown for the difficulties of the authorities. This tendency has been due
to the habit of seeing history as a clash between 'progressive' and
'reactionary' forces. All those who did not support German unification
or constitutional advance have all too often been regarded as incorri-
gibles who deserve only contempt.

The questioning of the entire concept of nationalism in general and
of its German version in particular has weakened this approach, but
not eradicated it altogether. For it led to new distortions arising from
an attempt to force the nineteenth century into twentieth-century
patterns or to trace the faults of the National Socialists to various
groups in the Frankfurt Parliament. Little mercy is shown even to-day

to those who are seen to have hampered constitutional progress. Historians have tended to accept at their face-value the claims about the feasibility of change made by its advocates, without examining sufficiently the various factors governing the situation at the time.

Governments were under pressure from various quarters to agree to often quite irreconcilable demands, as for instance when the Czechs asked the Austrian government to stop elections for the Frankfurt Parliament in Bohemia which were urged by the Germans. The instability of government in Austria due to the weakness of the authorities and to their desire always to please the elements on the spot liable to make the biggest trouble for them, illustrates the dangers of a gullible acceptance of any petition which it seemed unwise to refuse because of the risks involved for the rulers in saying 'no'. The reluctance of state governments to agree to innovation was not necessarily due to being 'reactionary'. From March 1848, most of the conservative ministers were displaced in the state capitals. The governments had a responsibility to their citizens for the maintenance of law and order, as well as defence. They were not entitled to surrender the existing order, however imperfect, for something untried, without giving the reform proposals which were being made full and detailed consideration. They had to be convinced that change was for the better. The authorities had a greater realisation of the amount of alteration which could be absorbed by the governmental machine than those who never faced the practical difficulties of application. They also appreciated more readily the lethargy of public opinion which was only prepared to accept innovation in small doses. Not all change would have been salutary or 'progressive'. Demands for a return to the guild system in some quarters in 1848, and for an abandonment of technical advance, were not necessarily 'progressive' because they were made by radicals. The division into a Right which was reactionary and a Left which was progressive does not do justice to the situation at the time. Conservatism was not confined to the Right or, indeed, to the upper classes of society.

The appointment of moderate liberals to ministerial office in the states hastened the division of the erstwhile opposition into two major groups. The radicals were dissatisfied with being denied power, but the conflict between the democrats and the moderate liberals ought not to be seen merely in terms of 'ins' and 'outs'. While the liberals readily fitted monarchical institutions into their system, the radicals fundamentally thought in republican terms, though many of them were prepared to work with the princes. The moderate liberals favoured a strong executive under a monarch whose prerogative included the appointment of ministers. These ministers must have or gain the confidence of parliament. The liberals visualised parliament mainly as a watchdog over the government, rather than as a breeding-ground for ministers. They advocated a measure of separation between the various powers, but stopped short of a full separation. They had no desire to make membership of the government incompatible with that of the popular chamber. Thus they did not wish to limit ministerial appointments to members of parliament. In spite of certain doctrinaire leanings in the Right Centre group on the Constitutional Committee of the Frankfurt Parliament, the moderate liberals on the whole appreciated the importance of the monarchical element, both in keeping the executive strong and in giving representation to the various states and regions. As long as there was effective parliamentary control, they saw little danger to the liberty of the subject in the preservation of monarchy. The strong parliament they had in mind was not compatible with regarding its membership merely as a stepping-stone to the executive. The liberals were quite satisfied as long as certain main points of their programme were achieved. They were adamant on securing a written constitution which provided adequate safeguards for the free functioning of a parliament whose assent was essential to the passing of legislation and which had a measure of effective control over the executive, particularly in the field of finance through annual budgets. Parliament and the verdict of the electorate were held in honour by the moderate liberals, however disappointed they might sometimes be with their manifestations.

The constitutional concepts of the radicals are more difficult to summarise, as they were not fully developed in opposition. The name of 'democrats' did not mean that they were necessarily prepared to respect the result of elections. Fundamentally, the radicals did not change their attitude after the constitutional developments of March 1848. Most of them were just as ready to try and overthrow moderate liberal governments by force as they had been to get rid of autocratic régimes during the Metternich period. Their disagreement with the liberals went far deeper than any difference of opinion over particular measures, such as the extent of the franchise. As 'men of the people', the democrats believed that they knew what the people wanted. This was a vague concept, of a general feeling or a general will, of which they belived they were the authentic interpreters. The radicals thus objected to any formalisation in certain matters which they regarded as their exclusive domain. Although they pressed the usual constitutional demands of March 1848 together with the moderate liberals, and were even more insistent about basic rights, the radicals were not genuine constitutionalists. They wanted to realise their ideas. If the constitution eventually stood in the way, then it would have to be modified, if necessary by force. Although the actions of the radical sponsors of the 'second revolution' in the spring of 1849 are not absolutely conclusive, many members of the Left certainly reserved to themselves the right to resort to force, even against constitutional régimes. The difference between the moderate liberals and the radicals is thus not one of degree, but of principle. On the whole the moderate liberals were in favour of gradualism, though there was an element of a mechanistic rationalist approach. The radicals were rationalists, who advocated wholesale change. As the words were used in 1848, the concept of 'liberal democracy' is a contradiction in terms. The fate of the Left Centre in the Frankfurt Parliament shows the difficulty of harmonising constitutionalism with radicalism. It is thus beside the point to blame the moderate liberals of 1848 for not being sufficiently radical in their attitude. From their premises, a 'second revolution' was not only unnecessary, but might endanger the achievements of March 1848. It might give scope to those who wished to attack property and to undermine the whole social order. One cannot simply dispose of this attitude of the moderate liberals as a manifestation of class prejudice.

The moderate liberals were no more 'bourgeois' in their class composition than the radicals. Liberalism in Germany was associated in this period with free trade, but not basically with a policy of *laisser-faire*. The importance of the Economic Committee of the Frankfurt Parliament illustrates the interest taken by all sections of the assembly, including the moderate liberals, in social and economic questions. It may well be that historians of later generations have read the class structure of their own time into the situation prevailing in 1848 in Germany. With the fluidity of the social structure at that time, class had quite different connotations from those it acquired later. Education was the highway to social betterment, open to many men of talent irrespective of their own starting point in life. There does not seem to have been any shame felt about parents from an 'inferior' social background. The attitude to class was completely different from that which has been prevailing for instance in Britain for some time. In a sense it is just as interesting and fruitful to examine social origins. The Frankfurt Parliament contained a number of members who had risen from comparatively lowly backgrounds, and the Right Centre had its share of them. The preoccupation of the Right Centre in the Frankfurt Parliament with political problems does not denote a lack of interest in social and economic questions. There was the view that social problems could only be solved satisfactorily once the political framework had been established. Later history has not necessarily proved wrong the general tenet of European liberalism that safeguards for the liberty of the individual deserve top priority.

Was unification and constitutional progress too big a task to be tackled simultaneously ? Would it have been wiser to have concentrated on the one or the other ? For the moderate liberals and the radicals, certainly in the Frankfurt Parliament, these two planks of the programme were aspects of the same problem. Most of the moderate liberals and all the radicals believed that the German Confederation had impeded political development, and that constitutional progress anywhere was thus only feasible after national reorganisation. Diplomatically, the system of the German Confederation had in the past left the door wide open to Russian influence, to the detriment of German political development. It was thus felt that constitutional progress in future might be endangered unless Germany was unified. In turn, the unification of Germany was unthinkable without discarding autocracy.

The carrying out of these dual and connected tasks placed the Left in a quandary. In the indisputably German territories, the Left had a contempt for historical rights and for tradition. The radicals would have been only too delighted to have mediatised many of the states, to have deprived princes of their thrones and to have established republics everywhere. But on the whole the Left was not prepared to yield territory belonging to the German Confederation (even if only incorporated in the spring of 1848) inhabited mainly by non-Germans, except in the Grand-Duchy of Posen. In order to justify claims to regions populated by non-Germans, the Left had to appeal to history. However much they wished to free themselves from conventional prejudices, many radicals were even more strongly influenced by the identification of the Holy Roman Empire with Germany and the romanticising of Germany's past than the moderate liberals. Their attitude to Limburg and to Schleswig-Holstein reveals a basically territorial rather than ethnic concept. Only the Poles stirred the conscience of the German radicals, but even to them many members of the Left visualised concessions mainly at the expense of the Austrians and the Russians. In a sense, the Left was more tyrannical to other nationalities, such as the Danes in Schleswig or the Limburgers belonging to the Kingdom of the Netherlands, than the Right Centre. This was because they tried to apply their general principle demanding the obedience of the states to the centre even to territories which had been only in very loose association with Germany. In the case of Limburg they appealed partly to historical rights and partly to recent innovation just as it suited them. The Left Centre in the Frankfurt Parliament was more logical and even less compromising. It tended to assert German rights and refused any concessions to the Poles.

The moderate liberals also based their concept of German unity in the first instance on historical memories. They showed on the whole more understanding of tradition inside the purely German territories than the radicals. But they were much readier than the Left and the Left Centre to abandon historical and territorial concepts. They adopted a more conciliatory attitude over Schleswig-Holstein and were not so adamant about holding elections for the Frankfurt Parliament in the non-German territories of the Habsburg Empire. The eventual support of most members of the Right Centre in the Frankfurt Parliament for the programme of the hereditary emperor implied letting the non-Germans in the Habsburg Empire go their own way, which was impossible as long as the insistence of the Left and of the Left Centre on preserving the unity of the German Confederation territories prevailed. The Right Centre was not so favourably inclined to the Poles as the Left.

In the end the failure of the constitution drafted by the Frankfurt Parliament to gain acceptance was not due mainly to some idiosyncrasy on Frederick William IV's part. There has often been too much readiness among historians to blame Prussia for anything which went wrong. In this case, the King of Prussia can certainly not be accused of 'militarism' or of territorial ambition. Frederick William IV refused the imperial crown offered by the Frankfurt Parliament because he realised that his acceptance would involve Germany and possibly Europe in war. None of the parties supporting national unification had worked out the details sufficiently, either internally or internationally. They all underrated the German states, most so the Left and the Left Centre, least at any rate parts of the Right Centre. The impulse for an excessive centralism came mainly from the Left. To the extent that a belief in centralism was found in parts of the Right Centre, it was due – for instance with Dahlmann – mainly to a methodical approach and to the desire to create a central authority sufficiently strong for internal and external purposes. The centralism of the Left was of a more far-reaching and more partisan nature. The Right Centre was pushed much further than it wished along the road towards an unduly unitary form of government by constant pressure from the Left, in the Pre-Parliament, the Committee of Fifty and the Frankfurt Parliament. Some of the centralism of the Right Centre was due to the fear that the states might prove difficult partners.

The question thus arises whether there was sufficient support among Germans for unification, at any rate in any but quite a loose form. There were deep political, religious, regional and economic divisions hampering the movement towards unity. The hatred of the Left for the moderate liberals, the fear of extremism so widespread in the Right Centre and on the Right, and the mistrust between Protestants and Catholics were not a good omen.

Neither of the two main groups supporting unification – the moderate liberals and the radicals – could command a united national movement. The moderate liberals suffered from an even greater lack of coherence than the radicals. There were several reasons for that. The moderate liberal programme was harder to summarise briefly than that of the radicals. The leading personalities among the moderate liberals inclined to an even stronger individualism than their opposite numbers among the democrats. Whatever attachment to federalism there was tended to weaken cohesion. Ministerial office in Frankfurt on the one hand and in the various states on the other tended to increase differences in outlook. It may be said that the liberals were at fault in carrying their individualism to extremes and that they had to pay dearly for it. But it is not really possible to speak of the failure of a liberal party, for such a party did not exist. In the confused political situation of 1848, the term liberalism is merely a historian's short-hand and should be used with this limitation in mind. Political parties in Germany at this time developed from local roots, from constituency organisations. The moderate liberals in Germany were the sum total of many local clubs with the most varied combinations of views on the relationship with Austria and on the role of the states, depending on the region.

The radicals were in a slightly happier position. They were able to link the various local groups in a national organisation, the *Zentral-märzverein*. Even then, membership of this organisation was taken up by people covering a wide range of political opinion, and extended from the extreme Left into the Left Centre, taking in a man like Wyden-brugk who was the chief minister in Weimar. Though the Left in several places went into action in support of the Reich constitution drawn up by the Frankfurt Parliament, it did so probably more because of the Basic Rights than because of national unity. The Left in some important states, particularly in Prussia, was certainly not all of one mind in the national cause.

Quite apart from this insufficient public backing for unity, the national movement in Germany during the period of the Frankfurt Parliament lacked the support of a powerful state. The scheme of the hereditary emperor was dependent on the agreement of the King of Prussia. Although the situation in Berlin was often confused, there could certainly not be any clear expectation of Frederick William's acceptance. Was Heinrich von Gagern right to stake everything on one card? By the spring of 1849 the offer of the imperial crown to Frederick William may well have been the only way to bring constitution-making to a successful conclusion. The tragedy of the moderate liberals in 1848 was that they had responsibility without sufficient power. Admittedly they cannot be exculpated from following the lead from the Left even if they regarded it as unwise. The Left prevented any fruitful collabora-tion of the Central Power with the state governments so that the ground could never be tested in time, while there was still a chance of enlisting Prussian co-operation. It must, however, be added that some members of the Right Centre were vulnerable to the idea that the Frankfurt Parliament could dictate the future order of Germany to the states.

The struggle for unity in 1848 and 1849 was not only lost inside Germany. The German radicals found the tide running against their ideas almost everywhere on the continent by the end of 1848. Things went badly for them not only in the West of the Habsburg Monarchy, but also in France, where Louis Napoleon became President in Decem-ber by popular election. While the moderate liberals were not sorry to see the defeat of radicalism in other parts of the European continent, they saw the danger of the pendulum swinging towards reaction as a result of constant radical pressure.

By the end of 1850, 'reaction' had triumphed in Germany. The Vicar of Empire and the Provisional Central Power had been eliminated, and the Federal Assembly of the German Confederation restored. Almost all the 'March ministers' had fallen. The radicals were mainly in exile, or in prison in Germany. Some, like Trützschler in Saxony, had been executed. The old powers had triumphed over both the two groups which had been at loggerheads with each other, the radicals and the moderate liberals. The two movements had a common interest to prevent the return of 'reaction', but apart from that little united them. Both were entitled to pursue their objectives. But the responsibility of the radicals for the failure of the moderate liberal governments, which they had constantly attacked, and thus for their own elimination in the short term, was considerable. The radicals lost out because they had misjudged the general climate in Europe and in their own country. They were opposed to the constitutionalism of the moderate liberals, as they were not convinced that it would eventually lead to a more democratic system. The liberals fell between two stools, because the princes were not persuaded that a proper balance could be found between the monarchical and the constitutional principle in view of the complexity and variety of state systems in Germany. These matters were not put to a test.

In spite of the apparent return of the old powers in the 1850's, the status quo ante 1848 could not be restored. Too much had happened in 1848–49, not least the work of the Frankfurt Parliament. All over Germany, the short-hand reports had been avidly read. In spite of the frustration which often affected the assembly, the solid achievement and immense work put in earned widespread recognition. The national cause and the importance of parliament found acceptance in circles which had so far been negatively inclined. In this respect, the development of Radowitz during the Frankfurt Parliament was quite remarkable. This conservative and friend of Frederick William IV, as Prussian Foreign Minister in 1850, tried to achieve German unification under Prussian leadership, until the surrender to the Austrians in the treaty of Olmütz put an end to these plans. Outside the Frankfurt Parliament, Bismarck himself is perhaps the outstanding example of a hostile observer whose thinking was deeply influenced by the German national movement and by constitutionalism in the 1848 period.

The parliamentary groups of the Frankfurt Parliament, with their publicity apparatus, became the forerunners of the German political parties. It remained to be seen who could tap the great reservoirs of mass voters, the workers and the Roman Catholics. The Catholics were among the first to appreciate the possibilities of large-scale political organisation. The question was who would capture the mass working-class vote. Only a party with a clear programme was likely to succeed in doing so. The German liberals of the 1860's and the 1870's were a coalition of the moderate liberals and radicals of 1848, and even of elements of the Right of the Frankfurt Parliament, notably Vincke. The liberals had been on both sides of the barricades in 1848 and they could never get over that. Most of the fervent revolutionaries of 1848 and 1849 had been well cured by 1860. Many of them never returned to German political life. Prominent moderate liberals of the 1848 period had a brief moment of glory from the end of the 1850's onwards. Mathy became chief minister of Baden in 1866 and died in harness two years later. It fell to Eduard Simson in 1870 as President of the North German Reichstag to ask King William I of Prussia on behalf of the assembly to accept the imperial dignity. But once again liberalism was threatened by a more radical party on its left flank. Marxism and other movements emphasising the rights of the working class secured mass backing, which was denied to the liberals. Some of the former radicals, like the Königsberg medical practitioner Johann Jacoby, who had towards the end belonged to the Frankfurt Parliament, parted from their political friends and joined the Social Democrats. The radical wing of the liberals during the Bismarckian period, the Progress Party (*Fortschrittspartei*), did its best to fuse constitutionalist and democratic ideals. A careful process of historical selection began: the strife between the moderate liberals and the radicals in the middle of the century was soon forgotten, and replaced by the notion of the *Forty-Eighter* (*Achtundvierziger*), which blurred all divisions except that between autocracy and freedom. The weak flame of parliamentary government in Germany was forever kept alight by memories of 1848 and of the work of the Frankfurt Parliament, in increasingly legendary form as the years went on.

Other countries in Europe affected by nationalist ideas in 1848 have also had their problems arising from the impact of politics on historical interpretation. The German Revolution is perhaps singular in 1848 owing to the equal importance played by national and ideological issues, and because of the special complexity of the many factors affecting the situation in Central Europe. The Frankfurt Parliament reflects more of the strains and stresses not only of the German Confederation territories, but also of the European continent generally at the time, than any other institution in 1848.

Sources

I. UNPUBLISHED

The following files of the German Federal Archives (Bundesarchiv, Aussenstelle Frankfurt am Main, quoted as Bundesarchiv):

The personal files of members of the Frankfurt Parliament, particularly the *Nachlassakten*.

The minutes and other papers of two committees of the assembly, the Economic Committee (*Volkswirtschaftlicher Ausschuss*) and the Naval Committee (*Marineausschuss*).

The minutes of one of the parliamentary groups, the *Westendhall* (Moderate Left).

Some of the press hand-outs (*Pressekorrespondenzen*).

Information was received from the Historical Institute of the Polish Academy (Polska Akademia Nauk, Instytut Historii) and from the archives of the German nobility (Deutsches Adelsarchiv, Marburg an der Lahn).

II. PUBLISHED

(a) Primary

ANDRIAN-WERBURG, Victor von (anonymously), *Österreich und dessen Zukunft* (2 vol., Hamburg, 1841, 1847).

ARNDT, Ernst Moritz, *Blätter der Erinnerung meistens aus der Paulskirche* (Leipzig, 1849).

ARNETH, Alfred Ritter von, *Aus meinem Leben* (2 vol., Stuttgart, 1893).

—— *Anton Ritter von Schmerling* (Vienna, 1895).

BAMBERGER, Ludwig, *Erinnerungen*, ed. Paul Nathan (Berlin, 1899).

BASSERMANN, Friedrich Daniel, *Denkwürdigkeiten* (Frankfurt am Main, 1926).

BERGSTRÄSSER, Ludwig, *Die Verfassung des deutschen Reiches vom Jahre 1849*, mit Vorentwürfen, Gegenvorschlägen und Modifikationen bis zum Erfurter Parlament (Bonn, 1913).

—— (ed.), *R.C.T. Eigenbrodt* (Darmstadt, 1914).

—— (ed.), 'Briefe des Präsident Lette aus dem Frankfurter Parlament', *Deutsche Rundschau* **178** (1919) 169–84.

—— (ed.), *Der politische Katholizismus* **1** (Munich, 1921).

—— (ed.), *Das Frankfurter Parlament in Briefen und Tagebuchblättern* (Frankfurt am Main, 1929).

BESELER, Georg, *Erlebtes und Erstrebtes 1809–1859* (Berlin, 1884).

BESELER, Hans von (ed.), 'Aus Georg Beselers Frankfurter Briefen 1848/49', *Deutsche Revue* **37** (1912) 2 101–13, 230–9, 360–9; 3 110–20, 231–41.

BIEDERMANN, Karl, *Erinnerungen aus der Paulskirche* (Leipzig, 1849).

—— *Beiträge zur Geschichte des Frankfurter Parlaments* (Historische Taschenbücher 5, Leipzig, 1877).

—— *Mein Leben und ein Stück Zeitgeschichte* (2 vol., Breslau, 1886–7).

—— *50 Jahre im Dienste des nationalen Gedankens*, Aufsätz und Reden (Berlin, 1892).

Biographische Umrisse der deutschen konstituirenden Nationalversammlung (4 vol., Frankfurt am Main, 1848).

BLUM, Robert, *Fortschrittsmänner der Gegenwart* (Leipzig, 1847).

BORN, Stephan (ed.), *Erinnerungen von J. Temme* (Leipzig, 1893).

BUNSEN, Christian Carl Josias Freiherr von, *Aus seinen Briefen und nach eigener Erinnerung geschildert von seiner Witwe*, ed. Friedrich Nippold (3 vol., Leipzig, 1868–1871).

DETMOLD, J. H. (with A. von Boddien), *Thaten und Meinungen des Herrn Piepmeyer, Abgeordneten zur Konstituierenden National-Versammlung* (Frankfurt and Main, 1848–9).

DIETERICI, F. W. C. (ed.), *Mitteilungen des Statistischen Bureaus in Berlin, 1848*, etc., **1–3** (Berlin, 1848–50).

DROYSEN, Johann Gustav, *Die Verhandlungen des Verfassungsausschusses der deutschen Nationalversammlung*, Erster Teil (Leipzig, 1849).

DUCKWITZ, Arnold, *Denkwürdigkeiten aus meinem öffentlichen Leben von 1841–1866* (Bremen, 1877).

DUNCKER, Max, *Zur Geschichte der deutschen Reichsversammlung in Frankfurt* (Berlin, 1849).

EGELHAAF, Gottlob, 'Briefe F. T. Vischers aus der Paulskirche', *Deutsche Rundschau*, **132** (1907) 203–26; *Deutsche Revue* **34** (1909) 4 212–25, 360–8; **35** (1910) 1 368–71; 2 106–21.

EISENMANN, Johann Gottfried, *Die Parteyen der teutschen Reichsversammlung* . . . (Erlangen, 1848).

FEIGL, Hans, and MOLDEN, Ernst (eds.), *Ph. Fallmerayer, Schriften und Tagebücher* (2 vol., Munich, 1913).

FICKER, Adolf, *Bevölkerung der österreichischen Monarchie* (Gotha, 1860).

FONTANE, Theodor, 'Von Zwanzig bis Dreissig', *Gesamtausgabe der erzählenden Schriften* 4 (Berlin, 1925).

FRÖBEL, Julius, *Ein Lebenslauf* (2 vol., Stuttgart, 1890–1).

FUCHS, Karl, *Parlamentsbriefe aus Frankfurt 1848/9*, (Breslau, 1875).

GAGERN, Heinrich von, *Das Leben des Generals Friedrich von Gagern* (3 vol., Heidelberg, 1856–7).

GAGERN, Max von, *Jugend-Erinnerungen aus dem Gebiete der Nationalität* (Regensburg, 1889).

GATTI, F. A., *Die Ereignisse des Jahres 1848 in der Steiermark* (Graz, 1850).

Gegenwart, Die, Eine encyklopädische Darstellung der neuesten Zeitgeschichte für alle Stande, 1 *et seq.* (Leipzig: F. A. Brockhaus, 1848 *et seq.*).

GEIGER, Ludwig (ed.), *Briefwechsel von Moritz Veit mit Michael Sachs* (Frankfurt am Main, 1897).

GERBER, Marie von (ed.), 'Briefe Wilhelm Stahls . . . aus der Paulskirche', *Historisch-Politisches Archiv zur deutschen Geschichte des 19. und 20. Jahrhunderts*, ed. Ludwig Dehio, 1 (Munich, 1930).

GERLACH, Leopold von, *Denkwürdigkeiten* 1 (Berlin, 1891).

GERVINUS, G. G., *Leben. Von ihm selbst, 1860* (Leipzig, 1893).

GERVINUS, V. (ed.), *Hinterlassene Schriften von G. G. Gervinus* (Leipzig, 1872).

GOLTZ, Robert Heinrich von der, *Ideen über die Reorganisation des deutschen Bundes* (Berlin, 1848).

HAIN, Joseph, *Handbuch der Statistik des österreichischen Kaiserstaates* (2 vol., Vienna, 1852–3).

HANSEN, Josef, *Rheinische Briefe und Akten zur Geschichte der politischen Bewegung 1830–1850* (2 vol., Essen, 1919, and Bonn, 1942).

HART, Friedrich, *Ein Tag in der Paulskirche* (Leipzig, 1848).

HARTMANN, Moritz, *Reimchronik des Pfaffen Maurizius* (Frankfurt am Main, 1849).

—— 'Bruchstücke revolutionärer Erinnerungen', *Demokratische Studien* 127–215, ed. Ludwig Walesrode (Hamburg, 1861).

—— *Briefe aus dem Vormärz*, ed. O. Wittner (Prague, 1911).

—— *Briefe*, ed. R. Wolkan (Vienna, 1921).

HASSLER, K. D., *Verhandlungen der deutschen verfassunggebenden Reichver-sammlung zu Frankfurt am Main* (6 vol., Frankfurt am Main, 1848–9).

HAYM, Rudolf, *Reden und Redner des ersten Preussischen Vereinigten Landtags* (Berlin, 1847).

—— *Die deutsche Nationalversammlung . . . Ein Bericht aus der Partei des rechten Centrum* (3 vol., Frankfurt am Main, 1848–50).

—— *Aus meinem Leben* (Berlin, 1902).

HÖFKEN, Gustav, 'England und Deutschland in Bezug auf die Peelschen Handelsreformen', *Unsere Gegenwart und Zukunft* 3 (1846).

HUBER, E. R., *Dokumente zur deutschen Verfassungsgeschichte* 1 (Stuttgart, 1961).

HÜBNER, Rudolf (ed.), *Aktenstücke und Aufzeichnungen zur Geschichte der Frankfurter Nationalversammlung aus dem Nachlass von Johann Gustav Droysen* (Stuttgart, 1924). Cited as Hübner, *Droysen.*

—— *Johann Gustav Droysen, Briefwechsel* (2 vol., Stuttgart, 1929). Cited as Hübner, *Droysen, Briefwechsel.*

IPPEL, E. (ed.), *Briefwechsel zwischen J. & W. Grimm, Dahlmann und Gervinus* (2 vol., Berlin, 1885–6).

ISLER, M. (ed.), *Gabriel Riessers Gesammelte Schriften* (4 vol., Frankfurt am Main, 1867–8).

JUCHO, F. (ed.), *Verhandlungen des deutschen Parlaments*, Officielle Ausgabe (Frankfurt am Main, 1848).

JÜRGENS, Karl, *Zur Geschichte des deutschen Verfassungswerkes 1848–49* (3 vol., Brunswick, 1850, and Hanover, 1857).

KALCHBERG, Joseph von, *Mein politisches Glaubensbekenntnis* (Vienna, 1881).

KERST, Samuel Gottfried, 'Briefe des Abgeordneten zum Frankfurter Parlament Kerst aus Meseritz', ed. Christian Meyer, *Zeitschrift für Geschichte und Landeskunde der Provinz Posen* 2 1 (1883) 319–69; 3 1 (1884) 43–73.

KETTELER, Wilhelm von, *Deutschland nach dem Kriege von 1866* (Mainz, 1867).

KLÜPFEL, K., 'Aus Johannes Fallatis Tagebüchern und Briefen', *Württembergische Vierteljahrshefte für Landesgeschichte* 8 (1885) 1–36.

KOCH-GONTARD, Clotilde, *Tagebuch . . . über die Konstituierende Deutsche Nationalversammlung zu Frankfurt am Main*, ed. Georg Küntzel (Frankfurt am Main, 1924).

KÜNSSBERG, H., *Das deutsche Verfassungswerk 1848* (Frankfurt am Main, 1849).

LAUBE, Heinrich, *Das erste deutsche Parlament* (3 vol., Leipzig, 1849).

MATHY, Ludwig (ed.), *Aus dem Nachlass von Karl Mathy. Briefe aus den Jahren 1846/48* (Leipzig, 1898).

MOHL, Robert, *Lebenserinnerungen* (2 vol., Stuttgart, 1902).

MOHL, Robert, *et al.*, *Entwurf einer Geschäfts-Ordnung für den verfassunggebenden Reichstag* (Frankfurt am Main, 1848).

MÖRING, Carl, *Sibyllinische Bücher aus Österreich* (2 vol., Hamburg, 1848).

NERRLICH, Paul (ed.), *Arnold Ruges Briefwechsel und Tagebuchblätter, 1825–1880* (2 vol., Berlin, 1886).

PAGENSTECHER, C. H., *Lebenserinnerungen* (3 vol., Leipzig, 1913).

PAUR, THEODOR, 'Briefe aus der Paulskirche', *Mitteilungen aus dem Literatur-Archive in Berlin*, Neue Folge **16** (1919).

PERTHALER, Johann, *Erbkaisertum Kleindeutschland* (Frankfurt am Main, 1849).

PFIZER, Paul, *Politische Aufsätze und Briefe*, ed. Georg Küntzel (Frankfurt am Main, 1924).

RADOWITZ, J. von, *Gesammelte Schriften* (5 vol., Berlin, 1852).

—— *Nachgelassene Briefe und Aufzeichnungen zur Geschichte der Jahre 1848–1853*, ed. Walter Möring (Stuttgart, 1922).

RANK, Josef, *Erinnerungen aus meinem Leben* (Prague, 1896).

RAPP, Adolf (ed.), *Grossdeutsch-Kleindeutsch*, Stimmen aus der Zeit von 1815 bis 1914 (Munich, 1922).

RAUMER, Friedrich von, *Briefe aus Frankfurt und Paris 1848/49* (2 vol., Leipzig, 1849).

—— *Lebenserinnerungen und Briefwechsel* (2 vol., Leipzig, 1861).

ROCHAU, A. L. von, *Grundsätze der Realpolitik* (Stuttgart, 1853).

ROSS, Edgar, *Erinnerungen aus meiner öffentlichen Wirksamkeit* (printed as manuscript, no year).

ROSSMÄSSLER, Emil Adolf, *Mein Leben und Streben*, ed. K. Russ (Hanover, 1874).

ROTH, Paul, and MERCK, Heinrich, *Quellensammlung zum deutschen öffentlichen Recht seit 1848* (2 vol., Erlangen, 1850–2).

RÜMELIN, Gustav, *Aus der Paulskirche. Berichte an den Schwäbischen Merkur aus den Jahren 1848 und 1849*, ed. H. R. Schäfer (Stuttgart, 1892).

SACHSEN-COBURG-GOTHA, Ernst II Herzog von, *Aus meinem Leben* 1 (Berlin, 1887).

SCHLOSSAR, A., 'Politisches von Anastasius Grün. Ungedruckte Briefe an Anton Laschan', *Deutsche Revue* **22** 1 (1897) 129 ff.

SCHORN, Carl, *Lebenserinnerungen* (2 vol., Bonn, 1898).

SCHRADER, Wilhelm, *Erfahrungen und Bekenntnisse* (Berlin, 1900).

SCHULTZE, J. (ed.), *Max Dunckers politischer Briefwechsel* (Stuttgart, 1923).

SCHUSELKA, Franz, *Österreichische Vor- und Rückschritte* (Hamburg, 1847).

—— *Deutsche Fahrten* (2 vol., Vienna, 1849).

SEPP, Johann Nepomuk, *An das Volk von Oberbayern von einem deutschen Parlamentsmitgliede* (Munich, 1848).

—— 'Erinnerungen an die Paulskirche', *Grenzboten*, 3. Heft (1903) 694 ff., 780 ff.

—— *Ein Bild seines Lebens* (Regensburg, 1916).

SIMSON, B. von (ed.), *Eduard von Simson, Erinnerungen aus seinem Leben* (Leipzig, 1900).

SPRINGER, Anton, *Aus meinem Leben* (Berlin, 1892).

STOCKMAR, Freiherr Christian Friedrich von, *Denkwürdigkeiten*, ed. Ernst von Stockmar (Brunswick, 1872).

STREMAYR, Carl von, *Erinnerungen aus dem Leben* (Vienna, 1899).

STÜVE, Gustav, *J.C.B. Stüve nach Briefen und persönlichen Erinnerungen* (2 vol., Hanover, 1900).

—— (ed.), *Briefwechsel zwischen Stüve und Detmold . . . 1848 bis 1850* (Hanover, 1903).

VARNHAGEN VON ENSE, Karl August, *Aus dem Nachlass*, ed. Ludmilla Assing (14 vol., Zürich and Hamburg, 1835–58).

Verhandlungen der Versammlung zur Vereinbarung der preussischen Staats-Verfassung (4 vol., Berlin, 1848).

VISCHER, Friedrich Theodor, 'Mein Lebensgang', *Altes und Neues* **3** (Stuttgart, 1882) 250–390.

VOGT, Carl, *Der achtzehnte September in Frankfurt am Main* (Frankfurt am Main, 1848).

—— *Aus meinem Leben* (Stuttgart, 1896).

WALDBURG-ZEIL, Konstantin Fürst zu, *Meine Grundsätze* (Schaffhausen, 1850).

WEBER, Beda, *Charakterbilder* (Frankfurt am Main, 1853).

WENTZCKE, Paul, and KLÖTZER, Wolfgang, *Der Deutsche Liberalismus im Vormärz:* Heinrich von Gagern, Briefe und Reden 1815–1848 (Göttingen, 1959).

o

WESENDONCK, H., 'Vom ersten deutschen Parlament. Erinnerungen', *Die Gegenwart* **54** (1898) 54–7, 72–5.

WICHMANN, Wilhelm, *Denkwürdigkeiten aus der Paulskirche* (Hanover, 1888).

WIGARD, Franz (ed.), *Stenographischer Bericht über die Verhandlungen der deutschen constituirenden Nationalversammlung zu Frankfurt am Main* (9 vol., Frankfurt am Main, 1848–9).

—— *Vollständiges Inhalts-Verzeichniss zu den Stenographischen Berichten über die Verhandlungen der deutschen constituirenden Nationalversammlung zu Frankfurt am Main und Stuttgart* (Frankfurt am Main, 1850).

WINTERWERB, Ph., *Album der deutschen Nationalversammlung. Nach Seibs Lichtbildern gezeichnet und litographiert von H. Hasselhorst,* etc. (Frankfurt, 1849).

WURM, Christian Friedrich, *Die Diplomatie, das Parlament und der deutsche Bundesstaat* (Brunswick, 1849).

WURZBACH, C. von, *Biographisches Lexikon des Kaisertums Österreich* (60 vol., Vienna, 1856–91). Cited as Wurzbach.

WYDENBRUGK, Oskar, *Die Neugestaltung des deutschen Vaterlandes* (Weimar, 1848).

ZIEGERT, August, *Die Aufgabe der konstituierenden Nationalversammlung zu Frankfurt am Main* (Minden, 1848).

ZIMMERMANN, Wilhelm, *Die Deutsche Revolution* (Karlsruhe, ²1851).

(*b*) *Secondary*

Allgemeine deutsche Biographie (56 vol., Leipzig, 1875–1912). Cited as *ADB*, with volume number only.

APIH, Joseph, 'Die Slovenische Bewegung im Frühjahr und Vorsommer 1848', *Österreichisches Jahrbuch* **16** (1892) 196 ff.

BACHEM, Karl, *Josef Bachem und die Entwicklung der katholischen Presse in Deutschland* (vol. 1 & 2, Bonn, 1912).

—— *Vorgeschichte, Geschichte und Politik der deutschen Zentrumspartei* (5 vol., Cologne, 1927–9).

BAMMEL, Ernst, 'Gagerns Plan und die Frankfurter Nationalversammlung', *Archiv für Frankfurts Geschichte,* 5. Folge **1** 1 (1948) 5–33.

—— 'Der Pakt Simon-Gagern und der Abschluss der Paulskirchen-Verfassung' ed. Alfred Herrmann, *Aus Geschichte und Politik.*

Festschrift zum 70. Geburtstag von Ludwig Bergsträsser (Düsseldorf, 1954) 57–87.

BECKER, 'Samuel Gottfried Kerst', *Grenzmärkische Heimatblätter*, 2. Jg (1926) 3. Heft 3–20, 4. Heft 5–21.

BEHREND-ROSENFELD, Elsbeth, 'Die politischen Ideen Oskar von Wydenbrugk's', *Zeitschrift des Vereins für Thüringens Geschichte*, Neue Folge **25** (2), **26** (1 & 2) (1924–5).

BERGSTRÄSSER, Ludwig, *Studien zur Vorgeschichte der Zentrumspartei*. Beiträge zur Parteigeschichte, ed. Adalbert Wahl, **1** (Tübingen, 1910).

—— 'Entstehung und Entwicklung der Partei-Korrespondenzen in Deutschland im Jahre 1848/49', *Zeitungswissenschaft*, **8**. Jahrgang 1 (1933) 12–25.

—— *Geschichte der politischen Parteien in Deutschland* (Munich, ⁹1955).

BESELER, O., *Wilhelm H. Beseler, Ein Lebensbild seines Vaters* (Brunswick, 1914).

BETTELHEIM, Anton, *Neue Österreichische Biographie* (Vienna, 1923–35).

BLUM, Hans, *Robert Blum* (Leipzig, 1878).

BÖMMELS, Nicolaus, 'Die Abgeordneten für Neuss in den Parlamenten 1848/9', *Neusser Jahrbuch* (1957).

BOVENSIEPEN, Rudolf, 'Bruno Hildebrand', *Lebensbilder aus Kurhessen und Waldeck*, ed. Ingeborg Schnack, **3** (1942) 205–19.

—— 'Sylvester Jordan', *Lebensbilder aus Kurhessen und Waldeck* **4** (1950) 163–86.

BRANDENBURG, Erich, *Die Reichsgründung* (vol. 1, Leipzig, ²1922).

BRANDIS, C. G. (ed.), 'Briefe von Ernst Moritz Arndt aus dem Frankfurter Parlament', *Deutsche Rundschau*, **81** (1894) 117–28.

BURIAN, Peter, *Die Nationalitäten in 'Cisleithanien' und das Wahlrecht der Märzrevolution 1848/9* (Cologne, 1962).

CARR, W., *Schleswig-Holstein* (Manchester, 1963).

CASPARY, Anna, *Ludolf Camphausens Leben* (Stuttgart, 1902).

CHARMATZ, Richard, *Minister Freiherr von Bruck* (Leipzig, 1916).

CHRISTERN, Hermann, *F. C. Dahlmanns politische Entwicklung bis 1848* (Leipzig, 1921).

CHROUST, Anton, 'Ein Kritiker König Ludwigs I. von Bayern (Carl von Giech)', *Zeitschrift für bayerische Landesgeschichte* **13** (1942) 53–86.

CONZE, Werner (ed.), *Staat und Gesellschaft im deutschen Vormärz 1815–1848* (Stuttgart, 1962).

DEUERLEIN, Ernst, *Der katholische Klerus in der ersten deutschen Nationalversammlung* (Munich dissertation, 1947).

DEYM, Franz Graf, *Friedrich Graf Deym und die österreiche Frage in der Paulskirche* (Leipzig, 1891).

DÖBERL, M., *Bayern und Deutschland* (Munich, 1922).

DOR, F., *Franz Josef Ritter von Buss* (Freiburg im Breisgau, 1911).

DROZ, Jacques, *Les Révolutions Allemandes de 1848* (Paris, 1957).

ERASMUS, Siegfried, *Die Juden in der ersten deutschen Nationalversammlung 1848/9* (Weimar, 1941).

ERDINGER, A., *J. Fessler, ein Lebensbild* (Brixen, 1874).

ERICKSON, John, *Panslavism*, Historical Association pamphlet (London, 1964).

EULER, Carl, *F. L. Jahn, sein Leben und Wirken* (Stuttgart, 1851).

EYCK, Erich, 'Freiheit und Demokratie 1848–1948', *Convegno di Scienze Morali Storiche e Filologiche*, 4–10 Ottobre 1948 (Rome, Accademia Nazionale, 1949) 23–95.

EYCK, Frank, *The Prince Consort* (London, 1959).

EYCK, F. Gunther, 'English and French Influences on German Liberalism before 1848', *Journal of the History of Ideas* 18 3 (1957) 313–41.

FENDRICH, Anton, *Die badische Bewegung der Jahre 1848/49* (Frankfurt am Main, 1924).

FEUZ, Ernst, *Julius Fröbel, seine politische Entwicklung, bis 1849* (Bern, 1932).

FRANZ, A., *H. Forster, Fürstbischof von Breslau* (Neisse, 1875).

FRANZ, Georg, *Liberalismus*, die deutschliberale Bewegung in der habsburgischen Monarchie (Munich, 1955).

FREYTAG, Gustav, *Karl Mathy* (Leipzig, 1870).

FRIEDJUNG, Heinrich, *Österreich von 1848 bis 1860* (vol. 1, Stuttgart, ⁴1918).

FRIEDLÄNDER, Fritz, *Das Leben Gabriel Riessers* (Berlin, 1926).

FRIEDRICH, J., *I. von Döllinger* (3 vol., Munich, 1899–1901).

FROMMANN, F. J., *Hermann Freiherr von Rotenhan* (Jena, 1882).

GAGERN, Max von, see under 'Liederbach'.

GERCKE, F., *Heinrich Thöl* (Göttingen, 1931).

GILBERT, Felix, *Johann Gustav Droysen und die preussisch-deutsche Frage* (Munich, 1931).

GOLLWITZER, H., *Friedrich Daniel Bassermann und das deutsche Bürgertum* (Mannheim, 1955).

GRAFENAUER, Bogo, *Ethnic Conditions in Carinthia* (Ljubljana, 1946).

HAGENAH, Hermann, 'Georg Waitz als Politiker', *Jahrbuch der Schleswig-Holsteinischen Universitätsgesellschaft* **31** (1931) 134–216.

HAMEROW, Theodore S., 'The Elections to the Frankfurt Parliament', *Journal of Modern History* **33** (1961) 15–32.

HANSEN, Joseph, *Gustav von Mevissen* (2 vol., Berlin, 1906).

HARDEGEN, Friedrich, *Hermann Heinrich Meier* (Berlin, 1920).

HARNACK, Axel von, *Friedrich Daniel Bassermann und die deutsche Revolution von 1848/9* (Munich, 1920).

HAUSE, Richard, *Der deutsche Nationalstaat in den Flugschriften von 1848/49* (Leipzig, 1915).

HAYM, Rudolf, *Das Leben Max Dunckers* (Berlin, 1891).

HELFERT, Josef Alexander von, *Geschichte der Österreichischen Revolution* (2 vol., Freiburg im Breisgau, 1907–9).

HENDERSON, W. O., *The Zollverein* (London, [2]1959).

HEUSS, Theodor, *Ein Vermächtnis*, Werk und Erbe von 1848 (Stuttgart, 1948).

HIRSCH, Felix, 'Eduard von Simson', *Geschichte in Wissenschaft und Unterricht*, Heft 5 (1965) 261–77.

HOCK, Wolfgang, *Liberales Denken im Zeitalter der Paulskirche*, Droysen und die Frankfurter Mitte (Münster, 1957).

HOLM, Th., *Georg Beseler als Politiker 1848–50* (Dissertation, Tübingen, 1935).

HOUBEN, H. H., *Verbotene Literatur von der klassischen Zeit bis zur Gegenwart* (Dessau, 1925).

HUBER, Ernst Rudolf, *Deutsche Verfassungsgeschichte seit 1789* (vol. 1 & 2, Stuttgart, 1957, 1960).

HÜTTERMANN, Wilhelm, 'Parteipolitisches Leben in Westfalen', *Zeitschrift für Vaterländische Geschichte und Altertumskunde* **68** (1910) 97–230.

IBLER, Hermann, 'Die Wahlen zur Frankfurter Nationalversammlung in Österreich 1848', *Mitteilungen des Österreichischen Instituts für Geschichtsforschung* **48** (1934) 103 ff.

ILWOF, Franz, *Franz Freiherr von Kalchberg* (Graz, 1897).

—— *Joseph Freiherr von Kalchberg* (Innsbruck, 1902).

ISLER, M., *Gabriel Riessers Leben* (Frankfurt am Main, [2]1871).

JACOBY, Johann, *Heinrich Simon* (Berlin, [2]1865).

KEDOURIE, Elie, *Nationalism* (London, [2]1961).

KLAIBER, Theodor, *Friedrich Theodor Vischer* (Stuttgart, 1920).

KLÖTZER, Wolfgang, 'Die nassauischen Petitionen an die Frankfurter

Nationalversammlung 1848–49', *Nassauische Annalen* **70** (1959) 145–70.

KÖHLER, Jutta, *Friedrich Römer als Politiker* (Stuttgart, 1929).

KOHN, Hans, *Pan-Slavism, its History and Ideology* (Notre Dame, 1953).

KOPSTADT, H., *Hermann von Beckerath, ein Lebensbild* (Brunswick, 1875).

KOSCH, Wilhelm, *Biographisches Staatshandbuch* (2 vol., Bern, 1963). Cited as *BSTH*.

KRAUTKRÄMER, Elmar, *Georg Friedrich Kolb* (Meisenheim, 1959).

KRONES, Franz von, *Moritz von Kaiserfeld* (Leipzig, 1888).

KURANDA, Peter, *Grossdeutschland und Grossösterreich . . . 1830–1848* (Vienna, 1928).

KUSCHE, Lucia, 'Schlesiens Anteil an der national-deutschen Entwicklung von 1840 bis 1848 und die schlesischen Abgeordneten im Frankfurter Parlament', *Zeitschrift des Vereins für Geschichte Schlesiens* **53** (1919) 29–54; **54** (1920) 63–90.

LANZNASTER, Franz A., *Alois Flir* (Innsbruck, 1899).

LAUBERT, Manfred, *Eduard Flottwell* (Berlin, 1919).

LEMPP, Richard, *Die Frage der Trennung von Kirche und Staat im Frankfurter Parlament*, Beiträge zur Parteigeschichte, ed. Adalbert Wahl, **7** (Tübingen, 1913).

LENHART, Ludwig, *Bischof Ketteler, Staatspolitiker, Sozialpolitiker, Kirchenpolitiker* (2 vol., Mainz, 1966–7).

'LIEDERBACH, M.' [Max von Gagern], *Hermann Müller* (Mainz, 1878).

LILIENTHAL, K. von, and MITTERMAIER, W., *Karl Mittermaier* (Berlin, 1922).

LILL, Rudolf, *Die ersten deutschen Bischofskonferenzen* (Freiburg, 1964).

MAETSCHKE, E., 'Heinrich Simons politische Entwicklung', *Zeitschrift des Vereins für Geschichte Schlesiens* **46** (1912).

MANFRONI, M., *Don Giovanni a Prato* (Milan, 1920).

MARCHETTI, Livio, *Il Trentino nel Risorgimento* (2 vol., Rome, 1913).

MEINECKE, Friedrich, *Radowitz und die deutsche Revolution* (Berlin, 1913).

—— *Weltbürgertum und Nationalstaat* (Munich, ³1915).

MEINEL, Kurt, *Otto Leonhard Heubner* (Dresden, 1928).

MEISSNER, Alfred, *Geschichte meines Lebens* (2 vol., Vienna, ³1884).

MENZ, S. H., 'Christian Minkus', *Oberschlesien*, **12**. Jahrgang (1913) 1 ff.

MISTELI, Hermann, *Carl Vogt . . . 1817–1849* (Zürich, 1938).

MOHL, Robert von, *Johannes Fallati* (Tübingen, 1856).

MOHR, Gustav, *A. von Soiron* (Cologne, 1939).

MOLISCH, P., 'Briefe J. Perthalers aus der Paulskirche', *Mitteilungen des österreichischen Instituts für Geschichtsforschung* 47 (1933) 309–17.

MOLLAT, Georg, *Reden und Redner des ersten deutschen Parlaments* (Osterwiek, 1895).

MÖLLER, Heidrun von, *Grossdeutsch und Kleindeutsch*, Die Enstehung der Worte in den Jahren 1848–1849 (Berlin, 1937).

MOMMSEN, Wilhelm, *Grösse und Versagen des deutschen Bürgertums* (Munich, 1964).

MÜNCH, Hermann, *Böhmische Tragödie* (Brunswick, 1949.)

NAMIER, L. B., *1848: The Revolution of the Intellectuals*, reprinted from *Proceedings of the British Academy*, originally in 30 (1944.)

—— 'Nationality and Liberty', *Convegno di Scienze Morali Storiche e Filologiche*, 4–10 Ottobre 1948 (Rome, Accademia Nazionale, 1949) 162–84. Published in Sir Lewis Namier, *Vanished Supremacies* (London, 1957) 31–53.

NATHAN, Helene, 'Graf O. Reichenbach', *Zeitschrift für die Geschichte Schlesiens* 49 (1915) 73–90.

NEHER, Walter, *Arnold Ruge* . . . (Heidelberg, 1933).

Neue deutsche Biographie, 1 ff. (Berlin, 1953 ff.). Cited as *NDB*.

NIEBOUR, Hermann,[1] 'Die Hannoverschen Abgeordneten zur Nationalversammlung 1848–49', *Zeitschrift des Historischen Vereins für Niedersachsen* (1911) 136–54.

—— 'Plauener in der Frankfurter Nationalversammlung', *Mitteilungen des Vereins für vogtländische Geschichte und Altertumskunde* 28 (1918) 55–61.

—— 'Die Abgeordneten Pommerns in der Frankfurter Nationalversammlung', *Monatsblätter der Gesellschaft für Pommersche Geschichte* (1911) 166–7.

—— 'Die Vertreter der Provinz Posen in der Frankfurter Nationalversammlung', *Historische Monatsblätter für die Provinz Posen* 12 5 (1911) 65–74.

—— 'Die Vertreter der Rheinpfalz in der Frankfurter Nationalversammlung', *Pfälzische Geschichtsblätter* 6 11 (1910) 97–101.

—— 'Die Abgeordneten der Provinz Sachsen in der Frankfurter Nationalversammlung', *Thüringisch-Sächsische Gesellschaft für Geschichte und Kunst* 4 1 (1914) 46–60.

—— 'Die Vertreter Schleswig-Holsteins in der Frankfurter National versammlung', *Die Heimat* 26 1 (1916) 50–3.

---

[1] The following entries are arranged alphabetically by regions.

NIEBOUR, Hermann, 'Die Abgeordneten Steiermarks in der Frankfurter Nationalversammlung, *Zeitschrift des Historischen Vereins für Steiermark*, **10**, 3 & 4 (1912) 241 ff.

—— 'Die Vertreter Thüringens in der Frankfurter Nationalversammlung', *Zeitschrift des Vereins für Thüringens Geschichte und Altertumskunde*, Neue Folge **20** Heft 2 (1911) 401–18.

—— 'Die westfälischen Abgeordneten der Frankfurter Nationalversammlung', *Westfalen* **3**. Heft 2 (1911) 33–45.

—— 'Biographisches', in the appendix to Th. Schnurre, *Die württembergischen Abgeordneten in der deutschen konstituierenden Nationalversammlung zu Frankfurt am Main* (Stuttgart, 1912).

Österreichisches Biographisches Lexikon **1** ff. (Graz, 1957 ff.). Cited as *ÖBL*.

ONCKEN, W., *Aus dem Leben . . . H. von Beckeraths* (Cologne, 1873).

PAILLER, Wilhelm, *Jodok Stülz* (Linz, 1876).

Parlaments-Kalender, Herausgegeben im Auftrage des Märzvereins durch A. Rösler (Frankfurt am Main, 1849).

PASTOR, Ludwig, *August Reichensperger* (2 vol., Freiburg, 1899).

—— *Leben des Freiherrn Max von Gagern 1810–1889* (Kempten, 1912).

PAYER, Friedrich, '*Anno 48*' (Frankfurt am Main, 1923).

PFÜLF, Otto, *Bischof von Ketteler* (3 vol., Mainz, 1899).

PHILIPPSON, Johanna, *Über den Ursprung und die Einführung des allgemeinen gleichen Wahlrechts in Deutschland . . .* (Freiburg, 1913).

PLESSNER, Helmuth, *Die verspätete Nation* (Stuttgart, [3]1962).

PÖLLNITZ, G. von, 'Georg Phillips', *Historische Zeitschrift* **155** (1937) 51–97.

PÖPPELMANN, O., *Georg Beseler und seine Tätigkeit für die Grundrechte des deutschen Volkes . . . 1848* (Greifswald, 1907).

RAAB, Karl Richard, *Hans von Raumer* (Erlangen, 1893).

RANSAUER, M., *Dr. J. Fessler* (Würzburg, 1876).

RAPP, Adolf, *Friedrich Theodor Vischer und die Politik* (Tübingen, 1911).

—— *Das Österreichische Problem in den Plänen der Kaiserpartei von 1848* (Tübingen, 1919).

REINKENS, J. H., *Melchior von Diepenbrock* (Leipzig, 1881).

REINÖHL, Walther, *Uhland als Politiker*, Beiträge zur Parteigeschichte, ed. Adalbert Wahl, **2** (Tübingen, 1911).

REPGEN, Konrad, *Märzbewegung und Maiwahlen . . . 1848 im Rheinland* (Bonn, 1955).

—— *Hitlers Machtergreifung und der deutsche Katholizismus* (Saarbrücken, 1967).

RÖNNE, Julius von, *Friedrich von Rönne* (Berlin, 1867).

ROSENBERG, Hans, *Rudolf Haym und die Anfänge des klassischen Liberalismus* (Munich, 1933).

ROSENTHAL, D. A., *Konvertitenbilder aus dem 19. Jahrhundert* (3 vol., Schaffhausen, 1871).

RÖSSLER, Hellmuth, *Zwischen Revolution und Reaktion. Ein Lebensbild des Reichsfreiherrn H. Chr. von Gagern* (Göttingen, 1958).

RÖSSLER, Hellmuth, and FRANZ, Günther, *Biographisches Wörterbuch zur deutschen Geschichte* (Munich, 1953).

ROTTENKOLBER, Josef, 'Johann Haggenmüller,' *Allgäuer Geschichtsfreund*, Neue Folge **25** (1926) 1–30.

RUGGIERO, Guido de, *The History of European Liberalism*, trs. R. G. Collingwood (Oxford, 1927).

RÜMELIN, Max, *Gustav Rümelin, Erinnerungen an meinem Vater* (Tübingen, 1927).

SCHÄRL, Walter, *Die Zusammensetzung der bayerischen Beamtenschaft . . . von 1806 bis 1918* (Kallmünz Opf., 1955).

SCHNABEL, Franz, *Der Zusammenschluss des politischen Katholizismus in Deutschland . . . 1848* (Heidelberg, 1910).

—— *Deutsche Geschichte im Neunzehnten Jahrhundert* (4 vol., Freiburg, 1929–37).

SCHNEIDER, Eugen F., *Grossdeutsch oder Kleindeutsch. Untersuchung zu K. Biedermanns 'Erinnerungen aus der Paulskirche'* (Berlin, 1939).

SCHNEIDER, K., *Altenburg in der revolutionären Bewegung 1848/49* (Altenburg, 1913).

SCHNEIDER, W., *Wirtschafts- und Sozialpolitik im Frankfurter Parlament 1848/9* (Frankfurt am Main, 1923).

SCHNIZER, Otto, *Gustav Rümelins politische Ideen*, Beiträge zur Parteigeschichte, ed. Adalbert Wahl, 9 (Tübingen, 1919).

SCHNURRE, Th., *Die württembergischen Abgeordneten in der konstituierenden deutschen Nationalversammlung zu Frankfurt* (Stuttgart, 1912).

SCHREIBMÜLLER, H., 'Heinrich Künssberg', *Historischer Verein für Mittelfranken* (1930) 223 ff.

SCHÜSSLER, Wilhelm, *Die nationale Politik der österreichischen Abgeordneten im Frankfurter Parlament* (Berlin, 1913).

SCHWARZ, Max, *MdR* [*Mitglied des Reichstags*]: *Biographisches Handbuch der Reichstage* (Hanover, 1965). Cited as *MdR*.

SCHWEICKHARDT, Gertrud, *Wilhelm Beseler als Politiker* (Kiel, 1927).

SIEBOURG, M., *H. von Beckerath* (Crefeld, 1890).

SPRINGER, Anton, *Geschichte Österreichs* (vol. 2, Leipzig, 1865).

—— *F. C. Dahlmann* (2 vol., Leipzig, 1870–2).

STADELMANN, Rudolf, *Soziale und politische Geschichte der Revolution von 1848* (Munich, 1948).

STEIGER, Günter, 'Die Teilnehmerliste des Wartburgfestes von 1817', *Darstellungen und Quellen zur Geschichte der deutschen Einheitsbewegung im neunzehnten und zwanzigsten Jahrhundert* 4 (Heidelberg, 1963) 65–133.

STENZEL, K. G. W., *G. A. H. Stenzels Leben* (Gotha, 1897).

STÖLZLE, Remigius, *Ernst von Lasaulx* (Münster, 1904).

STRAUSS, Herbert Arthur, *Staat, Bürger, Mensch*. Die Debatten der deutschen Nationalversammlung 1848/1849 über die Grundrechte (Aarau, 1947).

Süss, Edgar, *Die Pfälzer im 'Schwarzen Buch'* (Heidelberg, 1956).

SUTTER, Otto Ernst, *Die Linke der Paulskirche* (Frankfurt am Main, 1924).

SYBEL, Heinrich von, *Die Begründung des deutschen Reiches durch Wilhelm I*, 1 (Munich, ³1890).

THEISS, V., *Erzherzog Johann* (Graz, 1950).

TREITSCHKE, Heinrich von, *Deutsche Geschichte im 19. Jahrhundert* (5 vol., Leipzig, originally 1879–94).

—— *Historische und Politische Aufsätze* (Leipzig, 1867).

UHDE, W., 'Hermann Freiherr von Rotenhan', *Münchener Historische Abhandlungen*, Heft 3 (Munich, 1933).

VALENTIN, Veit, *Fürst Karl Leiningen und das deutsche Einheitsproblem* (Stuttgart, 1910).

—— *Die erste deutsche Nationalversammlung* (Munich, 1919).

—— *Geschichte der deutschen Revolution von 1848–49* (2 vol., Berlin, 1930–1).

VOMÁČKOVÁ, Věra, *Österreich und der deutsche Zollverein* (Prague, 1963).

WAITZ, Eberhard, *Georg Waitz* (Berlin, 1913).

WALKER, Mack, *Germany and the Emigration 1816–1885*, (Cambridge, Mass., 1954).

WARSCHAUER, M., *J. H. Detmold in der Opposition 1838–48* (Hildesheim, 1926).

WEECH, F. von, *Badische Biographien* (6 vol., Heidelberg, 1875–1935).

WEGENER, August, *Die vorparlamentarische Zeit Peter Reichenspergers* (Cologne, 1930).

WENTZCKE, Paul, 'Erinnerungen Rüders', *Jahrbuch für Geschichte des Herzogtum Oldenburg* **20** (Oldenburg, 1912) 1 ff.

—— 'Ostendorf', *Düsseldorfer Jahrbuch* **47** (1955) 297–317.

—— *Ideale und Irrtümer des ersten deutschen Parlaments (1848–1849)*. Abgeordnete und Beobachter: Kurzbiographien und Literaturnachweise von Wolfgang Klötzer. Darstellungen und Quellen zur Geschichte der deutschen Einheitsbewegung im neunzehnten und zwanzigsten Jahrhundert, **3** (Heidelberg, 1959).

WIEBER, W., *Die politischen Ideen von Sylvester Jordan* (Tübingen, 1913).

WILD, Karl, *Karl Theodor Welcker* (Heidelberg, 1913).

WILHELM, Theodor, *Die englische Verfassung und der vormärzliche deutsche Liberalismus* (Stuttgart, 1929).

WININGER, S., *Grosse Jüdische Nationalbiographie* (7 vol., Cernauti, etc., 1925–36). Cited as *GJNB*.

WITTNER, Otto, *Moritz Hartmanns Leben und Werke* (2 vol., Prague, 1906–7).

WOHLWILL, Adolf, 'Beiträge zu einer Lebensgeschichte C. F. Wurms', *Zeitschrift des Vereins für Hamburgische Geschichte* **22** (1918) 22–122.

WOLFF, Ernst, *Eduard von Simson* (Berlin, 1929).

WURM-ARNKREUZ, 'Mühlfeld', *Österreichische Rundschau* **55** (1918).

ZIEBURA, Gilbert, 'Anfänge des deutschen Parlamentarismus', ed. Gerhard A. Ritter and Gilbert Ziebura, *Faktoren der politischen Entscheidung*. Festgabe für Ernst Fraenkel zum 65. Geburtstag (Berlin, 1963) 185–236.

ZUCKER, A. E. (ed.), *The Forty-Eighters*, Political Refugees of the German Revolution of 1848 (New York, 1950).

ZWIEDINECK-SÜDENHORST, *Deutsche Geschichte*, **2** (Stuttgart, 1903).

Index

Entries are listed under English name wherever possible. Names of members of Frankfurt Parliament followed by asterisk and life-dates. Their main biographical references are in italic figures.

Croatia, *see under* Hungary

Cumberland, Duke of, *see* Ernest Augustus

Czechs, *see* Austria (Slavs; Bohemia)

Dahlmann, Friedrich Christoph* (1785–1860), 112, 296; and England, 6; Seventeen Men of Public Confidence, *41*; and Schleswig-Holstein, 94, 294–5, 297; Committee on Central Power, 167, 169–71, 178, 192, 194, 196; Constitutional Committee, 206–8, 210; attempt to form Reich government, 303–4; and Schmerling's fall, 344–5; and hereditary emperor, 363, 373; resignation from assembly, 385; Gotha meeting, 387

Danube Empire, *see* Austria

Darmstadt, *see* Hesse (Grand-Duchy)

Daxenberger, Sebastian* (1809–78), *96*

Denmark, 40, 46–9, 51, 118, 123, 254–6; Eider Danes, 47; Jutland, 49, 162. *See also* Malmö Armistice

Detmold, Johann Hermann* (1807–56), *99*, *150*, 190 n., 191, 195, 209, 250 n, 322 n., 366, 385

Deutsche Burschenschaft, see Universities

Deutsche Zeitung, Die, newspaper founded in 1847 to propagate constitutionalism and German unity, 22, 27, 41, 180, 187

Deutscher Bund, see German Confederation

Deutscher Hof (Main Left in Frankfurt Parliament), 132, 135, 138–9, 176, 197, 201, 209, 297, 301, 309, 313, 317

Deutschkatholizismus, 20–2, 27, 86, 98, 99, 134, 137, 209, 229, 232, 236–7, 243, 374–5

Deym, Friedrich v.* (1801–53), *324*

Dham, Carl* (1809–71), *226*

Diepenbrock, Melchior v.* (1798–1853), *141*, 144, 195, 321 n.

Dieringer, Franz Xaver* (1811–76), *98–9*

Dieskau, Julius v.* (1798–1878), *176–7*

Dietsch, Carl Theodor* (1819–57), *253*

Directory (*Reichsdirectorium*), proposal for, *see* Reich Constitution, Section III

Döllinger, Ignaz* (1799–1890), *82*, 98, 229, 238–9, 274, 281, 283, 285

Donnersberg (Extreme Left in Frankfurt Parliament), 121, 135, 138, 150, 176, 197, 248, 274, 297, 309, 313, 317

Droste-Vischering, Clemens August v., Archbishop of Cologne, 19

Droysen, Johann Gustav* (1808–84), 46, 100 n., 113, 148, *206–8*, 250, 297, 307, 328–9, 344–5, 362, 381

Duckwitz, Arnold, Bremen Senator and Reich minister of commerce, 204, 291 n.

Duncker, Max* (1811–86), 100 n.

Eider Danes, *see* Denmark

Eisenmann, Johann Gottfried* (1795–1867), *12*, 93

Eisenstuck, Bernhard* (*c.* 1805–71), *209*, 217–18, 372, 385

Elbe Duchies, *see* Schleswig-Holstein

Electoral law, for Reichstag (*Volkshaus*), 367–8, 373–4, 382

Engels, Friedrich, 87

Erbkaiserliche, see Prussian hereditary emperorship

Ernest Augustus, King of Hanover (Duke of Cumberland), 10, 38

Fallati, Johannes* (1809–55), *204*, 210

Federal Act (*Bundesakte*) of 1815, *see under* German Confederation

Federal Assembly (*Bundesversammlung*), *see under* German Confederation

Festi, Count Giuseppe* (1816–82), *74–5*

Fichte, Johann Gottlieb, 14–15

Fickler, Joseph, Baden revolutionary, 55 187

Ficquelmont, Karl Ludwig v., Austrian minister, 69

Flottwell, Eduard Heinrich* (1786–1865), *168*, 178, *183*

Flugblätter aus der Deutschen National-Versammlung, Die, press organ of Right Centre, 310

France, 15, 23, 29–31, 118, 157, 287, 289, 298; Alsace, 16, 129; and Germany, 4, 9–11, 14–17, 19, 29–31, 35, 42, 118–19, 148, 165, 191, 277, 293, 369

Francis Joseph, Emperor of Austria, 331, 370

Francke, Karl Philipp* (1805–70), *305*, 307

Franconia, *see* Bavaria

Frankfurt (on Main) (Free Town), 61; Putsch (*Wachensturm*), 1833, 11, 186; riots (September 1848), 246–7, 310–13, 315, 317

Frankfurt Parliament (German Constituent National Assembly, Reichstag):

420　INDEX